ドラゴン騎士団.13

DRAGON KNIGHTS 13

押上美猫

Mineko Ohkami

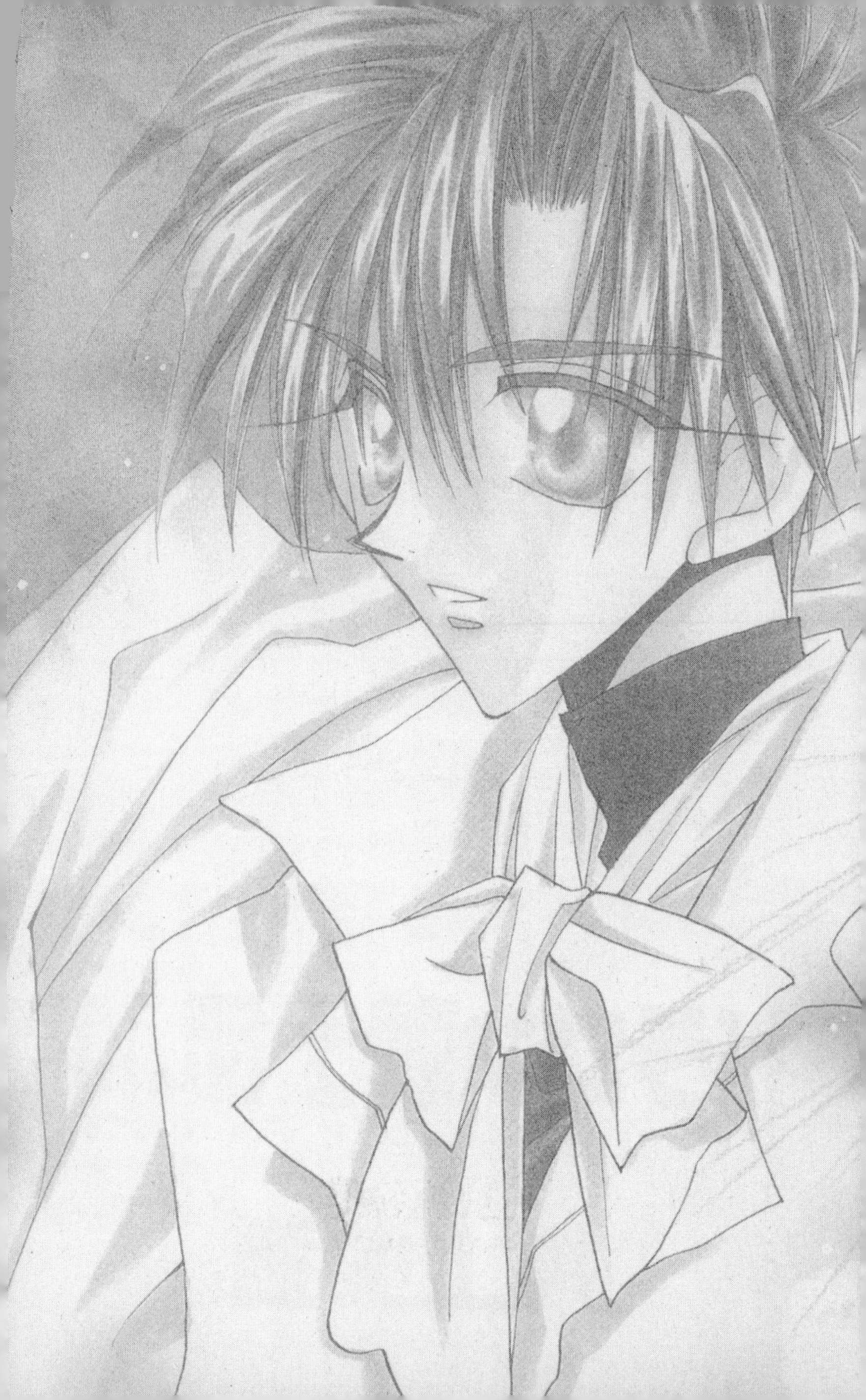

b16340668

Dragon Knights

Written and Illustrated by
Mineko Ohkami

Volume 13

TOKYOPOP®

Los Angeles • Tokyo • London

Translator - Yuki Nakamura
English Adaptation - Stephanie Sheh
Associate Editor - Tim Beedle
Copy Editor - Carol Fox
Retouch and Lettering - Vicente Rivera, Jr.
Cover Layout - Anna Kernbaum

Editors - Luis Reyes and Paul Morrissey
Digital Imaging Manager - Chris Buford
Pre-Press Manager - Antonio DePietro
Production Managers - Jennifer Miller, Mutsumi Miyazaki
Art Director - Matt Alford
Managing Editor - Jill Freshney
VP of Production - Ron Klamert
President & C.O.O. - John Parker
Publisher & C.E.O. - Stuart Levy

Email: info@TOKYOPOP.com
Come visit us online at www.TOKYOPOP.com

A  Manga

TOKYOPOP Inc.
5900 Wilshire Blvd. Suite 2000
Los Angeles, CA 90036

Dragon Knights Vol. 13

ISBN: 1-59182-441-9

First TOKYOPOP printing: April 2004

10 9 8 7 6 5 4 3 2 1

Printed in the USA

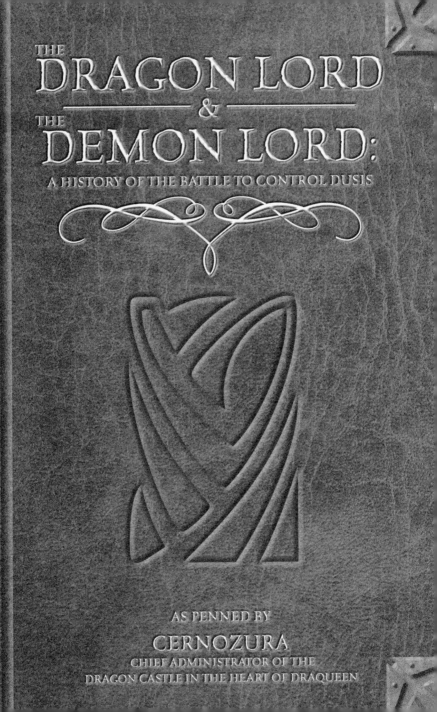

THE DRAGON LORD
& ——
THE DEMON LORD:
A HISTORY OF THE BATTLE TO CONTROL DUSIS

AS PENNED BY

CERNOZURA
CHIEF ADMINISTRATOR OF THE
DRAGON CASTLE IN THE HEART OF DRAQUEEN

Keeper of the Tome

On the eve of battle with the demon hordes, I toil myself with the demon sleeplessness and so have turned to the quill. My name is Cernozura and I am the chief administrator for the Dragon Castle, Draqueen in the heart of Dragoon, the Dragon Kingdom. Within these pages I will attempt to chronicle the events of yesteryear in the hopes that it will in turn offer some future understanding of the chaos that currently befalls us. Though candles and magic illuminate my chamber, the light still seems dim; perhaps more a reflection of my dour premonitions of what is to come. Our worst fears have come to pass. The Demon Lord Nadil has been resurrected despite our best efforts to keep his decapitated head safely locked away in the depths of the Castle, and he has stolen from the bosom of our care Cesia, who harbors an incredible magic that we have only begun to witness. In the service of a villain as pernicious as Nadil, Cesia, whether against her will or willingly giving into the seductive charm of the dreaded Demon Lord, may prove to be the most dangerous threat we've faced. I feel it imperative that I record a comprehensive, if somewhat cursory, history of the events that have led to this dark hour for a I fear that none will remain to tell the tale. My only hope is that this tome survive so that future generations will know of the valiance of the Dragon Tribe.

The End of Our Innocence

This epic clash between the Demon Hordes and the Dragon Kingdom began many years ago, at the height of peace throughout the allied kingdoms. Prosperity had flourished, and the Dragon Lord Lykouleon served as a powerful and beneficent Chief Secretary to all of Dusis. This is when Nadil, the Demon Lord, came into being. He infiltrated the admittedly vulnerable Dragon Castle and kidnapped the fair Lady Raseleane, Lykouleon's queen and the kingdom's one-time hope for an heir to the throne that could continue Lykouleon's legacy of strength and solidarity.

It was an unprecedented act of aggression towards Draqueen, and after several of his bravest warriors failed in their missions to rescue the kidnapped Queen, Lord Lykouleon himself, armed with his trusted sword and accompanied only by the Dragon of Light, Little Deus, journeyed to Kainaldia to defeat the Demon Lord and bring back his wife. Traveling in disguise, the trip was without incident, but upon crossing into the Demon Realm, the Dragon Lord found himself beset by Nadil's guardians, Crewger and Illuser. After the Lord freed the possessed Dragon Dogs from their restraints, Nadil's control over them was severed and with the dogs at his side, Lykouleon entered the palace.

While deeply loyal to their dark master, most of the Demon army had no wish to die on his behalf, and the Dragon Lord found he had little opposition while making his way through Nadil's palace. However, when at last he found the Demon Lord, the confrontation proved devastating. Both kings fought with skill and passion, and both were nearly overcome. However, in the end, the Demon Lord fell, thanks to the brave sacrifice of Illuser, who fearlessly gave his life in a charge against Nadil that gave the Dragon Lord the upper hand. With a swift blow, he cut the Demon Lord's head from his shoulders. But, victory was to be fleeting and bittersweet, for the Demon Lord, although weakened, wasn't dead. Nadil escaped with the assistance of his generals, Shydeman and Shyrendora, but not before casting a demon curse upon Raseleane, rendering our queen barren, unable to bear Lykouleon a child nor the Dragon Kingdom an heir.

The Call of the Warrior

The next several years found Lykouleon determined to build an army of soldiers strong enough to defend the allied kingdoms against any attack that might come from the Demon Hordes...and assemble a league of Dragon Knights powerful enough to infiltrate Rainaldia and destroy the Demon Lord once and for all. Nadil is not an enemy of mere flesh and bone but a magical beast born of the darkest powers this world has ever known. The only known way to destroy him is to cut off his head and take it far away from his body, else he will rise from mortal injury and live again.

The first of Lykouleon's Dragon Knights was the hot-tempered Rath, who came to us as a vivacious child, curious to a fault and blessed with the alacrity and determination that eventually led to his christening as the Dragon Knight of Fire. He's as much a son to Lykouleon as anyone could be. Our lord has even gone so far as to infuse Rath with the spirit of the slain Dragon Dog Illuser. But still through his blood courses the essence of a demon. Ever since coming to the Dragon Castle, the spry Rath has worn a magical Dragon Amulet to keep his demon spirit from completely possessing his body.

The second Dragon Knight to find his way into Lykouleon's elite league of warriors was the human thief Thatz. Bereft of funds and starving in the streets of outer Draqueen, the feisty rogue, part out of desperation and part out of pride, took a dare to slip into the Dragon Castle undetected and come out with the precious Earth Dragon Rock. The burglary was a particularly bungled affair.

However, the notoriously stubborn Earth Dragon took to Thatz, thus thrusting upon the criminal an honor he could never, and still probably, cannot imagine.

Rune, the Dragon Knight of Water, is the only elf in the history of the Dragon Kingdom to become a Dragon Knight. Promoting him to the position wasn't without its share of controversy, but the dragons choose their master, and Water chose Rune. Besides, it would be hard to argue that the brave elf was unworthy of the role. The Water Dragon had long been missing, and when it was revealed that it was engaged in a seemingly endless struggle with the Monster Fish Varawoo, a mighty demon with the power to drown the entire world, no one would have dared tried to claim it. Yet Rune, accompanied by Lykouleon, managed to trap the powerful Varawoo within a magical seal and heal the Water Dragon, who readily accepted the elf as his master. Unfortunately, the victory came at a high price. Tintlet, Rune's lover, was caught within the seal as well, where she fell into a deep sleep, her powers focused on keeping the Monster Fish subdued.

With his triptych assembled, Lykouleon dispatched his Dragon Knights on their most harrowing adventure yet...to retrieve the head of Nadil and bring it back to the Dragon Castle to be locked behind five magical seals, never to be fused again with the body of the vile Demon Lord. Much to our collective relief, the Knights were victorious. Nadil, at least temporarily, had been vanquished.

The Long Road Home

Although their orders were to return to the Dragon Kingdom as soon as they completed their mission, the journey home wrapped circuitously around Rath's overwhelming passion for killing demons and Thatz's overwhelming hunger for cash and fine cuisine. However, their distracted trek back to Dragoon proved rather fortunate when they arrived in the Misty Valley. It was here that the Dragon Knights first encountered Cesia, the half-demon fortune-teller who has come to play a crucial role in the war with Nadil. Living in the care of the vile Man-Eating Witch, Cesia was instructed by her mistress to trap the Dragon Knights so that the witch could feed upon them. Needless to say, things didn't go as planned, and in the process, the witch was killed, leaving Cesia and Zoma, her faithful demon companion, without a home. Perhaps this explains why she later chose to endear herself to the Dragon Lord by bringing Nadil's head to Draqueen herself, the trusted, incredibly distracted Dragon Knights having lost it in the twilight of their journey home.

The Horizon Grows Dark

The Dragon Knights did, indeed, make it home, and for a brief time, the Dragon court was complete. But signs of trouble started almost immediately. Word had arrived that the Demon Army, now commanded by Shydeman and Shyrendora, had begun its march toward the Dragon Kingdom. Also, the magical barrier that Lykouleon had constructed to repel any demon energy began showing signs of weakness. Some of the craftier demons, such as the Yokai Bierrez, managed to penetrate the shield, hoping to scout the strength of the Dragon forces, which were too slim to combat entire legions of Demon warriors--a devastating truth that remains even now, in the face of monumental doom. In one of these furtive incursions past the magical barrier, demons ravaged the castle. It required the combined might of the Dragon Knights and the Dragon Officers to fend off the attack. And it was at this time the sinister Bierrez engaged Rath in combat and would have killed the young Dragon Knight were it not for the valiant efforts of Cesia, Zoma and the Dragon Dog Crewger. Crewger met his mortal end saving Cesia from the poisonous grip of Garfakcy, the servant of Kharl the Alchemist, a threat perhaps even more dangerous than the Demon Army. It was then we learned of Bierrez's collusion with Kharl to gain control of Dusis for themselves. The day was a dark one, having lost the other of Lord Lykouleon's precious Dragon Dogs and faced with the daunting reality that there were multiple threats looming on our horizon. Rath himself, faced with his own mortality, began to withdraw deeper into his fractured psyche, his demon spirit tightening its grip on his human will.

Missions of Hope

Much was done diplomatically to strengthen the alliances Dragoon holds with other peaceful lands in the hope that unity would stave the imminent Demon attack. Much to our chagrin, however, many leaders were reluctant to provide aid, either grossly underestimating the strength of the Demon Army or ambivalent about the fate of Dusis. Lykouleon then, loath to once again divide the Dragon Tribe but unable to deny the need for more magical power, sent the Dragon Knights out, this time on three different quests.

Lykouleon partnered Thatz with his old thieving companion Ritchel, a woman who has continually betrayed him but for whom he harbors latent feelings. At least that is the way I understand their relationship, but mine is a heart starved to see a little hope for happiness in this unraveling tapestry of horror and pain. Thatz and Ritchel set off for the East in search for the powerful Three Treasures.

Rath once again allied with Cesia on a journey North to Mt. Emphaza in search of a legendary creature, a great beast with the power of resurrection that may have been able to revive the slain Dragon Dog Crewger. This mysterious creature could have proven to be the lost Wind Dragon, and we all held hope that Cesia, with her remarkable skill in the use of Wind magic, might indeed be the lost Dragon Knight of Wind. Had this proven true, Cesia, with Lykouleon and his Dragon of Light, would complete the Dragon Knight Circle.

Rune returned to the Faerie Forest, determined to break the seal that held Varawoo, release his love Tintlet, and discover the cause of what seemed to be a mass eradication of the Faeries. The journey united him with Nohiro, a human with a strong affinity for Faeries who turned out to be an important ally to us all.

The Eve of Hopelessness

The details of their individual missions teem with tales of adventure, harrowing conflict, and enlightening moments of self-realization, but the urgency of my situation requires me to forego these glorious stories and instead focus on the matter at hand. Should the resplendent hand of good fortune intervene on our behalf and the crisis we now face be overcome, perhaps one day I shall return to this chronicle to record these worthy tales. If not, may they be passed through the generations by playwright and by bard, for I fear there shall be none of us left to recount them.

Nadil's Army has already penetrated the Dragon Castle, resurrected their leader, and kidnapped Cesia. Needless to say, the missions as of yet have all failed. Thatz has become separated from Ritchel and her new companion Ringleys, and the pair was last seen trapped within the Cave of the Three Treasures on the lost continent of Arinas. Cesia and Rath discovered that the Wind Dragon had been killed, most likely by Nadil himself, who was revealed as the lost Dragon Knight of Wind. Rune did indeed release Tintlet by absorbing the Monster Fish Varawoo into his body, only to see his victory twisted into defeat when a demon-possessed Rath drove Varawoo from Rune, releasing one of the most dangerous demons again upon the world.

Yes, that's correct. Though I claimed the particulars of the missions were inconsequential to the matter at hand, one detail must be revealed. On his journey to Mt. Emphaza, Rath began losing his continual struggle to keep his demon spirit at bay. When at last he returned to the castle, his humanity had been stripped away, though he kept this well hidden from us all. For days he slumbered, a new evil festering inside him. When awoken, he was no longer our Dragon Knight of Fire, but a possessed Yokai. The Rath we knew was dead, a nightmare that became heartbreakingly real when he murdered Alfeegi, the White Dragon Officer. This act was the first blow in an ambush that would create havoc unimaginable throughout Dragoon and lead directly to Nadil's resurrection and Cesia's capture. Rath himself was slain, a pawn willingly used and sacrificed by the Demon Lord to achieve this vile goal. But in the aftermath of the incursion, Rai-Stern, the Blue Dragon Officer and a close friend to the Dragon Knight of Fire, surrendered his life essence so that Rath may live again. So, Rath is back, but the guilt he feels will leave scars on his heart that may never heal. The souls of Alfeegi, Rai-Stern, and countless Dusisians forever to burden his slim shoulders.

As for the Demon Army, we await its return, for we have had but a taste of its bitter poison. Nadil has chosen to spare us, temporarily. He will no doubt return soon, leading an army that is tens of thousands strong, each soldier a devil thirsty for human blood. And it is here that I reveal Cesia's significance. She has a unique gift, which in the hands of the righteous could help the whole of Dusis, but in evil's possession may prove to bring the Dragon Tribe to its knees. It is the power of amplification. The natural or magical abilities bestowed upon an individual become magnified in the presence of this divine marvel. Obviously the possession of such power by a demon as mighty as Nadil would render the Dragon Army ineffectual in protecting the unsuspecting lands of Dusis.

But I have lingered too long over these few scraps of parchment. Already the light of dawn creeps through my casement, and I know I must ready the kitchen for breakfast. It will be a somber meal, reflective of the night past and uncertain of the day ahead. A meal served with sorrow, anger and fear. I have tarried too long. I leave you with a map of the continents and a promise to return to these pages and record the events to come, until the day that my quill runs dry and my blood spills across my chamber floor.

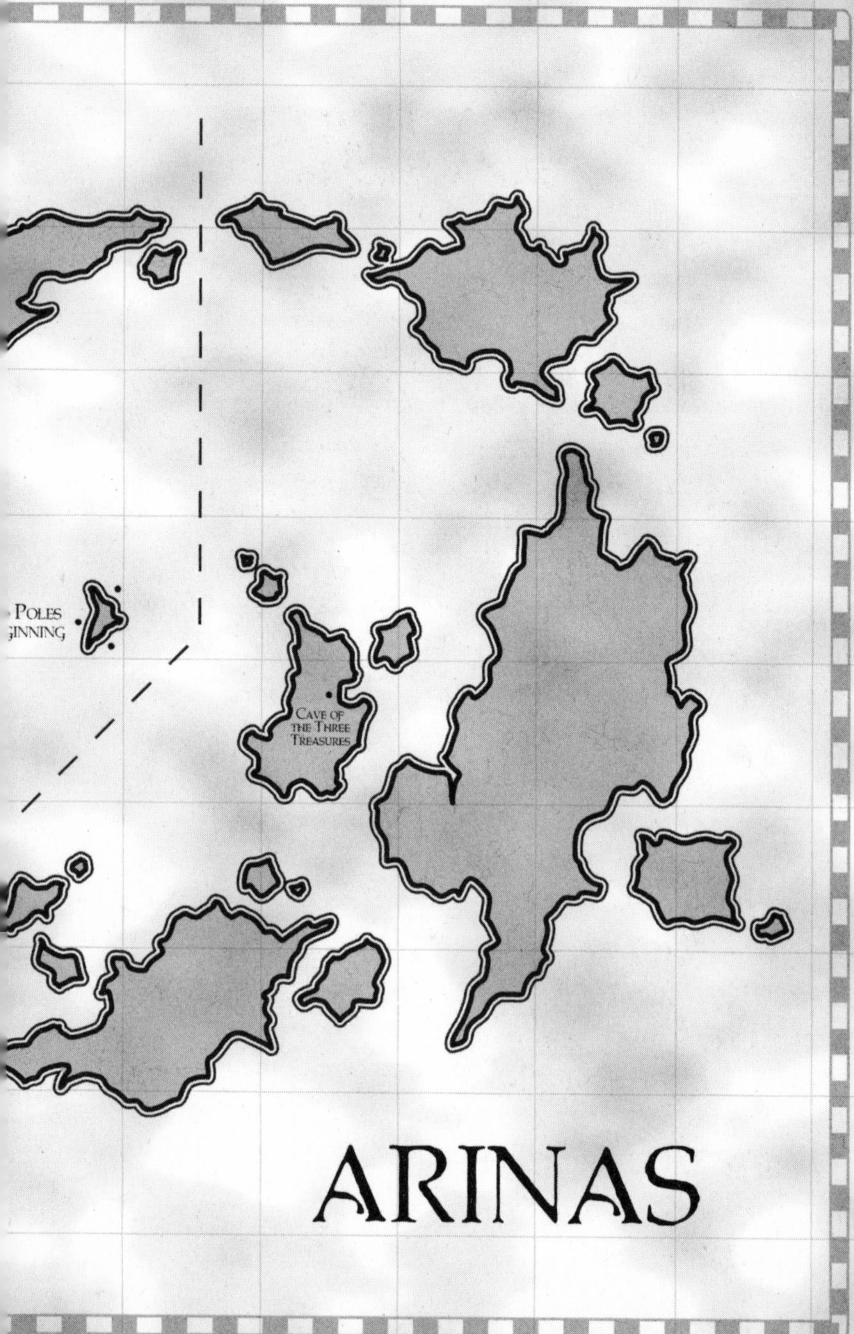

Poles
ginning
Cave of
the Three
Treasures
ARINAS

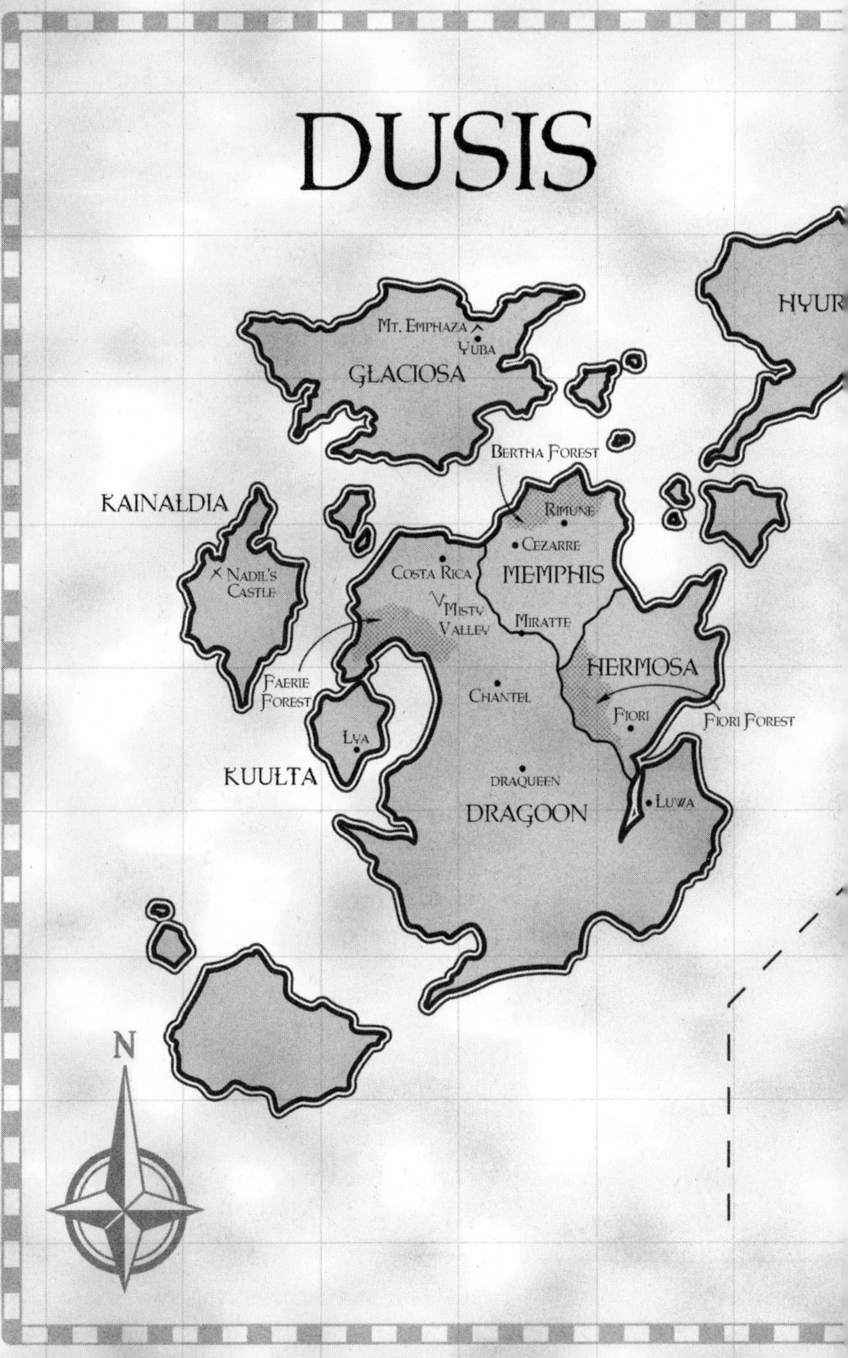
DUSIS
Mt. Emphaza
Yuba
Glaciosa
Bertha Forest
Hyur
Kainaldia
Rimune
Cezarre
Nadil's Castle
Costa Rica
Memphis
Misty Valley
Miratte
Hermosa
Faerie Forest
Chantel
Fiori
Fiori Forest
Lya
Kuulta
draqueen
Luwa
Dragoon
N

CONTENTS

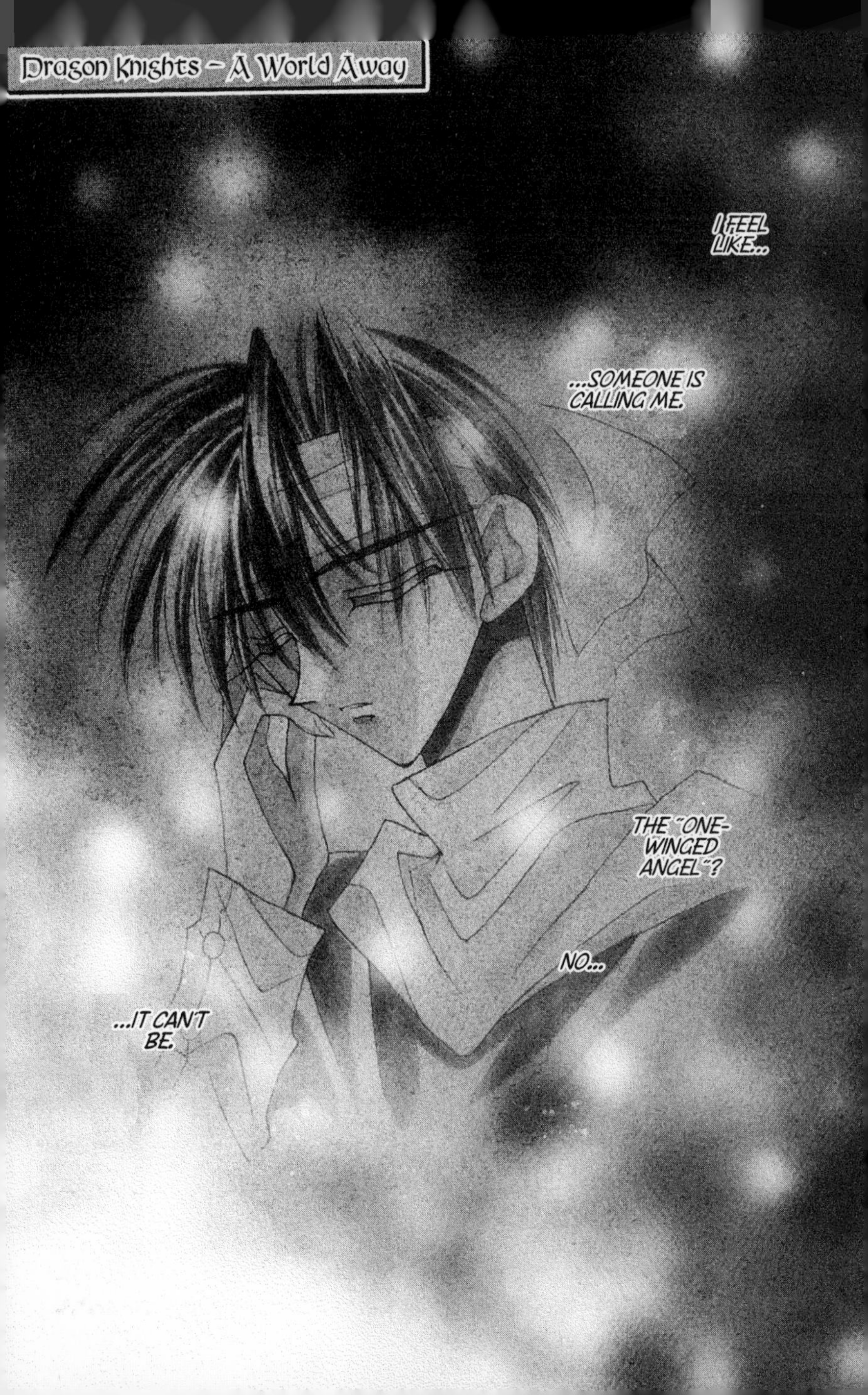
I FEEL LIKE...
...SOMEONE IS CALLING ME.
THE "ONE-WINGED ANGEL"?
NO...
...IT CAN'T BE.

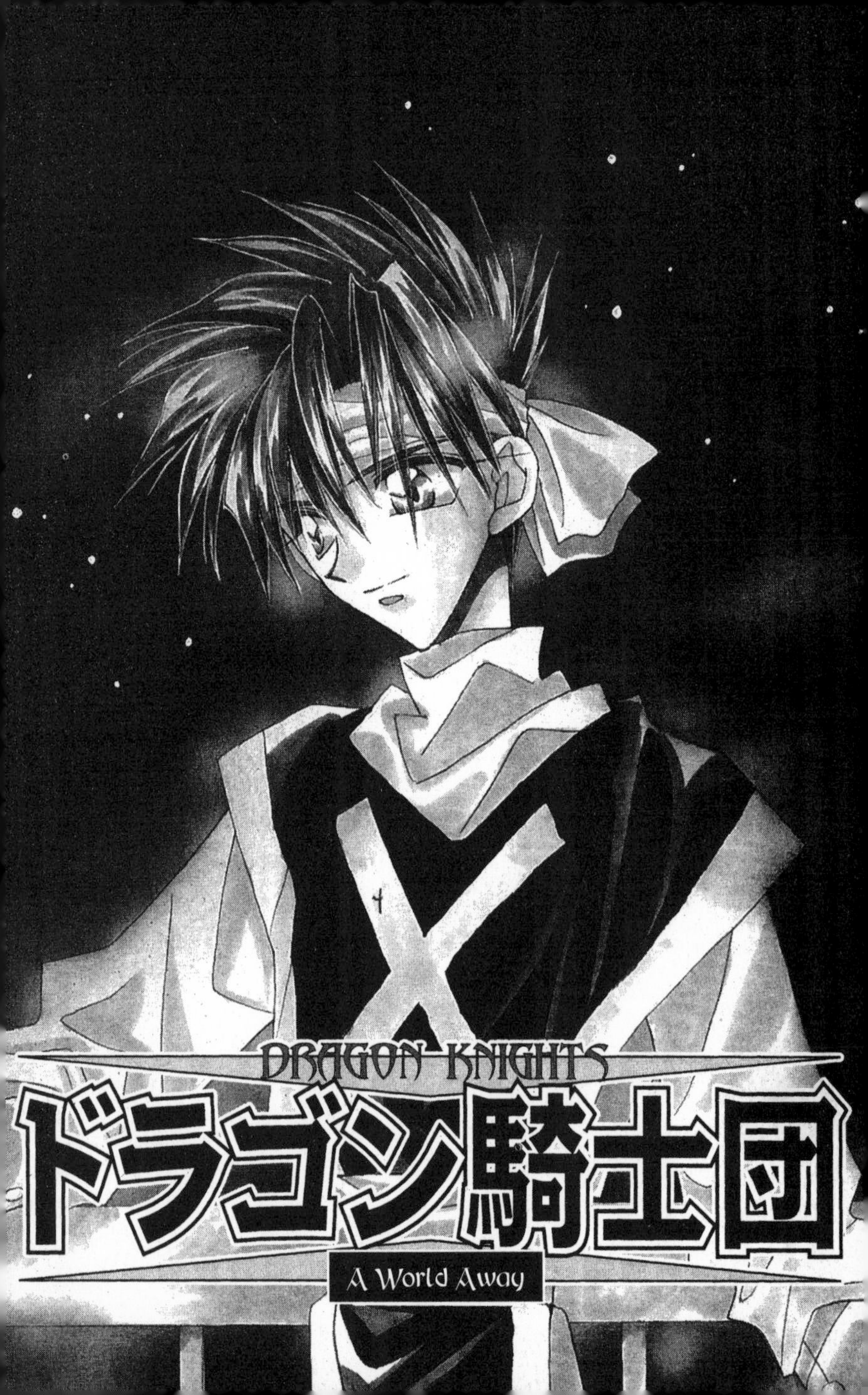
DRAGON KNIGHTS
ドラゴン騎士団
A World Away

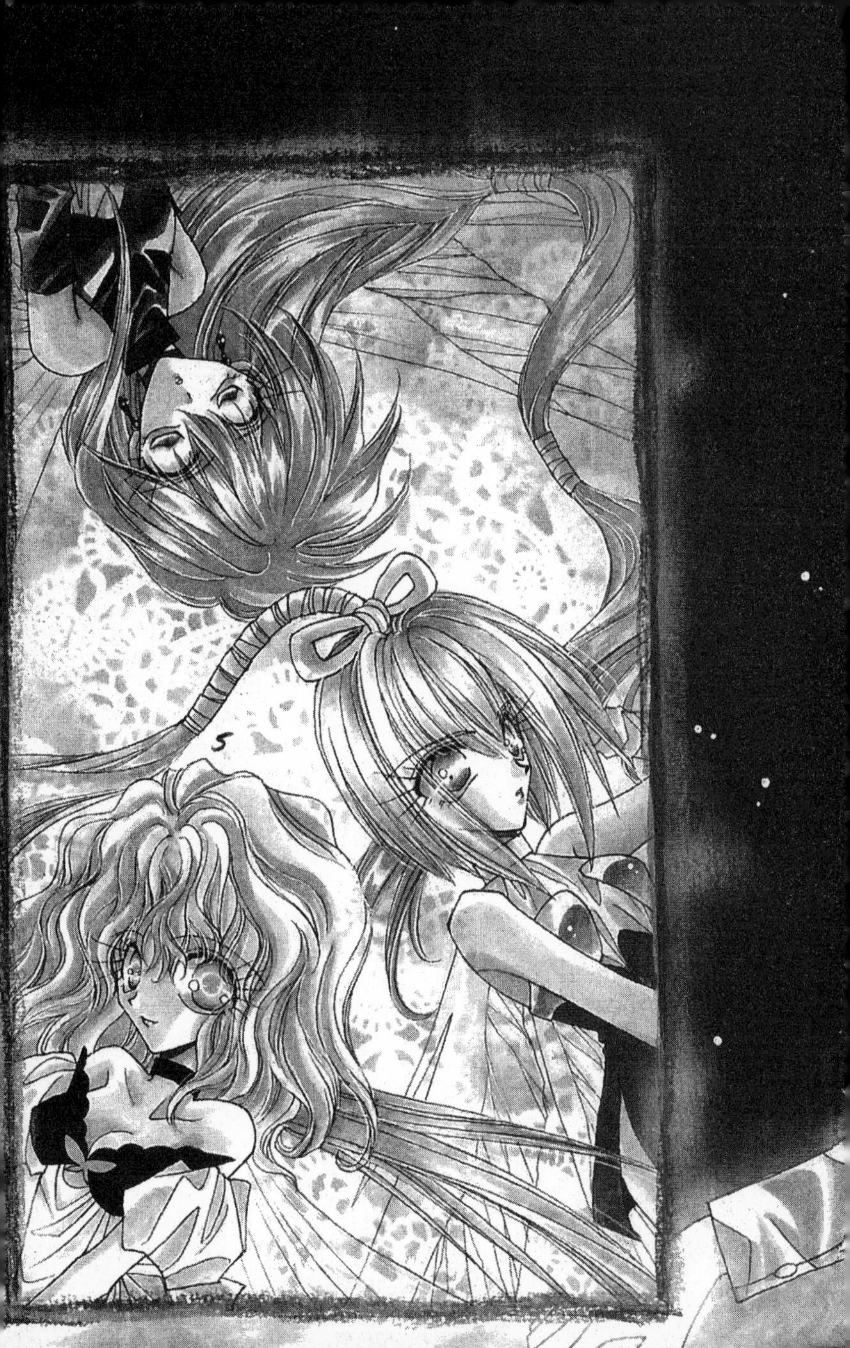

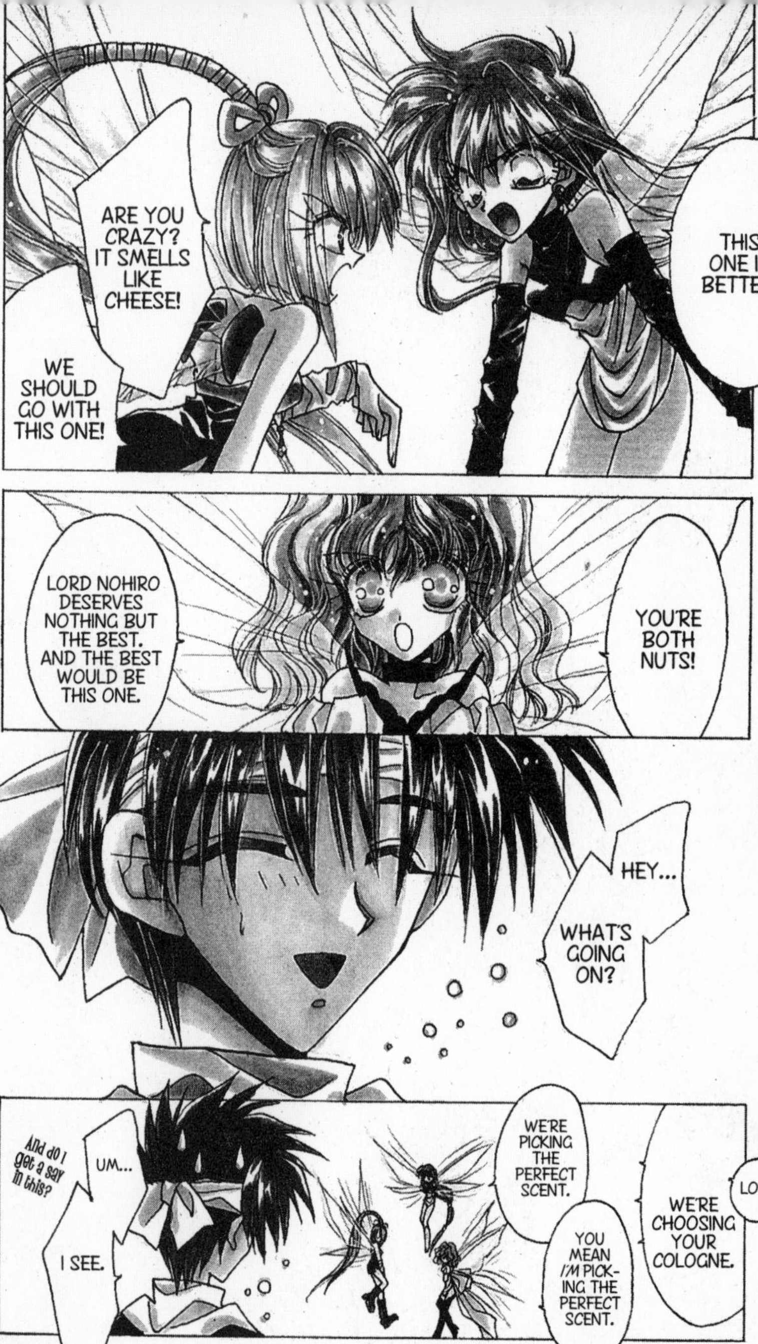
THIS ONE IS BETTER!
ARE YOU CRAZY? IT SMELLS LIKE CHEESE!
WE SHOULD GO WITH THIS ONE!
YOU'RE BOTH NUTS!
LORD NOHIRO DESERVES NOTHING BUT THE BEST. AND THE BEST WOULD BE THIS ONE.
HEY...
WHAT'S GOING ON?
LORD!
WE'RE CHOOSING YOUR COLOGNE.
WE'RE PICKING THE PERFECT SCENT.
YOU MEAN I'M PICKING THE PERFECT SCENT.
UM...
I SEE.
And do I get a say in this?

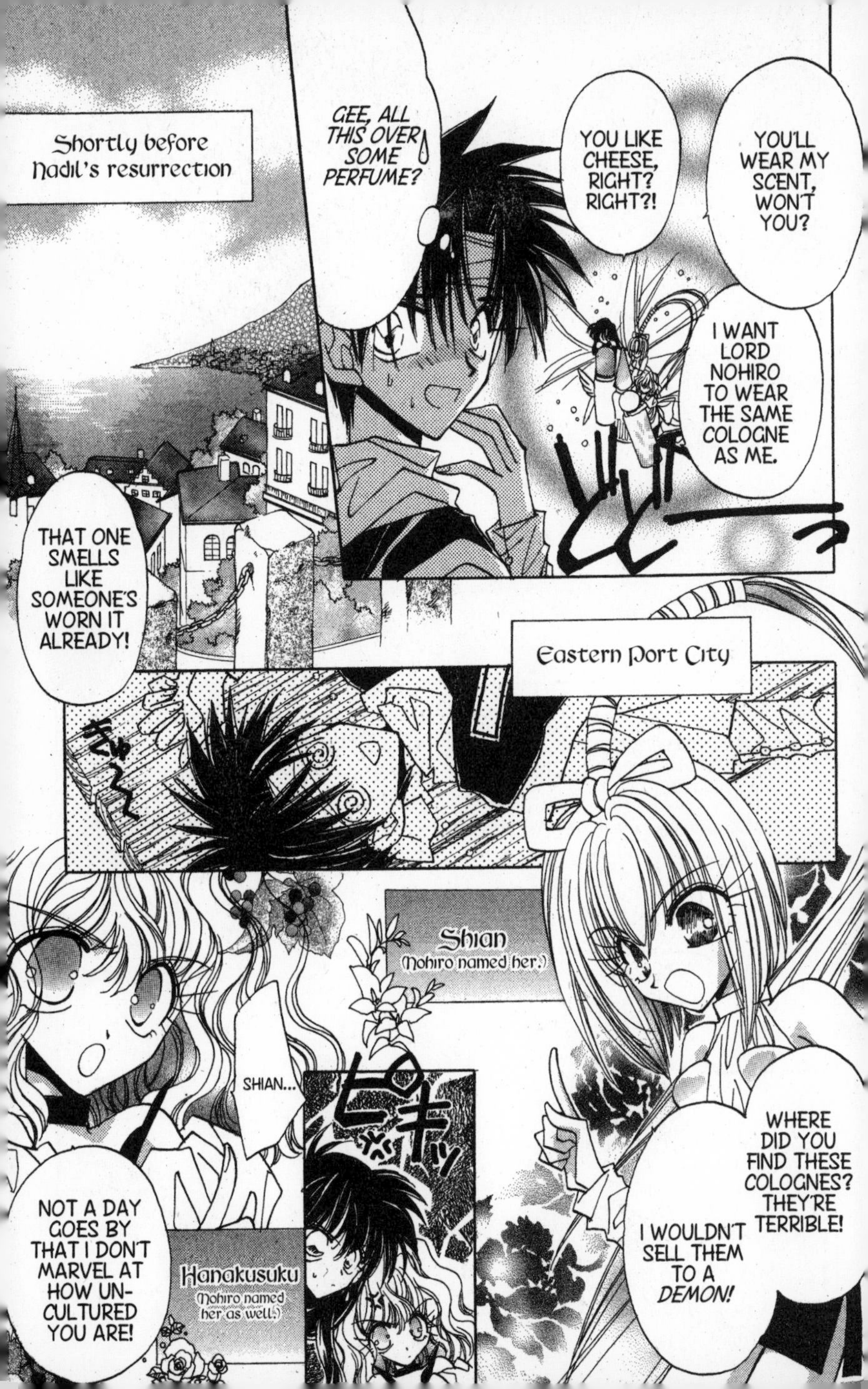
YOU'LL WEAR MY SCENT, WON'T YOU?
YOU LIKE CHEESE, RIGHT? RIGHT?!
I WANT LORD NOHIRO TO WEAR THE SAME COLOGNE AS ME.
GEE, ALL THIS OVER SOME PERFUME?
Shortly before Nadil's resurrection
THAT ONE SMELLS LIKE SOMEONE'S WORN IT ALREADY!
Eastern Port City
Shian
(Nohiro named her.)
WHERE DID YOU FIND THESE COLOGNES? THEY'RE TERRIBLE!
I WOULDN'T SELL THEM TO A *DEMON!*
SHIAN...
NOT A DAY GOES BY THAT I DON'T MARVEL AT HOW UN-CULTURED YOU ARE!
Hanakusuku
(Nohiro named her as well.)

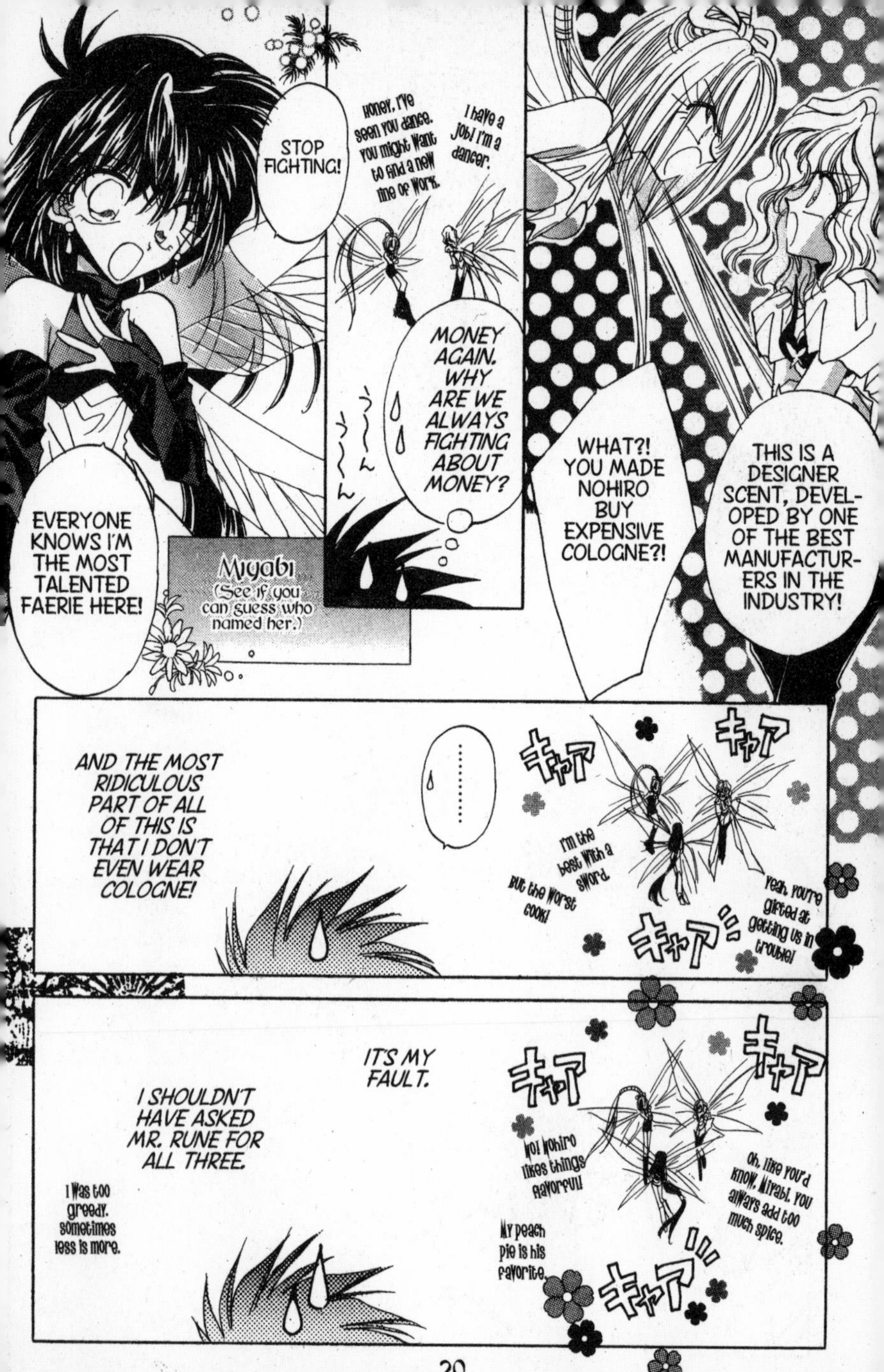
THIS IS A DESIGNER SCENT, DEVELOPED BY ONE OF THE BEST MANUFACTURERS IN THE INDUSTRY!
WHAT?! YOU MADE NOHIRO BUY EXPENSIVE COLOGNE?!
I have a job! I'm a dancer.
Honey, I've seen you dance. You might want to find a new line of work.
MONEY AGAIN. WHY ARE WE ALWAYS FIGHTING ABOUT MONEY?
う～ん う～ん
STOP FIGHTING!
EVERYONE KNOWS I'M THE MOST TALENTED FAERIE HERE!
Miyabi (See if you can guess who named her.)
キャア
キャア
I'm the best with a sword.
Yeah, you're gifted at getting us in trouble!
But the worst cook!
キャア!!!
......
AND THE MOST RIDICULOUS PART OF ALL OF THIS IS THAT I DON'T EVEN WEAR COLOGNE!
キャア
キャア
No! Nohiro likes things flavorful!
Oh, like you'd know, Miyabi. You always add too much spice.
My peach pie is his favorite.
キャア!!!
IT'S MY FAULT.
I SHOULDN'T HAVE ASKED MR. RUNE FOR ALL THREE.
I was too greedy. Sometimes less is more.

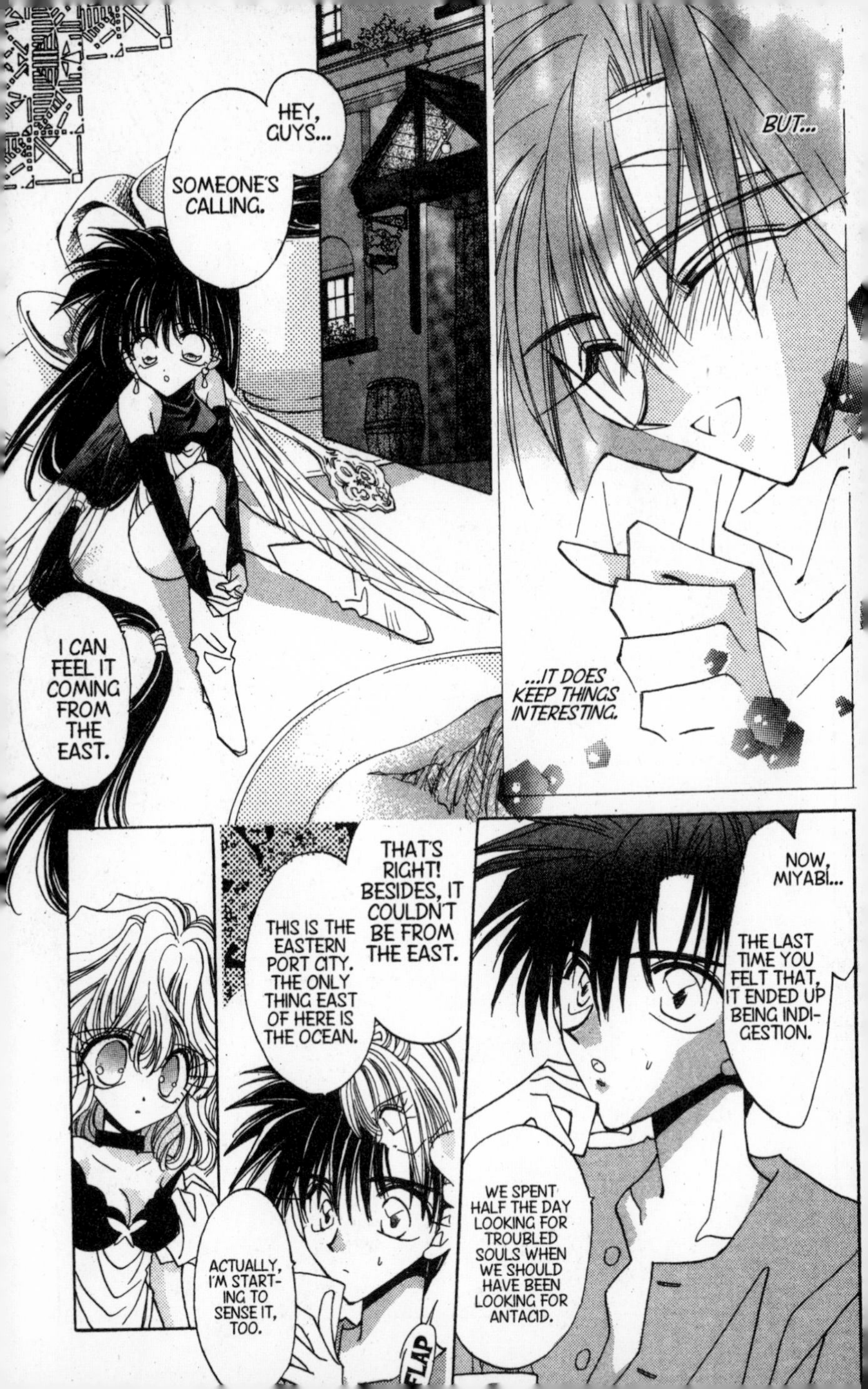
BUT...
...IT DOES KEEP THINGS INTERESTING.
HEY, GUYS...
SOMEONE'S CALLING.
I CAN FEEL IT COMING FROM THE EAST.
NOW, MIYABI...
THE LAST TIME YOU FELT THAT, IT ENDED UP BEING INDI-GESTION.
WE SPENT HALF THE DAY LOOKING FOR TROUBLED SOULS WHEN WE SHOULD HAVE BEEN LOOKING FOR ANTACID.
THAT'S RIGHT! BESIDES, IT COULDN'T BE FROM THE EAST.
THIS IS THE EASTERN PORT CITY. THE ONLY THING EAST OF HERE IS THE OCEAN.
ACTUALLY, I'M START-ING TO SENSE IT, TOO.
FLAP

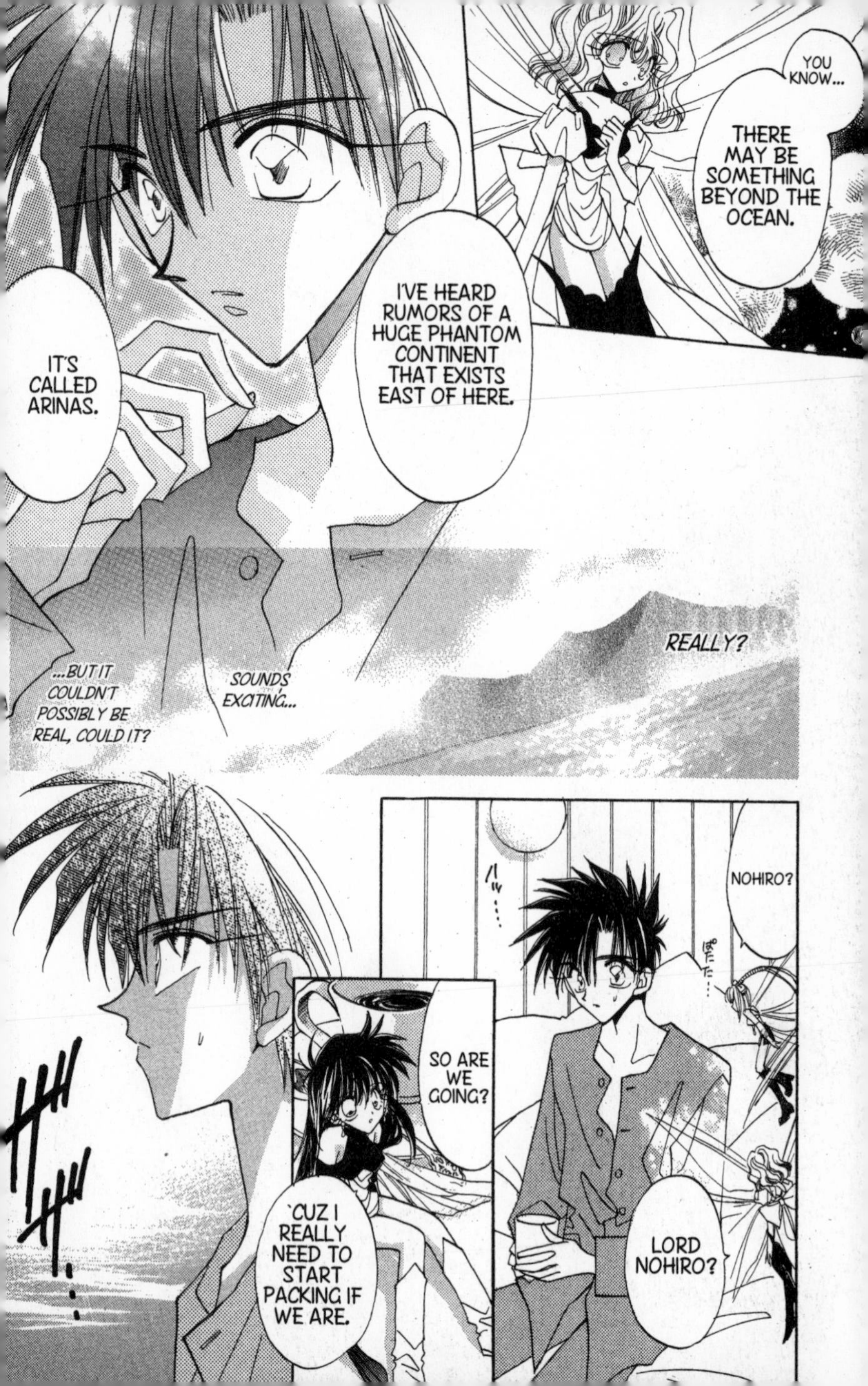
YOU KNOW...
THERE MAY BE SOMETHING BEYOND THE OCEAN.
I'VE HEARD RUMORS OF A HUGE PHANTOM CONTINENT THAT EXISTS EAST OF HERE.
IT'S CALLED ARINAS.
REALLY?
SOUNDS EXCITING...
...BUT IT COULDN'T POSSIBLY BE REAL, COULD IT?
NOHIRO?
LORD NOHIRO?
SO ARE WE GOING?
'CUZ I REALLY NEED TO START PACKING IF WE ARE.

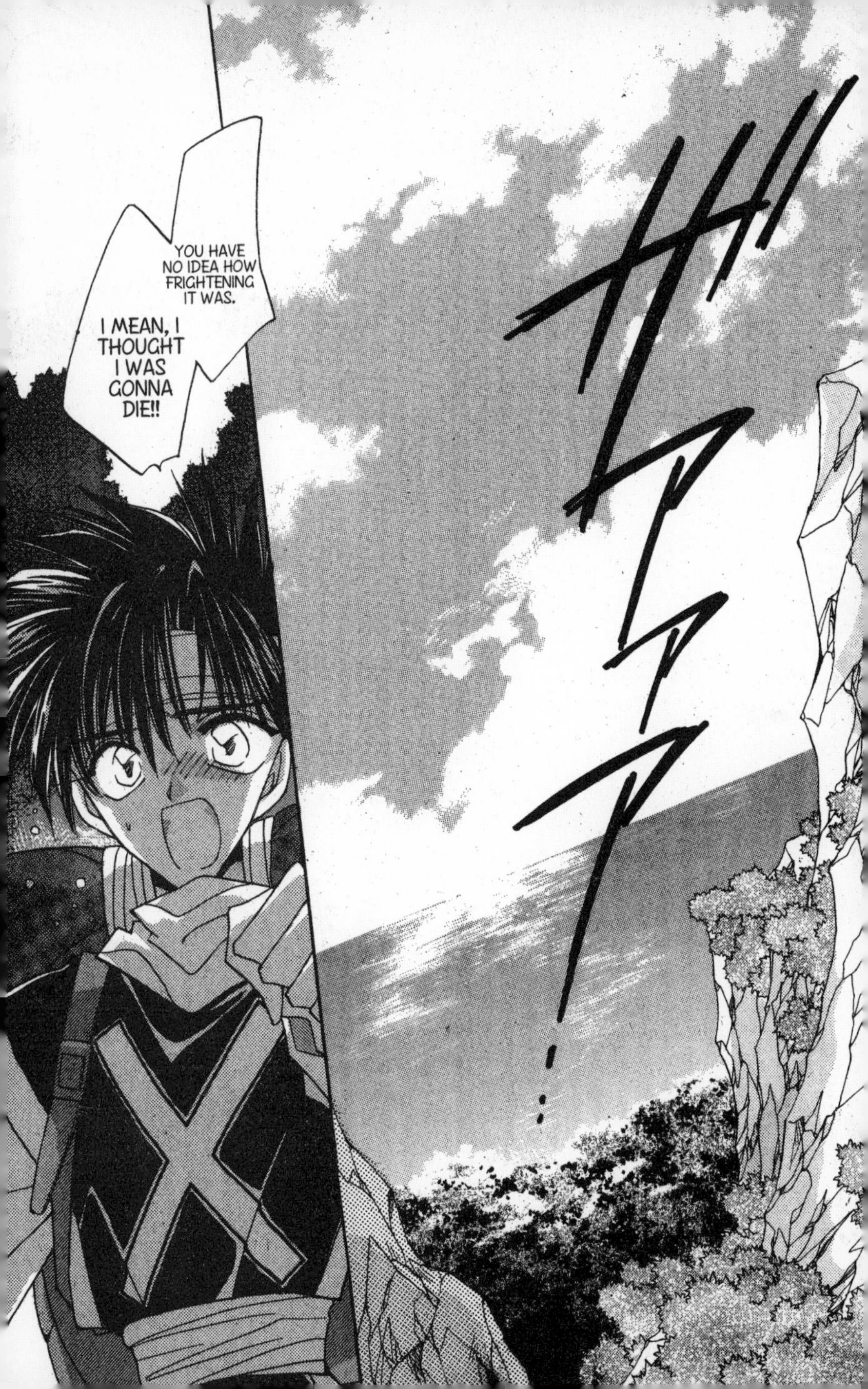
YOU HAVE NO IDEA HOW FRIGHTENING IT WAS.
I MEAN, I THOUGHT I WAS GONNA DIE!!
ザァァァ…

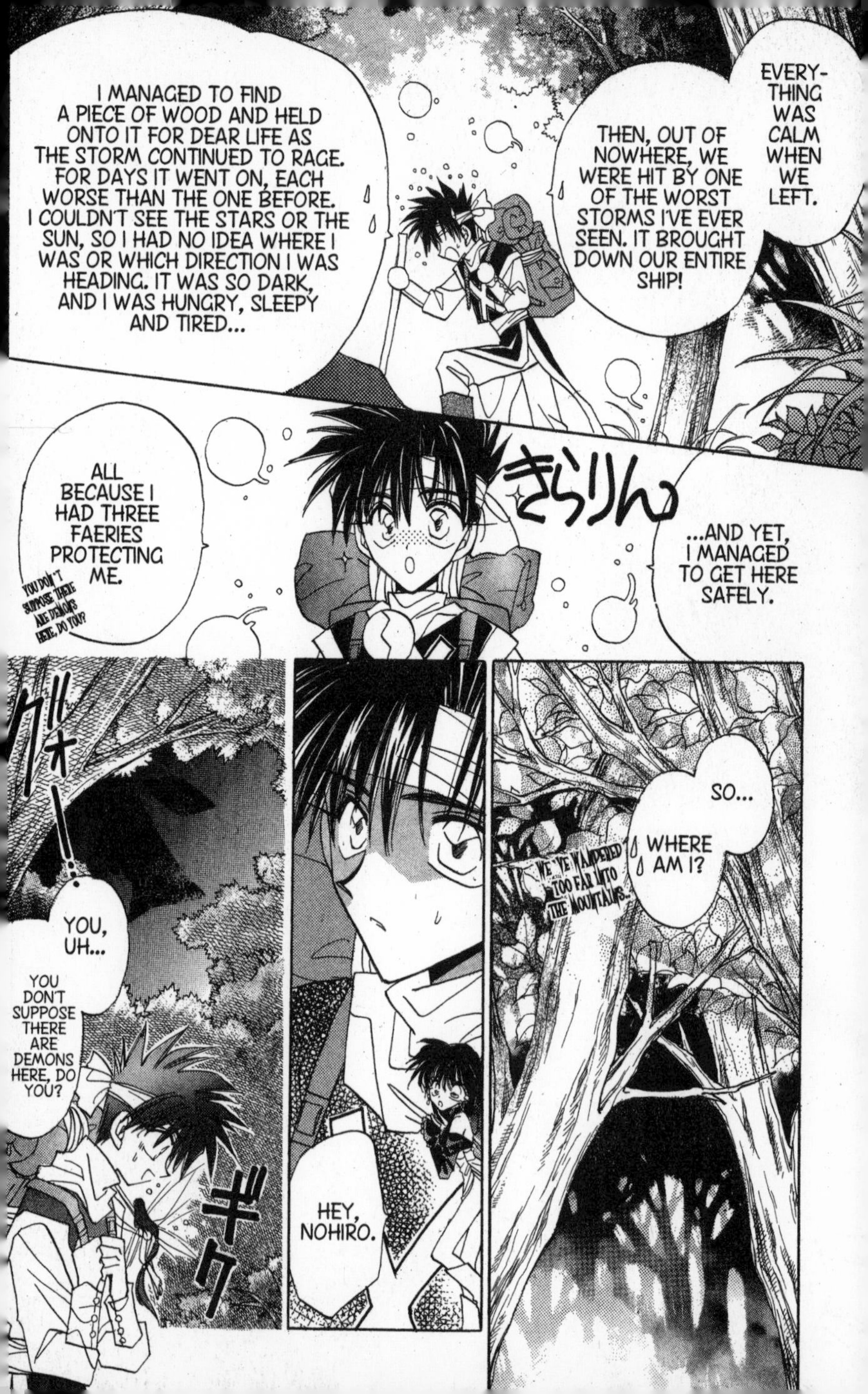
EVERY-THING WAS CALM WHEN WE LEFT.
THEN, OUT OF NOWHERE, WE WERE HIT BY ONE OF THE WORST STORMS I'VE EVER SEEN. IT BROUGHT DOWN OUR ENTIRE SHIP!
I MANAGED TO FIND A PIECE OF WOOD AND HELD ONTO IT FOR DEAR LIFE AS THE STORM CONTINUED TO RAGE. FOR DAYS IT WENT ON, EACH WORSE THAN THE ONE BEFORE. I COULDN'T SEE THE STARS OR THE SUN, SO I HAD NO IDEA WHERE I WAS OR WHICH DIRECTION I WAS HEADING. IT WAS SO DARK, AND I WAS HUNGRY, SLEEPY AND TIRED...
...AND YET, I MANAGED TO GET HERE SAFELY.
きらりん
ALL BECAUSE I HAD THREE FAERIES PROTECTING ME.
YOU DON'T SUPPOSE THERE ARE DEMONS HERE, DO YOU?
SO...
WHERE AM I?
WE'VE WANDERED TOO FAR INTO THE MOUNTAINS...
HEY, NOHIRO.
グォー
YOU, UH...
YOU DON'T SUPPOSE THERE ARE DEMONS HERE, DO YOU?
ギク

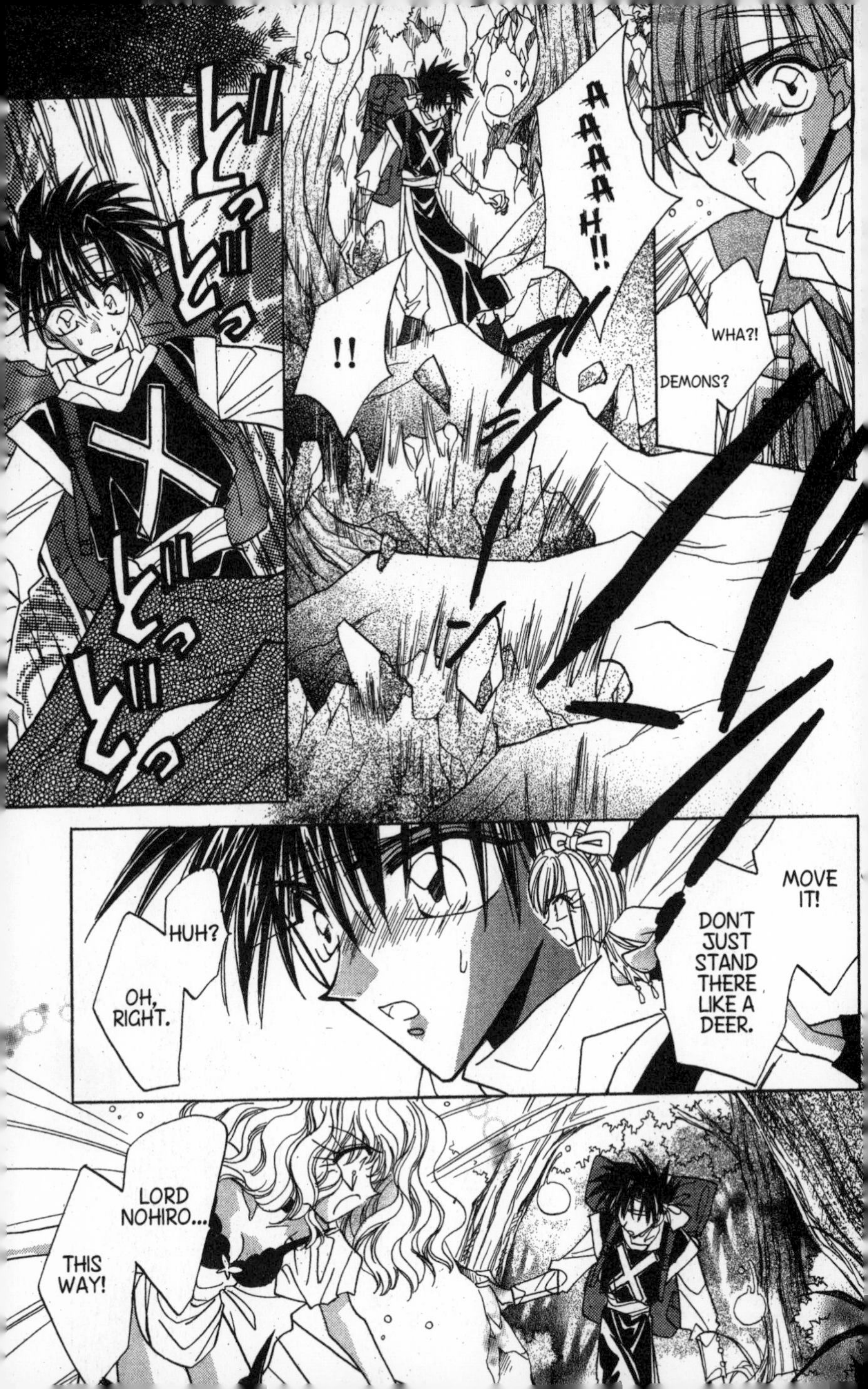

AAAAH!!
WHA?!
DEMONS?
!!
MOVE IT!
DON'T JUST STAND THERE LIKE A DEER.
HUH?
OH, RIGHT.
LORD NOHIRO...
THIS WAY!

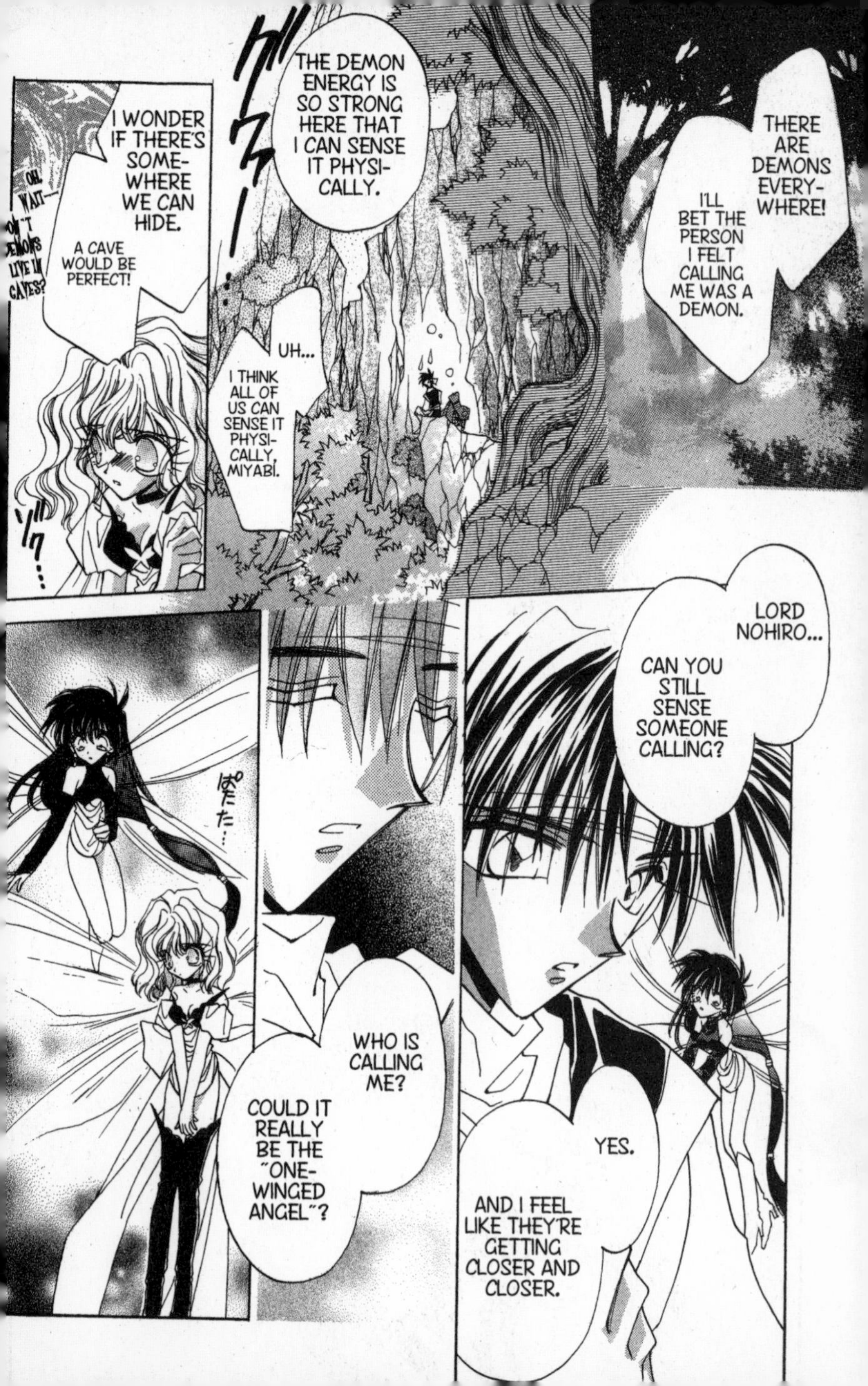
THERE ARE DEMONS EVERY-WHERE!
I'LL BET THE PERSON I FELT CALLING ME WAS A DEMON.
THE DEMON ENERGY IS SO STRONG HERE THAT I CAN SENSE IT PHYSI-CALLY.
UH...
I THINK ALL OF US CAN SENSE IT PHYSI-CALLY, MIYABI.
I WONDER IF THERE'S SOME-WHERE WE CAN HIDE.
A CAVE WOULD BE PERFECT!
OH, WAIT— DON'T DEMONS LIVE IN CAVES?
LORD NOHIRO...
CAN YOU STILL SENSE SOMEONE CALLING?
YES.
AND I FEEL LIKE THEY'RE GETTING CLOSER AND CLOSER.
WHO IS CALLING ME?
COULD IT REALLY BE THE "ONE-WINGED ANGEL"?
ぱたた…

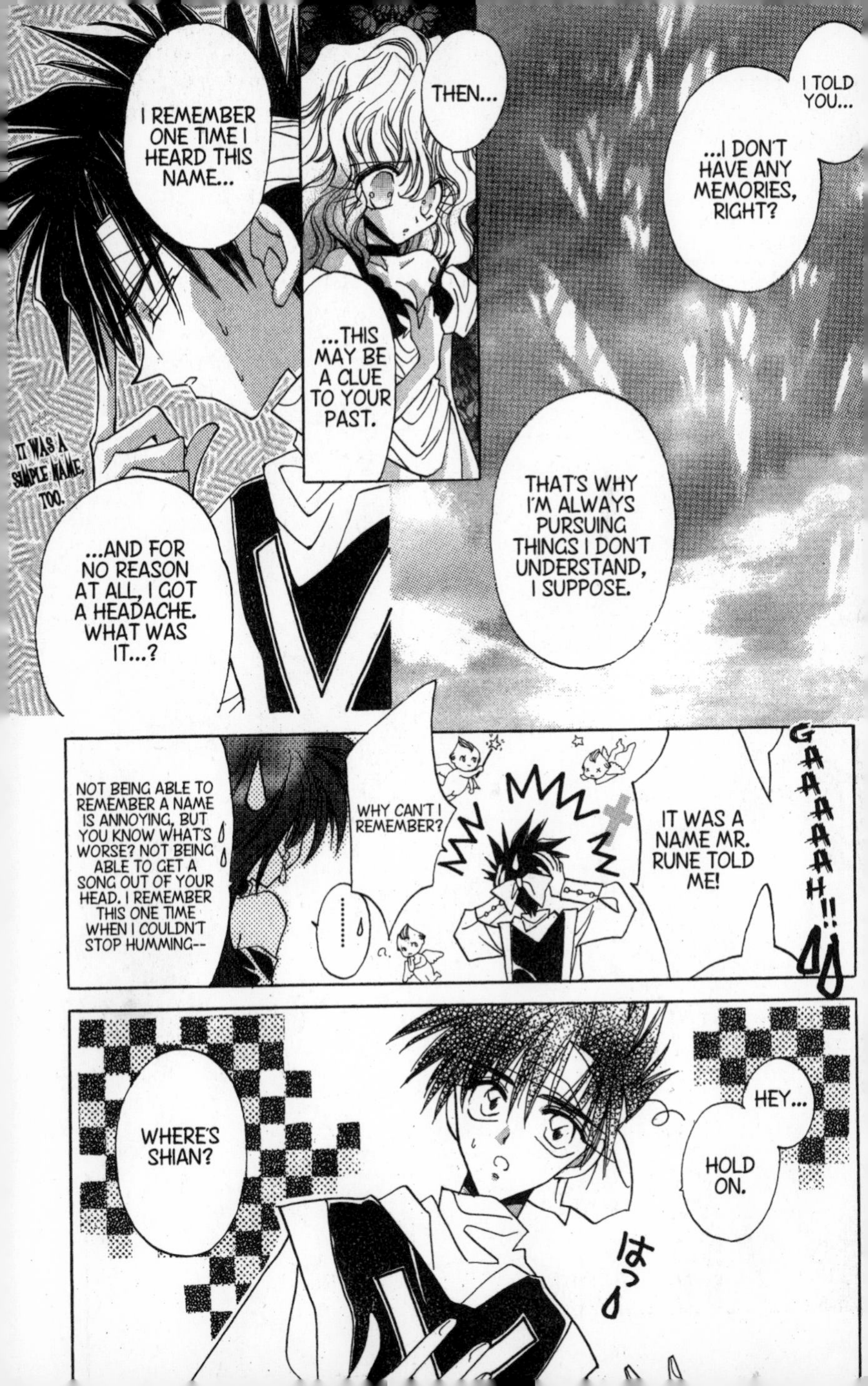
I TOLD YOU...
...I DON'T HAVE ANY MEMORIES, RIGHT?
THAT'S WHY I'M ALWAYS PURSUING THINGS I DON'T UNDERSTAND, I SUPPOSE.
THEN...
...THIS MAY BE A CLUE TO YOUR PAST.
I REMEMBER ONE TIME I HEARD THIS NAME...
IT WAS A SIMPLE NAME, TOO.
...AND FOR NO REASON AT ALL, I GOT A HEADACHE. WHAT WAS IT...?
GAAAAAH!!
IT WAS A NAME MR. RUNE TOLD ME!
WHY CAN'T I REMEMBER?
....
NOT BEING ABLE TO REMEMBER A NAME IS ANNOYING, BUT YOU KNOW WHAT'S WORSE? NOT BEING ABLE TO GET A SONG OUT OF YOUR HEAD. I REMEMBER THIS ONE TIME WHEN I COULDN'T STOP HUMMING--
HEY...
HOLD ON.
はっ
WHERE'S SHIAN?

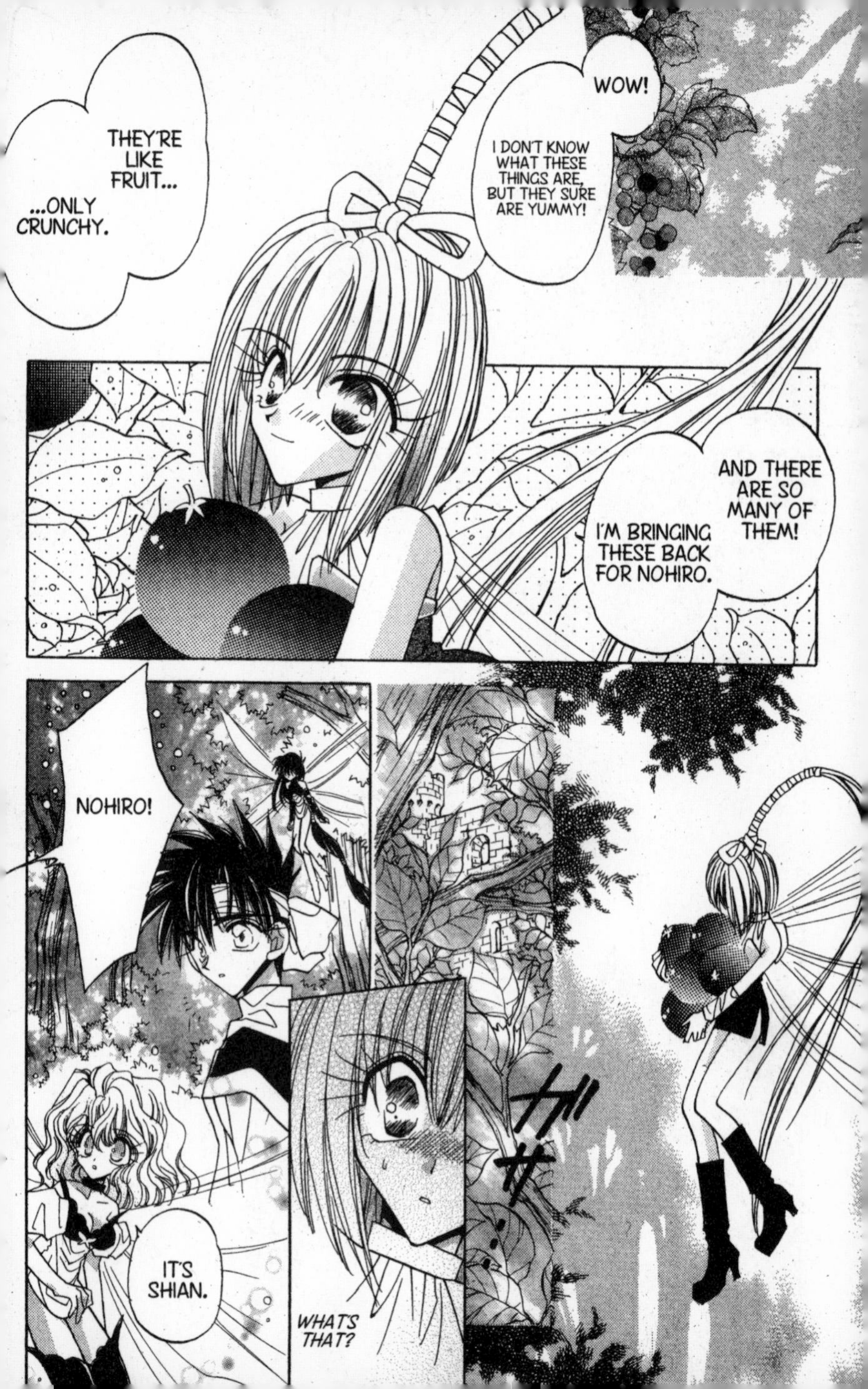
WOW!
I DON'T KNOW WHAT THESE THINGS ARE, BUT THEY SURE ARE YUMMY!
THEY'RE LIKE FRUIT...
...ONLY CRUNCHY.
AND THERE ARE SO MANY OF THEM!
I'M BRINGING THESE BACK FOR NOHIRO.
WHAT'S THAT?
NOHIRO!
IT'S SHIAN.

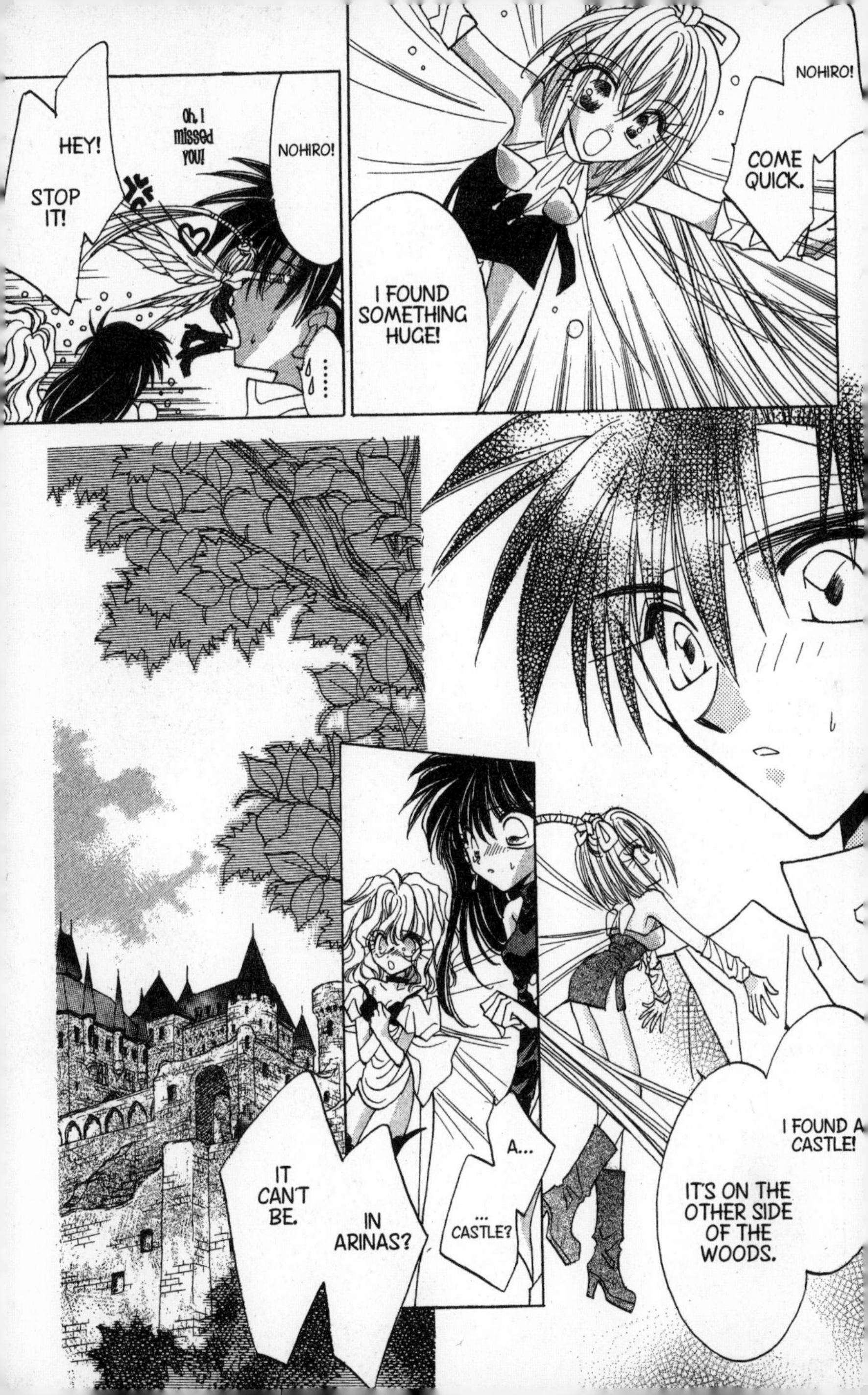
NOHIRO!
COME QUICK.
I FOUND SOMETHING HUGE!
NOHIRO!
Oh, I missed you!
HEY!
STOP IT!
......
I FOUND A CASTLE!
IT'S ON THE OTHER SIDE OF THE WOODS.
A...
...CASTLE?
IN ARINAS?
IT CAN'T BE.

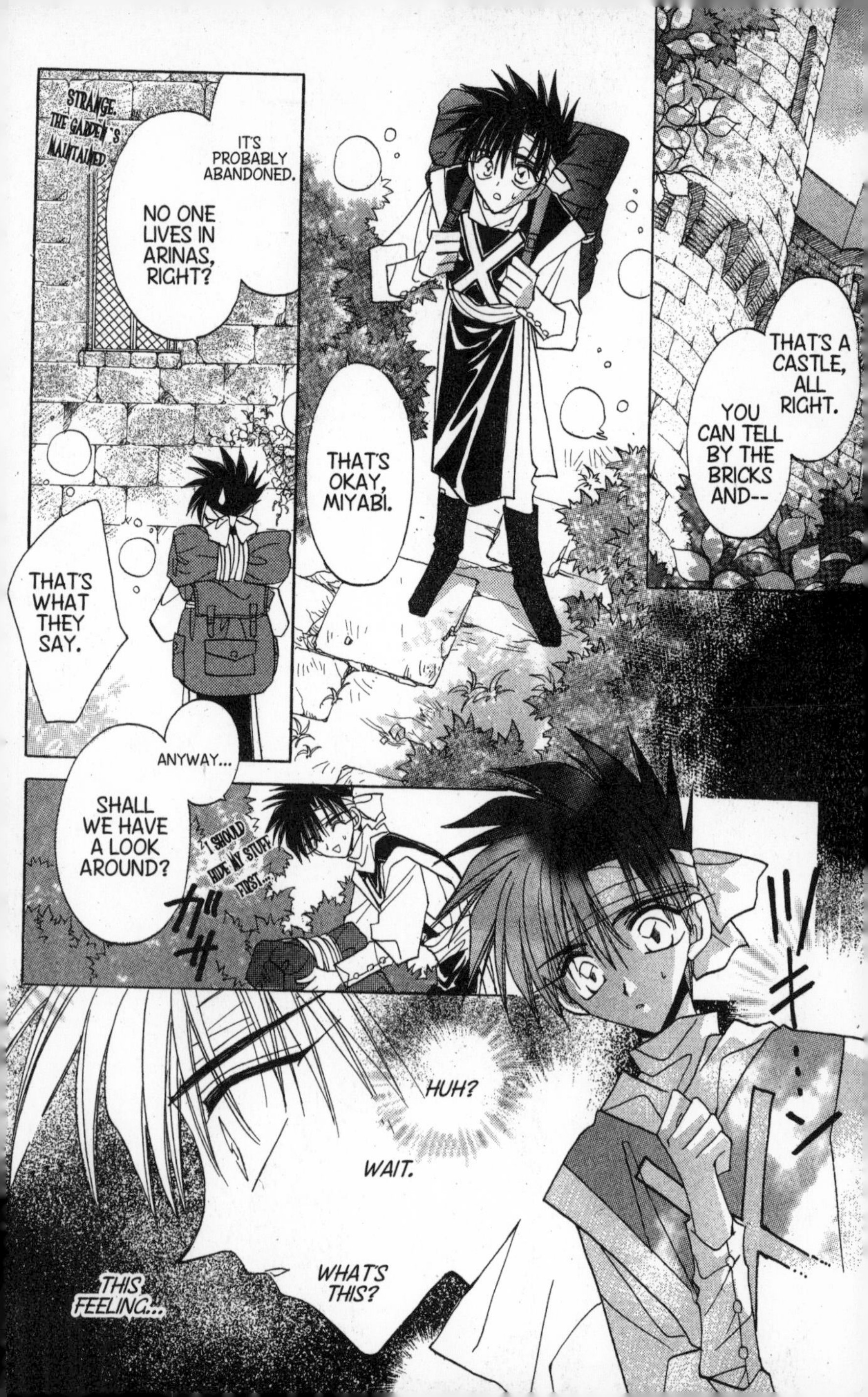
THAT'S A CASTLE, ALL RIGHT.
YOU CAN TELL BY THE BRICKS AND--
THAT'S OKAY, MIYABI.
IT'S PROBABLY ABANDONED.
NO ONE LIVES IN ARINAS, RIGHT?
STRANGE. THE GARDEN'S MAINTAINED.
THAT'S WHAT THEY SAY.
ANYWAY...
SHALL WE HAVE A LOOK AROUND?
I SHOULD HIDE MY STUFF FIRST...
HUH?
WAIT.
WHAT'S THIS?
THIS FEELING...

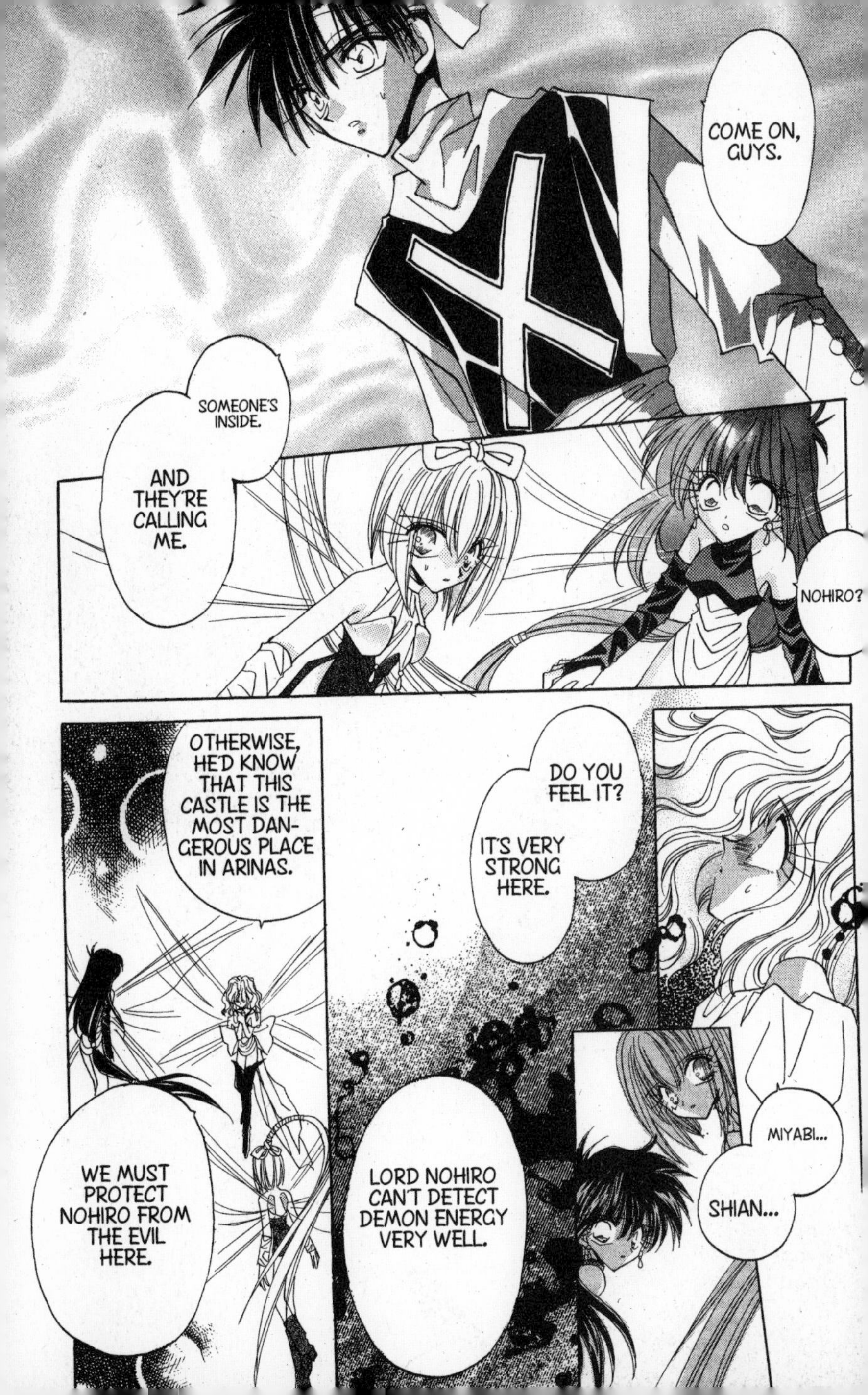
COME ON, GUYS.
NOHIRO?
SOMEONE'S INSIDE.
AND THEY'RE CALLING ME.
DO YOU FEEL IT?
IT'S VERY STRONG HERE.
MIYABI...
SHIAN...
LORD NOHIRO CAN'T DETECT DEMON ENERGY VERY WELL.
OTHERWISE, HE'D KNOW THAT THIS CASTLE IS THE MOST DAN-GEROUS PLACE IN ARINAS.
WE MUST PROTECT NOHIRO FROM THE EVIL HERE.

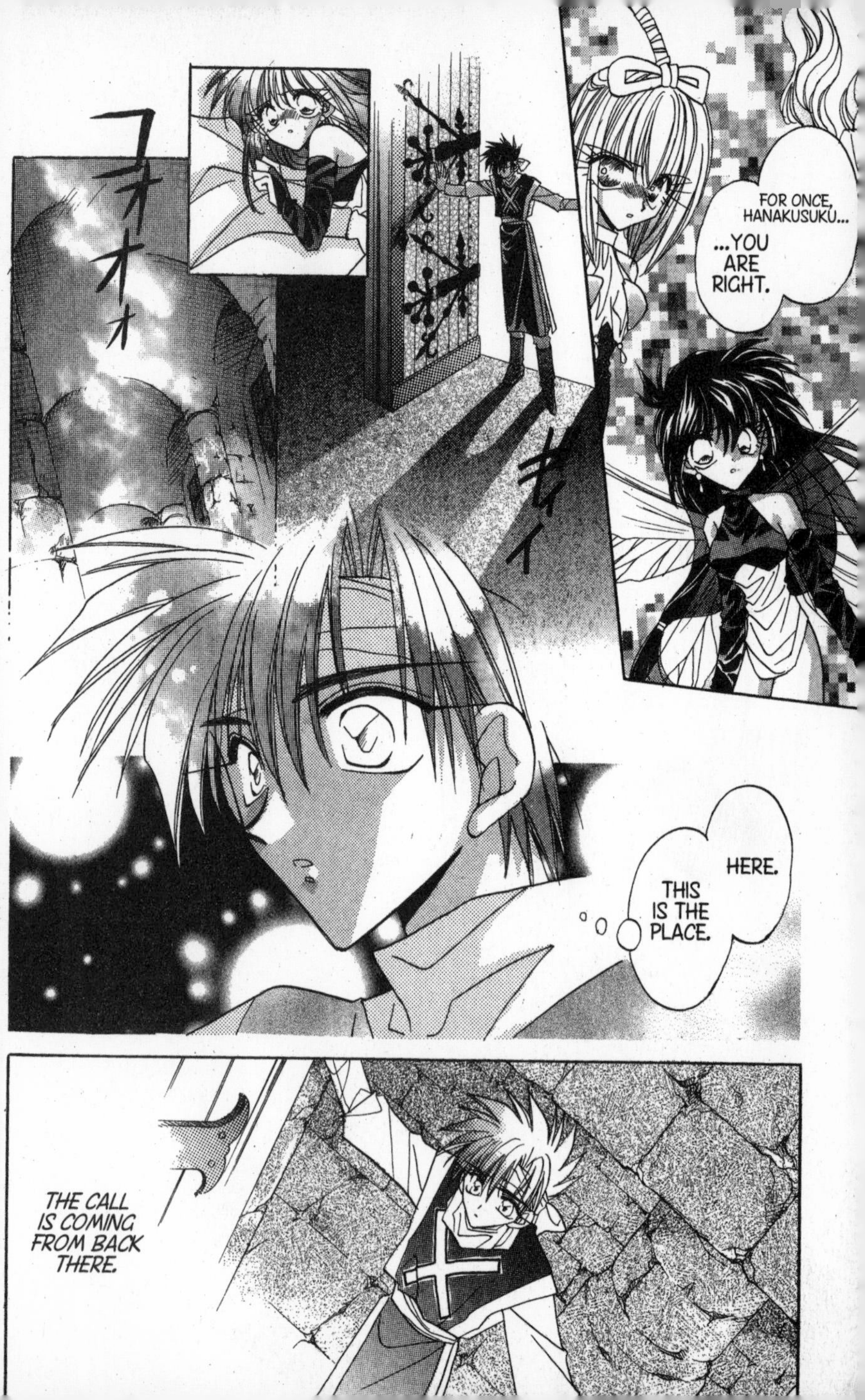
FOR ONCE, HANAKUSUKU...
...YOU ARE RIGHT.
キィ
コオオオ
HERE. THIS IS THE PLACE.
THE CALL IS COMING FROM BACK THERE.

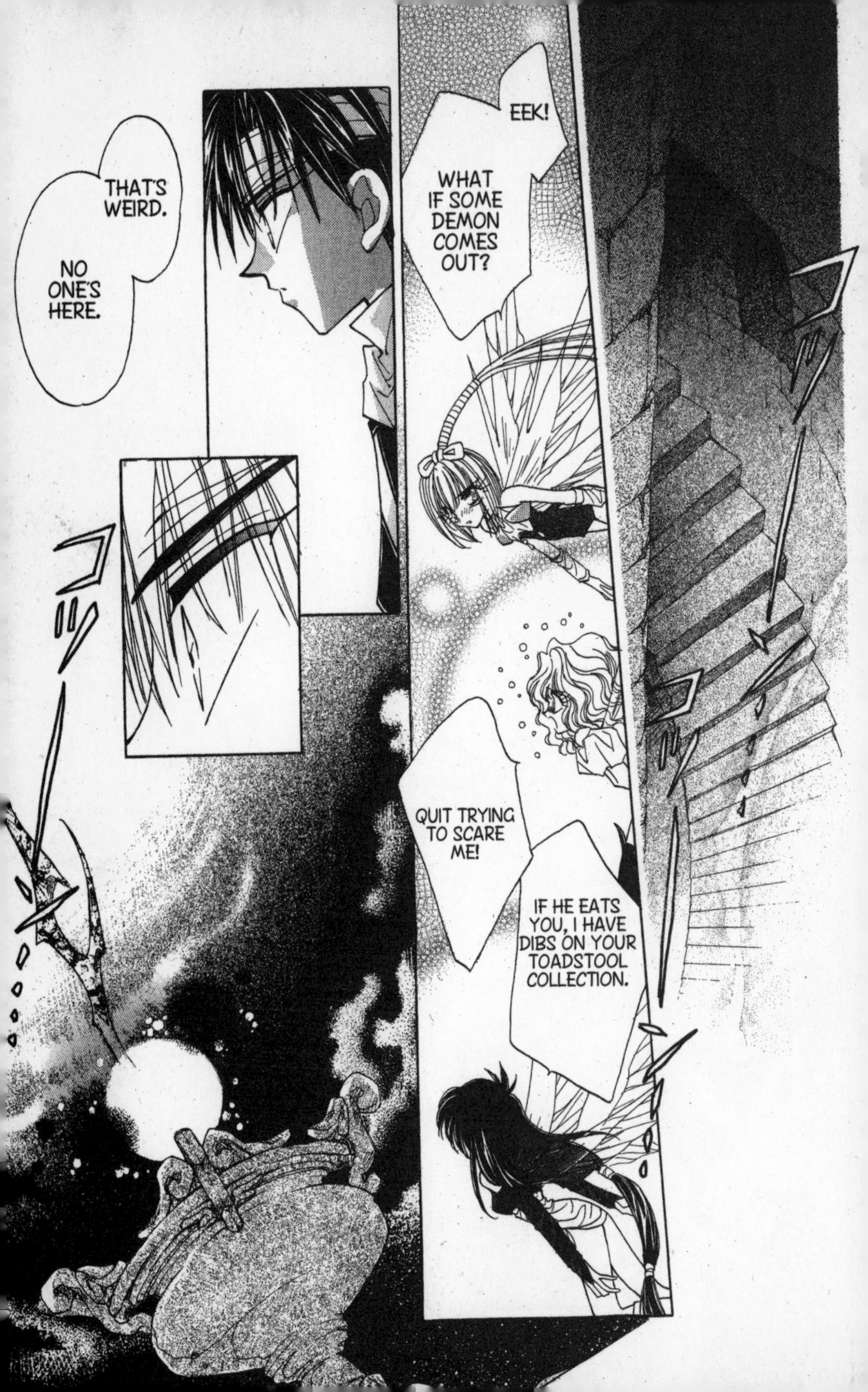
EEK!
WHAT IF SOME DEMON COMES OUT?
QUIT TRYING TO SCARE ME!
IF HE EATS YOU, I HAVE DIBS ON YOUR TOADSTOOL COLLECTION.
THAT'S WEIRD.
NO ONE'S HERE.

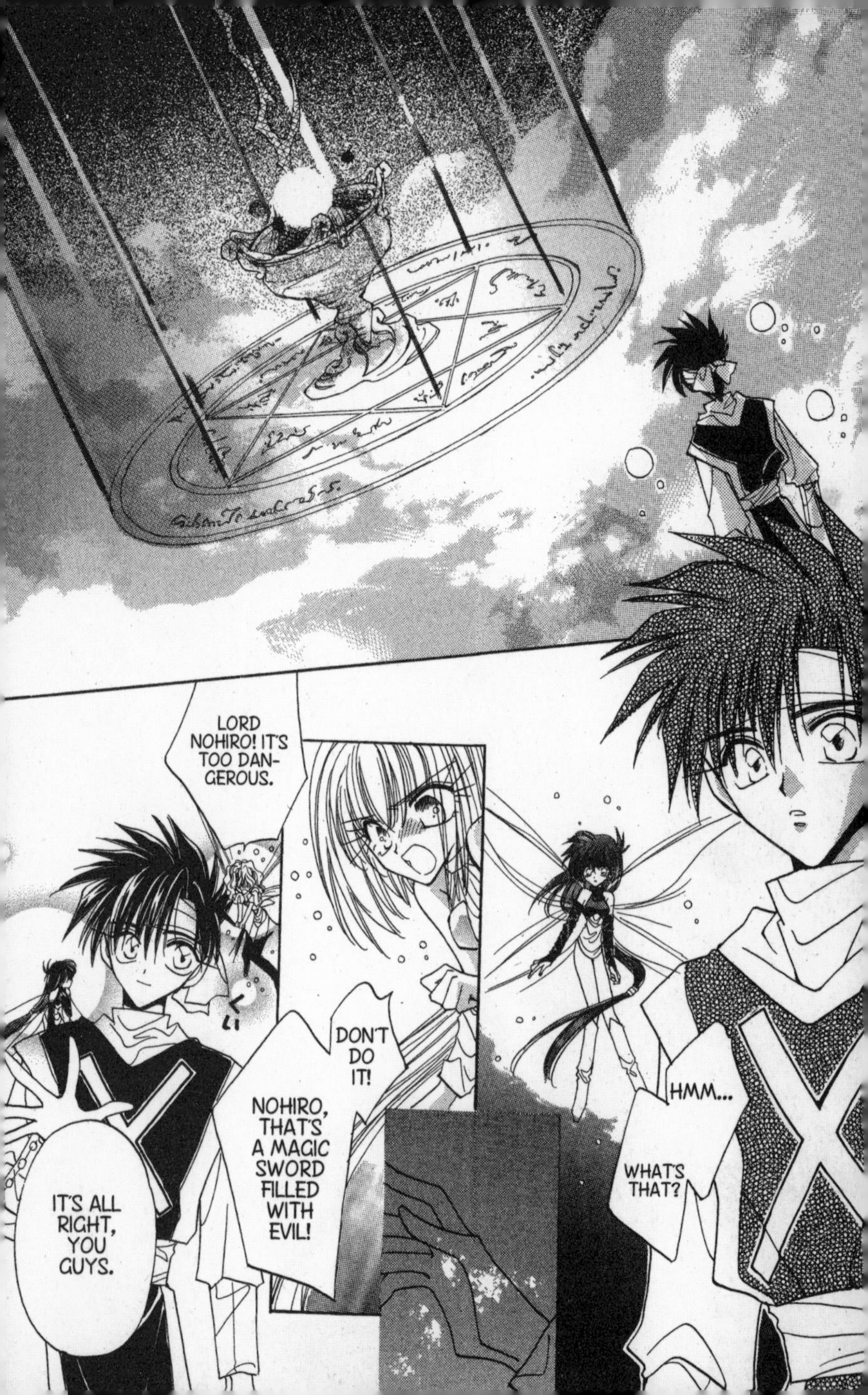

HMM...
WHAT'S THAT?
DON'T DO IT!
NOHIRO, THAT'S A MAGIC SWORD FILLED WITH EVIL!
LORD NOHIRO! IT'S TOO DANGEROUS.
IT'S ALL RIGHT, YOU GUYS.

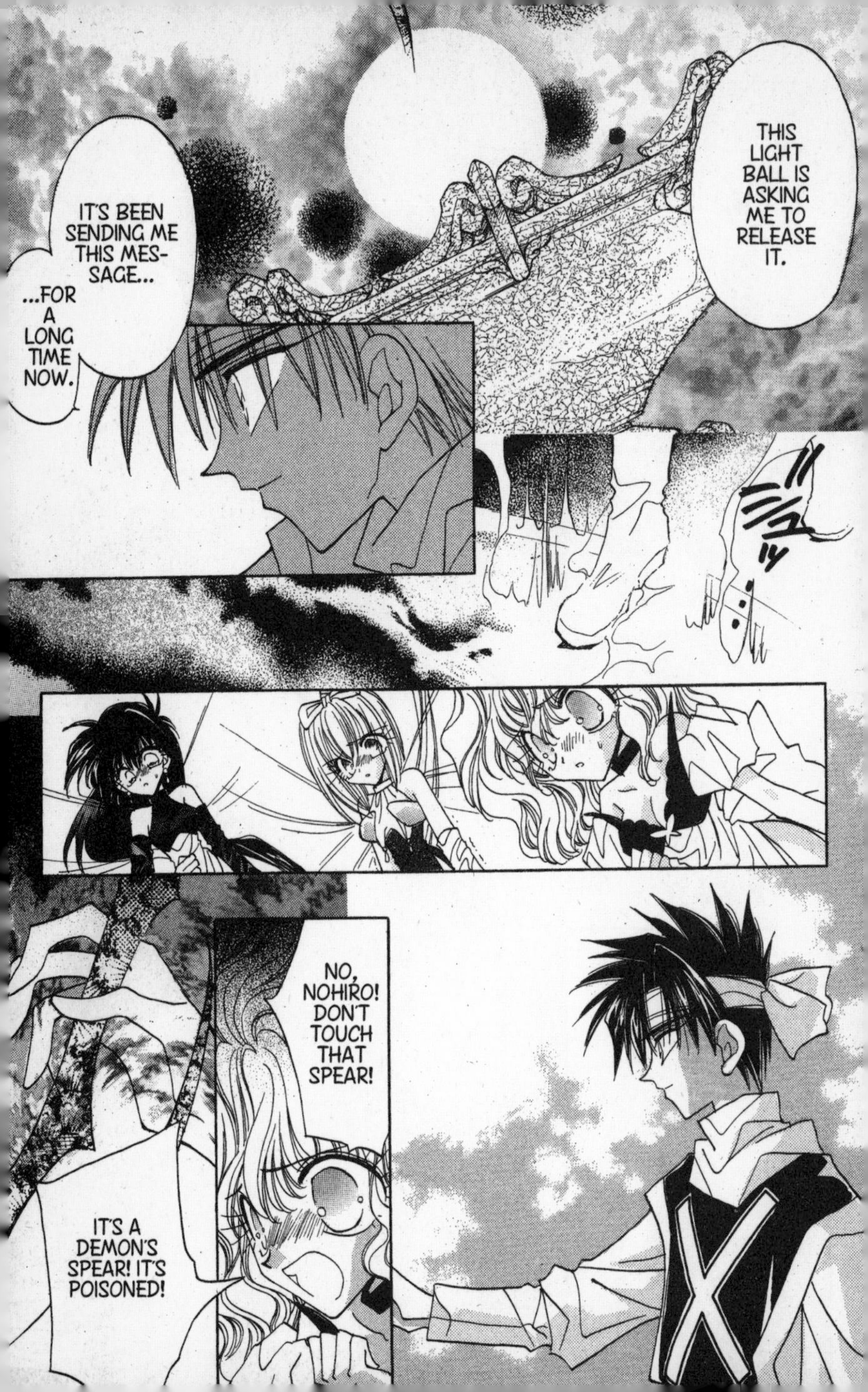
THIS LIGHT BALL IS ASKING ME TO RELEASE IT.
IT'S BEEN SENDING ME THIS MES-SAGE...
...FOR A LONG TIME NOW.
NO, NOHIRO! DON'T TOUCH THAT SPEAR!
IT'S A DEMON'S SPEAR! IT'S POISONED!

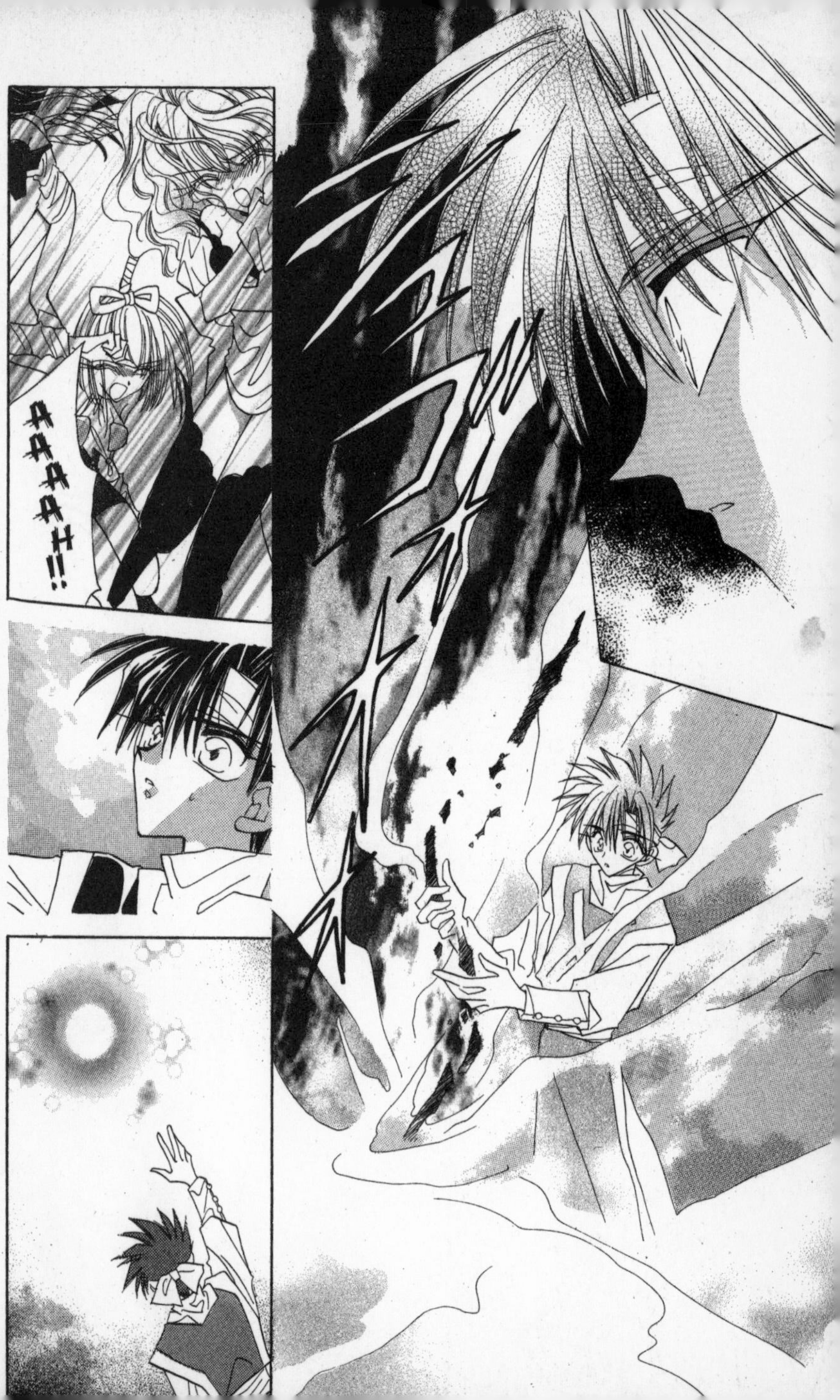
AAAAAH!!

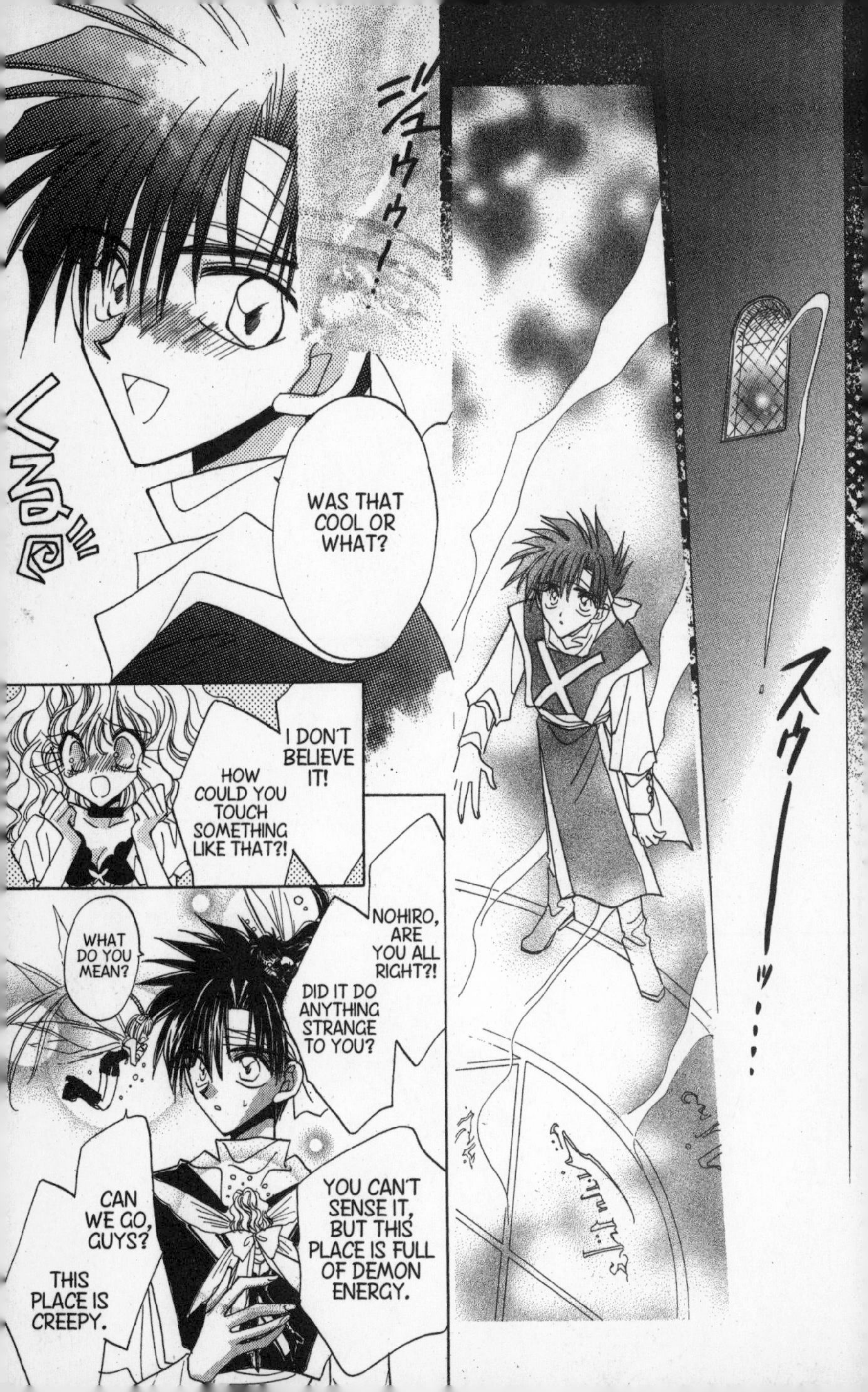
スウーーッ…
ジュウウー…
WAS THAT COOL OR WHAT?
くるっ!!
I DON'T BELIEVE IT!
HOW COULD YOU TOUCH SOMETHING LIKE THAT?!
NOHIRO, ARE YOU ALL RIGHT?!
DID IT DO ANYTHING STRANGE TO YOU?
WHAT DO YOU MEAN?
YOU CAN'T SENSE IT, BUT THIS PLACE IS FULL OF DEMON ENERGY.
CAN WE GO, GUYS?
THIS PLACE IS CREEPY.

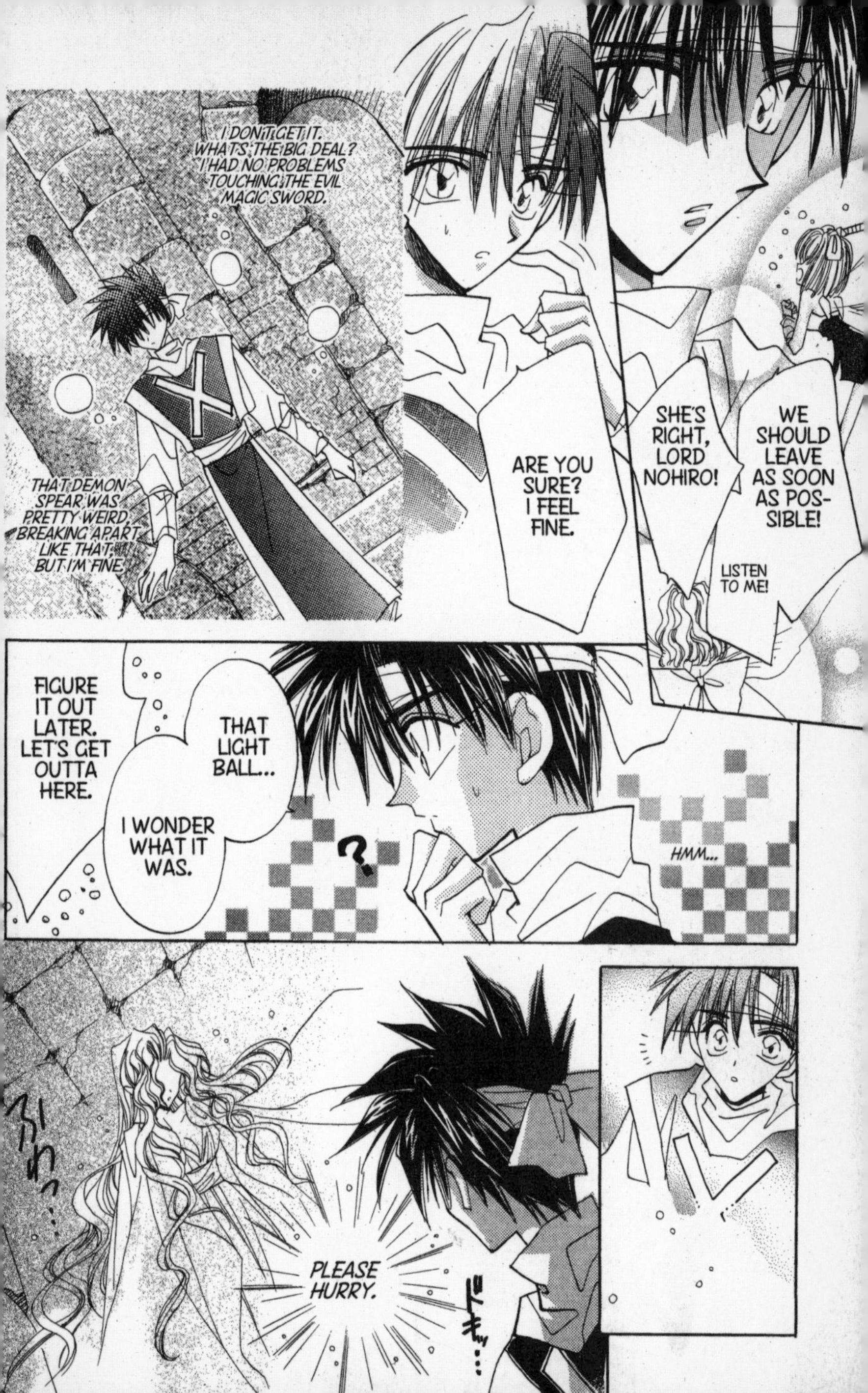

WE SHOULD LEAVE AS SOON AS POS-SIBLE!
SHE'S RIGHT, LORD NOHIRO!
LISTEN TO ME!
ARE YOU SURE? I FEEL FINE.
I DON'T GET IT. WHAT'S THE BIG DEAL? I HAD NO PROBLEMS TOUCHING THE EVIL MAGIC SWORD.
THAT DEMON SPEAR WAS PRETTY WEIRD, BREAKING APART LIKE THAT, BUT I'M FINE.
HMM...
?
THAT LIGHT BALL...
I WONDER WHAT IT WAS.
FIGURE IT OUT LATER. LET'S GET OUTTA HERE.
ドキッ…
PLEASE HURRY.
ふわっ…

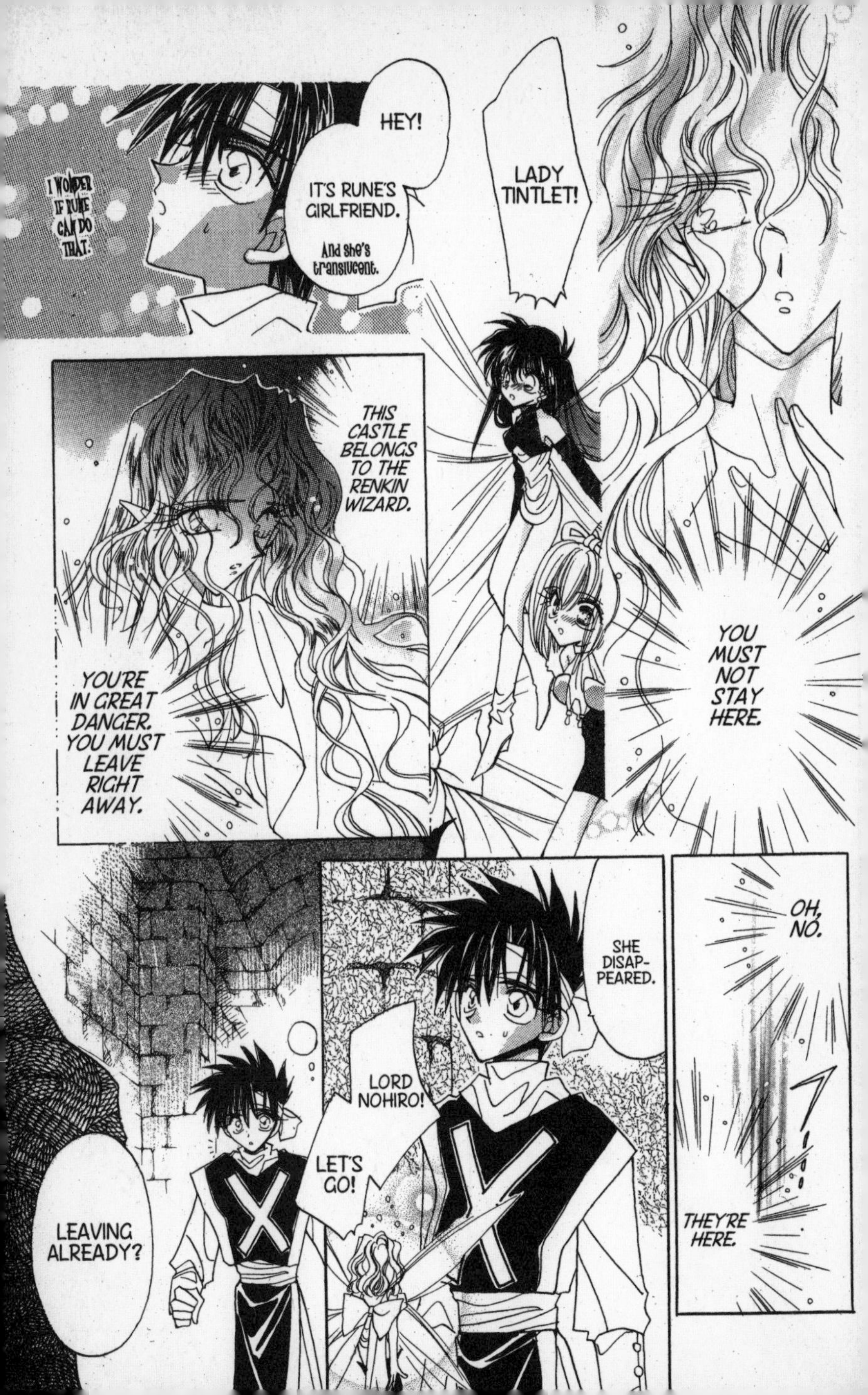

LADY TINTLET!
HEY!
IT'S RUNE'S GIRLFRIEND.
And she's translucent.
I WONDER IF RUNE CAN DO THAT.
THIS CASTLE BELONGS TO THE RENKIN WIZARD.
YOU'RE IN GREAT DANGER. YOU MUST LEAVE RIGHT AWAY.
YOU MUST NOT STAY HERE.
OH, NO.
THEY'RE HERE.
SHE DISAPPEARED.
LORD NOHIRO!
LET'S GO!
LEAVING ALREADY?

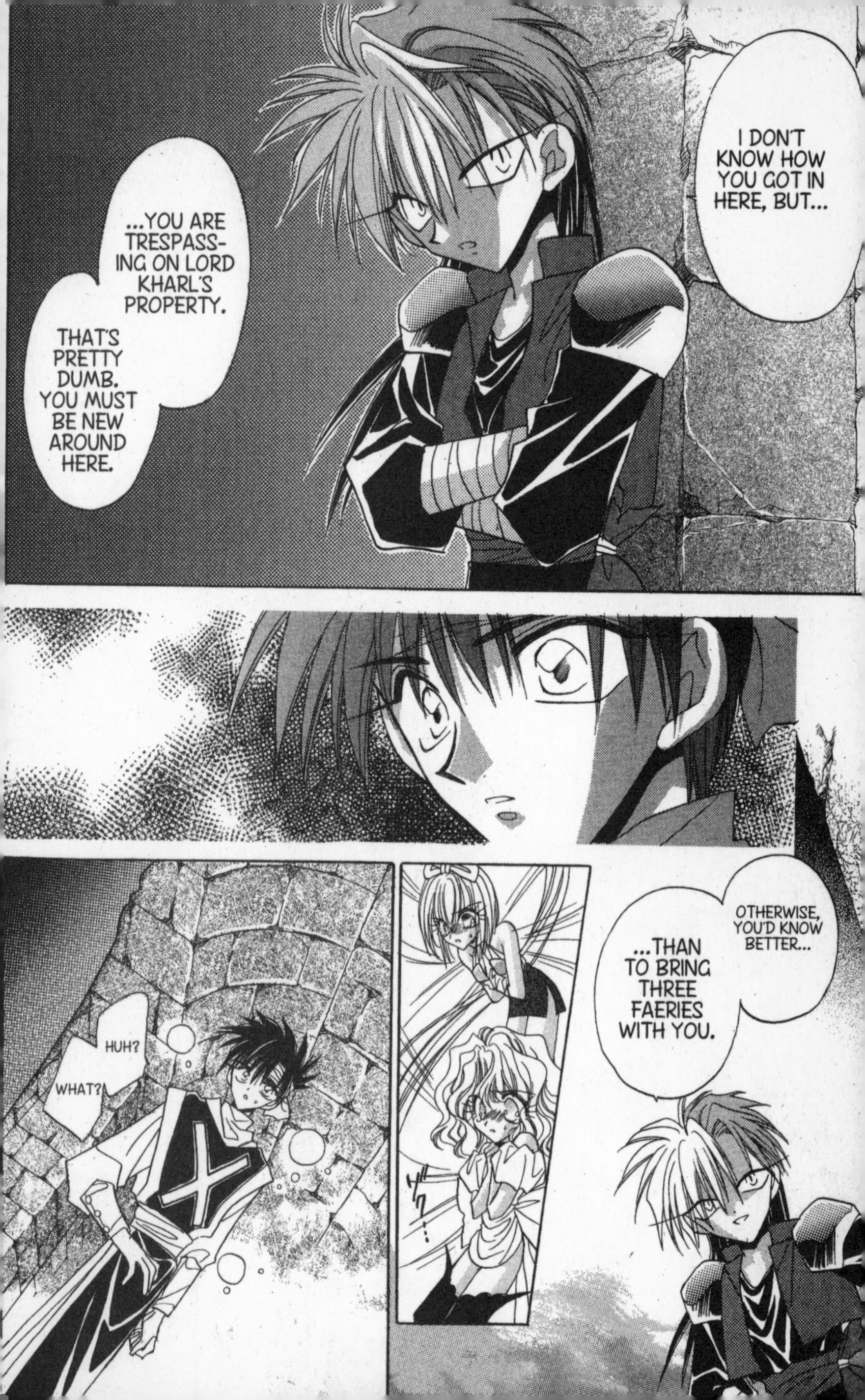

I DON'T KNOW HOW YOU GOT IN HERE, BUT...
...YOU ARE TRESPASS-ING ON LORD KHARL'S PROPERTY.
THAT'S PRETTY DUMB. YOU MUST BE NEW AROUND HERE.
OTHERWISE, YOU'D KNOW BETTER...
...THAN TO BRING THREE FAERIES WITH YOU.
HUH?
WHAT?

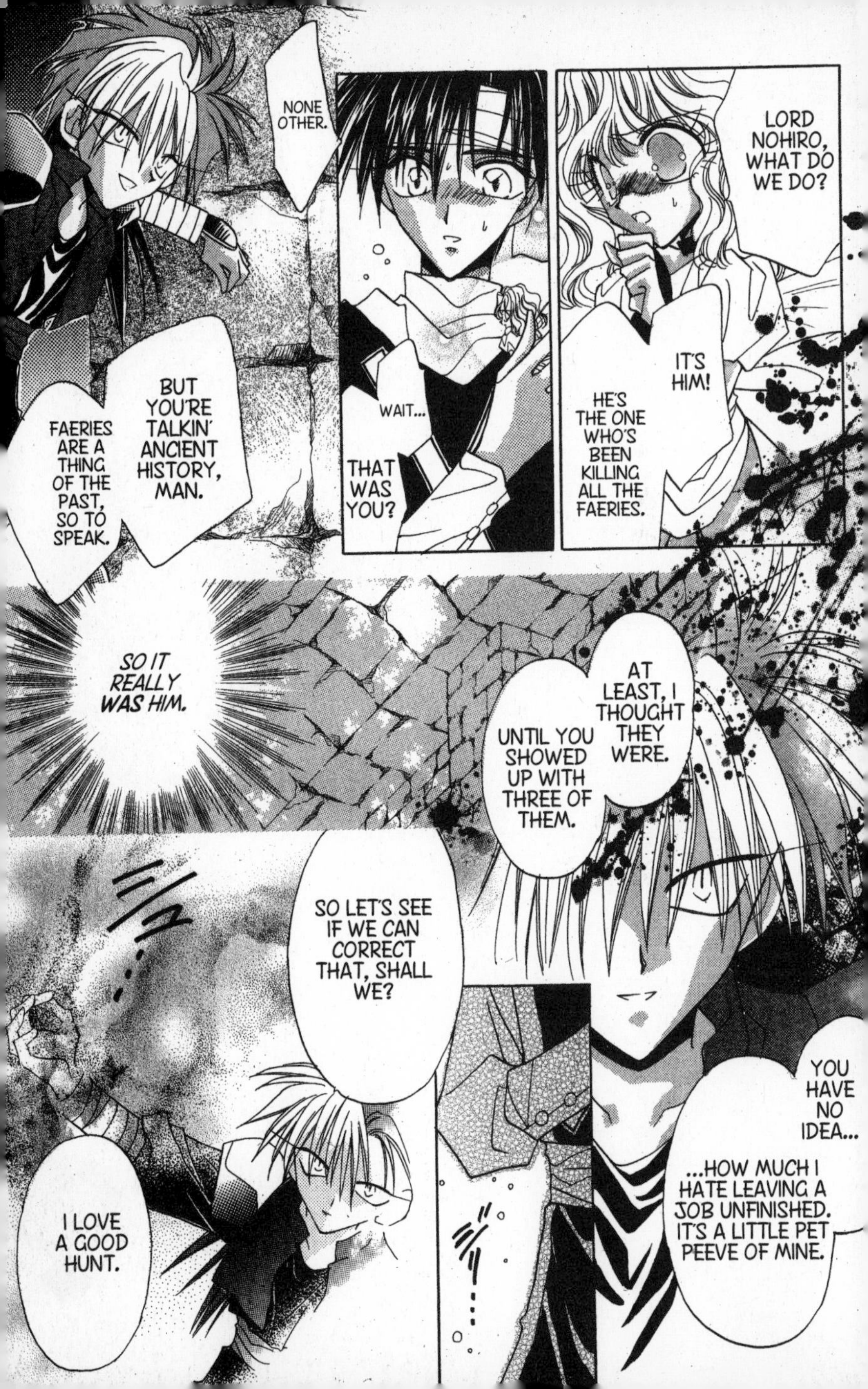
LORD NOHIRO, WHAT DO WE DO?
IT'S HIM!
HE'S THE ONE WHO'S BEEN KILLING ALL THE FAERIES.
WAIT...
THAT WAS YOU?
NONE OTHER.
BUT YOU'RE TALKIN' ANCIENT HISTORY, MAN.
FAERIES ARE A THING OF THE PAST, SO TO SPEAK.
AT LEAST, I THOUGHT THEY WERE.
UNTIL YOU SHOWED UP WITH THREE OF THEM.
SO IT REALLY ***WAS*** HIM.
YOU HAVE NO IDEA...
...HOW MUCH I HATE LEAVING A JOB UNFINISHED. IT'S A LITTLE PET PEEVE OF MINE.
SO LET'S SEE IF WE CAN CORRECT THAT, SHALL WE?
I LOVE A GOOD HUNT.

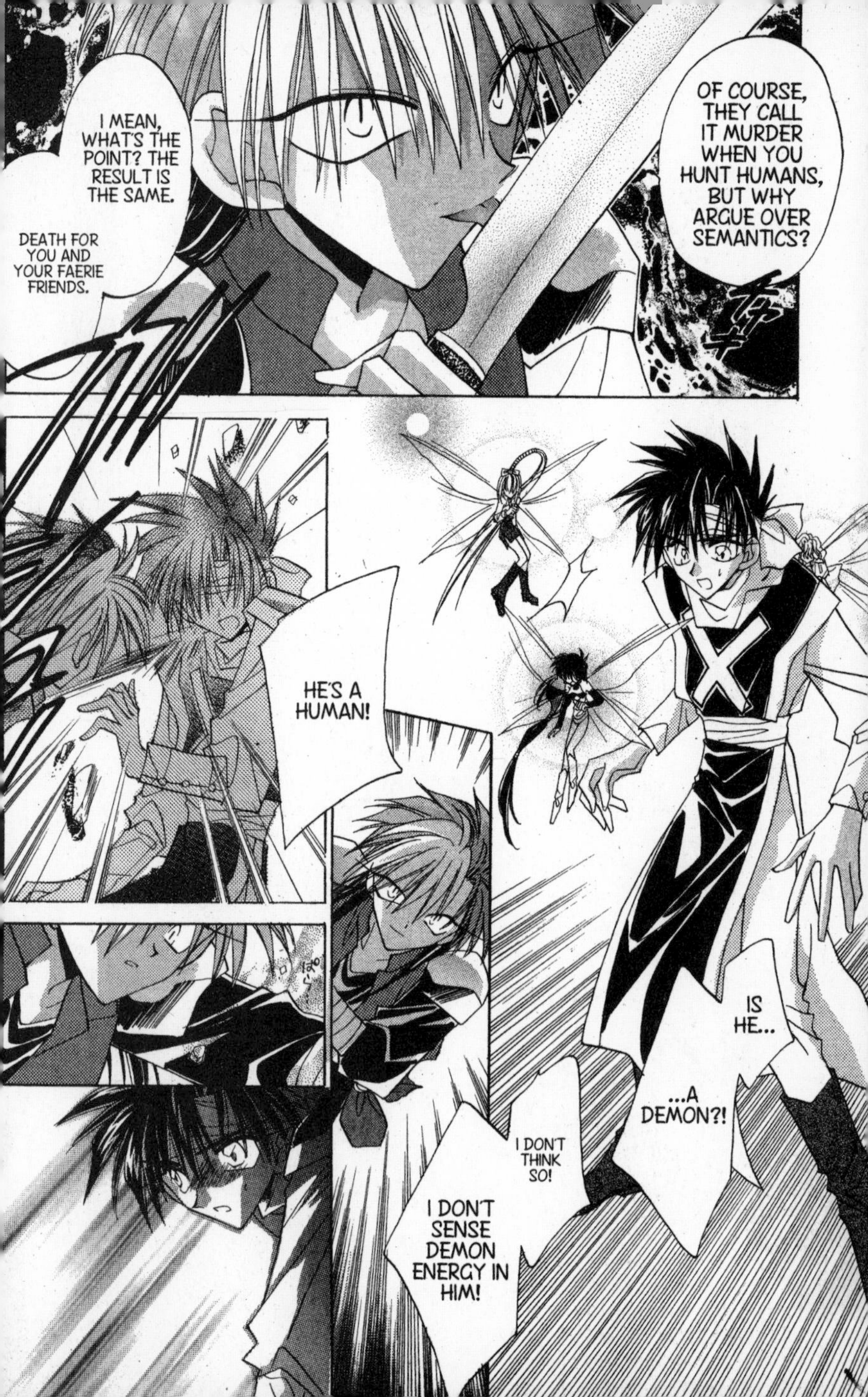
OF COURSE, THEY CALL IT MURDER WHEN YOU HUNT HUMANS, BUT WHY ARGUE OVER SEMANTICS?
I MEAN, WHAT'S THE POINT? THE RESULT IS THE SAME.
DEATH FOR YOU AND YOUR FAERIE FRIENDS.
IS HE...
...A DEMON?!
HE'S A HUMAN!
I DON'T THINK SO!
I DON'T SENSE DEMON ENERGY IN HIM!

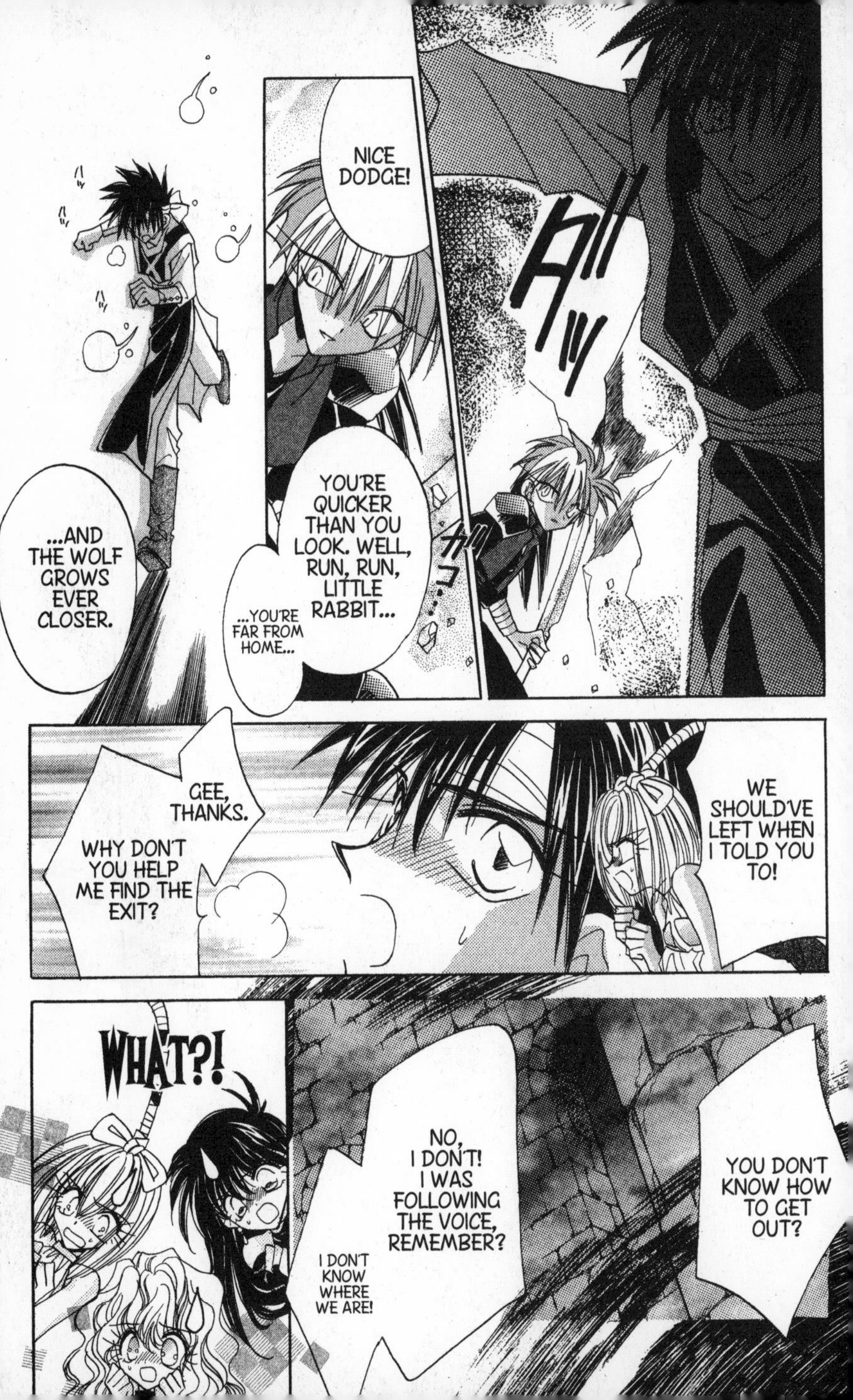
NICE DODGE!
YOU'RE QUICKER THAN YOU LOOK. WELL, RUN, RUN, LITTLE RABBIT...
...YOU'RE FAR FROM HOME...
...AND THE WOLF GROWS EVER CLOSER.
WE SHOULD'VE LEFT WHEN I TOLD YOU TO!
GEE, THANKS.
WHY DON'T YOU HELP ME FIND THE EXIT?
YOU DON'T KNOW HOW TO GET OUT?
NO, I DON'T! I WAS FOLLOWING THE VOICE, REMEMBER?
I DON'T KNOW WHERE WE ARE!
WHAT?!

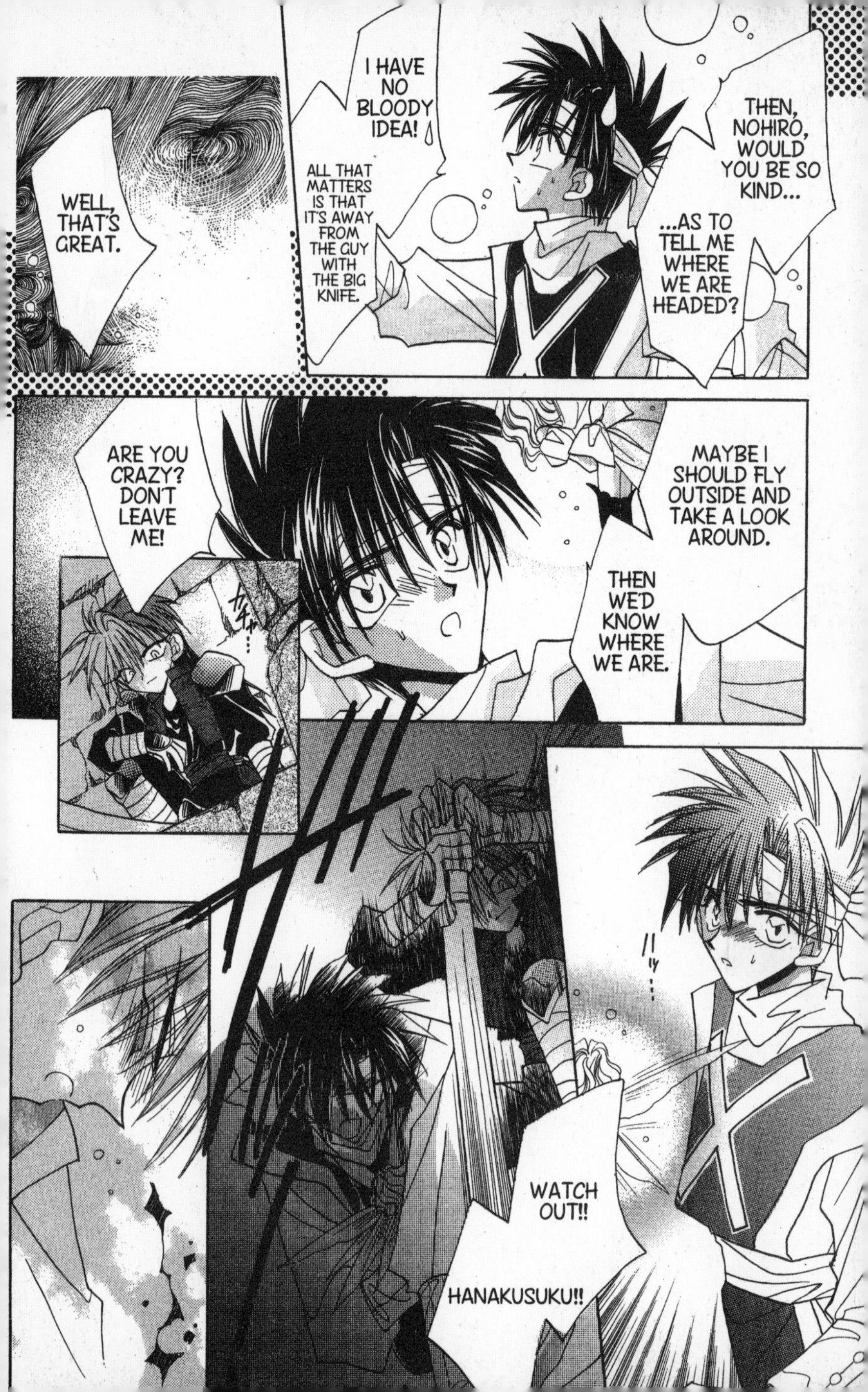
THEN, NOHIRO, WOULD YOU BE SO KIND...
...AS TO TELL ME WHERE WE ARE HEADED?
I HAVE NO BLOODY IDEA!
ALL THAT MATTERS IS THAT IT'S AWAY FROM THE GUY WITH THE BIG KNIFE.
WELL, THAT'S GREAT.
MAYBE I SHOULD FLY OUTSIDE AND TAKE A LOOK AROUND.
THEN WE'D KNOW WHERE WE ARE.
ARE YOU CRAZY? DON'T LEAVE ME!
WATCH OUT!!
HANAKUSUKU!!

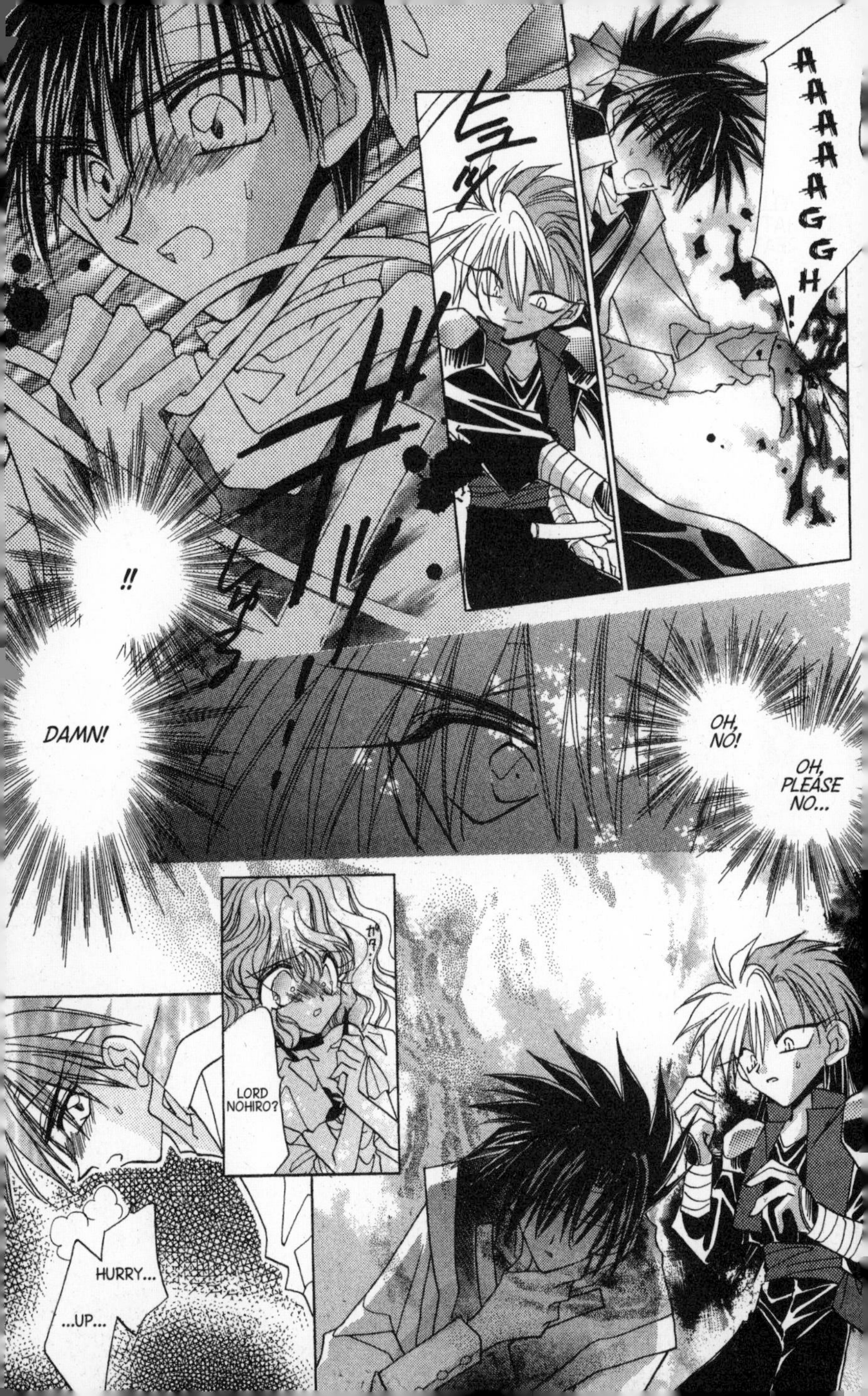
AAAAAAGGH!
!!
DAMN!
OH, NO!
OH, PLEASE NO...
LORD NOHIRO?
HURRY...
...UP...

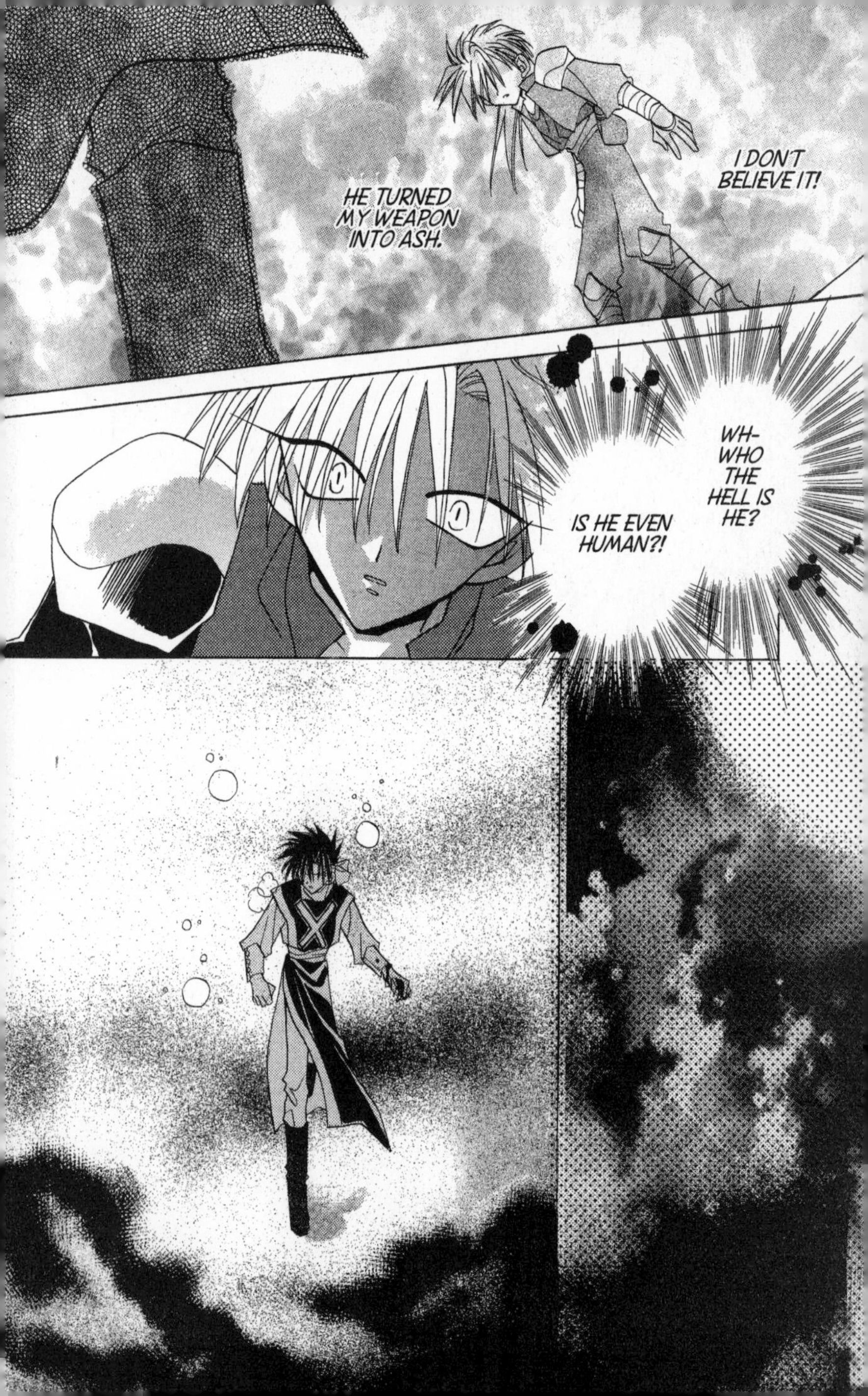
I DON'T BELIEVE IT!
HE TURNED MY WEAPON INTO ASH.
WH- WHO THE HELL IS HE?
IS HE EVEN HUMAN?!

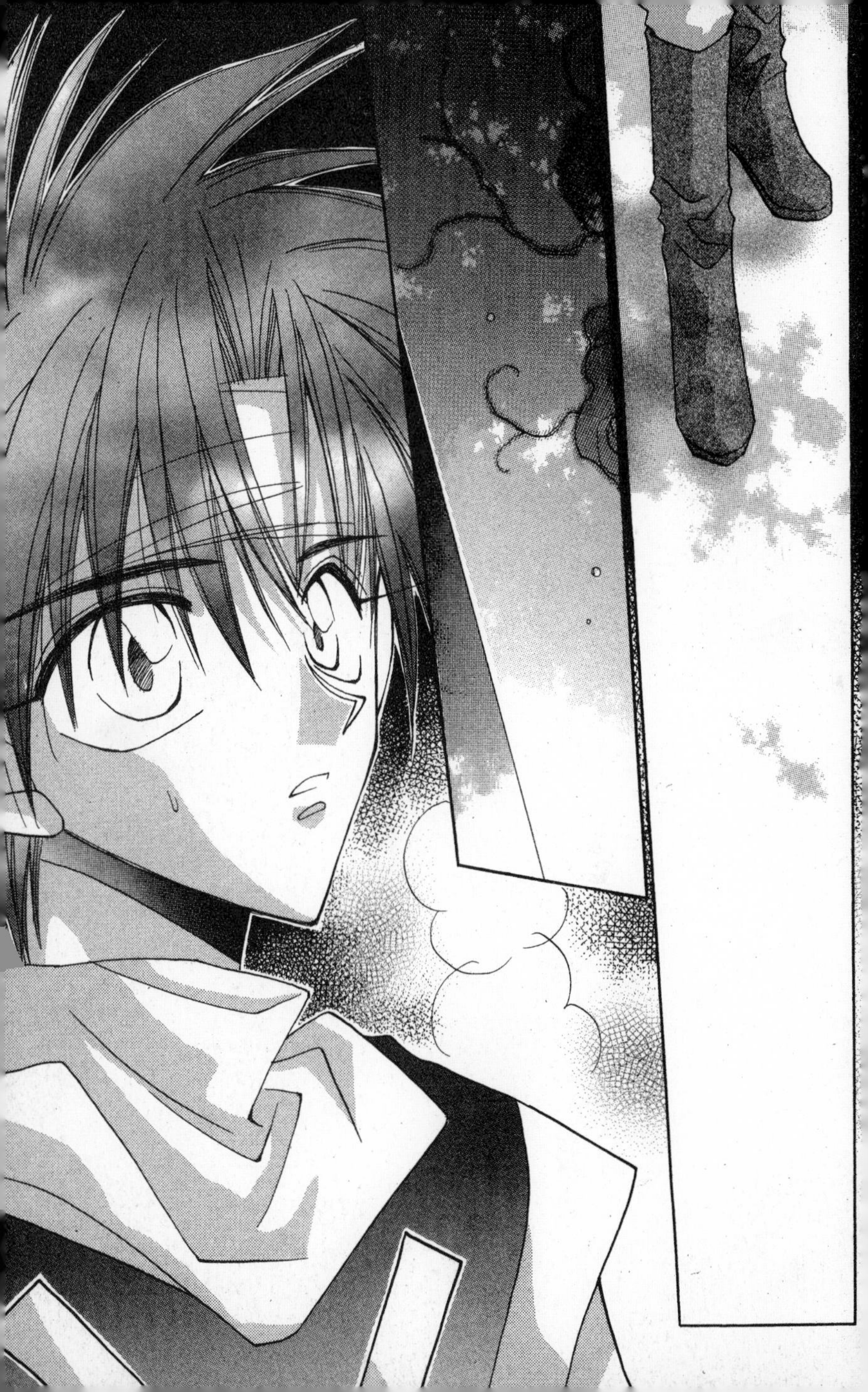

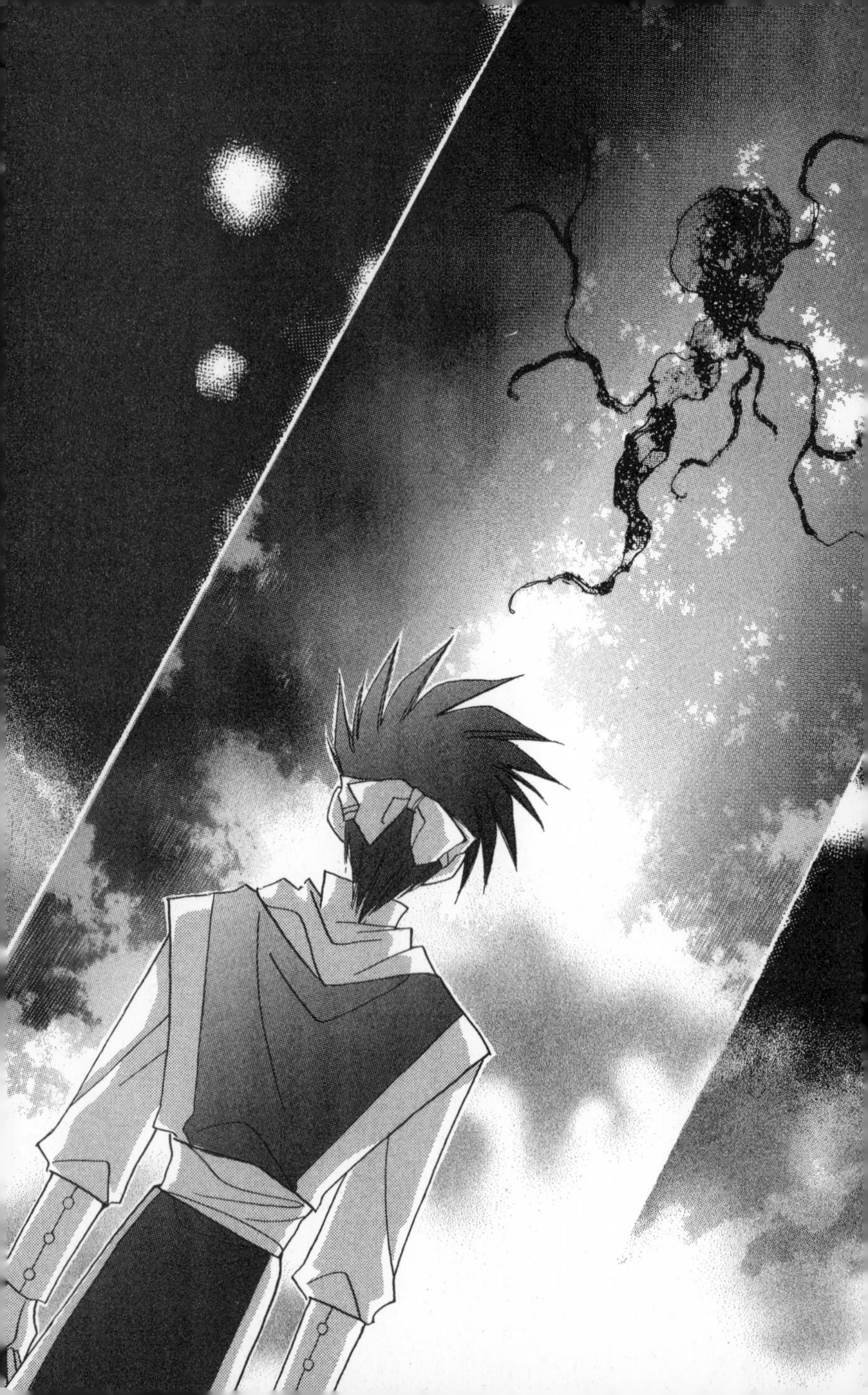

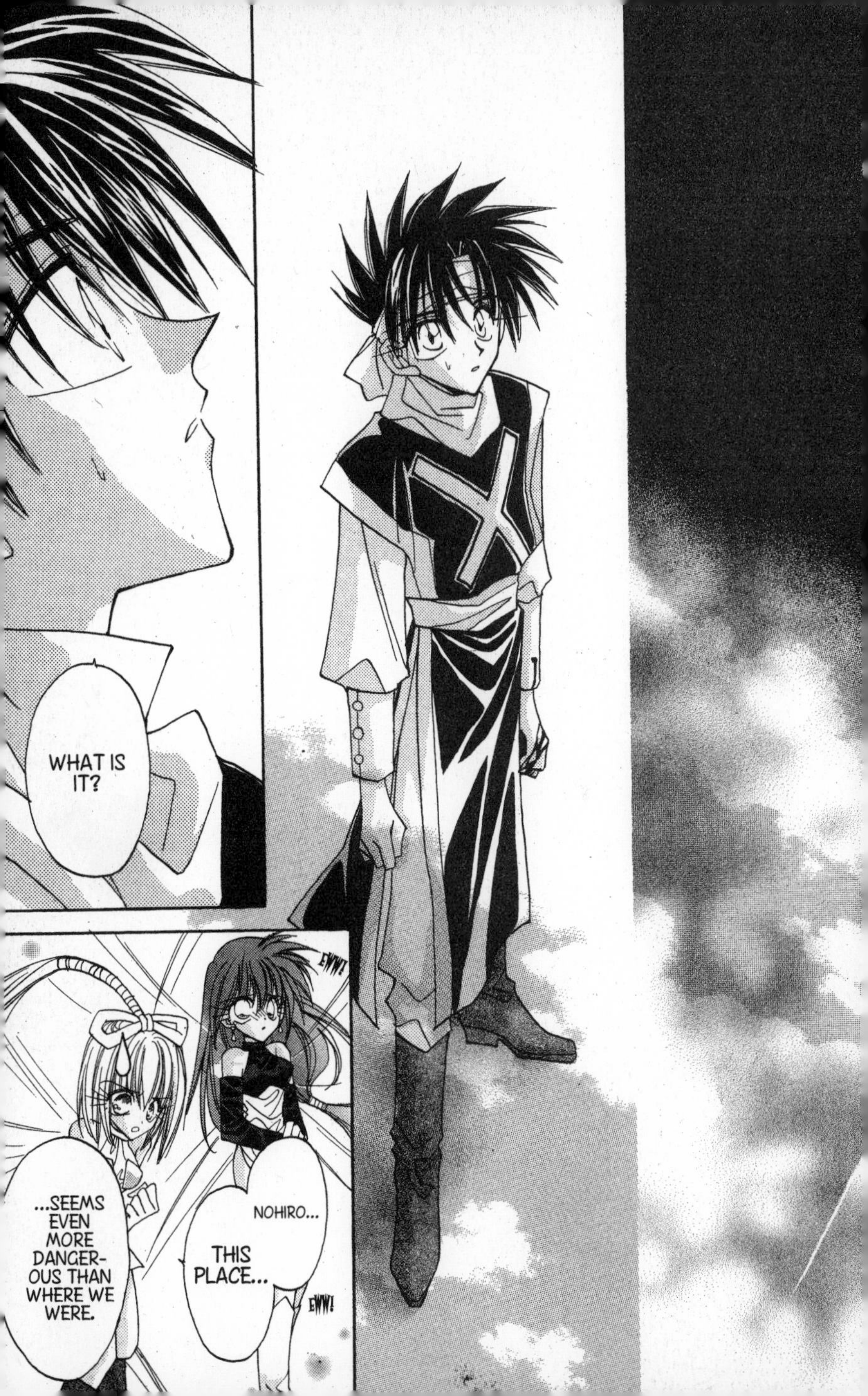
WHAT IS IT?
EWW!
NOHIRO...
THIS PLACE...
EWW!
...SEEMS EVEN MORE DANGER-OUS THAN WHERE WE WERE.

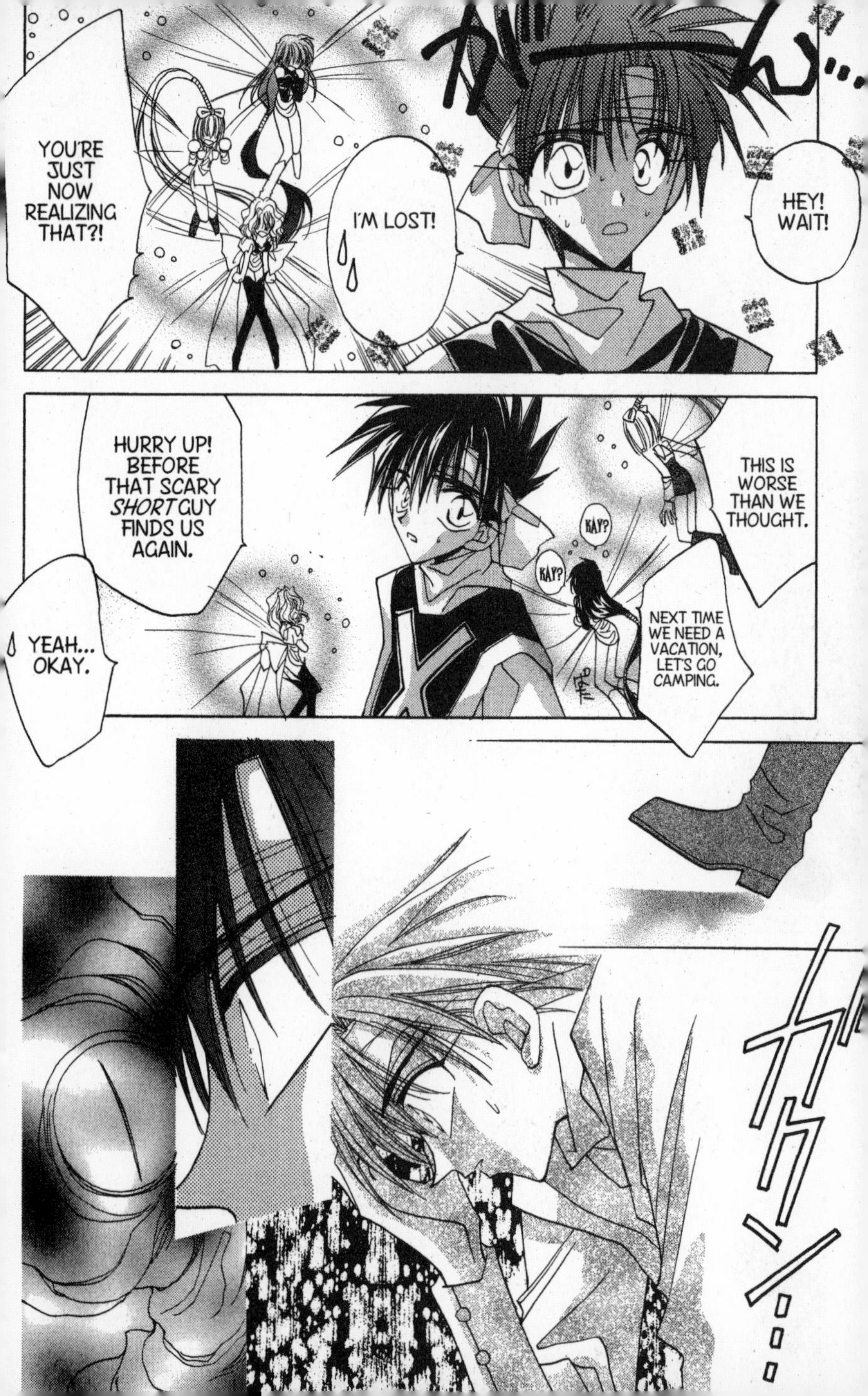
HEY! WAIT!
I'M LOST!
YOU'RE JUST NOW REALIZING THAT?!
THIS IS WORSE THAN WE THOUGHT.
KAY?
KAY?
NEXT TIME WE NEED A VACATION, LET'S GO CAMPING.
HURRY UP! BEFORE THAT SCARY *SHORT* GUY FINDS US AGAIN.
YEAH... OKAY.

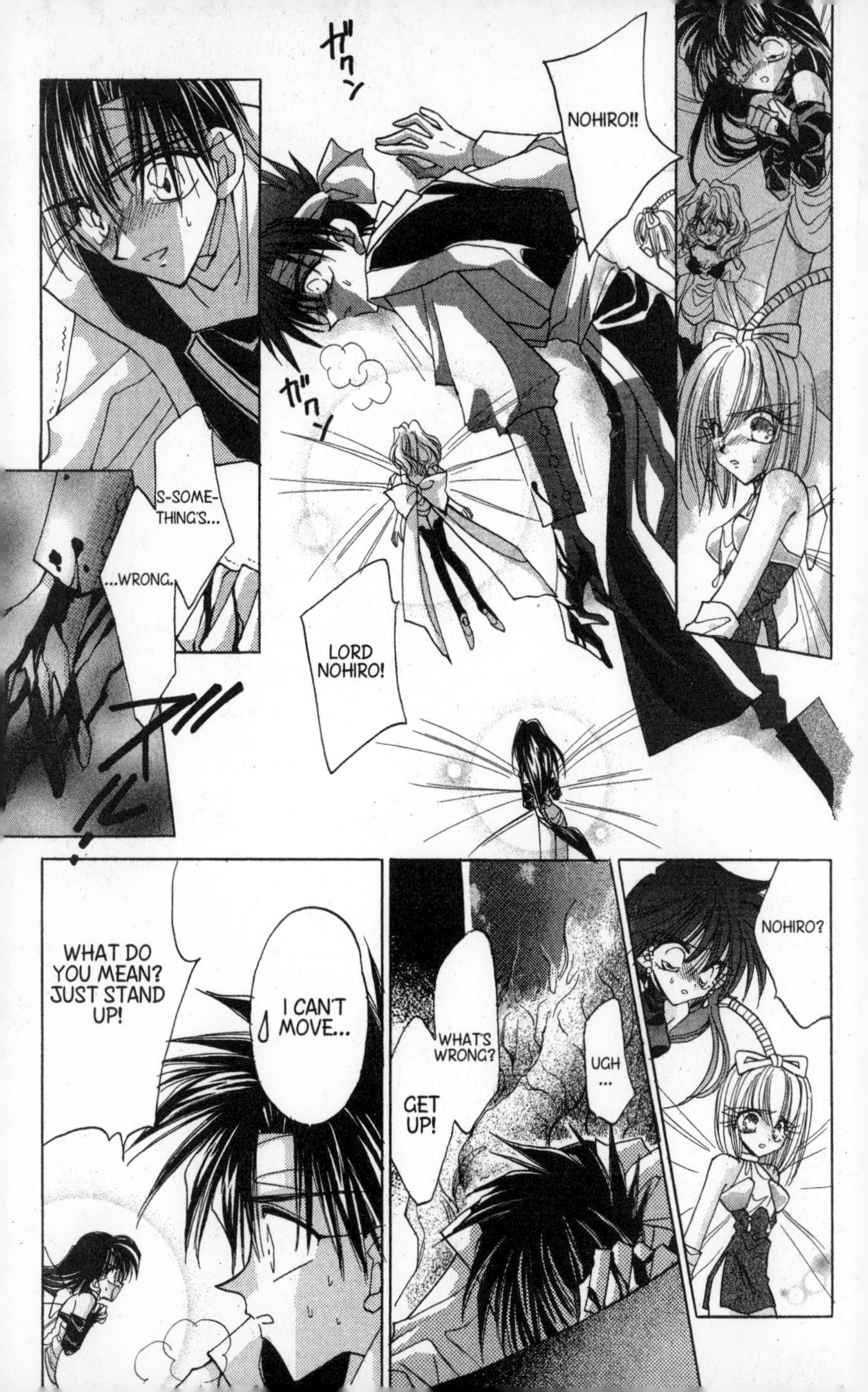
NOHIRO!!
ガクン
ガクン
LORD NOHIRO!
S-SOMETHING'S...
...WRONG.
NOHIRO?
WHAT'S WRONG?
UGH ...
GET UP!
I CAN'T MOVE...
WHAT DO YOU MEAN? JUST STAND UP!

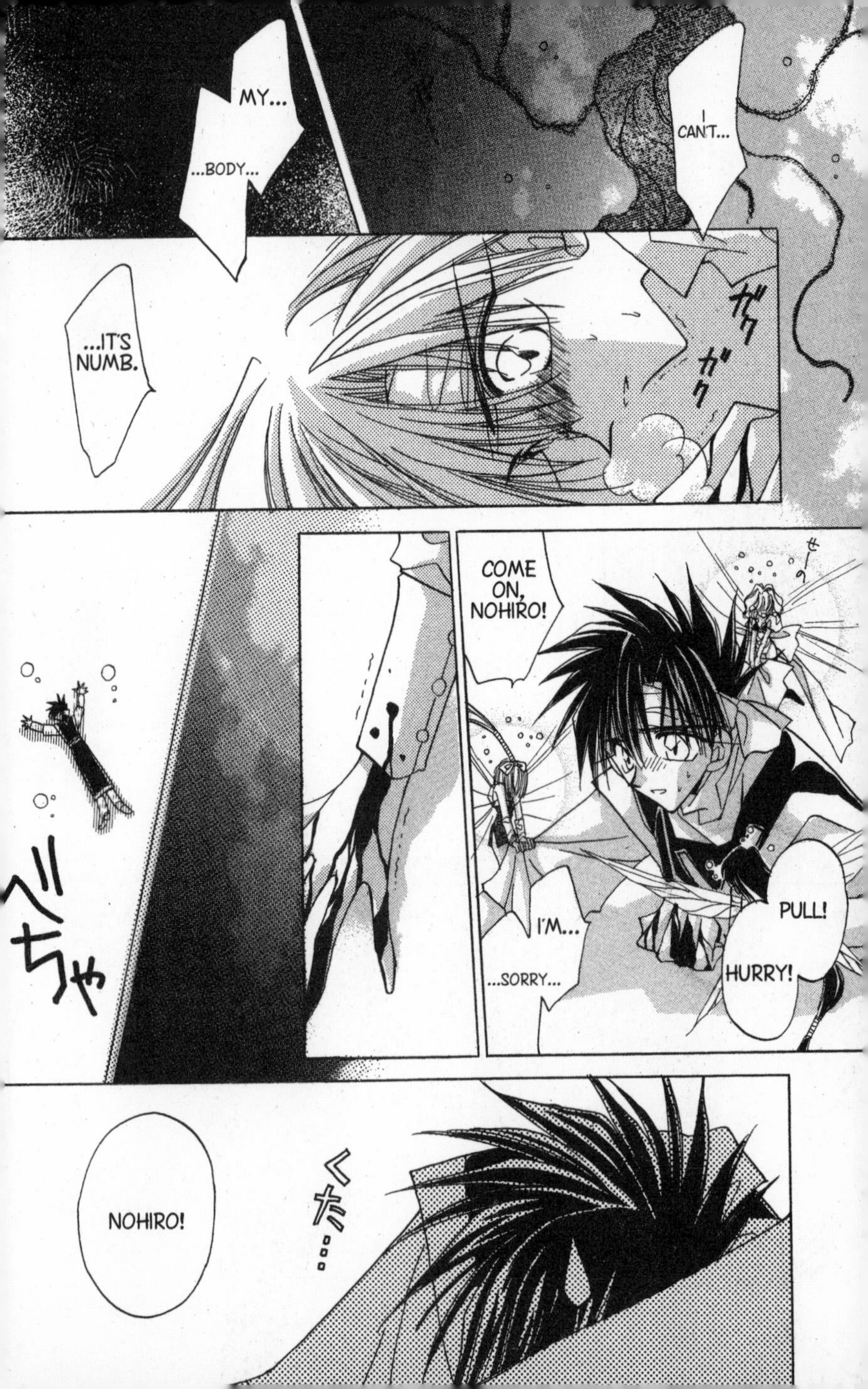
I CAN'T...
MY...
...BODY...
ガク ガク
...IT'S NUMB.
せーの
COME ON, NOHIRO!
PULL!
HURRY!
I'M...
...SORRY...
べちゃ
くた...
NOHIRO!

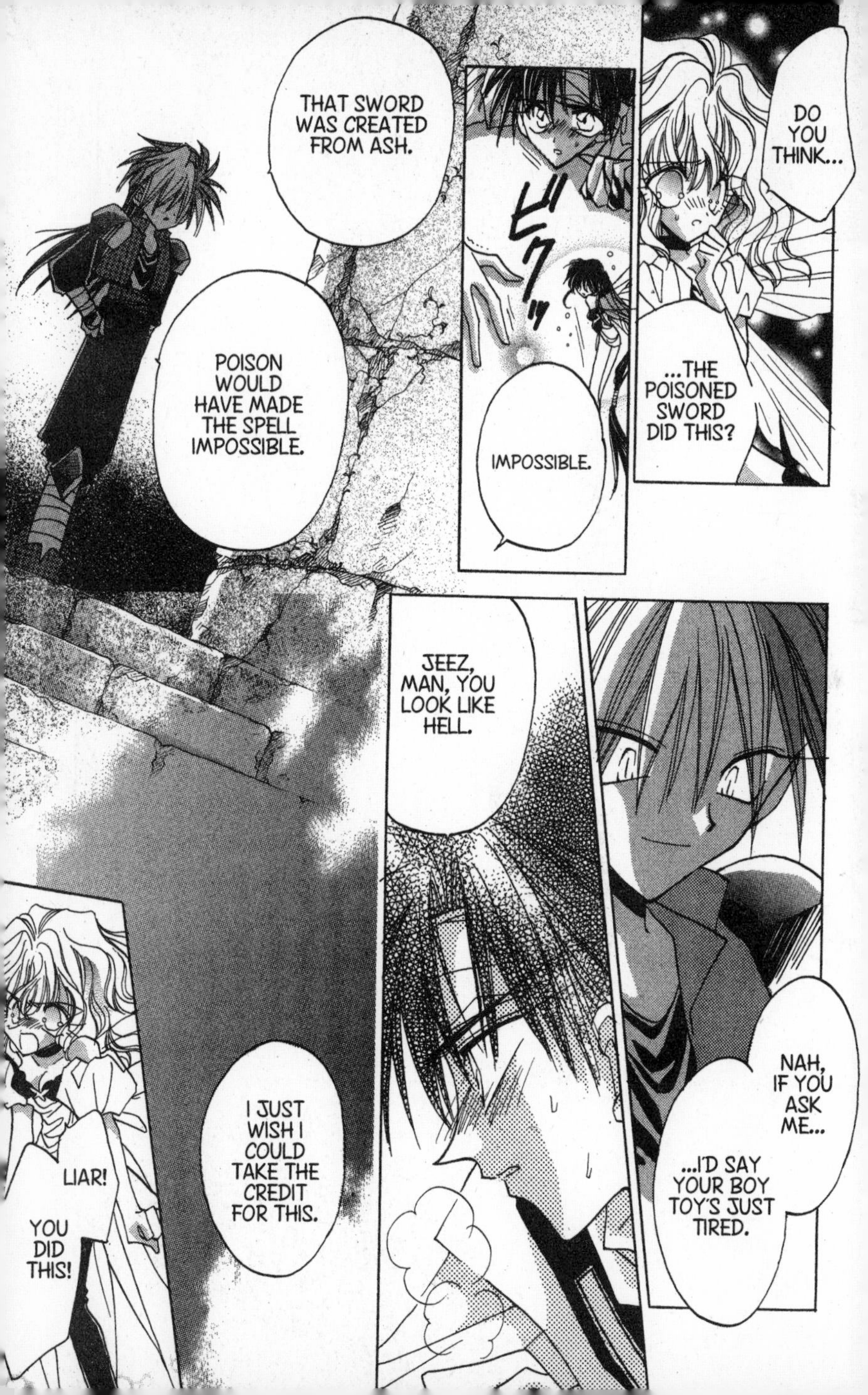
DO YOU THINK...
...THE POISONED SWORD DID THIS?
ビクッ
IMPOSSIBLE.
THAT SWORD WAS CREATED FROM ASH.
POISON WOULD HAVE MADE THE SPELL IMPOSSIBLE.
JEEZ, MAN, YOU LOOK LIKE HELL.
NAH, IF YOU ASK ME...
...I'D SAY YOUR BOY TOY'S JUST TIRED.
I JUST WISH I COULD TAKE THE CREDIT FOR THIS.
LIAR!
YOU DID THIS!

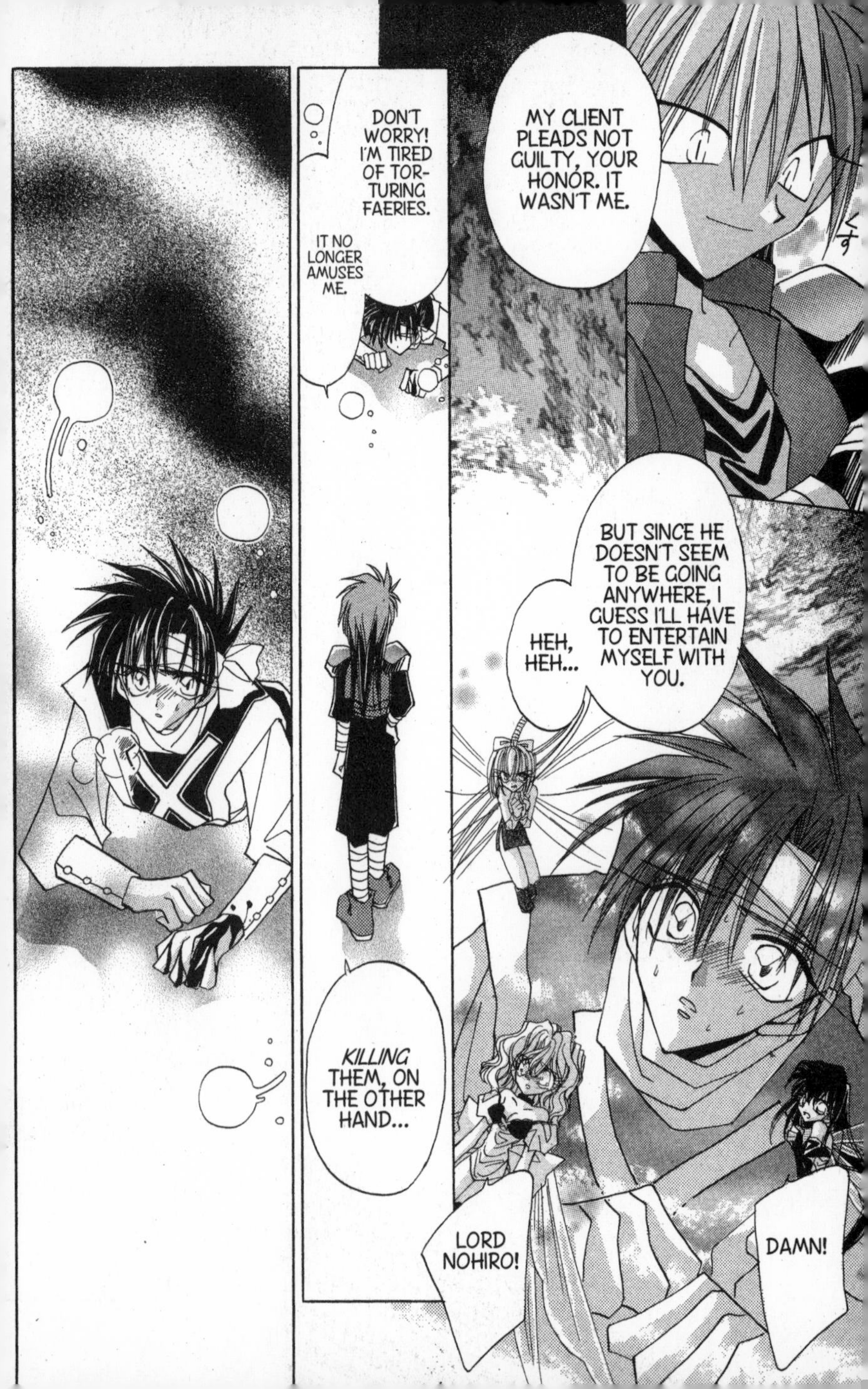
MY CLIENT PLEADS NOT GUILTY, YOUR HONOR. IT WASN'T ME.
くす
BUT SINCE HE DOESN'T SEEM TO BE GOING ANYWHERE, I GUESS I'LL HAVE TO ENTERTAIN MYSELF WITH YOU.
HEH, HEH...
DAMN!
LORD NOHIRO!
DON'T WORRY! I'M TIRED OF TOR-TURING FAERIES.
IT NO LONGER AMUSES ME.
KILLING THEM, ON THE OTHER HAND...

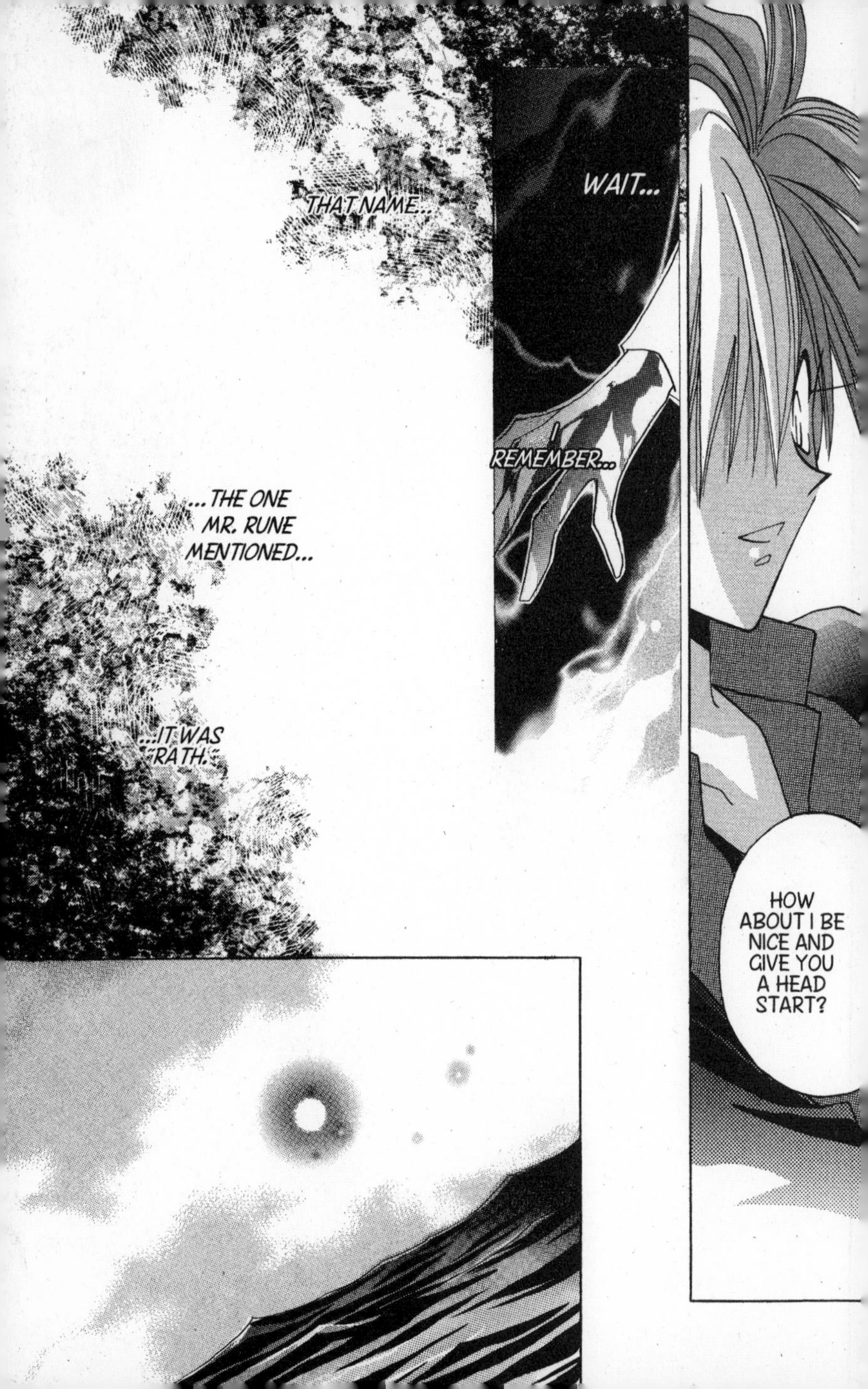
HOW ABOUT I BE NICE AND GIVE YOU A HEAD START?
WAIT...
I REMEMBER...
THAT NAME...
...THE ONE MR. RUNE MENTIONED...
...IT WAS RATH.

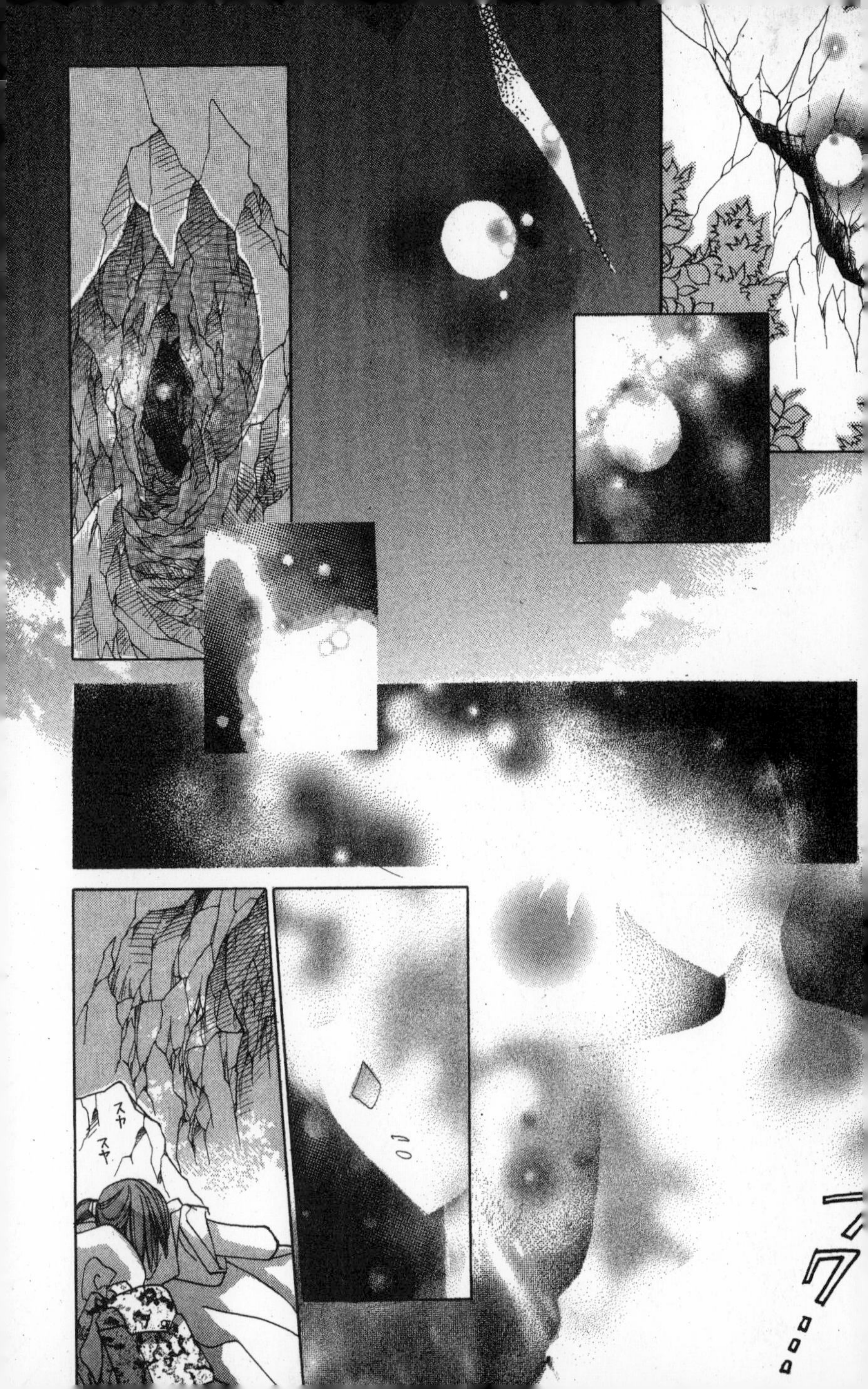
スヤ
スヤ

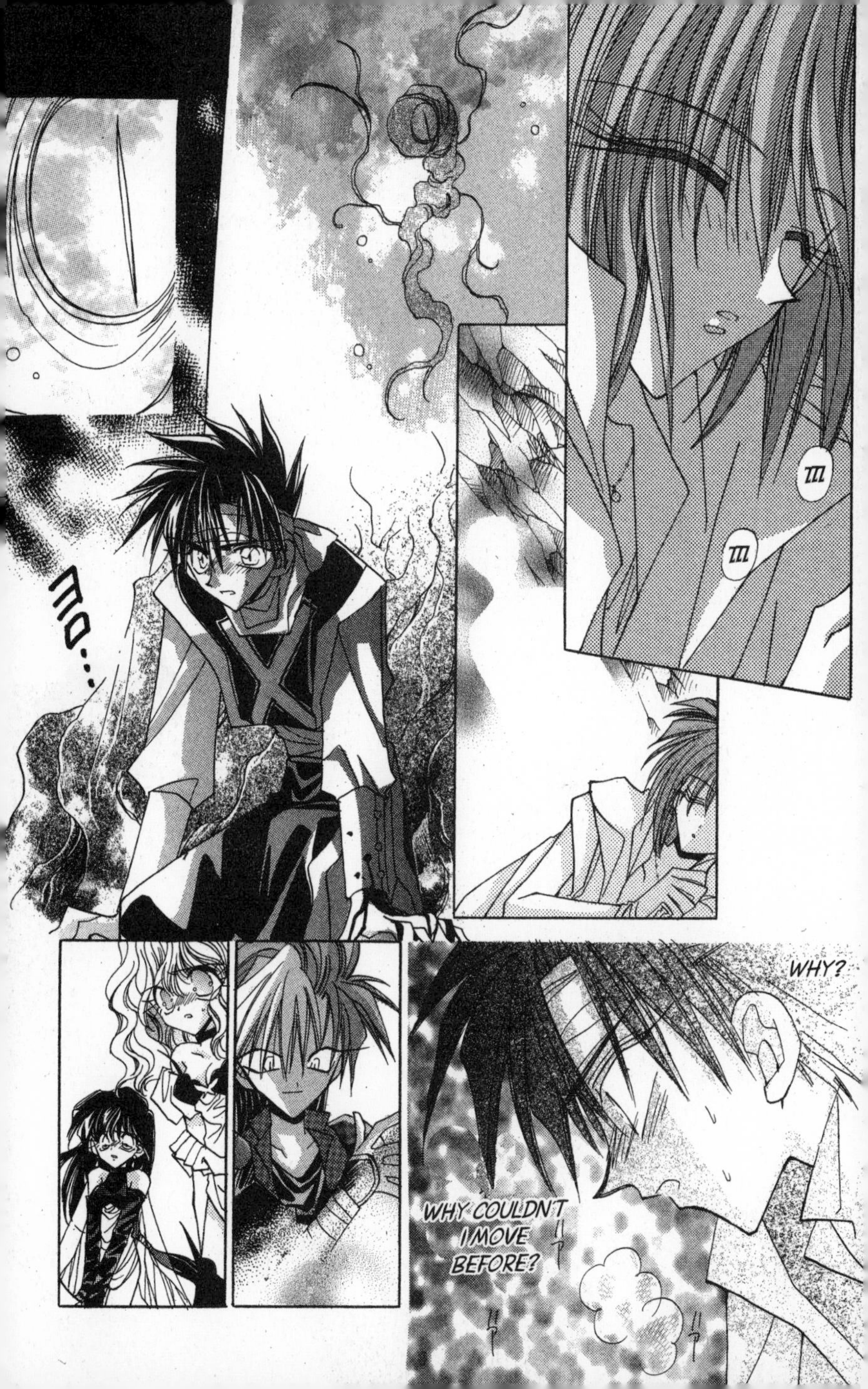
mo...
WHY?
WHY COULDN'T I MOVE BEFORE?
ハァ
ハァ
ハァ

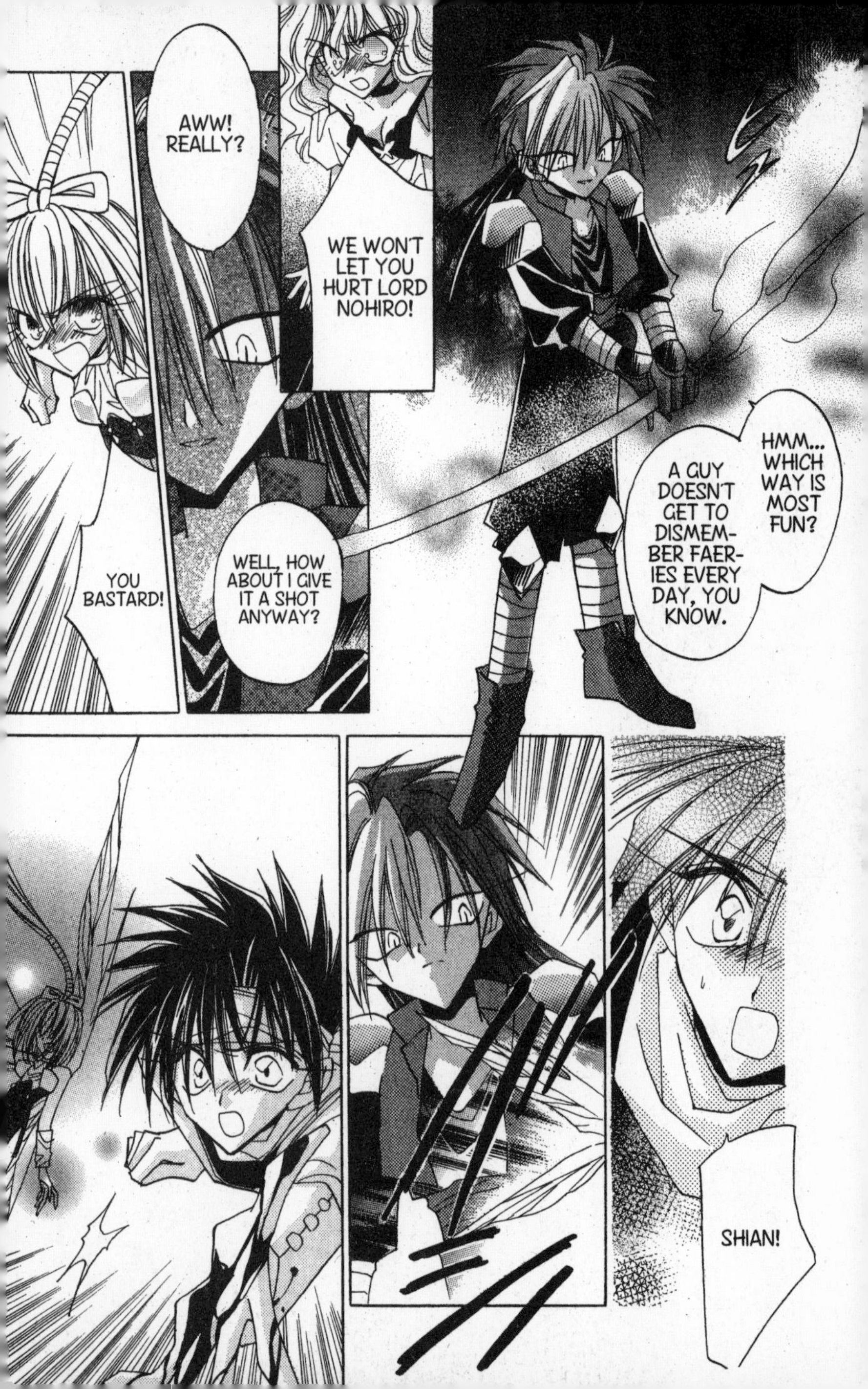
HMM... WHICH WAY IS MOST FUN?
A GUY DOESN'T GET TO DISMEMBER FAERIES EVERY DAY, YOU KNOW.
WE WON'T LET YOU HURT LORD NOHIRO!
AWW! REALLY?
WELL, HOW ABOUT I GIVE IT A SHOT ANYWAY?
YOU BASTARD!
SHIAN!

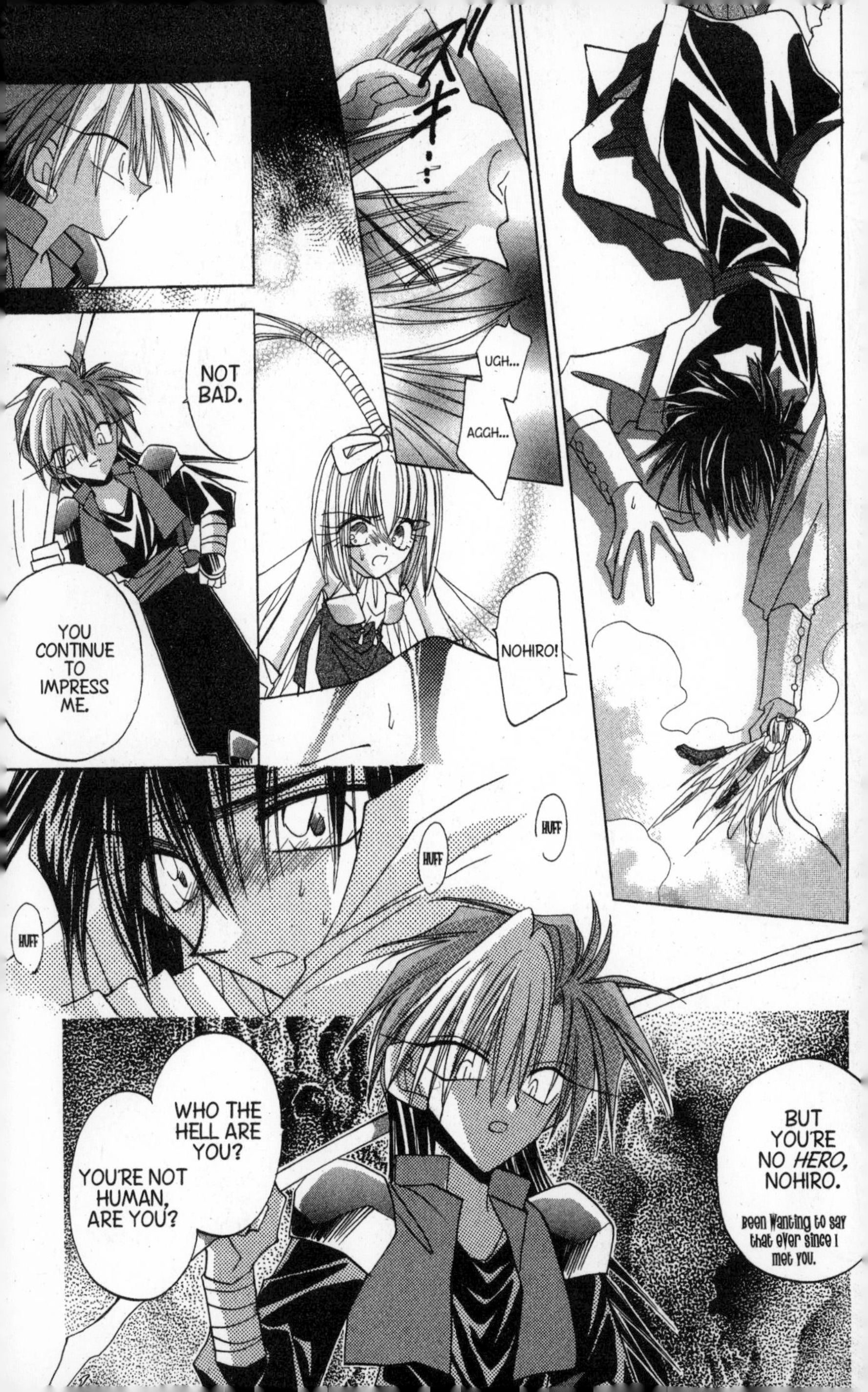
ズギ…!!
UGH...
AGGH...
NOHIRO!
NOT BAD.
YOU CONTINUE TO IMPRESS ME.
HUFF
HUFF
HUFF
BUT YOU'RE NO *HERO*, NOHIRO.
Been wanting to say that ever since I met you.
WHO THE HELL ARE YOU?
YOU'RE NOT HUMAN, ARE YOU?

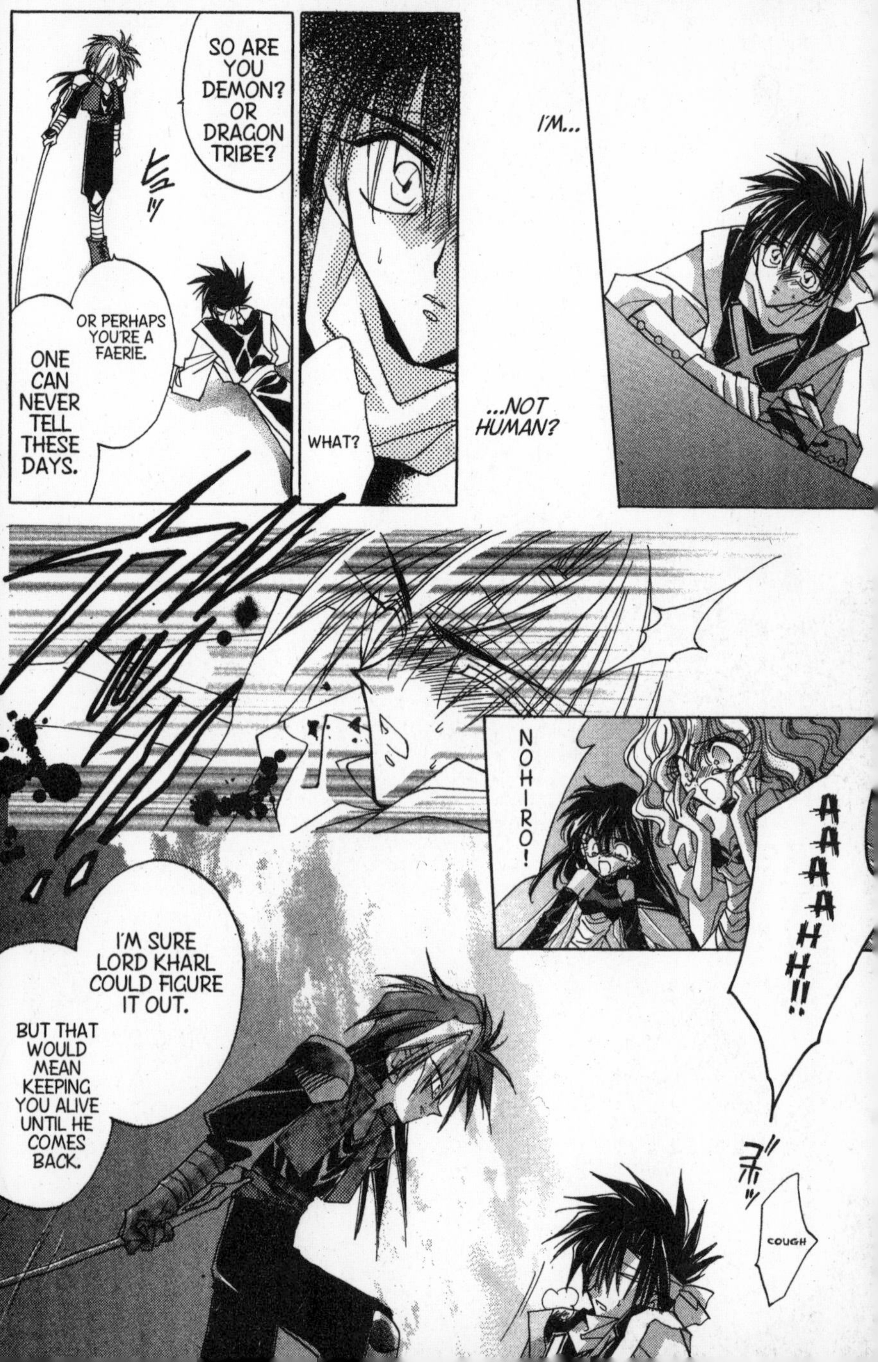
I'M...
...NOT HUMAN?
WHAT?
SO ARE YOU DEMON? OR DRAGON TRIBE?
OR PERHAPS YOU'RE A FAERIE.
ONE CAN NEVER TELL THESE DAYS.
NOHIRO!
AAAAAHH!!
COUGH
I'M SURE LORD KHARL COULD FIGURE IT OUT.
BUT THAT WOULD MEAN KEEPING YOU ALIVE UNTIL HE COMES BACK.

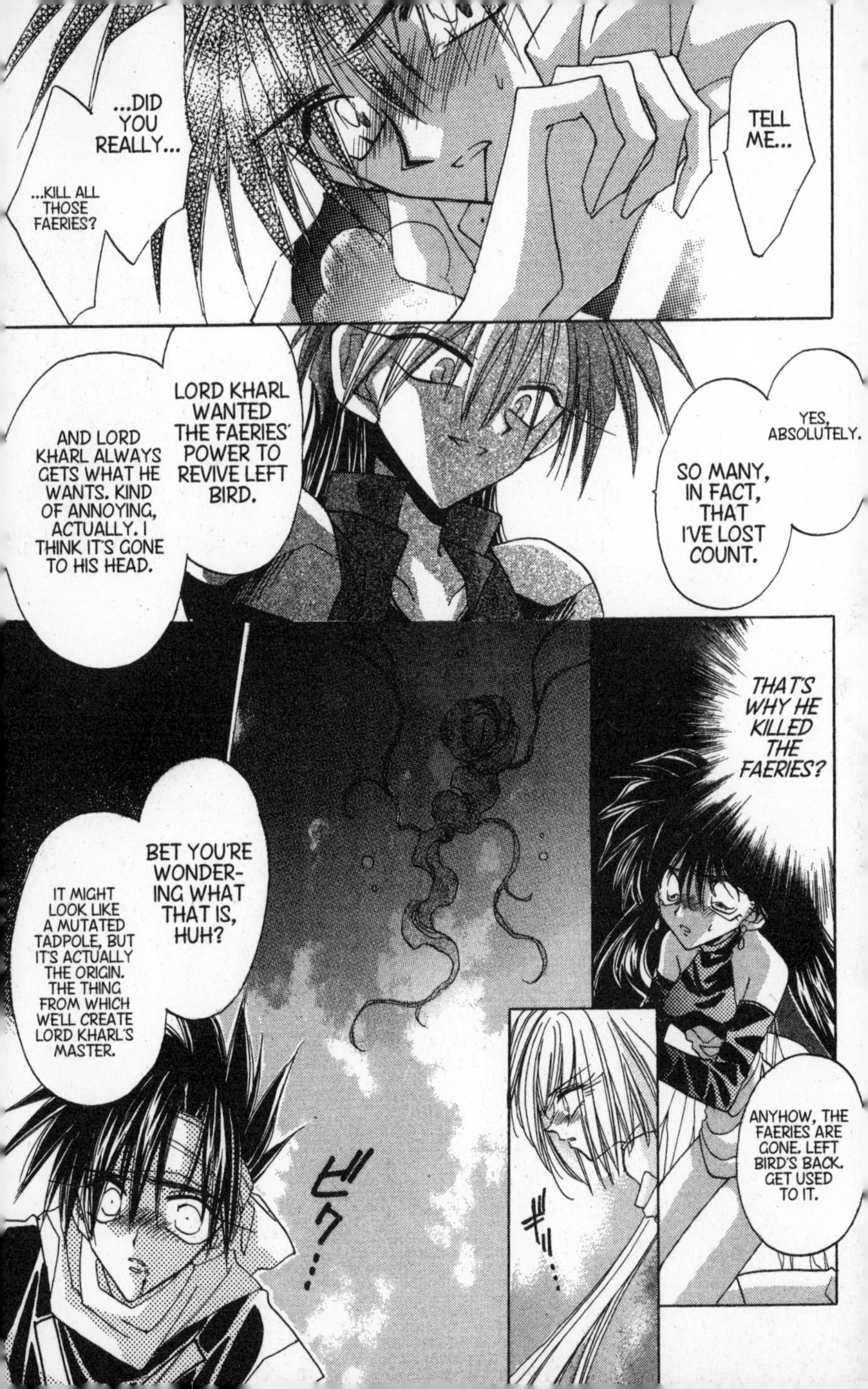
TELL ME...
...DID YOU REALLY...
...KILL ALL THOSE FAERIES?
YES, ABSOLUTELY.
SO MANY, IN FACT, THAT I'VE LOST COUNT.
LORD KHARL WANTED THE FAERIES' POWER TO REVIVE LEFT BIRD.
AND LORD KHARL ALWAYS GETS WHAT HE WANTS. KIND OF ANNOYING, ACTUALLY. I THINK IT'S GONE TO HIS HEAD.
THAT'S WHY HE KILLED THE FAERIES?
ANYHOW, THE FAERIES ARE GONE. LEFT BIRD'S BACK. GET USED TO IT.
ギリ...
BET YOU'RE WONDERING WHAT THAT IS, HUH?
IT MIGHT LOOK LIKE A MUTATED TADPOLE, BUT IT'S ACTUALLY THE ORIGIN. THE THING FROM WHICH WE'LL CREATE LORD KHARL'S MASTER.
ビク...

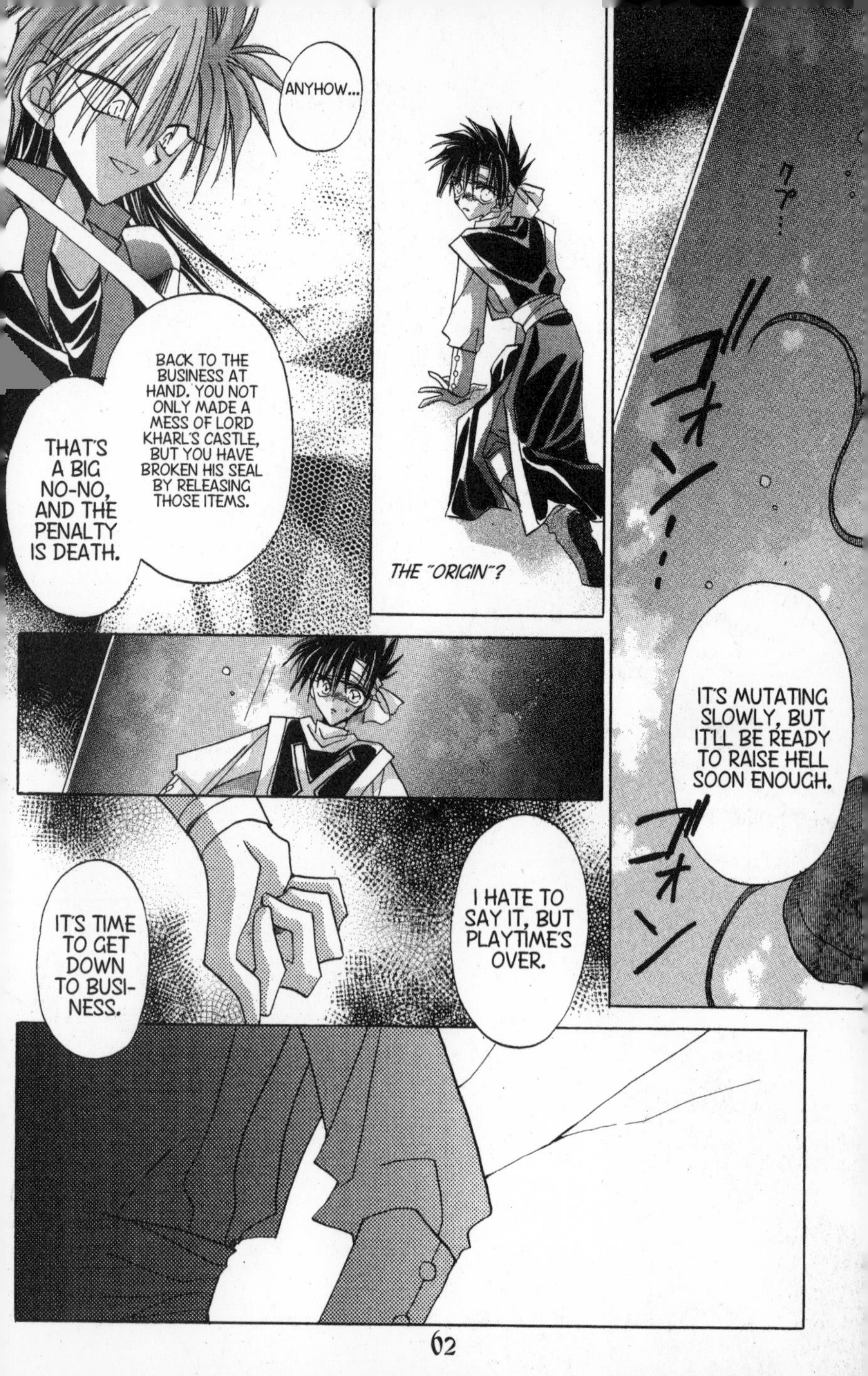

クプ…
ゴォン…
IT'S MUTATING SLOWLY, BUT IT'LL BE READY TO RAISE HELL SOON ENOUGH.
ゴォン
THE "ORIGIN"?
ANYHOW...
BACK TO THE BUSINESS AT HAND. YOU NOT ONLY MADE A MESS OF LORD KHARL'S CASTLE, BUT YOU HAVE BROKEN HIS SEAL BY RELEASING THOSE ITEMS.
THAT'S A BIG NO-NO, AND THE PENALTY IS DEATH.
I HATE TO SAY IT, BUT PLAYTIME'S OVER.
IT'S TIME TO GET DOWN TO BUSI-NESS.

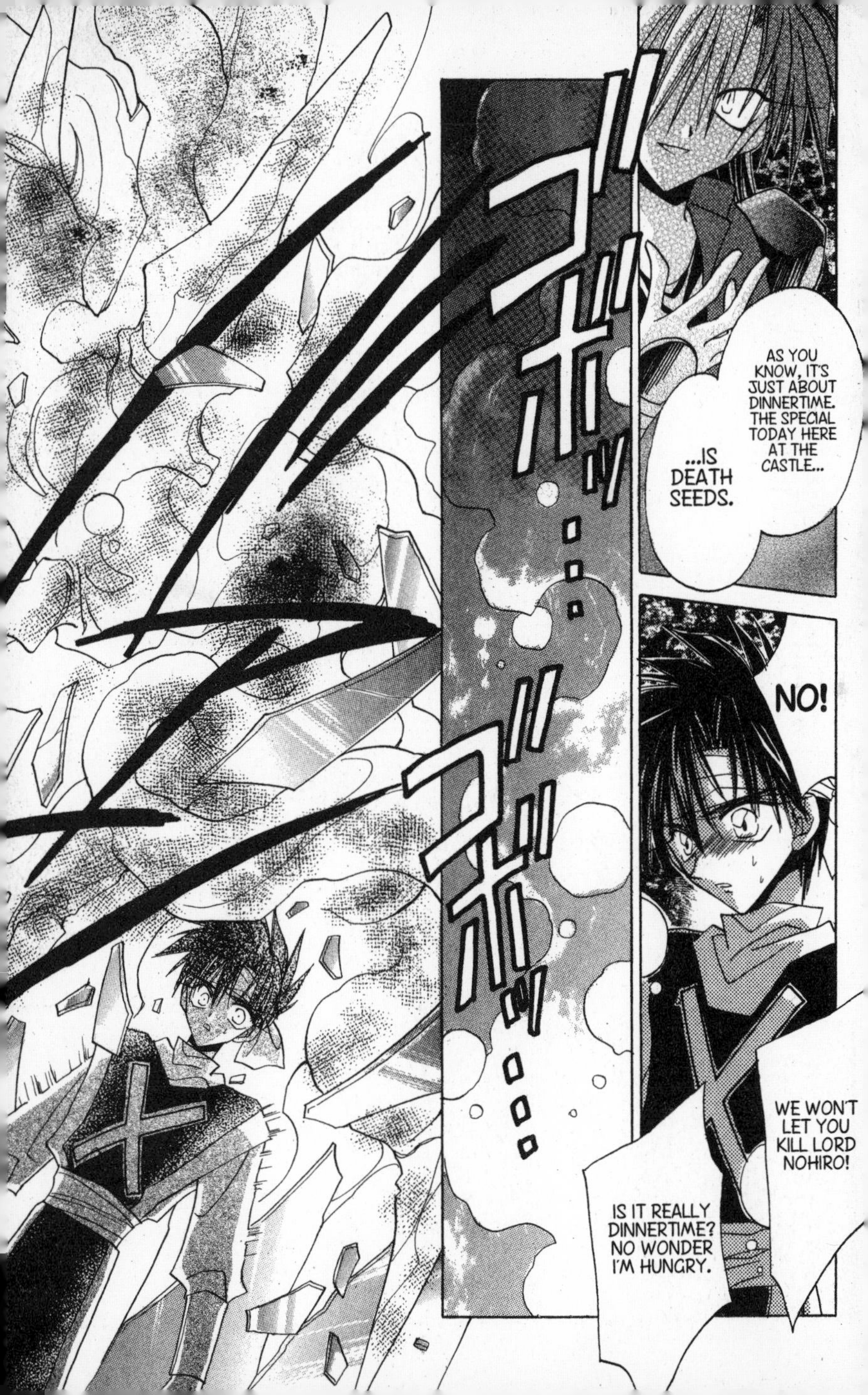
AS YOU KNOW, IT'S JUST ABOUT DINNERTIME. THE SPECIAL TODAY HERE AT THE CASTLE...
...IS DEATH SEEDS.
NO!
WE WON'T LET YOU KILL LORD NOHIRO!
IS IT REALLY DINNERTIME? NO WONDER I'M HUNGRY.
ゴボッ...
ゴボッ...

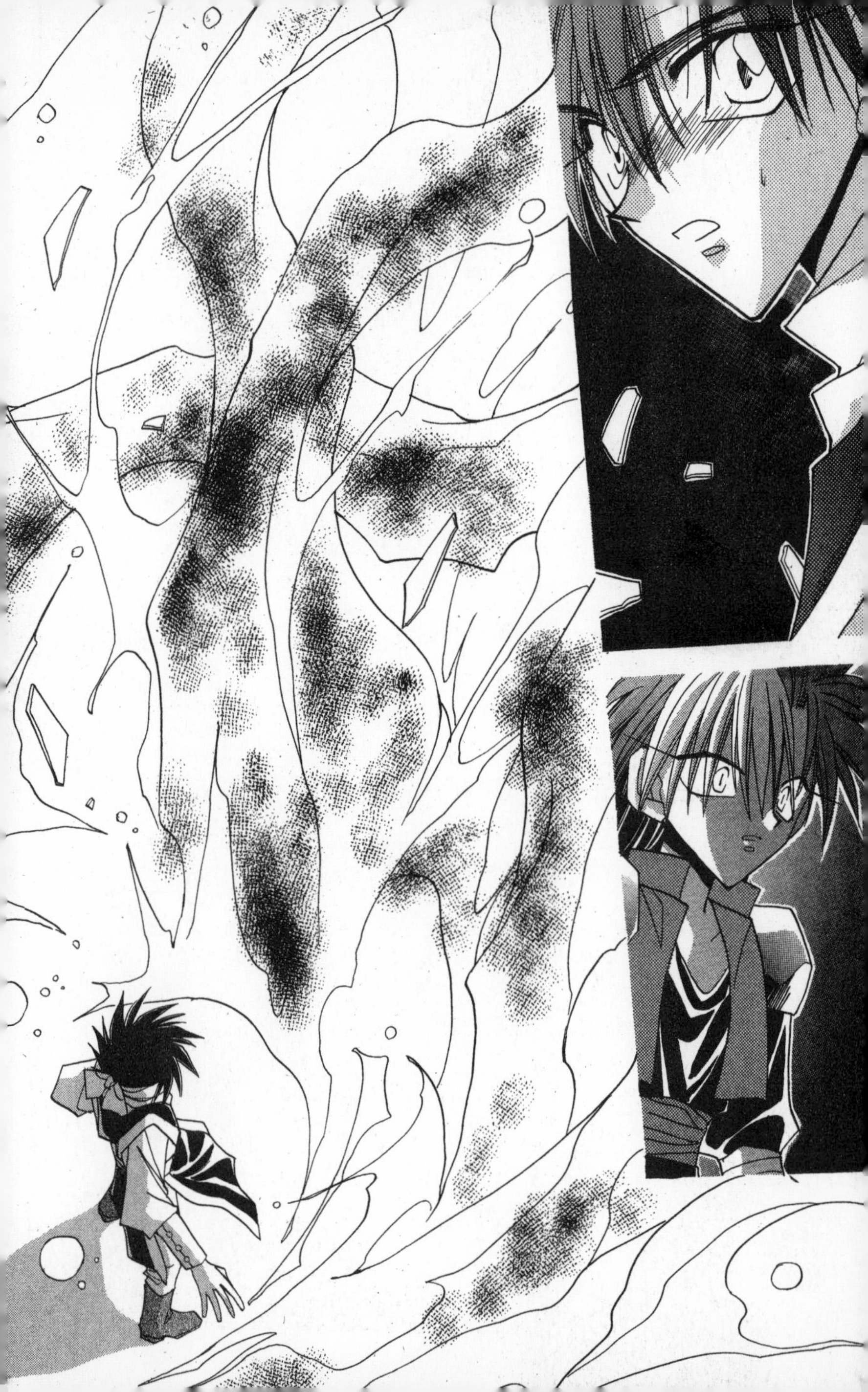

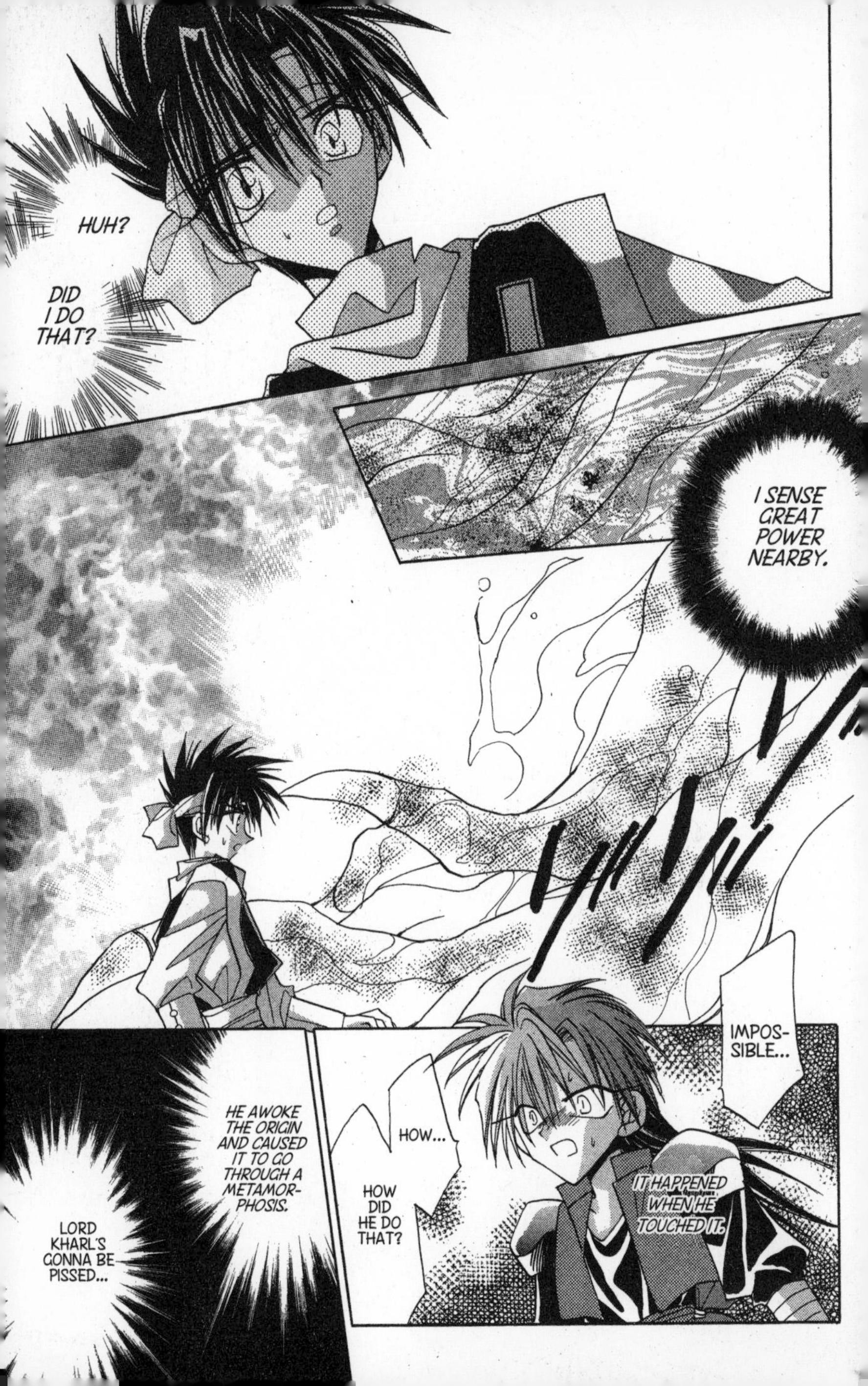
HUH?
DID I DO THAT?
I SENSE GREAT POWER NEARBY.
IMPOSSIBLE...
HOW...
HOW DID HE DO THAT?
IT HAPPENED WHEN HE TOUCHED IT.
HE AWOKE THE ORIGIN AND CAUSED IT TO GO THROUGH A METAMORPHOSIS.
LORD KHARL'S GONNA BE PISSED...

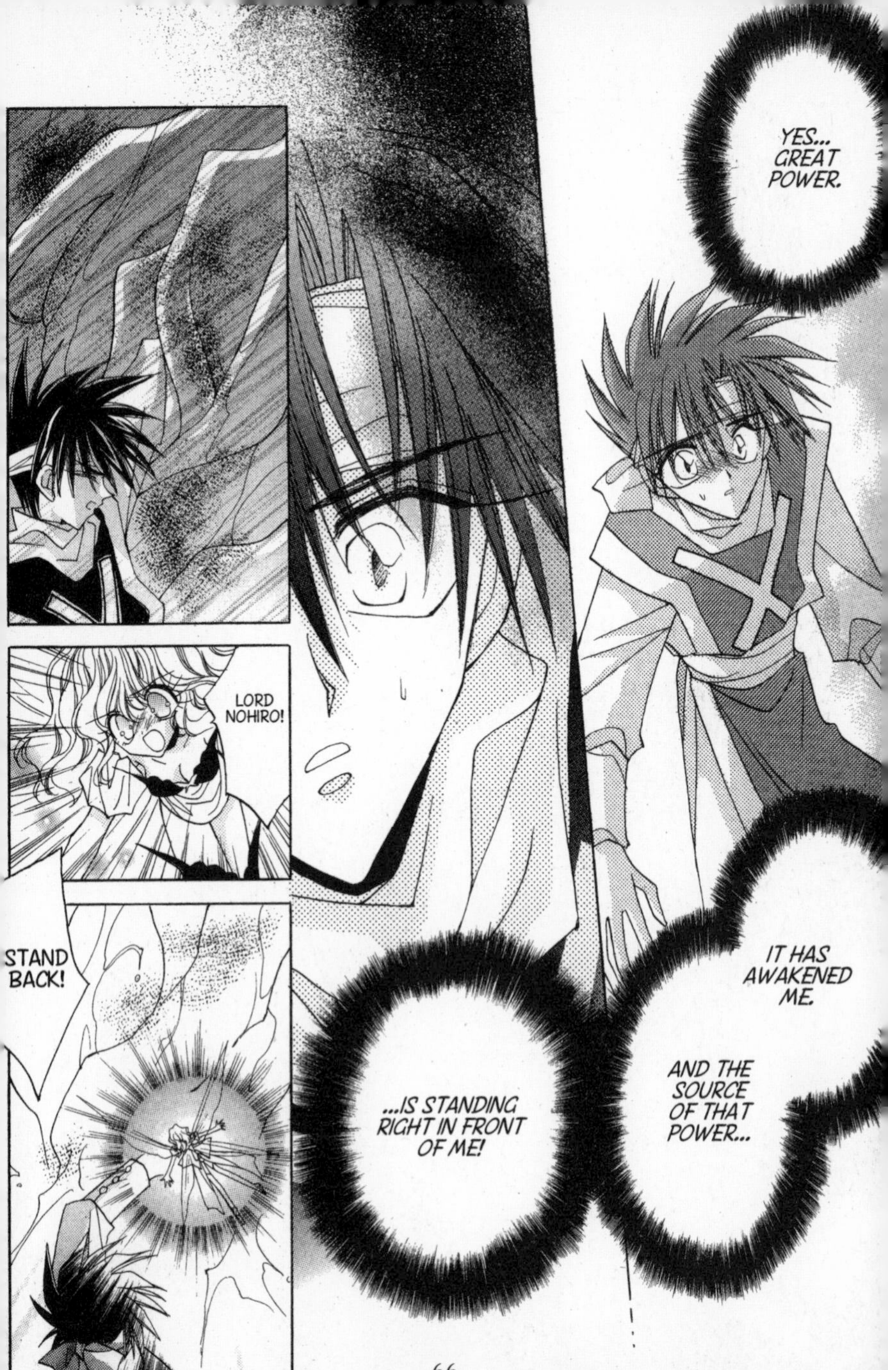
YES... GREAT POWER.
IT HAS AWAKENED ME.
AND THE SOURCE OF THAT POWER...
...IS STANDING RIGHT IN FRONT OF ME!
LORD NOHIRO!
STAND BACK!

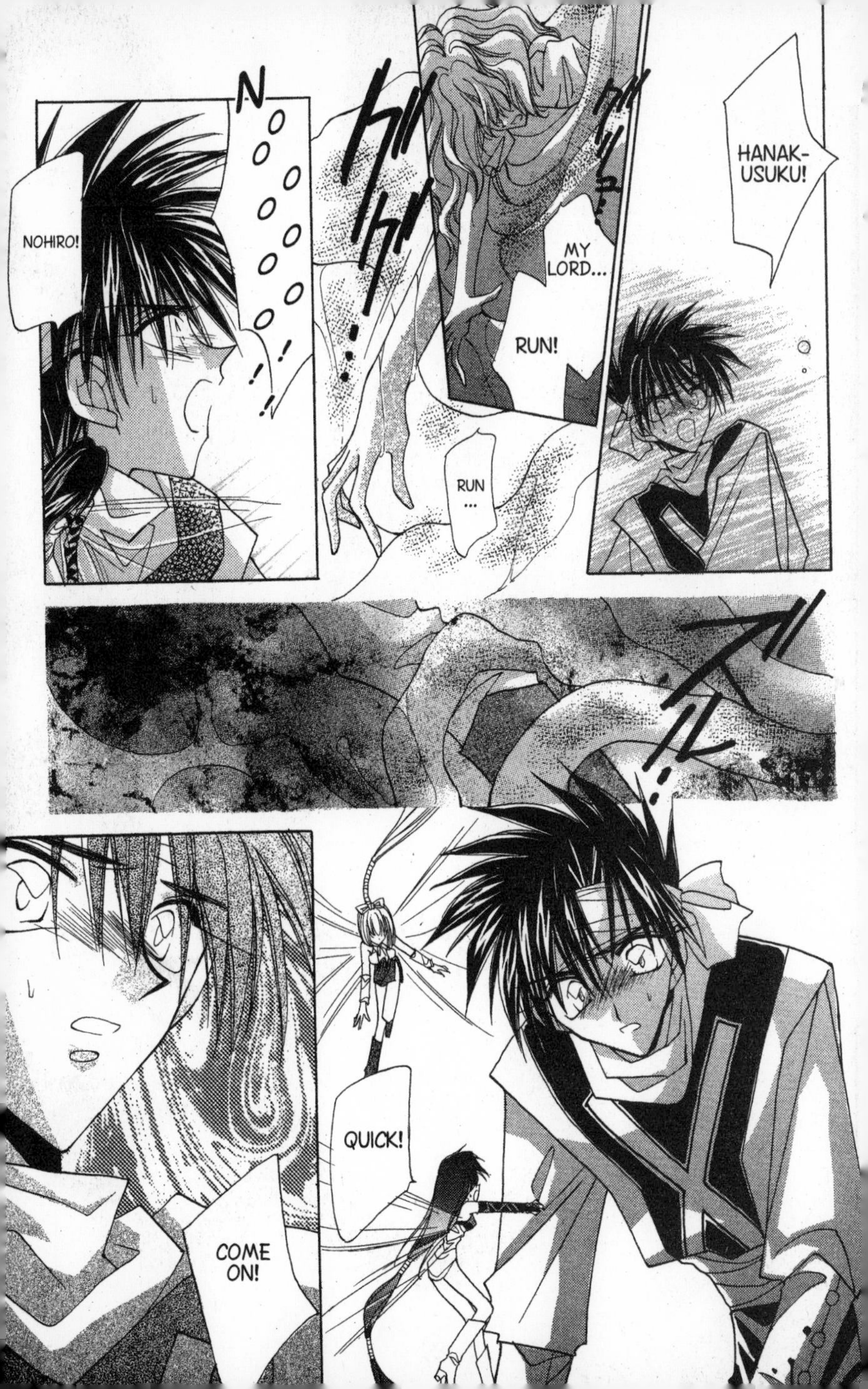
HANAK-USUKU!
MY LORD...
RUN!
RUN ...
NOHIRO!
NOOOOOOOO!!!
QUICK!
COME ON!

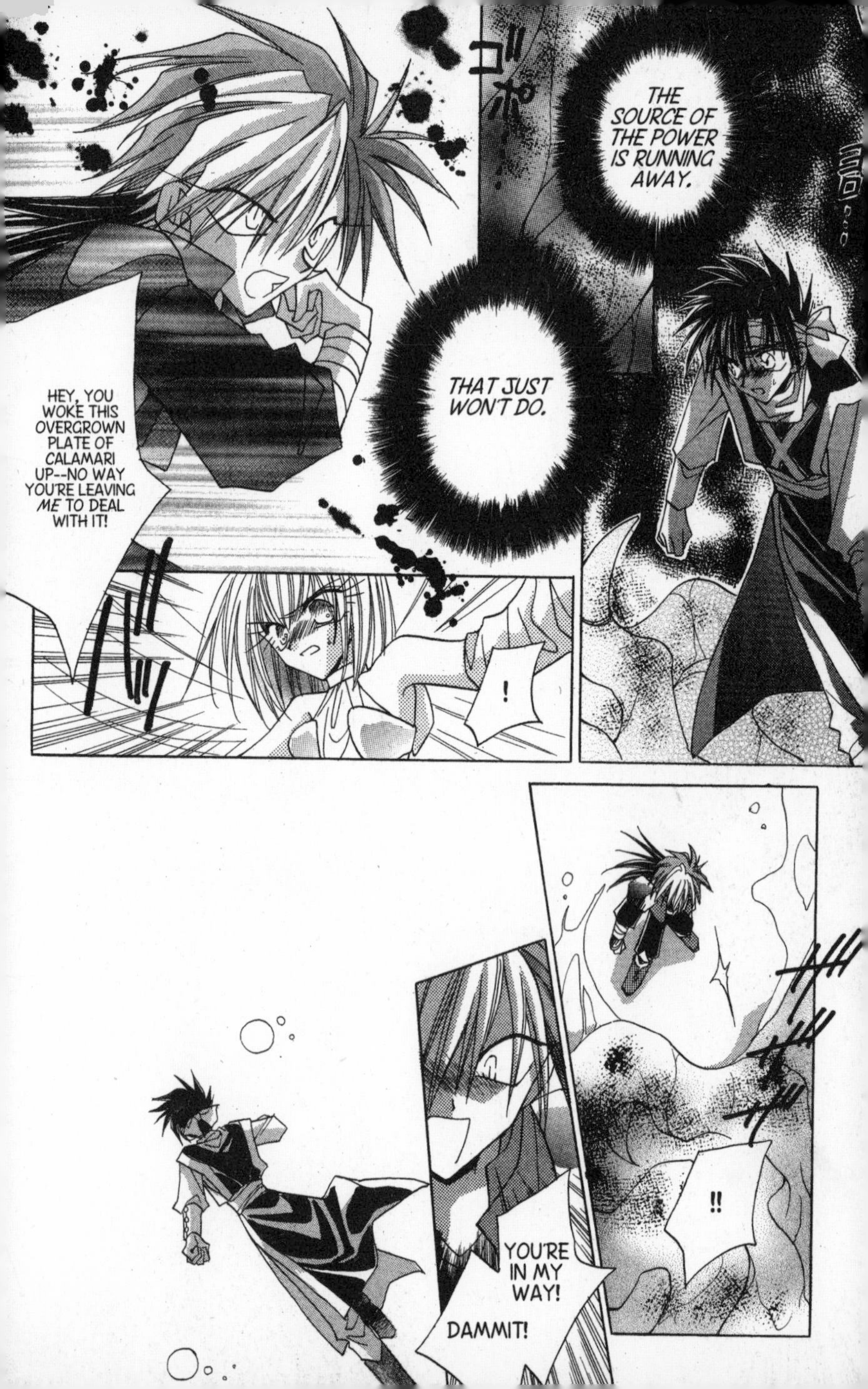
THE SOURCE OF THE POWER IS RUNNING AWAY.
THAT JUST WON'T DO.
HEY, YOU WOKE THIS OVERGROWN PLATE OF CALAMARI UP--NO WAY YOU'RE LEAVING *ME* TO DEAL WITH IT!
!
!!
YOU'RE IN MY WAY!
DAMMIT!

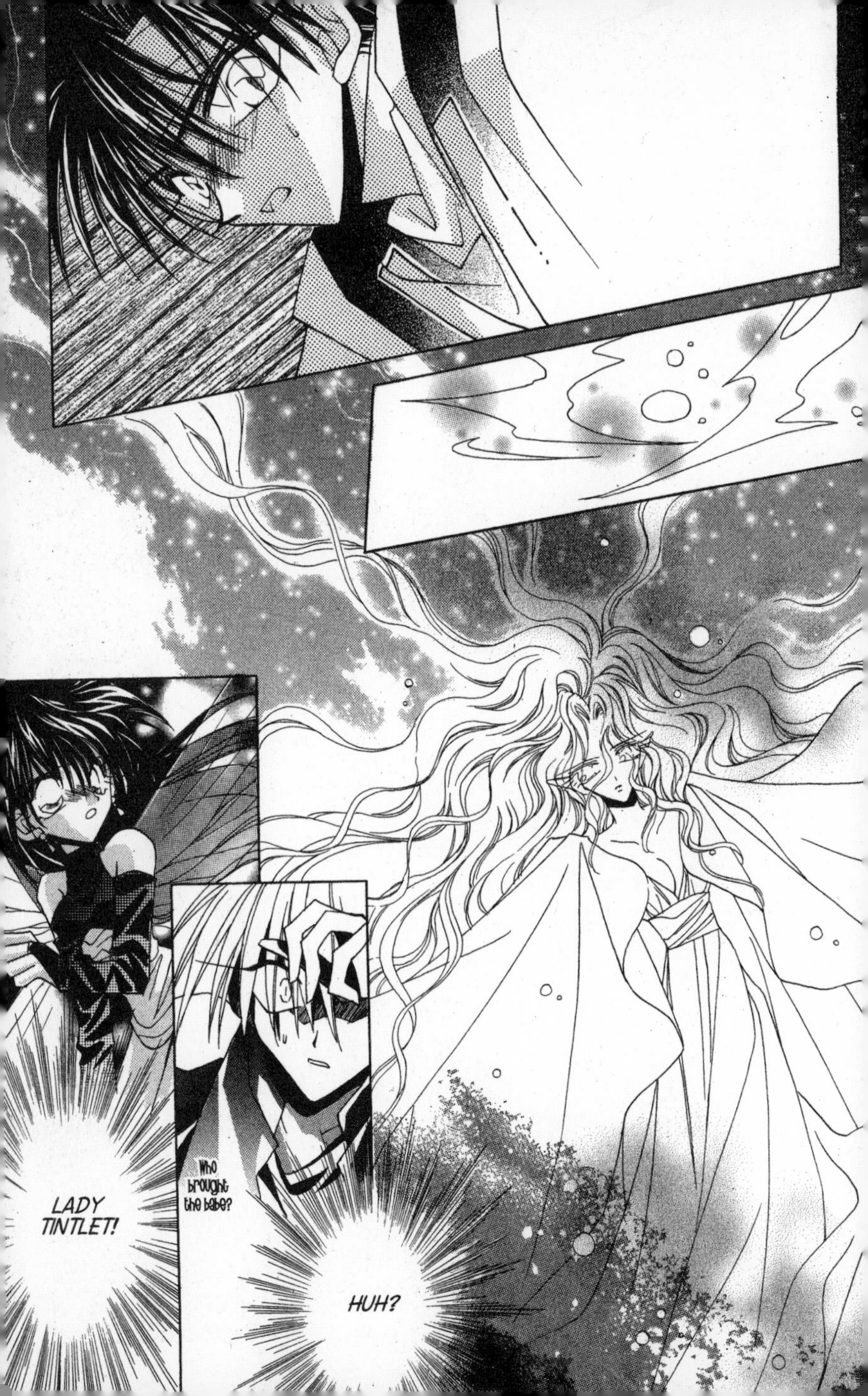
HUH?
Who brought the babe?
LADY TINTLET!

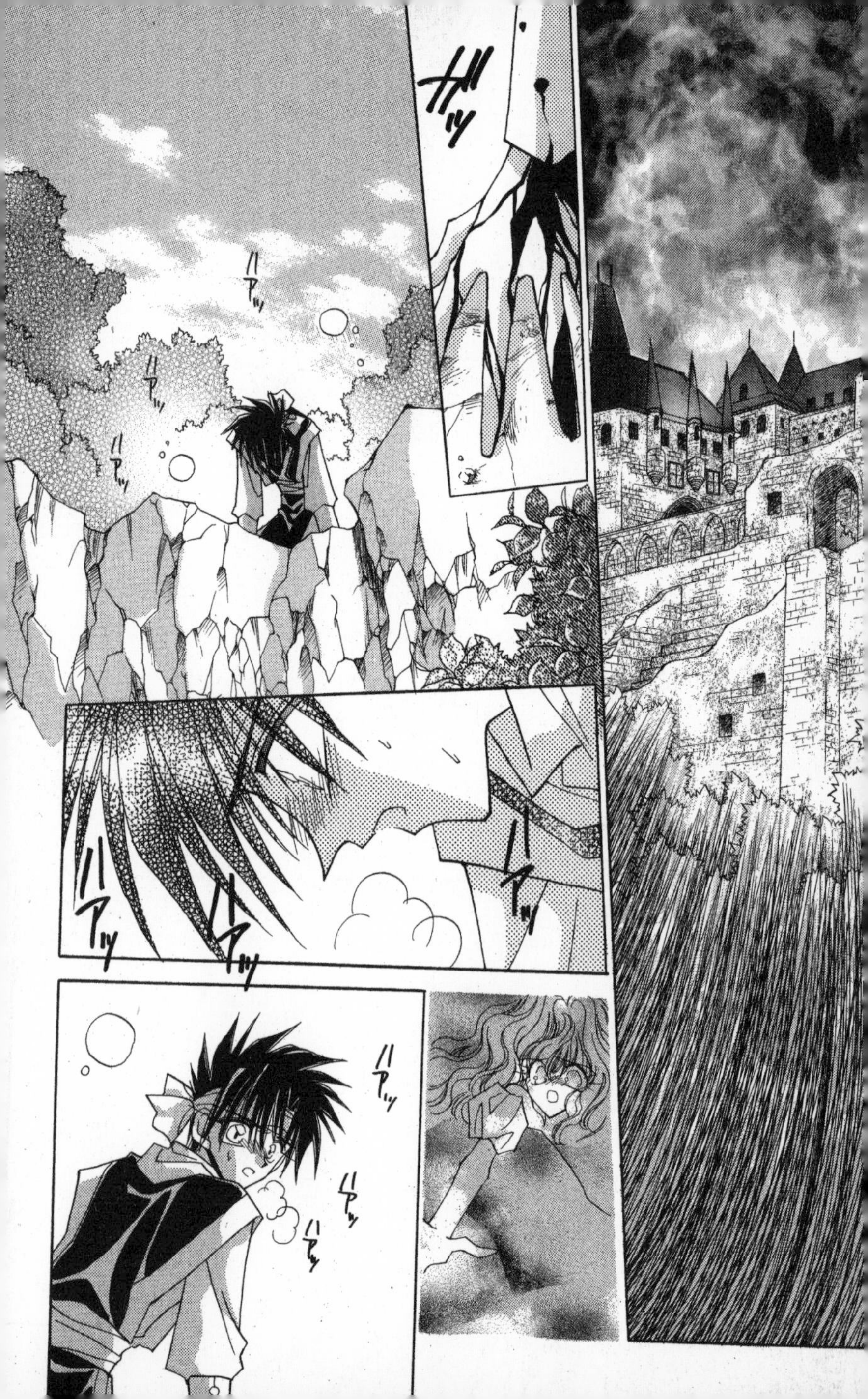

ガッ
ハアッ
ハアッ
ハアッ
ハアッ
ハアッ
ハアッ
ハアッ
ハアッ
ハアッ

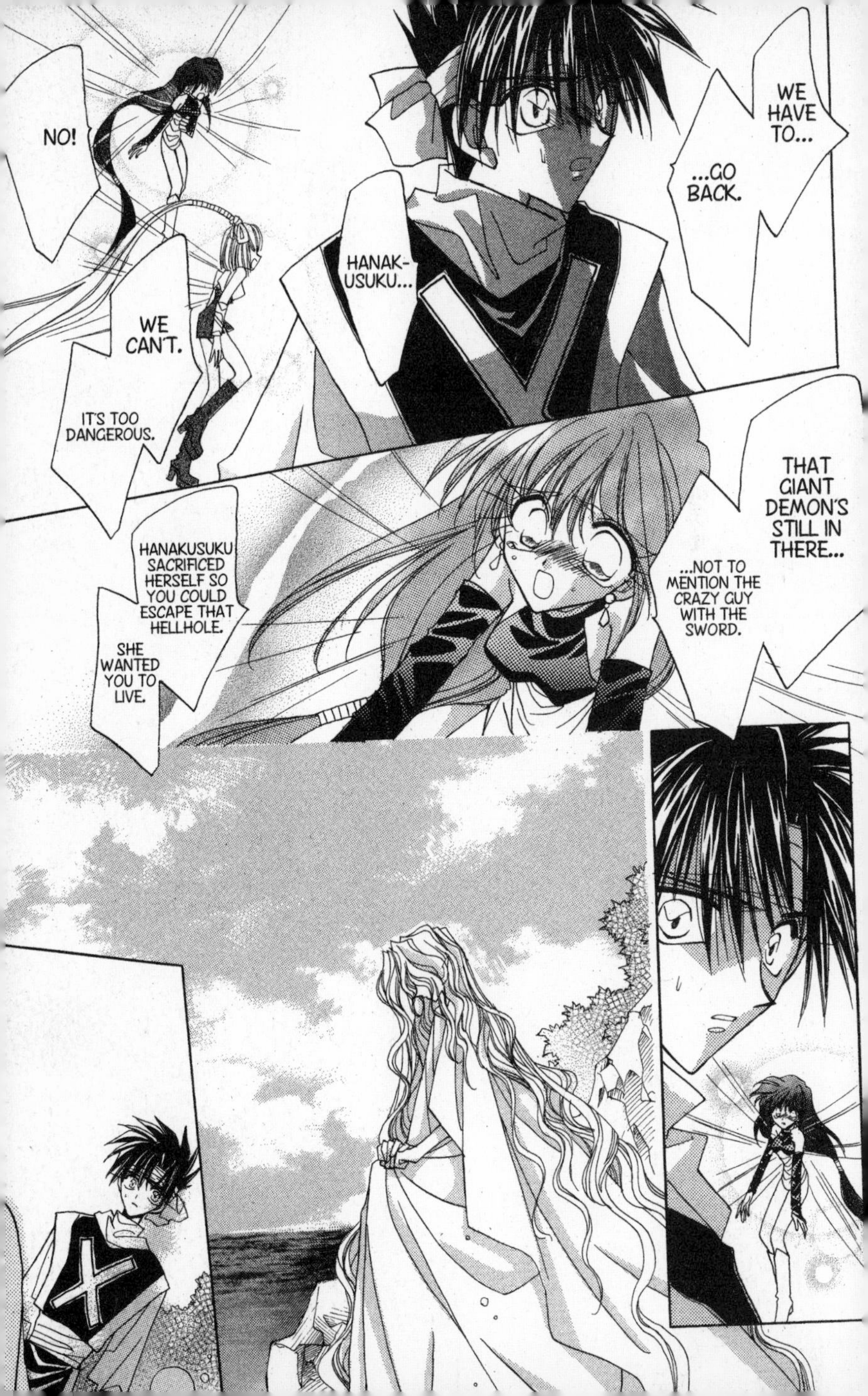
WE HAVE TO...
...GO BACK.
HANAK-USUKU...
NO!
WE CAN'T.
IT'S TOO DANGEROUS.
THAT GIANT DEMON'S STILL IN THERE...
...NOT TO MENTION THE CRAZY GUY WITH THE SWORD.
HANAKUSUKU SACRIFICED HERSELF SO YOU COULD ESCAPE THAT HELLHOLE.
SHE WANTED YOU TO LIVE.

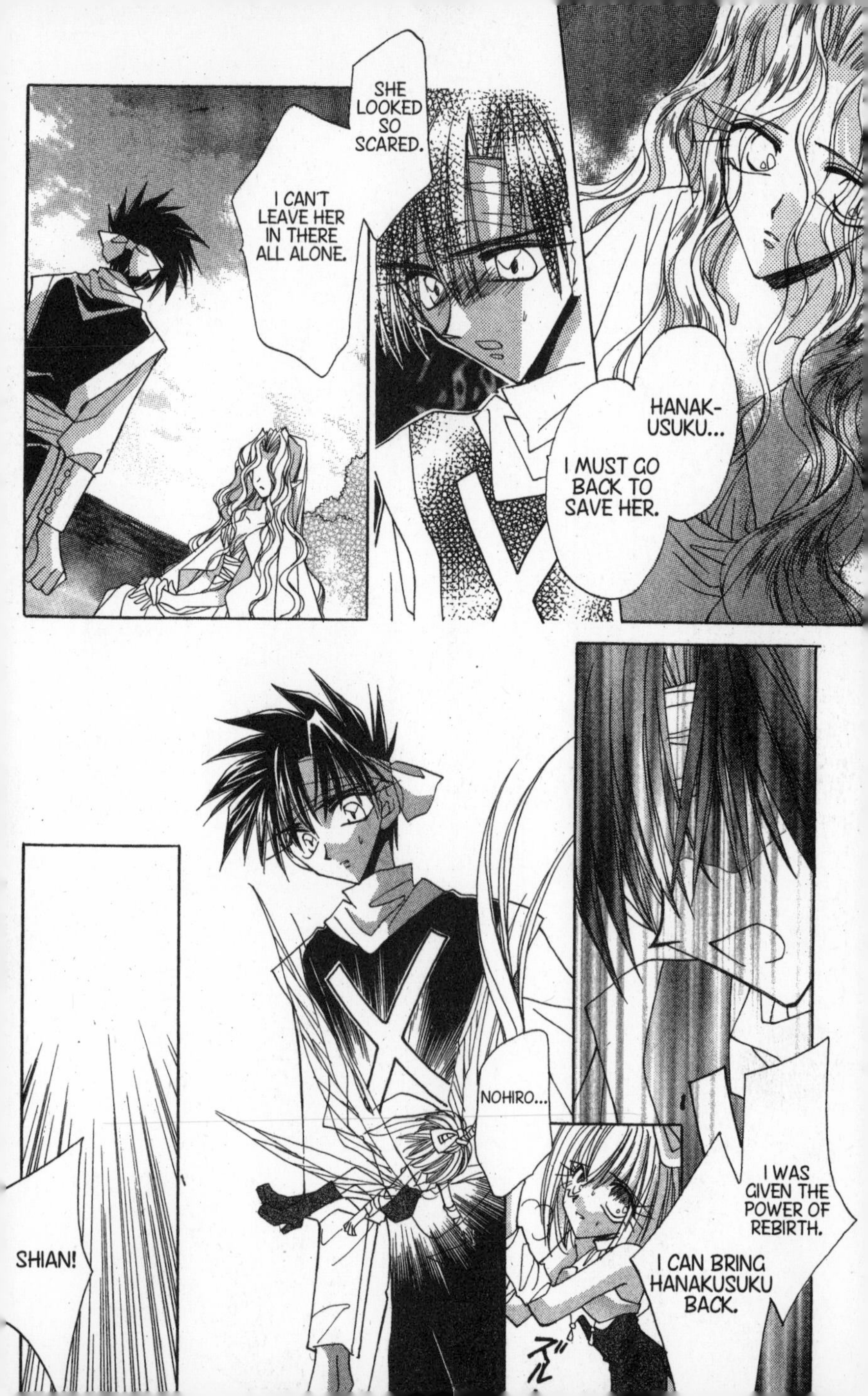
HANAK-USUKU...
I MUST GO BACK TO SAVE HER.
SHE LOOKED SO SCARED.
I CAN'T LEAVE HER IN THERE ALL ALONE.
I WAS GIVEN THE POWER OF REBIRTH.
I CAN BRING HANAKUSUKU BACK.
NOHIRO...
ズル
SHIAN!

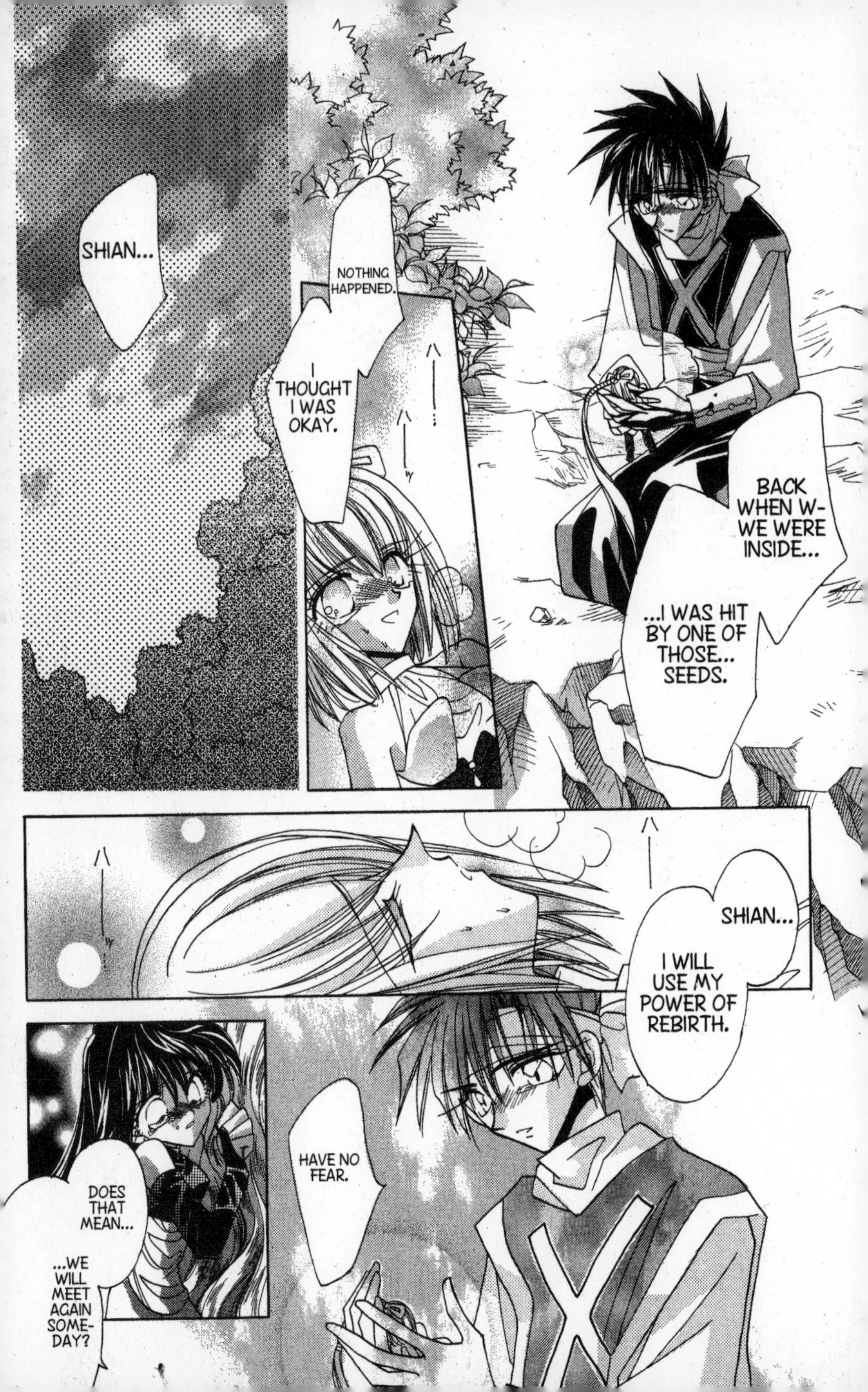
BACK WHEN W- WE WERE INSIDE...
...I WAS HIT BY ONE OF THOSE... SEEDS.
NOTHING HAPPENED.
I THOUGHT I WAS OKAY.
SHIAN...
SHIAN...
I WILL USE MY POWER OF REBIRTH.
HAVE NO FEAR.
DOES THAT MEAN...
...WE WILL MEET AGAIN SOME-DAY?

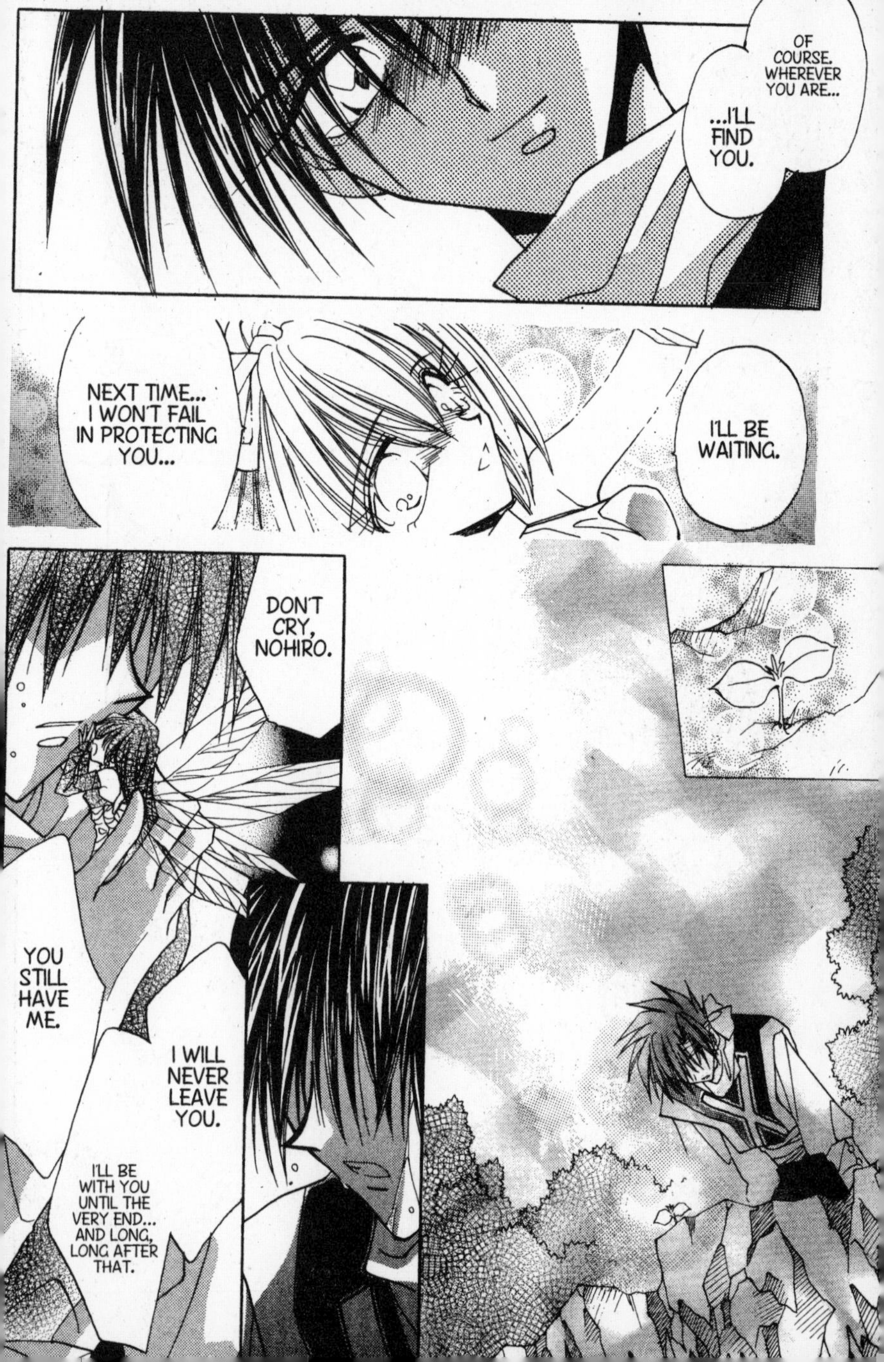
OF COURSE. WHEREVER YOU ARE...
...I'LL FIND YOU.
I'LL BE WAITING.
NEXT TIME... I WON'T FAIL IN PROTECTING YOU...
DON'T CRY, NOHIRO.
YOU STILL HAVE ME.
I WILL NEVER LEAVE YOU.
I'LL BE WITH YOU UNTIL THE VERY END... AND LONG, LONG AFTER THAT.

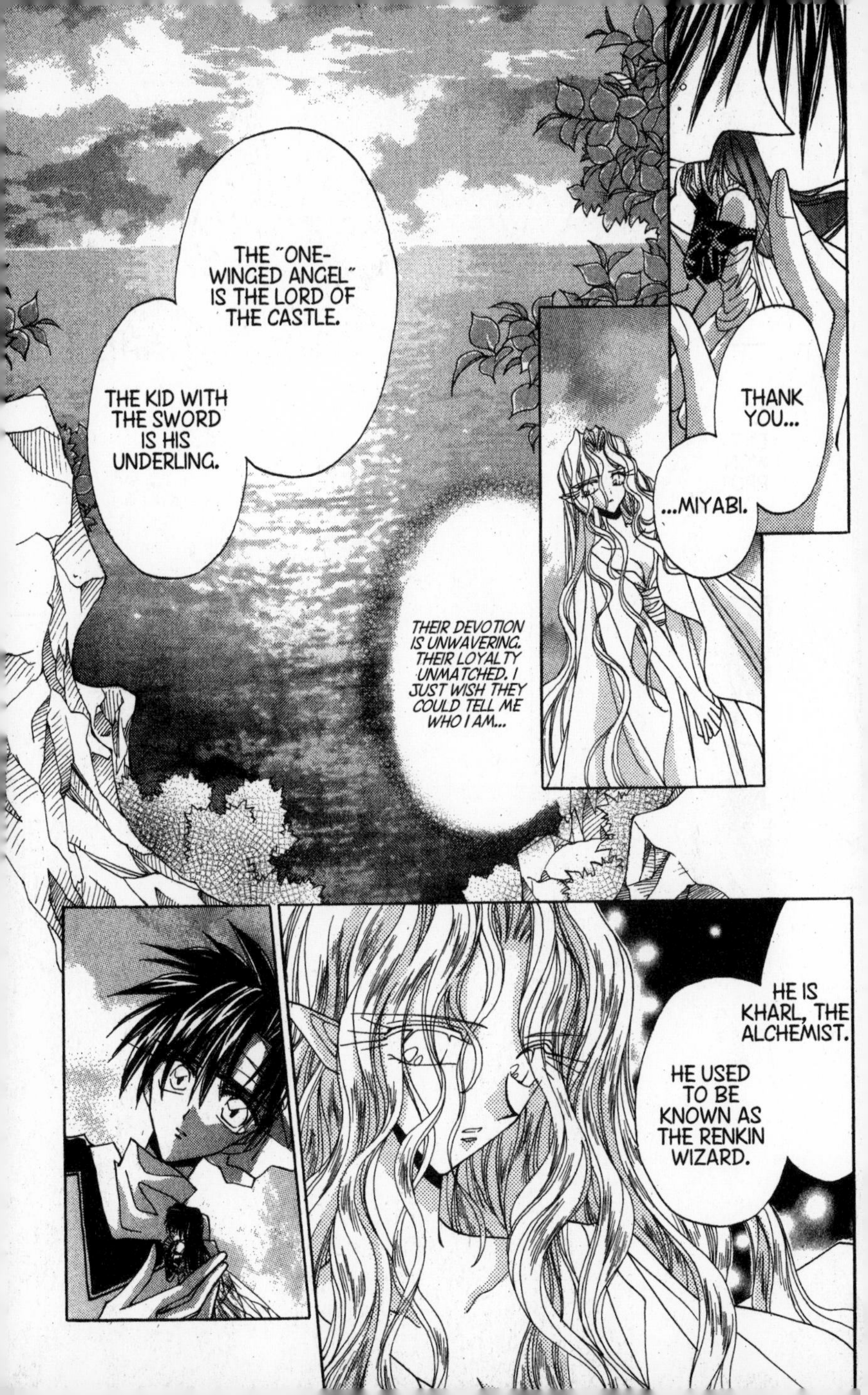
THANK YOU...
...MIYABI.
THEIR DEVOTION IS UNWAVERING. THEIR LOYALTY UNMATCHED. I JUST WISH THEY COULD TELL ME WHO I AM...
THE "ONE-WINGED ANGEL" IS THE LORD OF THE CASTLE.
THE KID WITH THE SWORD IS HIS UNDERLING.
HE IS KHARL, THE ALCHEMIST.
HE USED TO BE KNOWN AS THE RENKIN WIZARD.

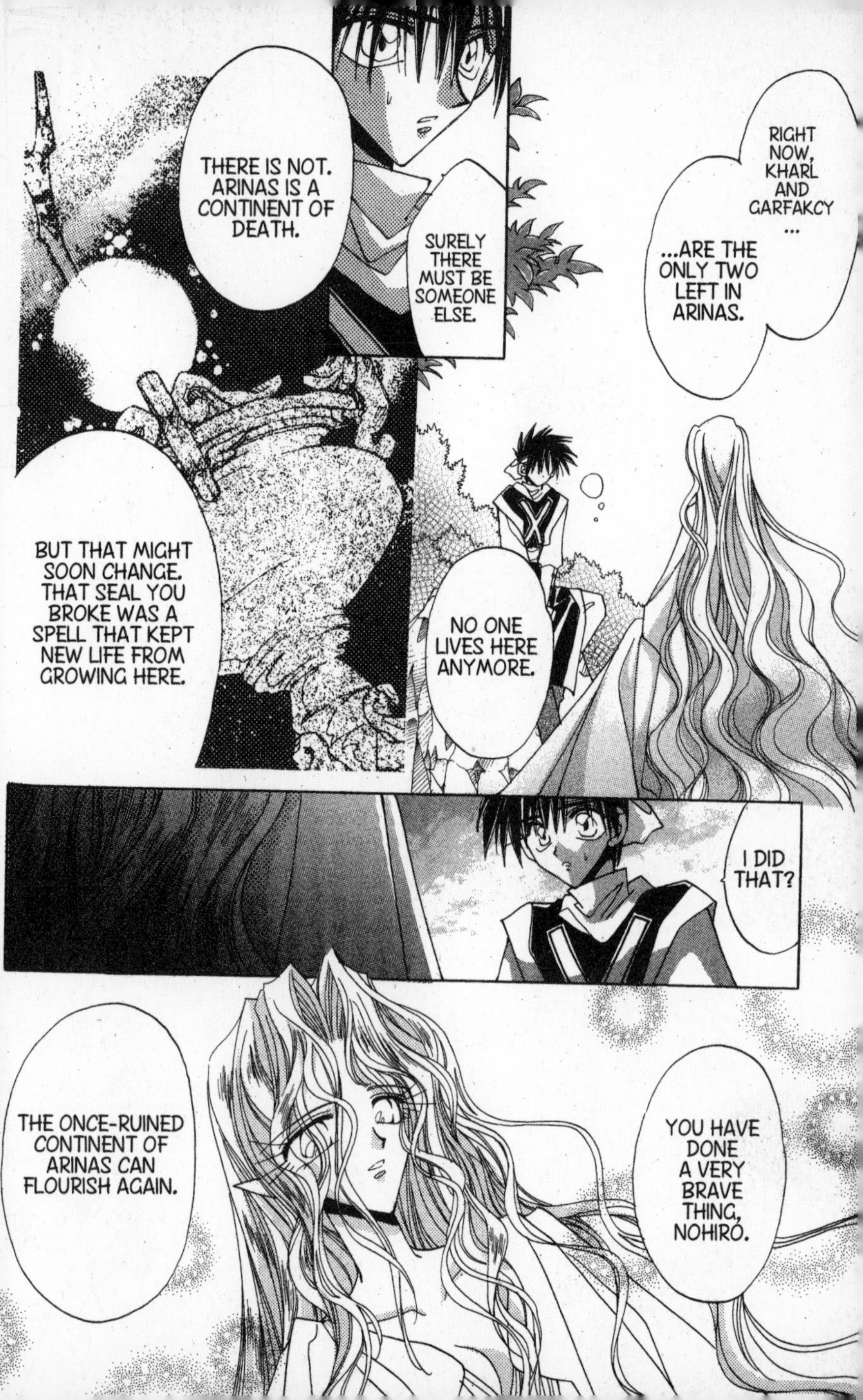
RIGHT NOW, KHARL AND GARFAKCY...
...ARE THE ONLY TWO LEFT IN ARINAS.
NO ONE LIVES HERE ANYMORE.
SURELY THERE MUST BE SOMEONE ELSE.
THERE IS NOT. ARINAS IS A CONTINENT OF DEATH.
BUT THAT MIGHT SOON CHANGE. THAT SEAL YOU BROKE WAS A SPELL THAT KEPT NEW LIFE FROM GROWING HERE.
I DID THAT?
YOU HAVE DONE A VERY BRAVE THING, NOHIRO.
THE ONCE-RUINED CONTINENT OF ARINAS CAN FLOURISH AGAIN.

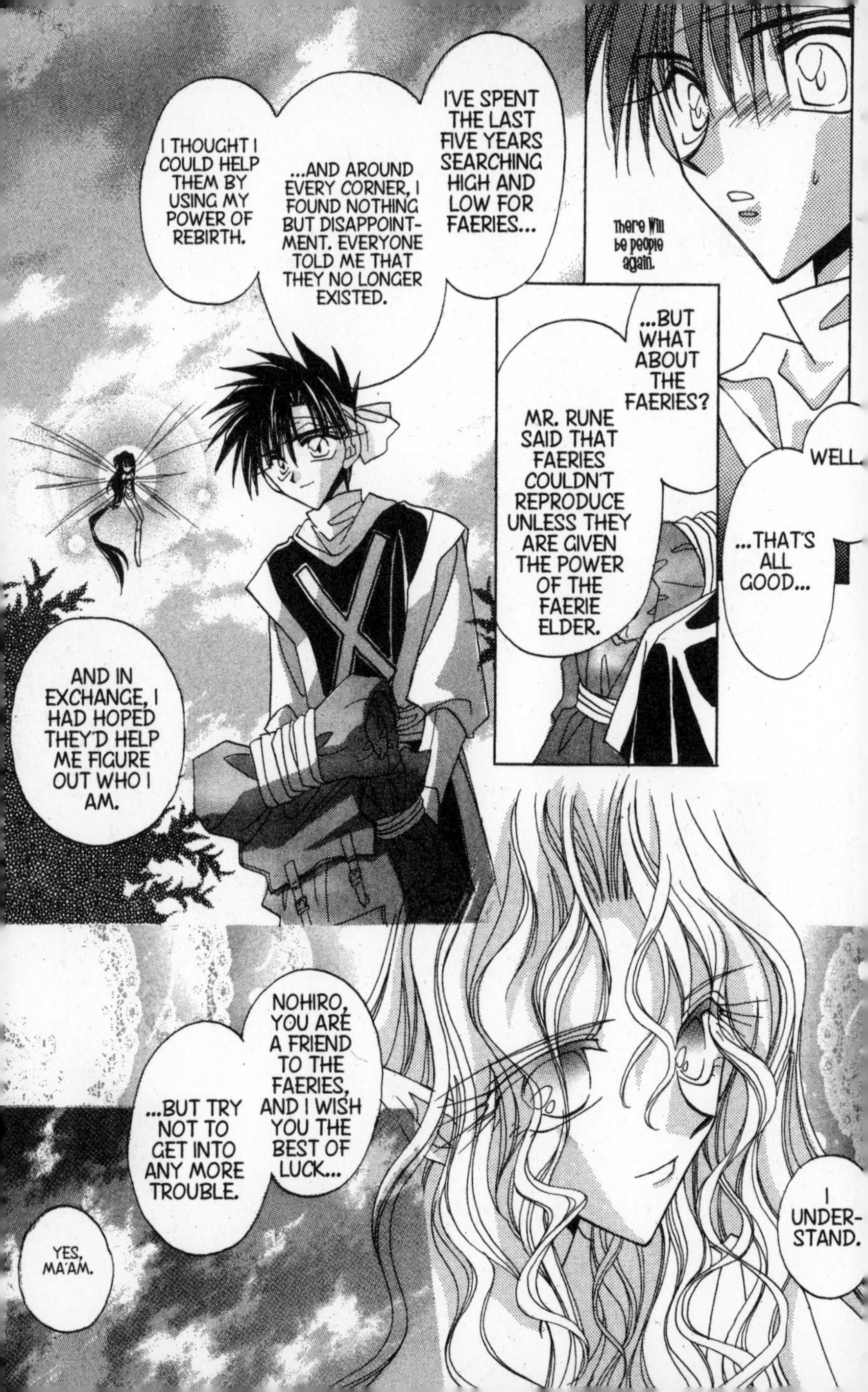
There will be people again.
...BUT WHAT ABOUT THE FAERIES?
MR. RUNE SAID THAT FAERIES COULDN'T REPRODUCE UNLESS THEY ARE GIVEN THE POWER OF THE FAERIE ELDER.
WELL.
...THAT'S ALL GOOD...
I'VE SPENT THE LAST FIVE YEARS SEARCHING HIGH AND LOW FOR FAERIES...
...AND AROUND EVERY CORNER, I FOUND NOTHING BUT DISAPPOINT-MENT. EVERYONE TOLD ME THAT THEY NO LONGER EXISTED.
I THOUGHT I COULD HELP THEM BY USING MY POWER OF REBIRTH.
AND IN EXCHANGE, I HAD HOPED THEY'D HELP ME FIGURE OUT WHO I AM.
I UNDER-STAND.
NOHIRO, YOU ARE A FRIEND TO THE FAERIES, AND I WISH YOU THE BEST OF LUCK...
...BUT TRY NOT TO GET INTO ANY MORE TROUBLE.
YES, MA'AM.

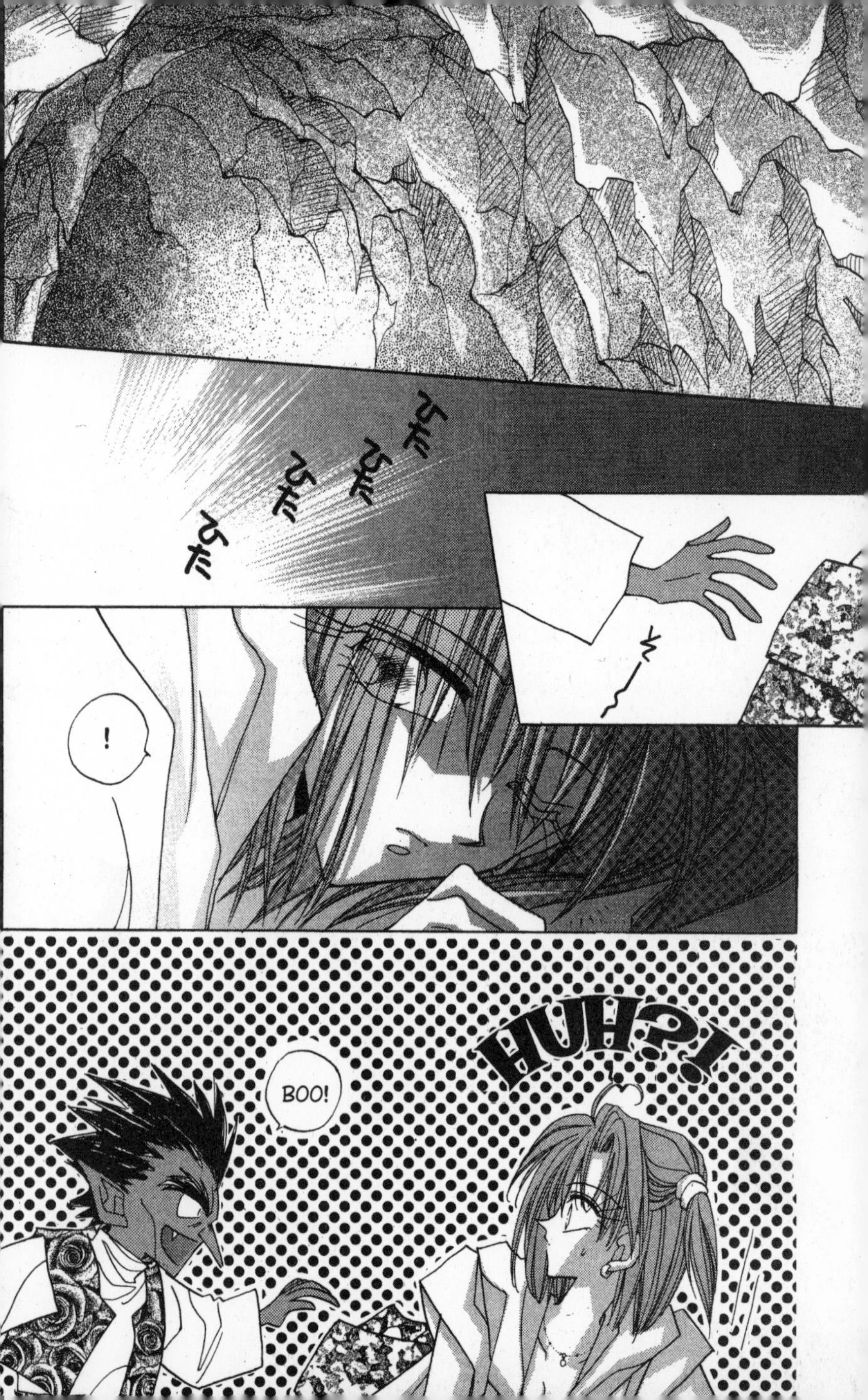
ひた ひた ひた ひた
!
HUH?!
BOO!

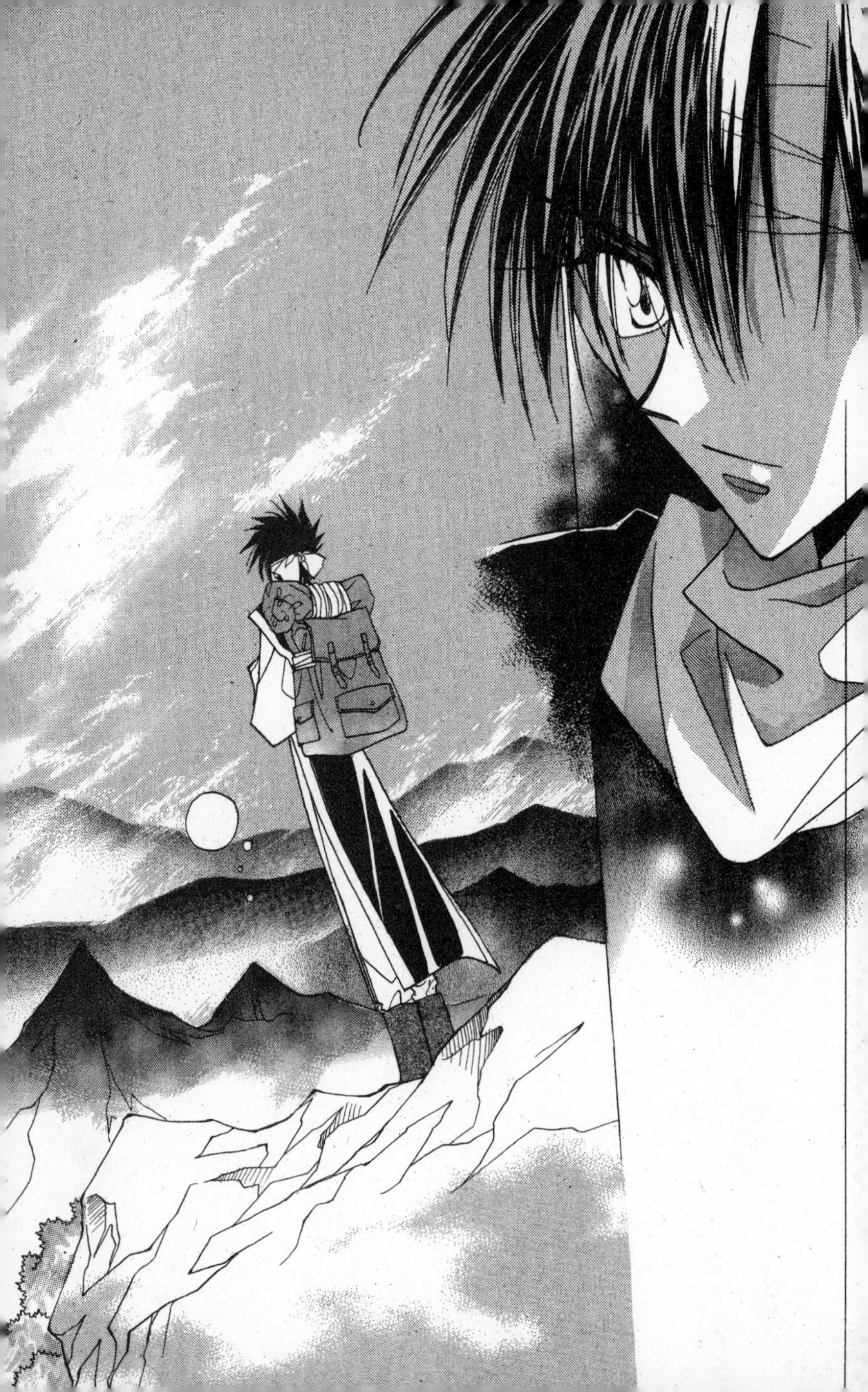

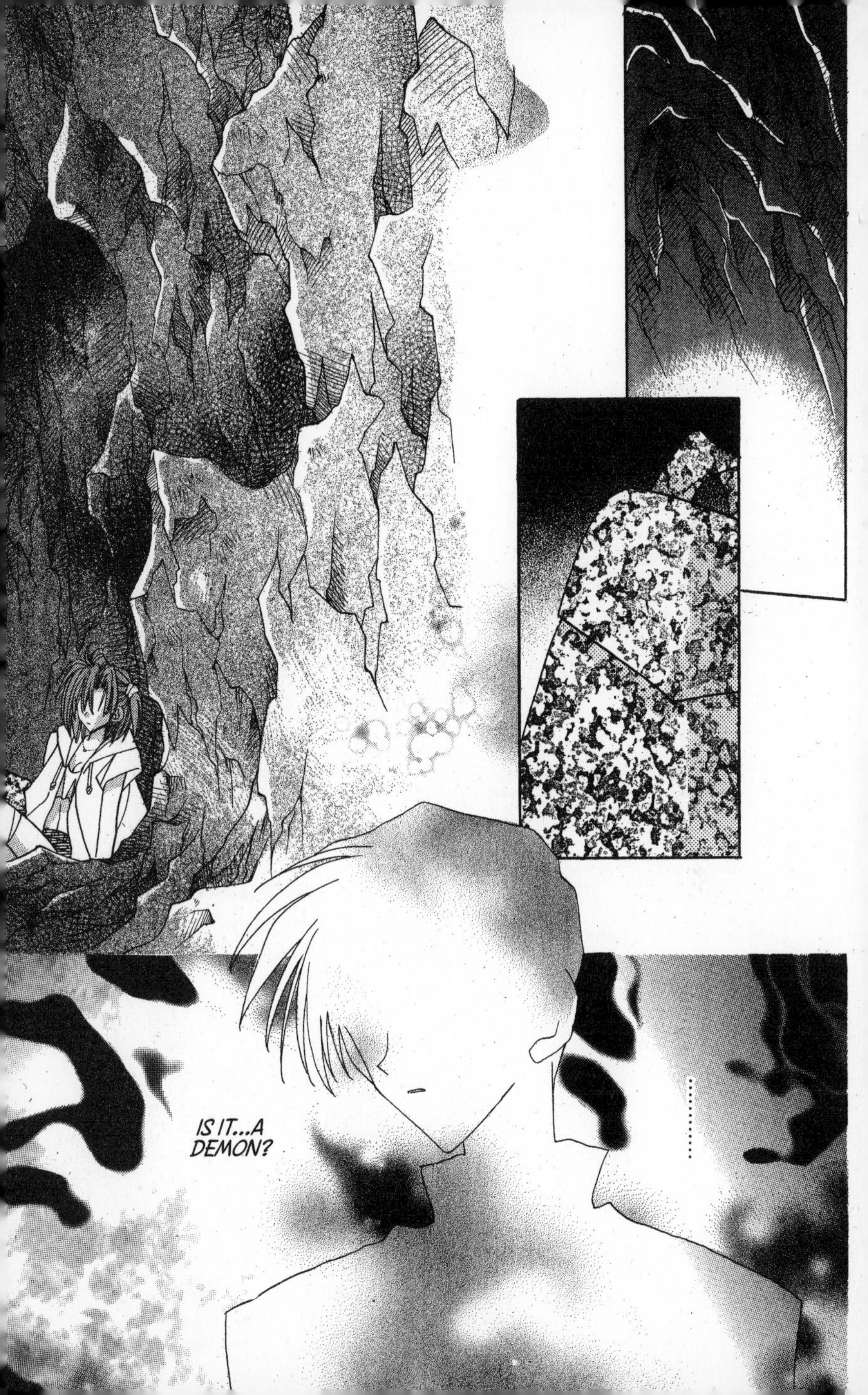
......
IS IT...A DEMON?

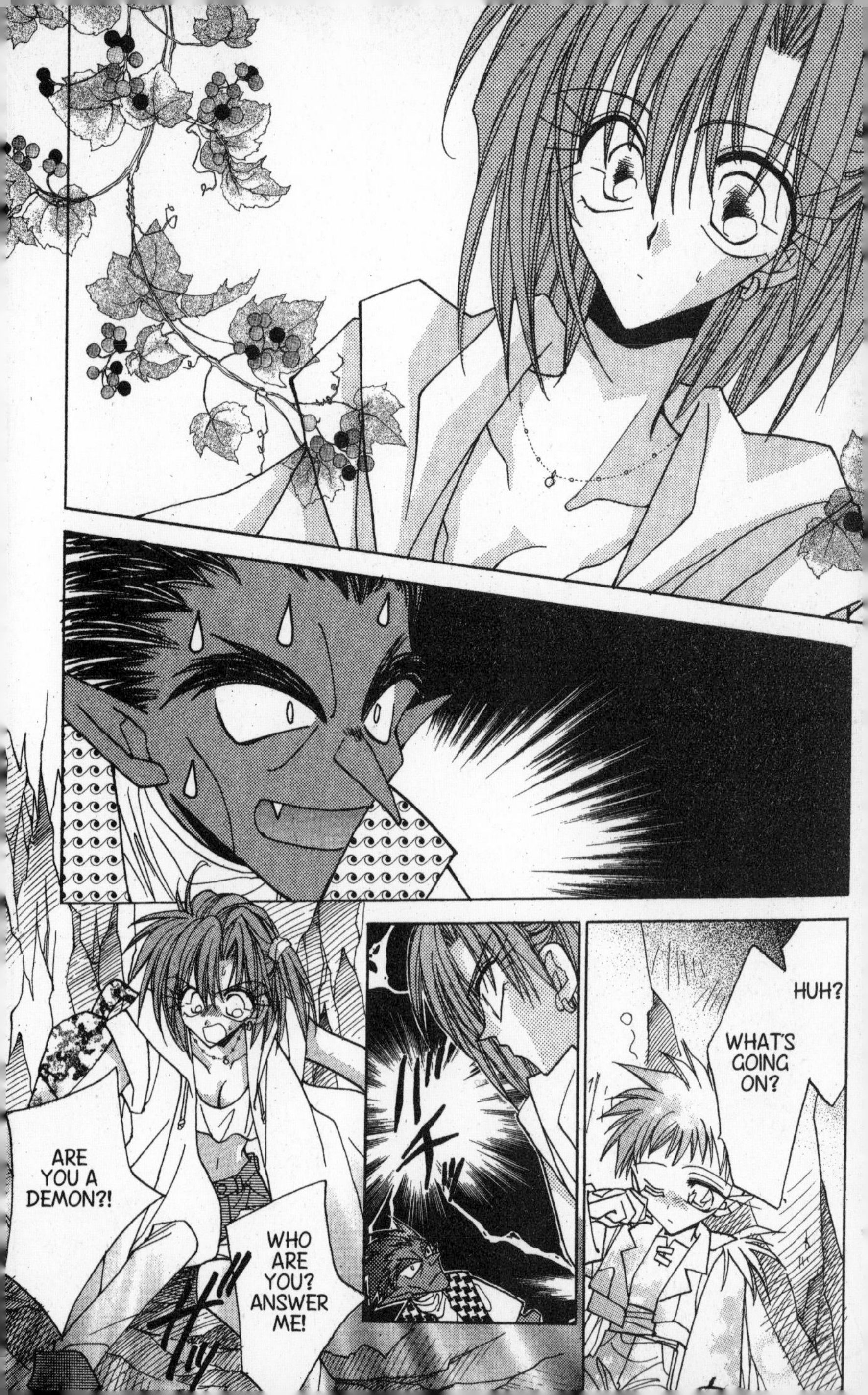
HUH?
WHAT'S GOING ON?
WHO ARE YOU? ANSWER ME!
ARE YOU A DEMON?!

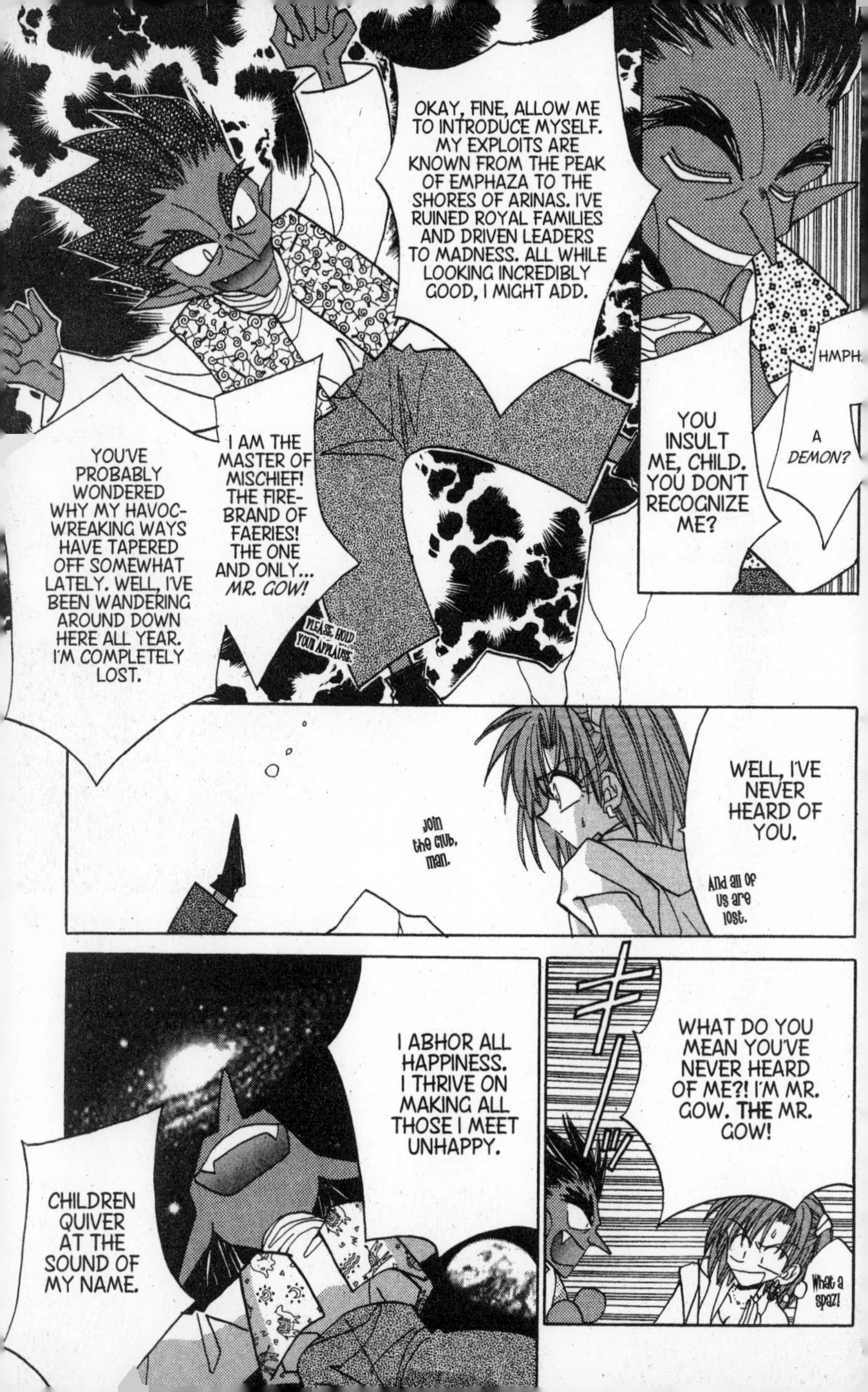
HMPH.
A DEMON?
YOU INSULT ME, CHILD. YOU DON'T RECOGNIZE ME?
OKAY, FINE, ALLOW ME TO INTRODUCE MYSELF. MY EXPLOITS ARE KNOWN FROM THE PEAK OF EMPHAZA TO THE SHORES OF ARINAS. I'VE RUINED ROYAL FAMILIES AND DRIVEN LEADERS TO MADNESS. ALL WHILE LOOKING INCREDIBLY GOOD, I MIGHT ADD.
I AM THE MASTER OF MISCHIEF! THE FIRE-BRAND OF FAERIES! THE ONE AND ONLY... *MR. GOW!*
PLEASE HOLD YOUR APPLAUSE.
YOU'VE PROBABLY WONDERED WHY MY HAVOC-WREAKING WAYS HAVE TAPERED OFF SOMEWHAT LATELY. WELL, I'VE BEEN WANDERING AROUND DOWN HERE ALL YEAR. I'M COMPLETELY LOST.
WELL, I'VE NEVER HEARD OF YOU.
And all of us are lost.
Join the club, man.
WHAT DO YOU MEAN YOU'VE NEVER HEARD OF ME?! I'M MR. GOW. **THE** MR. GOW!
What a spaz!
I ABHOR ALL HAPPINESS. I THRIVE ON MAKING ALL THOSE I MEET UNHAPPY.
CHILDREN QUIVER AT THE SOUND OF MY NAME.

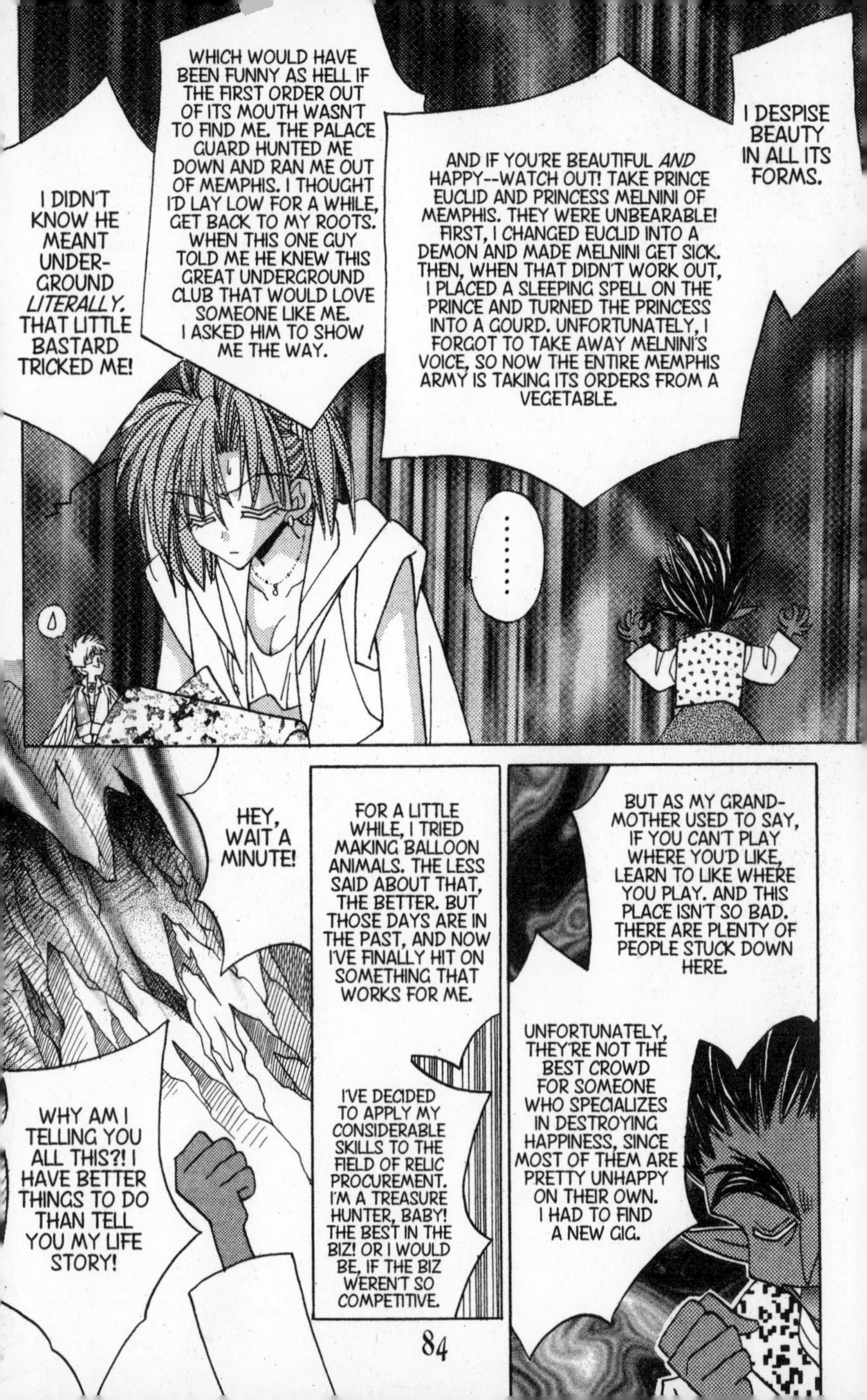
I DESPISE BEAUTY IN ALL ITS FORMS.
AND IF YOU'RE BEAUTIFUL *AND* HAPPY--WATCH OUT! TAKE PRINCE EUCLID AND PRINCESS MELNINI OF MEMPHIS. THEY WERE UNBEARABLE! FIRST, I CHANGED EUCLID INTO A DEMON AND MADE MELNINI GET SICK. THEN, WHEN THAT DIDN'T WORK OUT, I PLACED A SLEEPING SPELL ON THE PRINCE AND TURNED THE PRINCESS INTO A GOURD. UNFORTUNATELY, I FORGOT TO TAKE AWAY MELNINI'S VOICE, SO NOW THE ENTIRE MEMPHIS ARMY IS TAKING ITS ORDERS FROM A VEGETABLE.
WHICH WOULD HAVE BEEN FUNNY AS HELL IF THE FIRST ORDER OUT OF ITS MOUTH WASN'T TO FIND ME. THE PALACE GUARD HUNTED ME DOWN AND RAN ME OUT OF MEMPHIS. I THOUGHT I'D LAY LOW FOR A WHILE, GET BACK TO MY ROOTS. WHEN THIS ONE GUY TOLD ME HE KNEW THIS GREAT UNDERGROUND CLUB THAT WOULD LOVE SOMEONE LIKE ME. I ASKED HIM TO SHOW ME THE WAY.
I DIDN'T KNOW HE MEANT UNDER-GROUND *LITERALLY*. THAT LITTLE BASTARD TRICKED ME!
....
BUT AS MY GRAND-MOTHER USED TO SAY, IF YOU CAN'T PLAY WHERE YOU'D LIKE, LEARN TO LIKE WHERE YOU PLAY. AND THIS PLACE ISN'T SO BAD. THERE ARE PLENTY OF PEOPLE STUCK DOWN HERE.
UNFORTUNATELY, THEY'RE NOT THE BEST CROWD FOR SOMEONE WHO SPECIALIZES IN DESTROYING HAPPINESS, SINCE MOST OF THEM ARE PRETTY UNHAPPY ON THEIR OWN. I HAD TO FIND A NEW GIG.
FOR A LITTLE WHILE, I TRIED MAKING BALLOON ANIMALS. THE LESS SAID ABOUT THAT, THE BETTER. BUT THOSE DAYS ARE IN THE PAST, AND NOW I'VE FINALLY HIT ON SOMETHING THAT WORKS FOR ME.
I'VE DECIDED TO APPLY MY CONSIDERABLE SKILLS TO THE FIELD OF RELIC PROCUREMENT. I'M A TREASURE HUNTER, BABY! THE BEST IN THE BIZ! OR I WOULD BE, IF THE BIZ WEREN'T SO COMPETITIVE.
HEY, WAIT A MINUTE!
WHY AM I TELLING YOU ALL THIS?! I HAVE BETTER THINGS TO DO THAN TELL YOU MY LIFE STORY!

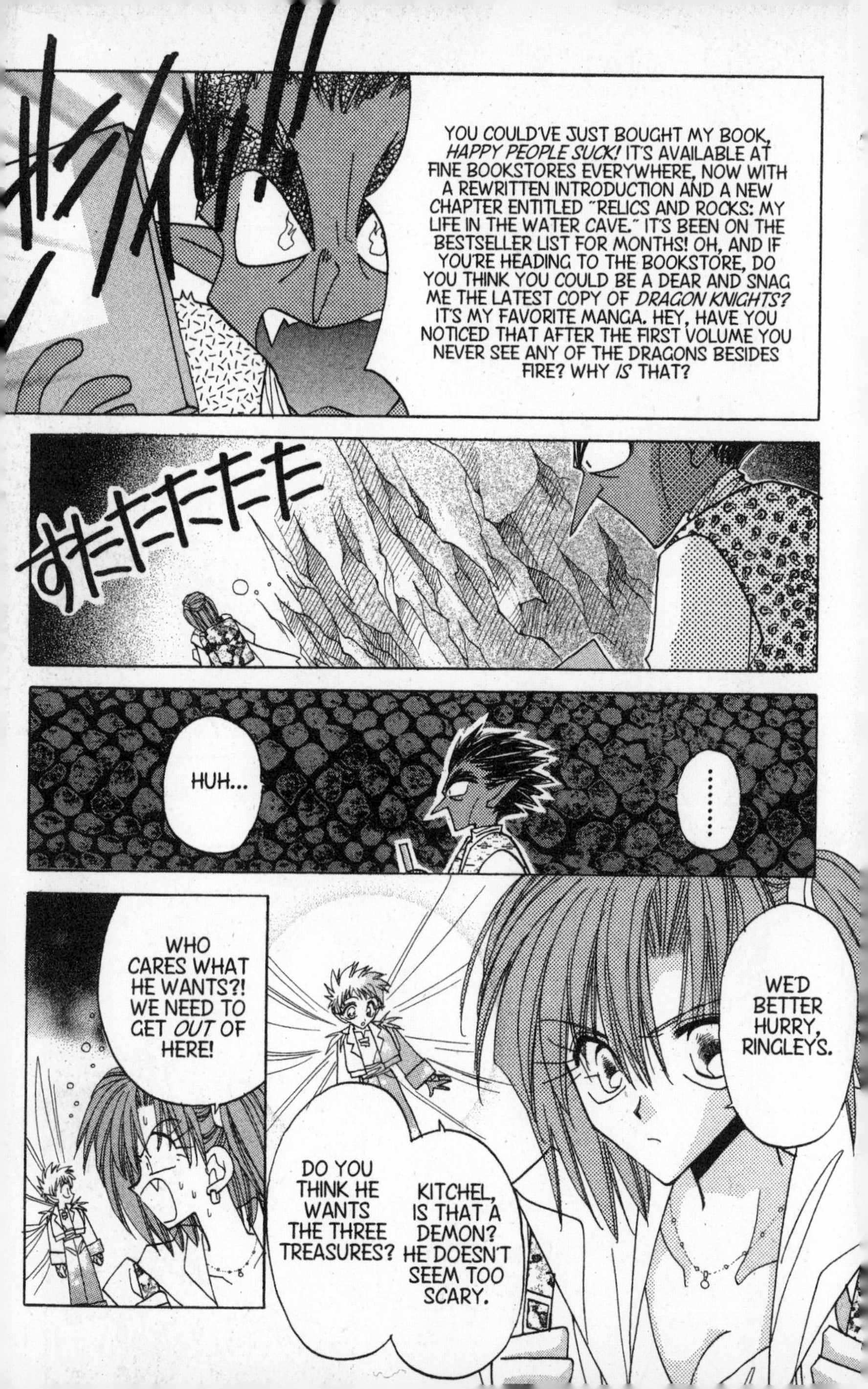
YOU COULD'VE JUST BOUGHT MY BOOK, *HAPPY PEOPLE SUCK!* IT'S AVAILABLE AT FINE BOOKSTORES EVERYWHERE, NOW WITH A REWRITTEN INTRODUCTION AND A NEW CHAPTER ENTITLED "RELICS AND ROCKS: MY LIFE IN THE WATER CAVE." IT'S BEEN ON THE BESTSELLER LIST FOR MONTHS! OH, AND IF YOU'RE HEADING TO THE BOOKSTORE, DO YOU THINK YOU COULD BE A DEAR AND SNAG ME THE LATEST COPY OF *DRAGON KNIGHTS?* IT'S MY FAVORITE MANGA. HEY, HAVE YOU NOTICED THAT AFTER THE FIRST VOLUME YOU NEVER SEE ANY OF THE DRAGONS BESIDES FIRE? WHY *IS* THAT?
すたたたたた
....
HUH...
WE'D BETTER HURRY, RINGLEYS.
KITCHEL, IS THAT A DEMON? HE DOESN'T SEEM TOO SCARY.
DO YOU THINK HE WANTS THE THREE TREASURES?
WHO CARES WHAT HE WANTS?! WE NEED TO GET *OUT* OF HERE!

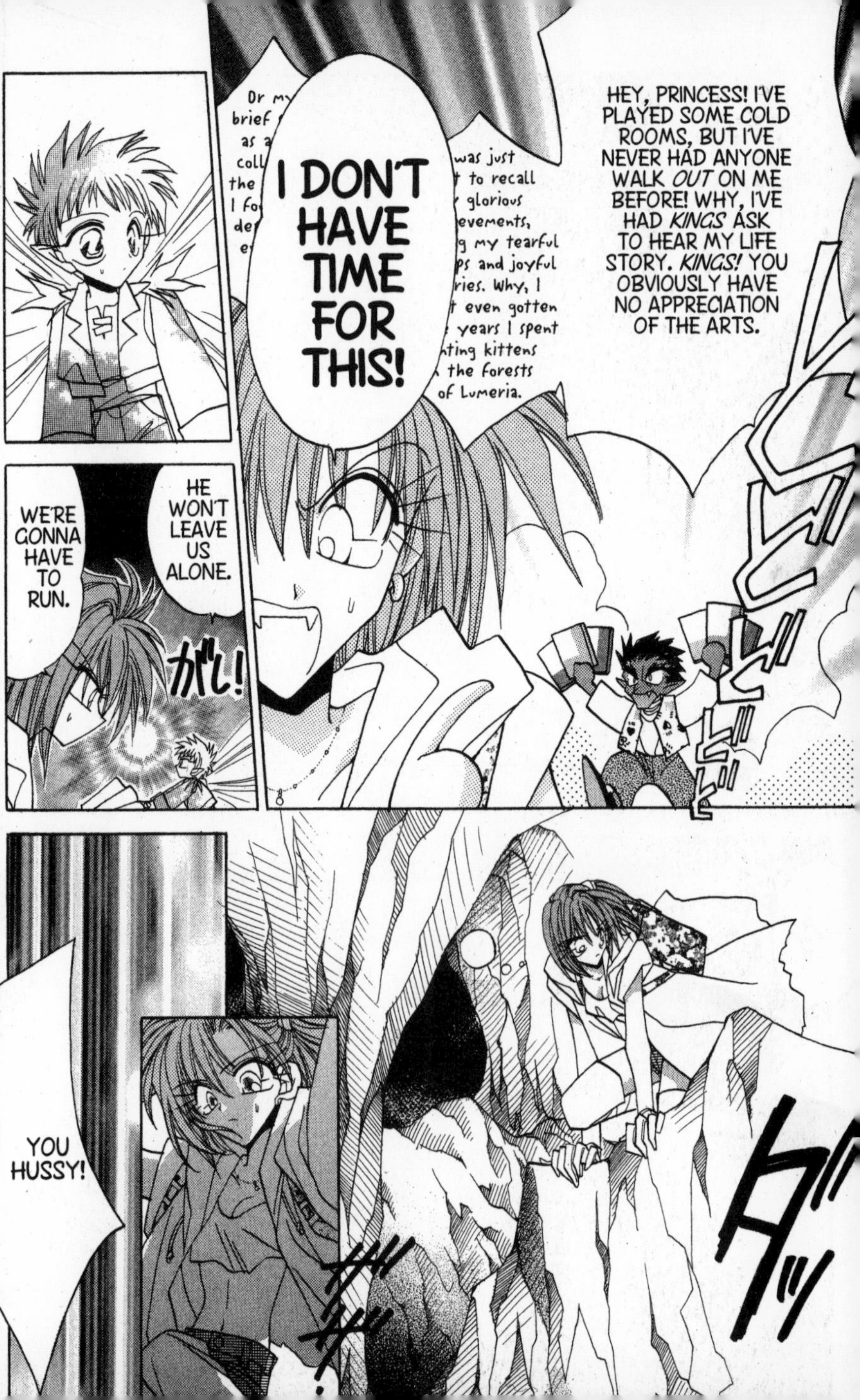
HEY, PRINCESS! I'VE PLAYED SOME COLD ROOMS, BUT I'VE NEVER HAD ANYONE WALK *OUT* ON ME BEFORE! WHY, I'VE HAD *KINGS* ASK TO HEAR MY LIFE STORY. *KINGS!* YOU OBVIOUSLY HAVE NO APPRECIATION OF THE ARTS.
I DON'T HAVE TIME FOR THIS!
of Lumeria.
HE WON'T LEAVE US ALONE.
WE'RE GONNA HAVE TO RUN.
がし!
YOU HUSSY!

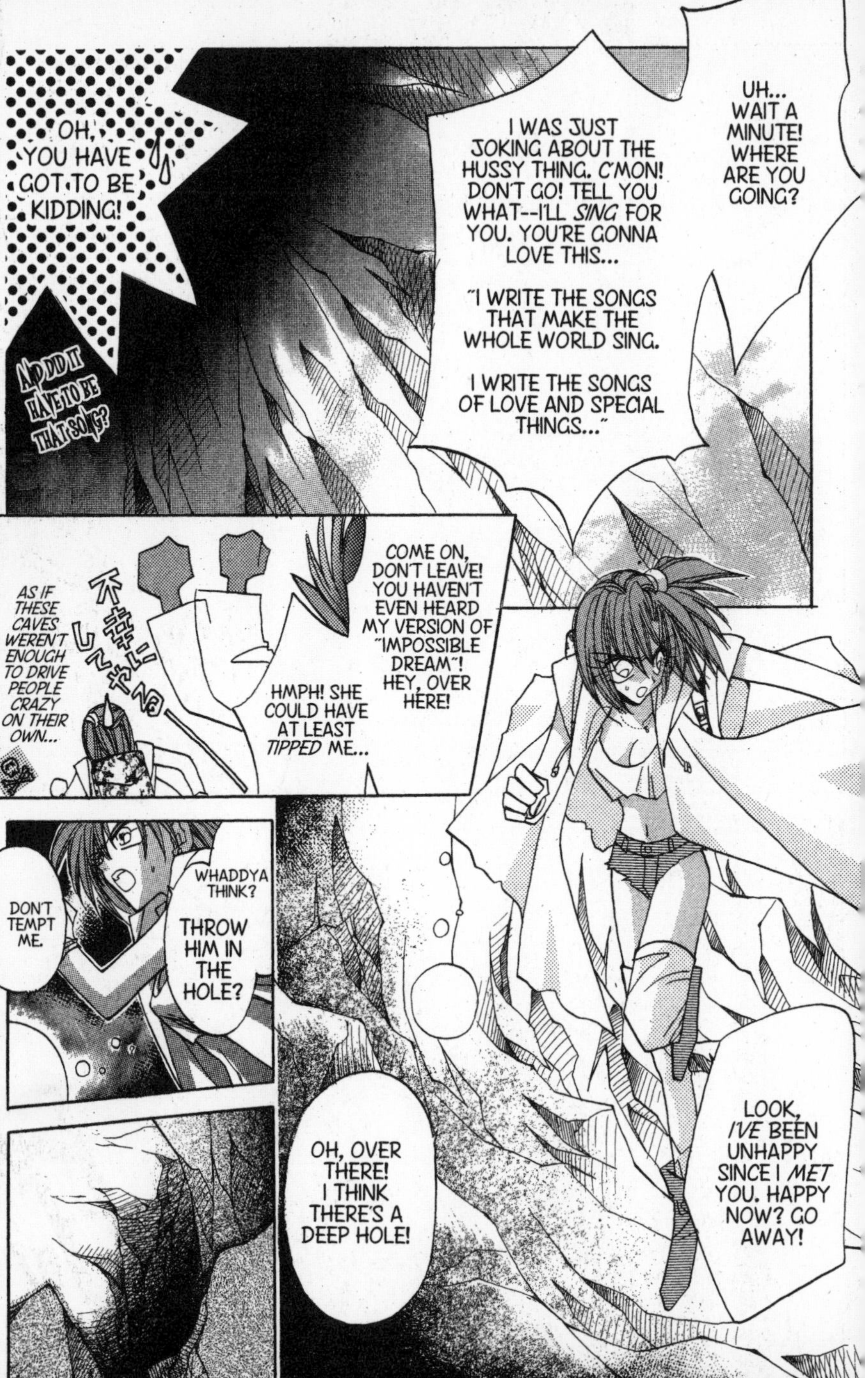
UH... WAIT A MINUTE! WHERE ARE YOU GOING?
I WAS JUST JOKING ABOUT THE HUSSY THING. C'MON! DON'T GO! TELL YOU WHAT--I'LL *SING* FOR YOU. YOU'RE GONNA LOVE THIS...
"I WRITE THE SONGS THAT MAKE THE WHOLE WORLD SING.
I WRITE THE SONGS OF LOVE AND SPECIAL THINGS..."
OH, YOU HAVE GOT TO BE KIDDING!
AND DID IT HAVE TO BE THAT SONG?
LOOK, *I'VE* BEEN UNHAPPY SINCE I *MET* YOU. HAPPY NOW? GO AWAY!
OH, OVER THERE! I THINK THERE'S A DEEP HOLE!
COME ON, DON'T LEAVE! YOU HAVEN'T EVEN HEARD MY VERSION OF "IMPOSSIBLE DREAM"! HEY, OVER HERE!
HMPH! SHE COULD HAVE AT LEAST *TIPPED* ME...
不幸にしてやる
AS IF THESE CAVES WEREN'T ENOUGH TO DRIVE PEOPLE CRAZY ON THEIR OWN...
WHADDYA THINK?
THROW HIM IN THE HOLE?
DON'T TEMPT ME.

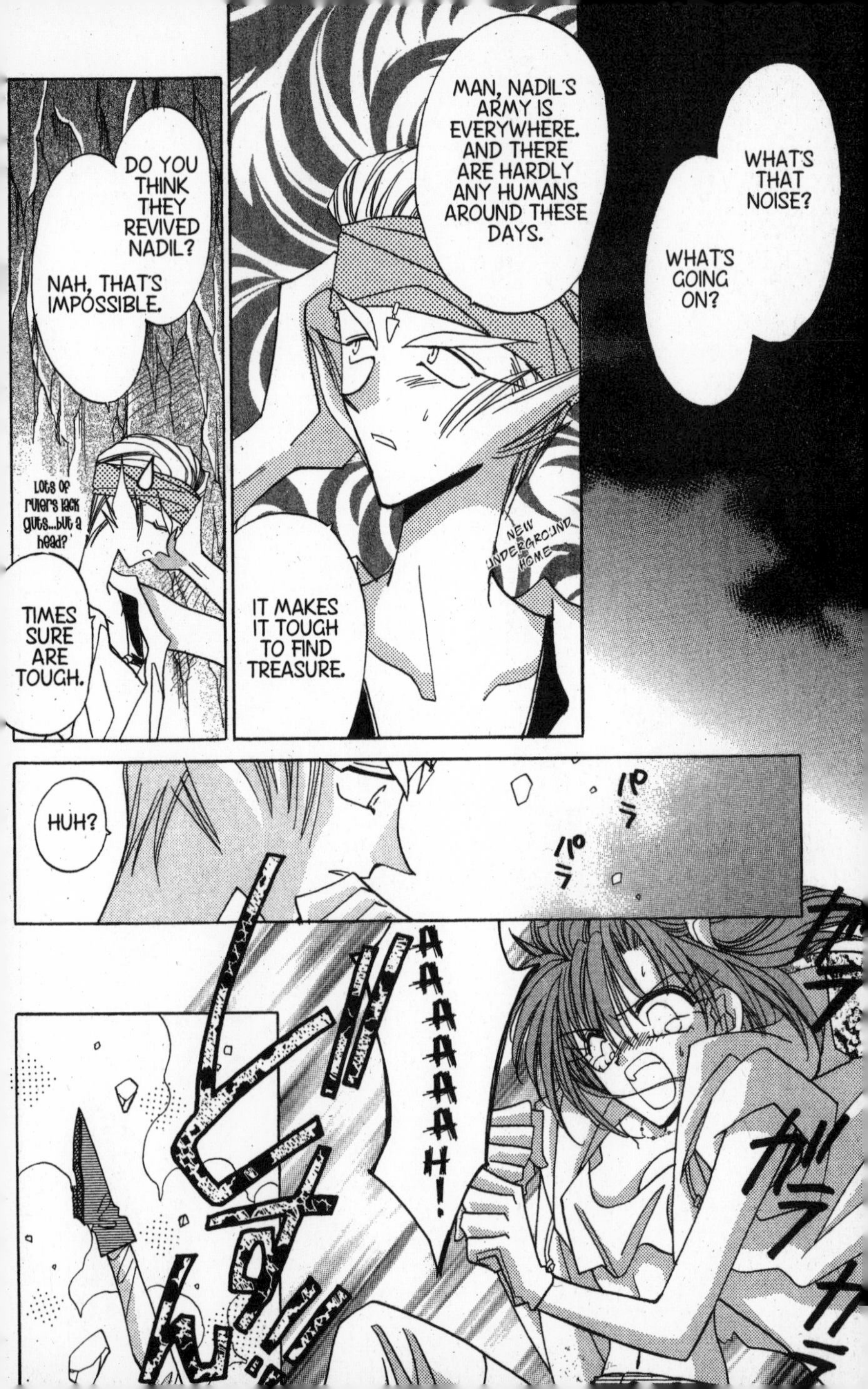
WHAT'S THAT NOISE?
WHAT'S GOING ON?
MAN, NADIL'S ARMY IS EVERYWHERE. AND THERE ARE HARDLY ANY HUMANS AROUND THESE DAYS.
IT MAKES IT TOUGH TO FIND TREASURE.
NEW UNDERGROUND HOME
DO YOU THINK THEY REVIVED NADIL?
NAH, THAT'S IMPOSSIBLE.
Lots of rulers lack guts...but a head?
TIMES SURE ARE TOUGH.
パラ
パラ
HUH?
AAAAAAAAH!

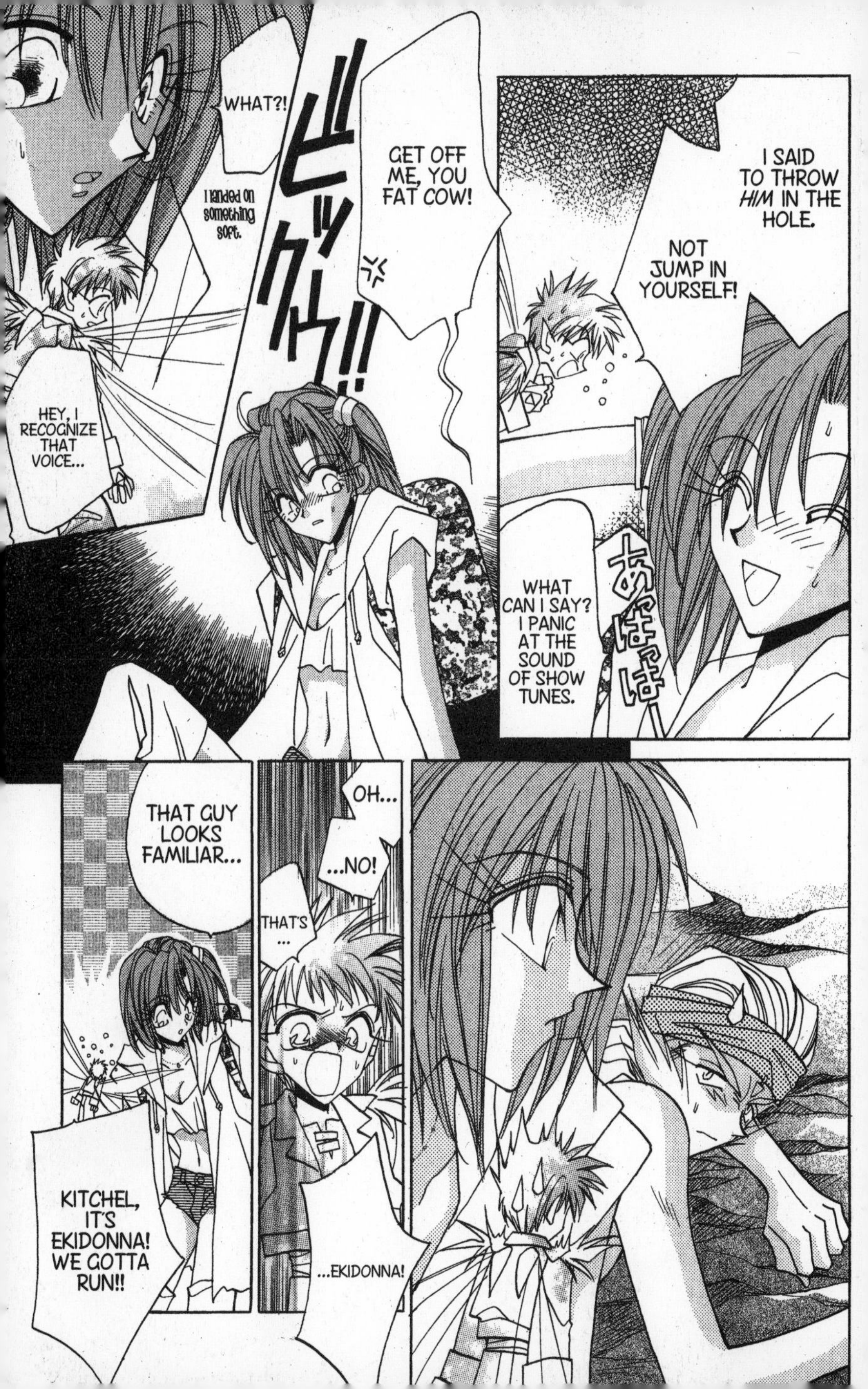
I SAID TO THROW *HIM* IN THE HOLE.
NOT JUMP IN YOURSELF!
WHAT CAN I SAY? I PANIC AT THE SOUND OF SHOW TUNES.
あはは
WHAT?!
ビックゥ!!
GET OFF ME, YOU FAT COW!
I landed on something soft.
HEY, I RECOGNIZE THAT VOICE...
OH...
...NO!
THAT'S ...
...EKIDONNA!
THAT GUY LOOKS FAMILIAR...
KITCHEL, IT'S EKIDONNA! WE GOTTA RUN!!

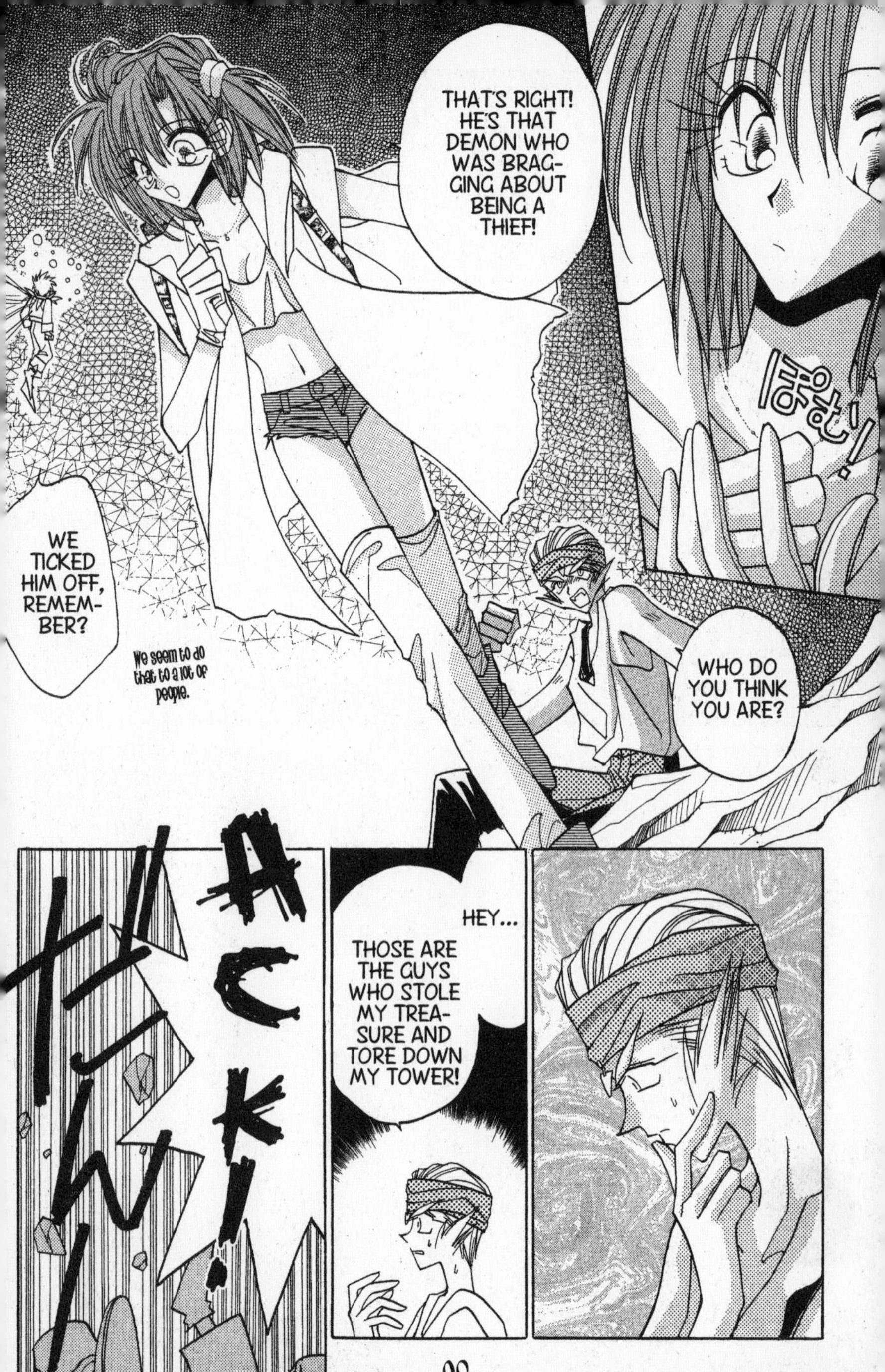
ぽむ!
THAT'S RIGHT! HE'S THAT DEMON WHO WAS BRAG-GING ABOUT BEING A THIEF!
WHO DO YOU THINK YOU ARE?
WE TICKED HIM OFF, REMEMBER?
We seem to do that to a lot of people.
HEY...
THOSE ARE THE GUYS WHO STOLE MY TREA-SURE AND TORE DOWN MY TOWER!
HACK

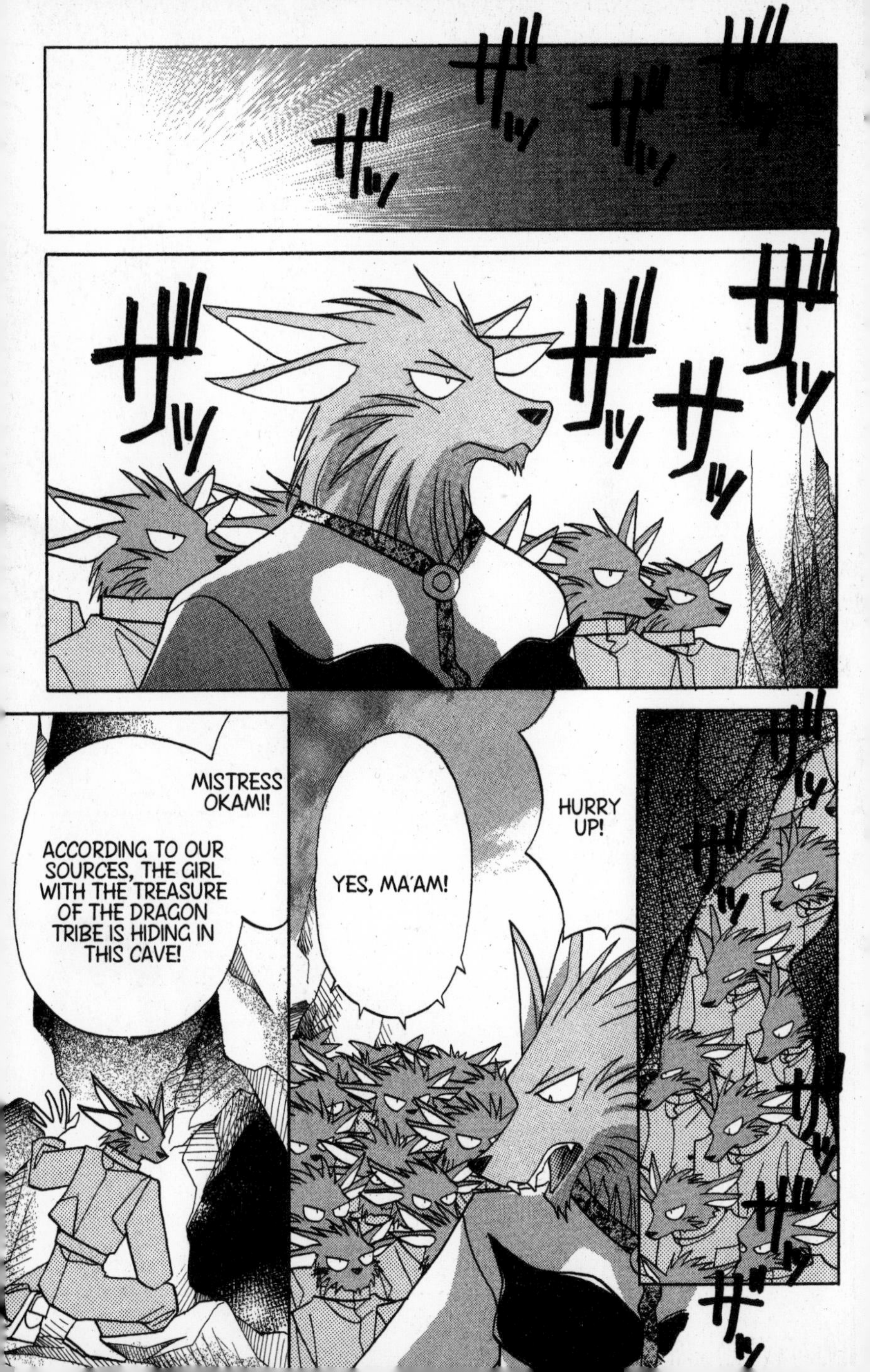
ザッ ザッ ザッ ザッ
ザッ ザッ サッ ザッ
ザッ ザッ ザッ ザッ ザッ
HURRY UP!
YES, MA'AM!
MISTRESS OKAMI!
ACCORDING TO OUR SOURCES, THE GIRL WITH THE TREASURE OF THE DRAGON TRIBE IS HIDING IN THIS CAVE!

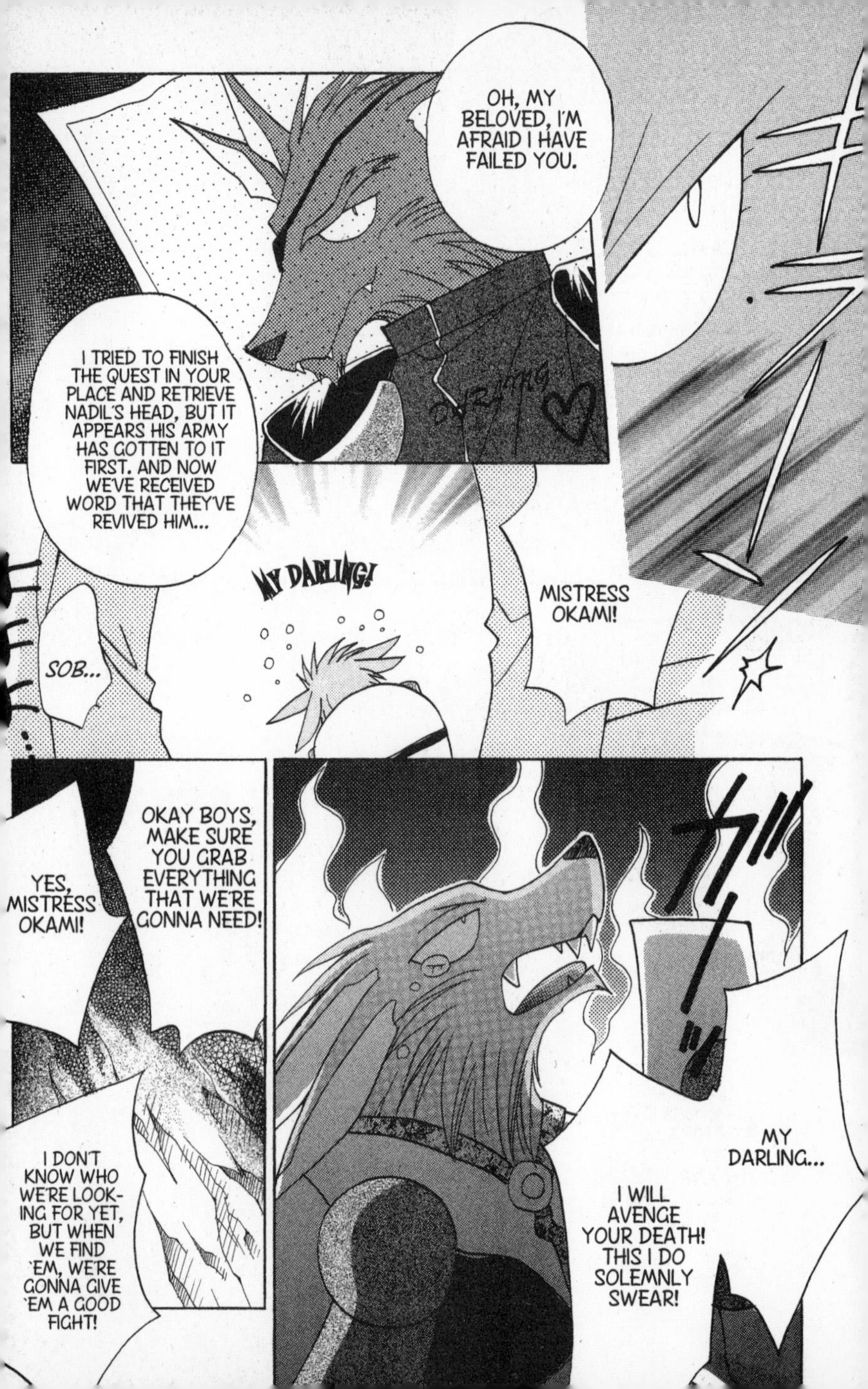

OH, MY BELOVED, I'M AFRAID I HAVE FAILED YOU.
I TRIED TO FINISH THE QUEST IN YOUR PLACE AND RETRIEVE NADIL'S HEAD, BUT IT APPEARS HIS ARMY HAS GOTTEN TO IT FIRST. AND NOW WE'VE RECEIVED WORD THAT THEY'VE REVIVED HIM...
MISTRESS OKAMI!
MY DARLING!
SOB...
MY DARLING...
I WILL AVENGE YOUR DEATH! THIS I DO SOLEMNLY SWEAR!
OKAY BOYS, MAKE SURE YOU GRAB EVERYTHING THAT WE'RE GONNA NEED!
YES, MISTRESS OKAMI!
I DON'T KNOW WHO WE'RE LOOKING FOR YET, BUT WHEN WE FIND 'EM, WE'RE GONNA GIVE 'EM A GOOD FIGHT!

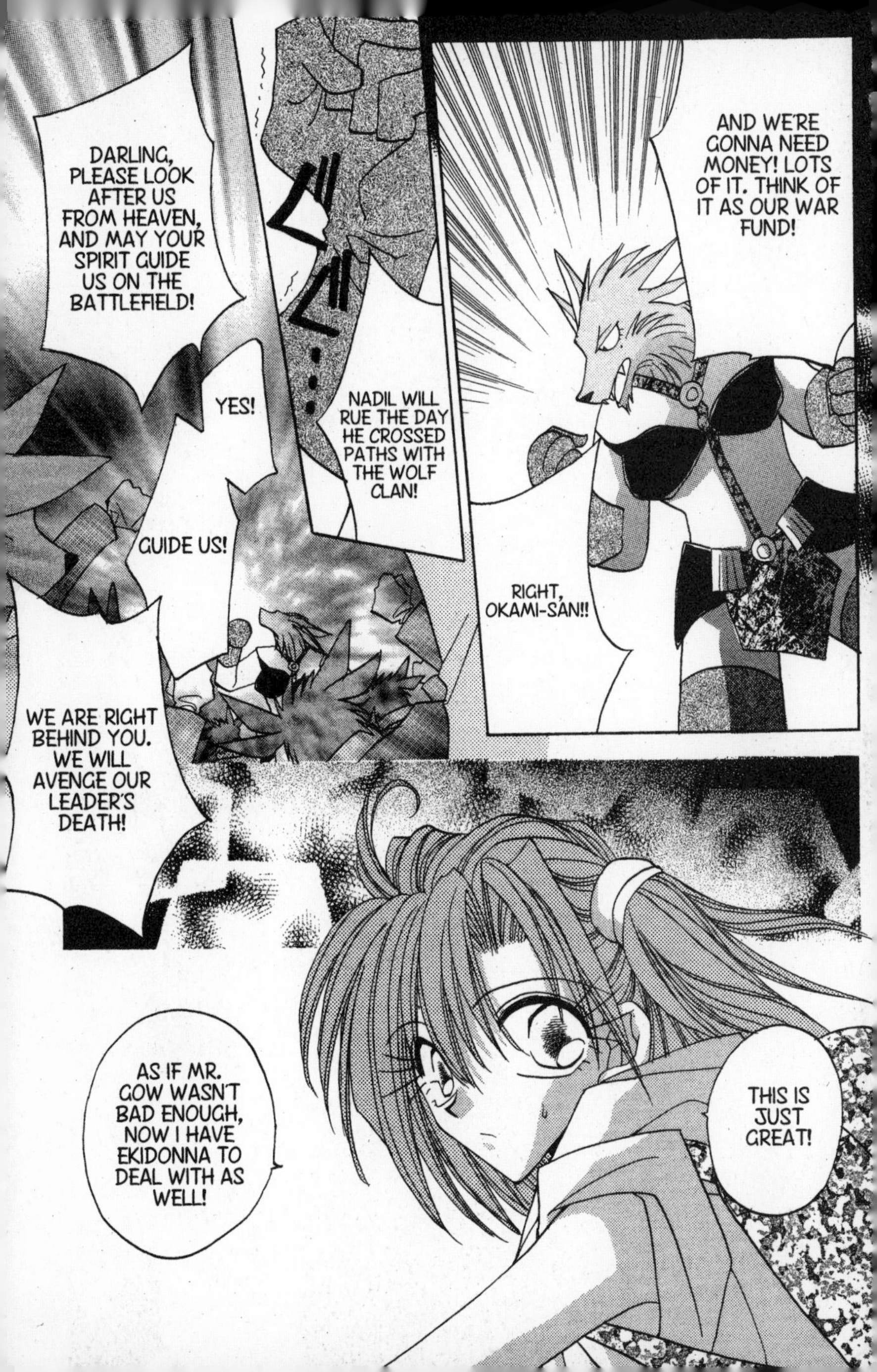
AND WE'RE GONNA NEED MONEY! LOTS OF IT. THINK OF IT AS OUR WAR FUND!
RIGHT, OKAMI-SAN!!
NADIL WILL RUE THE DAY HE CROSSED PATHS WITH THE WOLF CLAN!
DARLING, PLEASE LOOK AFTER US FROM HEAVEN, AND MAY YOUR SPIRIT GUIDE US ON THE BATTLEFIELD!
YES!
GUIDE US!
WE ARE RIGHT BEHIND YOU. WE WILL AVENGE OUR LEADER'S DEATH!
THIS IS JUST GREAT!
AS IF MR. GOW WASN'T BAD ENOUGH, NOW I HAVE EKIDONNA TO DEAL WITH AS WELL!

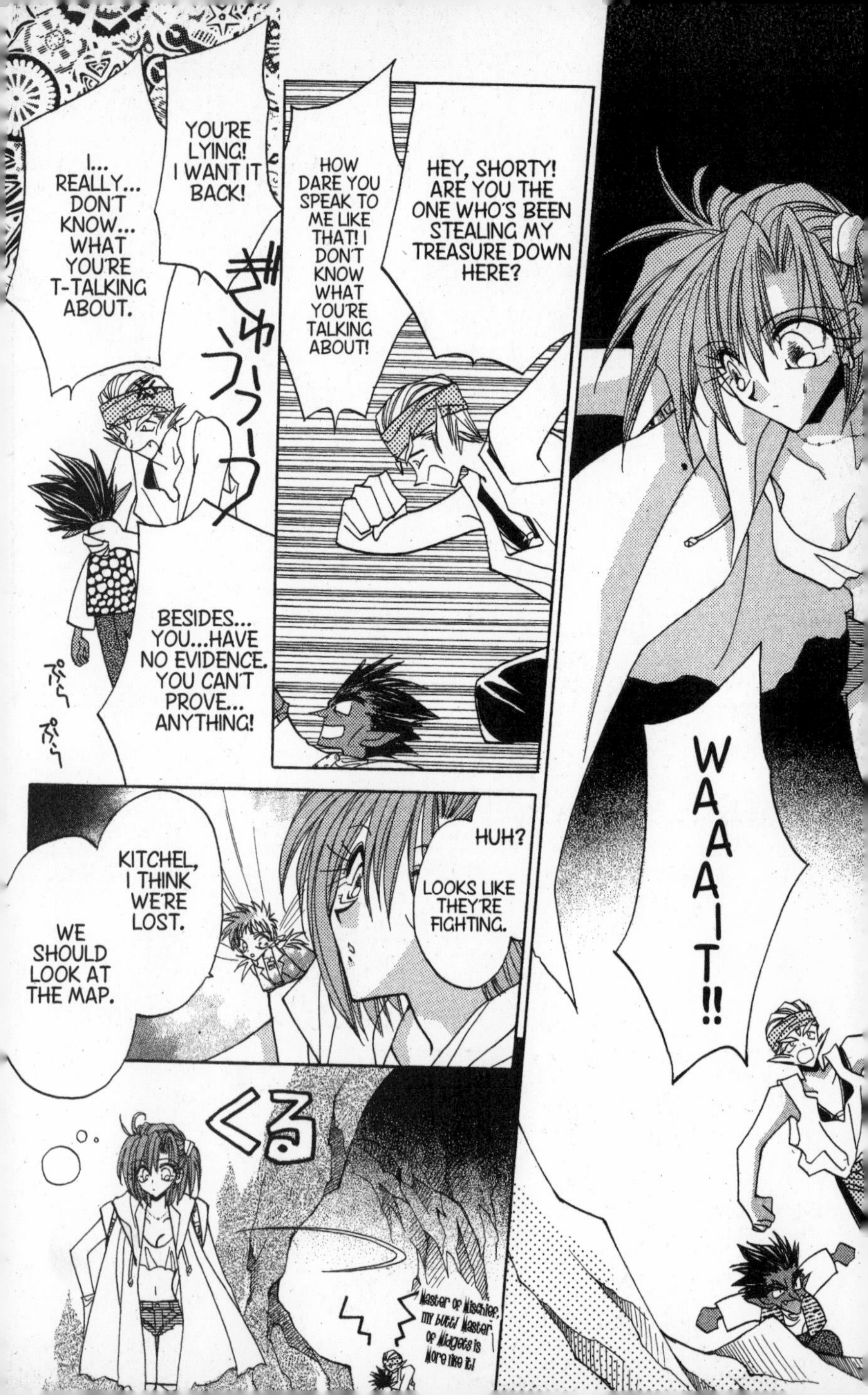
WAAAIT!!
HEY, SHORTY! ARE YOU THE ONE WHO'S BEEN STEALING MY TREASURE DOWN HERE?
HOW DARE YOU SPEAK TO ME LIKE THAT! I DON'T KNOW WHAT YOU'RE TALKING ABOUT!
YOU'RE LYING! I WANT IT BACK!
I... REALLY... DON'T KNOW... WHAT YOU'RE T-TALKING ABOUT.
ぎゅううーっ
BESIDES... YOU...HAVE NO EVIDENCE. YOU CAN'T PROVE... ANYTHING!
ぷら ぷら
HUH?
LOOKS LIKE THEY'RE FIGHTING.
KITCHEL, I THINK WE'RE LOST.
WE SHOULD LOOK AT THE MAP.
くる
Master of Mischief, my butt! Master of Midgets is more like it!

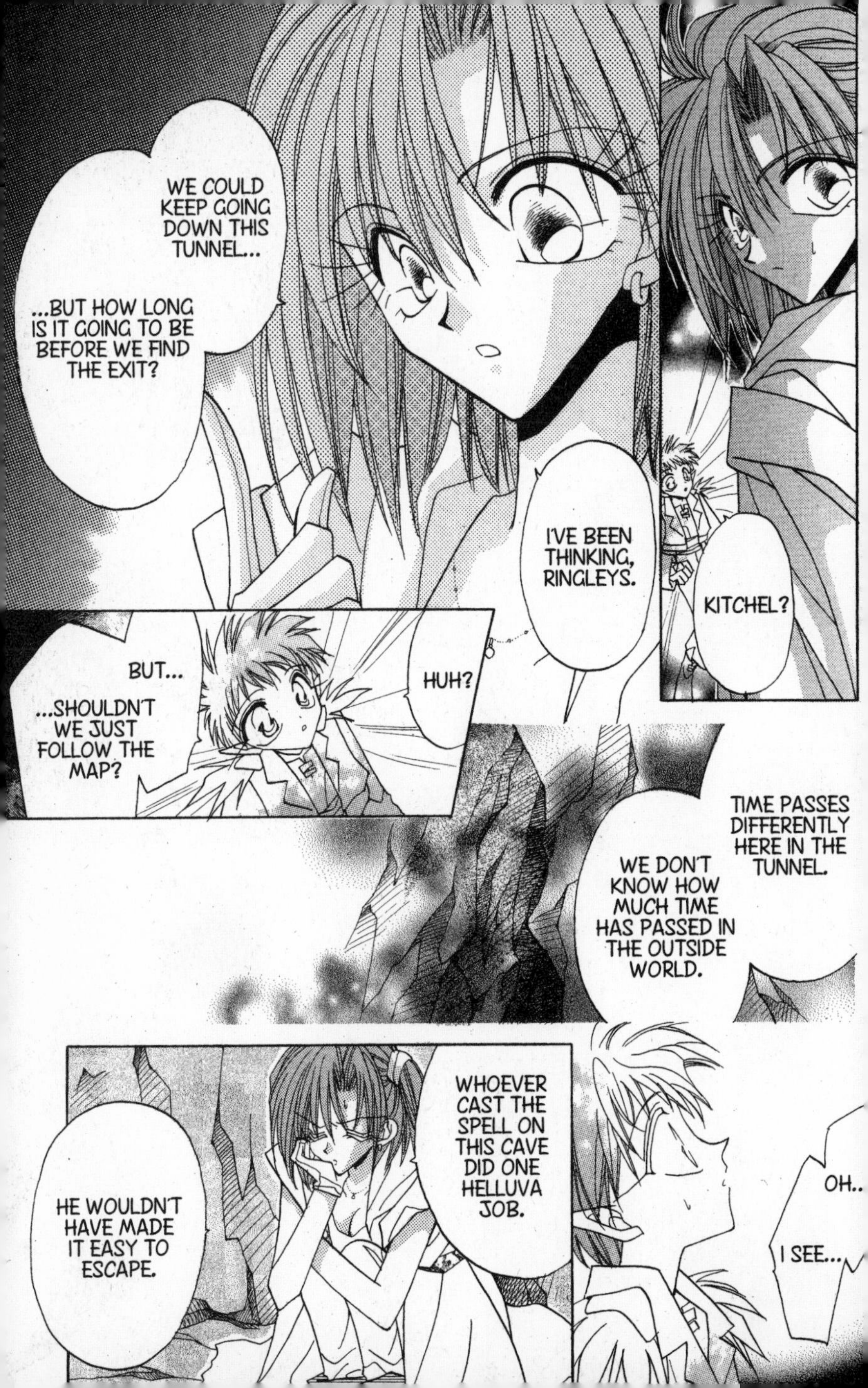
KITCHEL?
I'VE BEEN THINKING, RINGLEYS.
HUH?
WE COULD KEEP GOING DOWN THIS TUNNEL...
...BUT HOW LONG IS IT GOING TO BE BEFORE WE FIND THE EXIT?
BUT...
...SHOULDN'T WE JUST FOLLOW THE MAP?
TIME PASSES DIFFERENTLY HERE IN THE TUNNEL.
WE DON'T KNOW HOW MUCH TIME HAS PASSED IN THE OUTSIDE WORLD.
OH..
I SEE...
WHOEVER CAST THE SPELL ON THIS CAVE DID ONE HELLUVA JOB.
HE WOULDN'T HAVE MADE IT EASY TO ESCAPE.

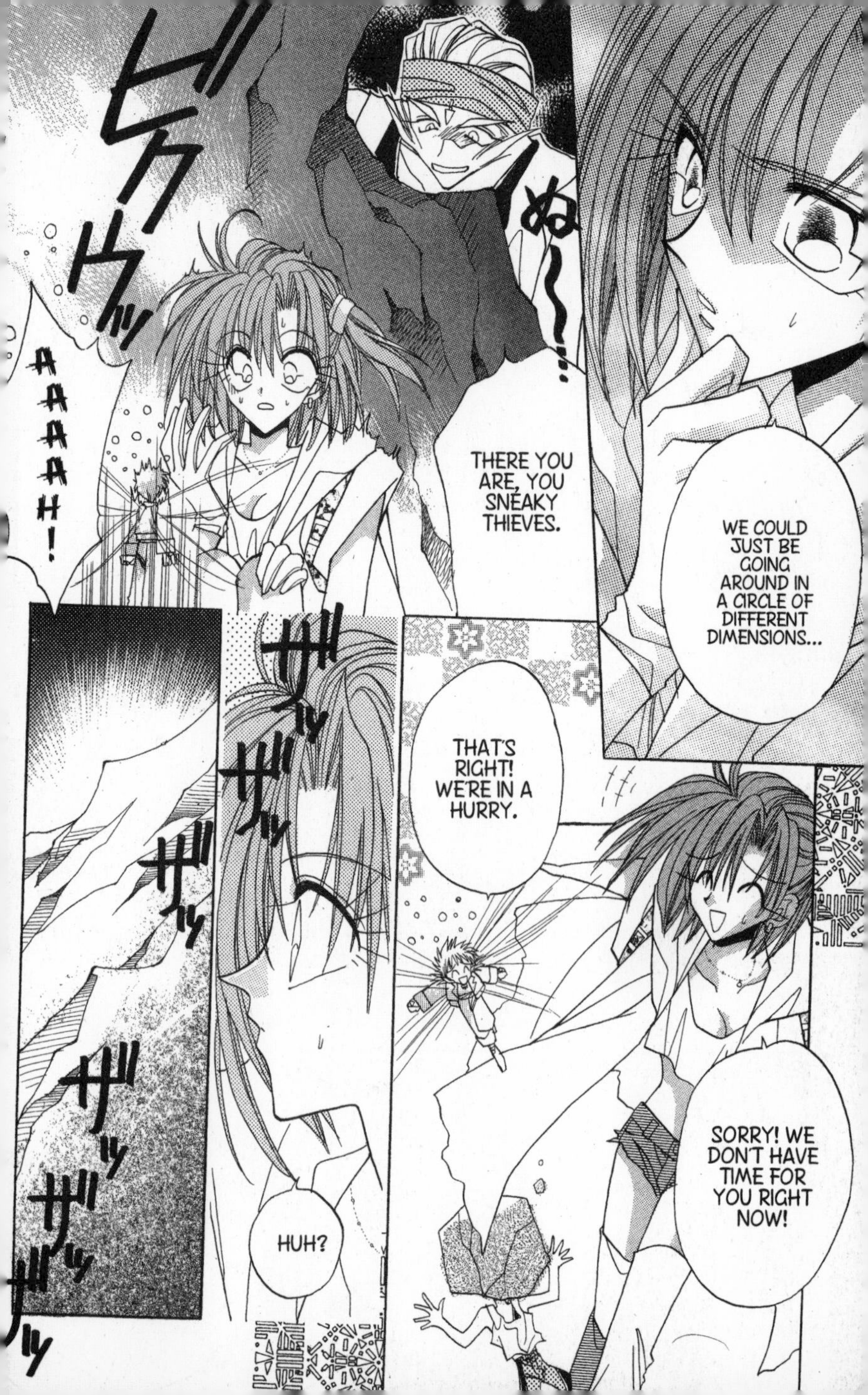

WE COULD JUST BE GOING AROUND IN A CIRCLE OF DIFFERENT DIMENSIONS...
ぬ～～…
THERE YOU ARE, YOU SNEAKY THIEVES.
ビクゥッ
AAAAAH!
THAT'S RIGHT! WE'RE IN A HURRY.
SORRY! WE DON'T HAVE TIME FOR YOU RIGHT NOW!
ザッ ザッ
HUH?
ザッ ザッ ザッ ザッ ザッ

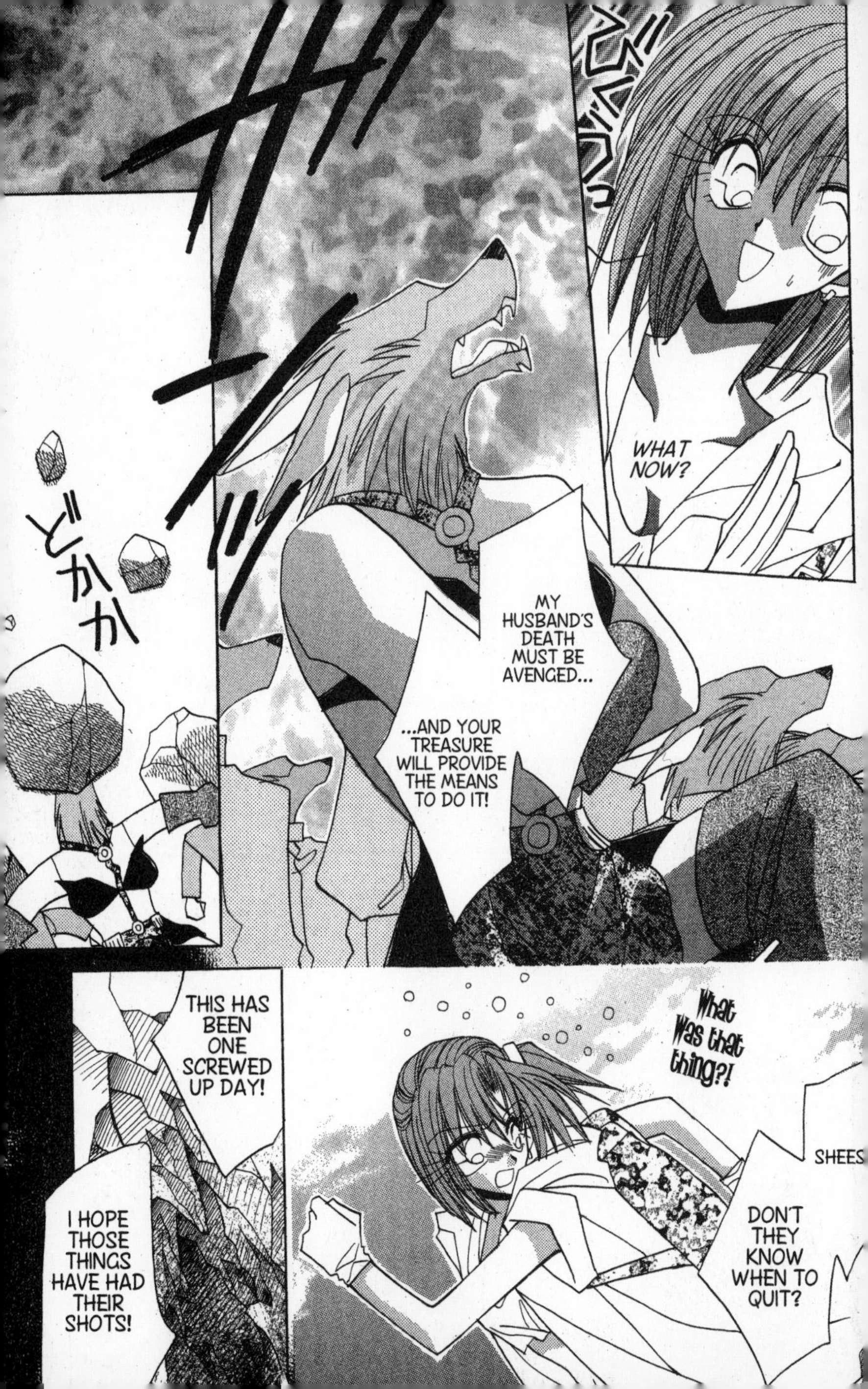
WHAT NOW?
MY HUSBAND'S DEATH MUST BE AVENGED...
...AND YOUR TREASURE WILL PROVIDE THE MEANS TO DO IT!
どかか
What was that thing?!
SHEES
DON'T THEY KNOW WHEN TO QUIT?
THIS HAS BEEN ONE SCREWED UP DAY!
I HOPE THOSE THINGS HAVE HAD THEIR SHOTS!

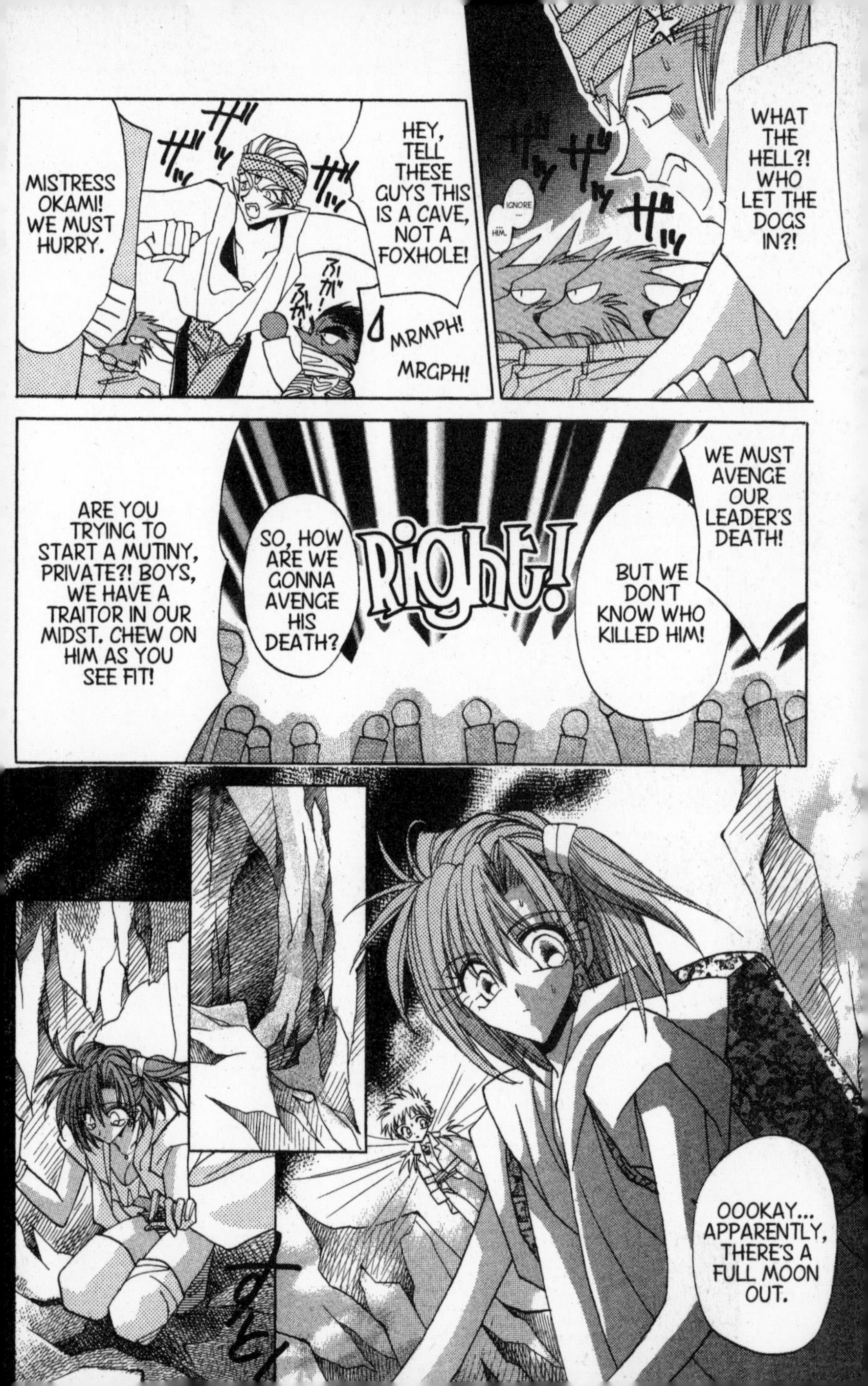
WHAT THE HELL?! WHO LET THE DOGS IN?!
IGNORE ... HIM.
HEY, TELL THESE GUYS THIS IS A CAVE, NOT A FOXHOLE!
MISTRESS OKAMI! WE MUST HURRY.
MRMPH!
MRGPH!
WE MUST AVENGE OUR LEADER'S DEATH!
BUT WE DON'T KNOW WHO KILLED HIM!
Right!
SO, HOW ARE WE GONNA AVENGE HIS DEATH?
ARE YOU TRYING TO START A MUTINY, PRIVATE?! BOYS, WE HAVE A TRAITOR IN OUR MIDST. CHEW ON HIM AS YOU SEE FIT!
OOOKAY... APPARENTLY, THERE'S A FULL MOON OUT.

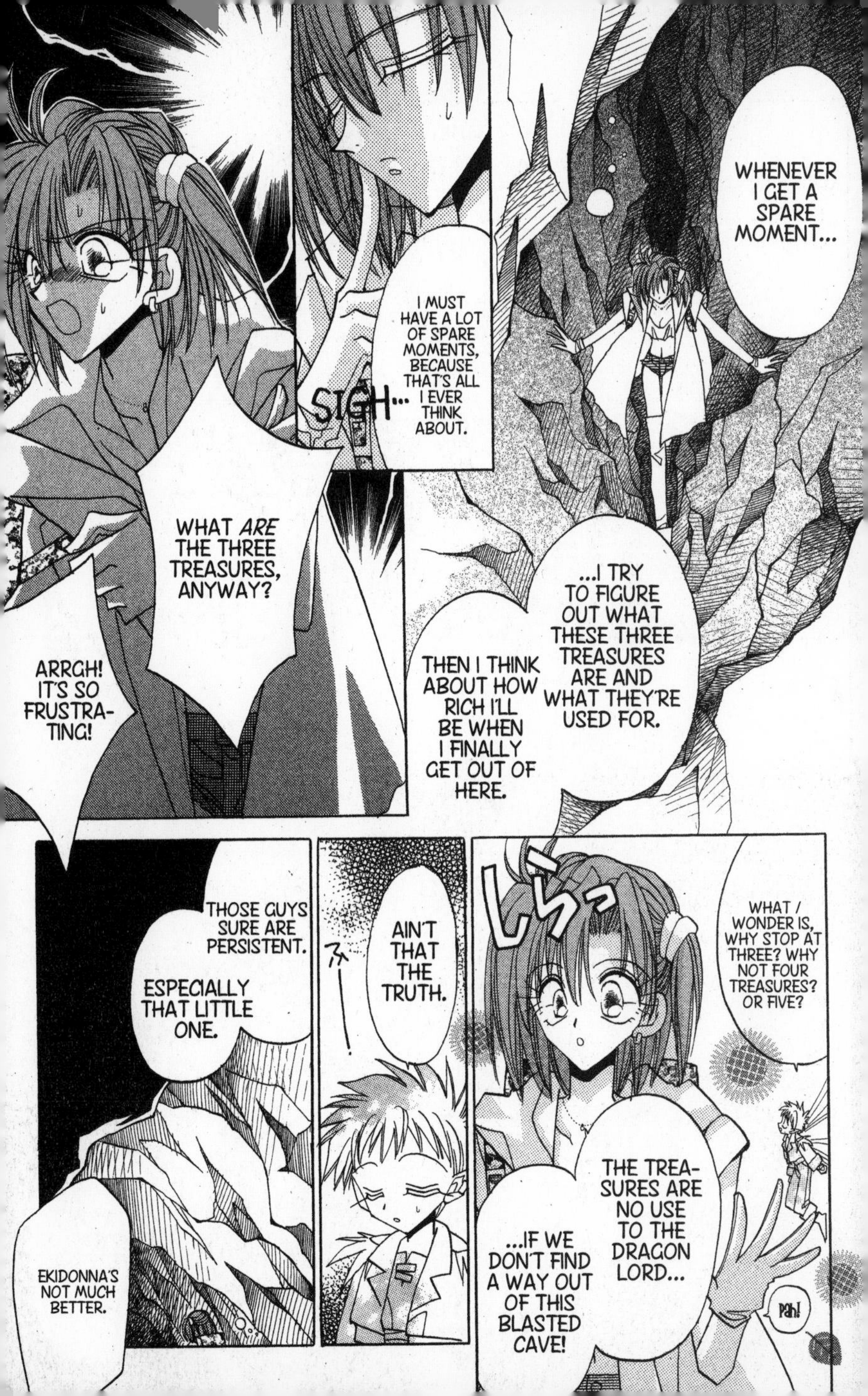
WHENEVER I GET A SPARE MOMENT...
...I TRY TO FIGURE OUT WHAT THESE THREE TREASURES ARE AND WHAT THEY'RE USED FOR.
THEN I THINK ABOUT HOW RICH I'LL BE WHEN I FINALLY GET OUT OF HERE.
SIGH...
I MUST HAVE A LOT OF SPARE MOMENTS, BECAUSE THAT'S ALL I EVER THINK ABOUT.
WHAT *ARE* THE THREE TREASURES, ANYWAY?
ARRGH! IT'S SO FRUSTRA-TING!
しらっ
WHAT *I* WONDER IS, WHY STOP AT THREE? WHY NOT FOUR TREASURES? OR FIVE?
THE TREA-SURES ARE NO USE TO THE DRAGON LORD...
...IF WE DON'T FIND A WAY OUT OF THIS BLASTED CAVE!
Pah!
AIN'T THAT THE TRUTH.
THOSE GUYS SURE ARE PERSISTENT.
ESPECIALLY THAT LITTLE ONE.
EKIDONNA'S NOT MUCH BETTER.

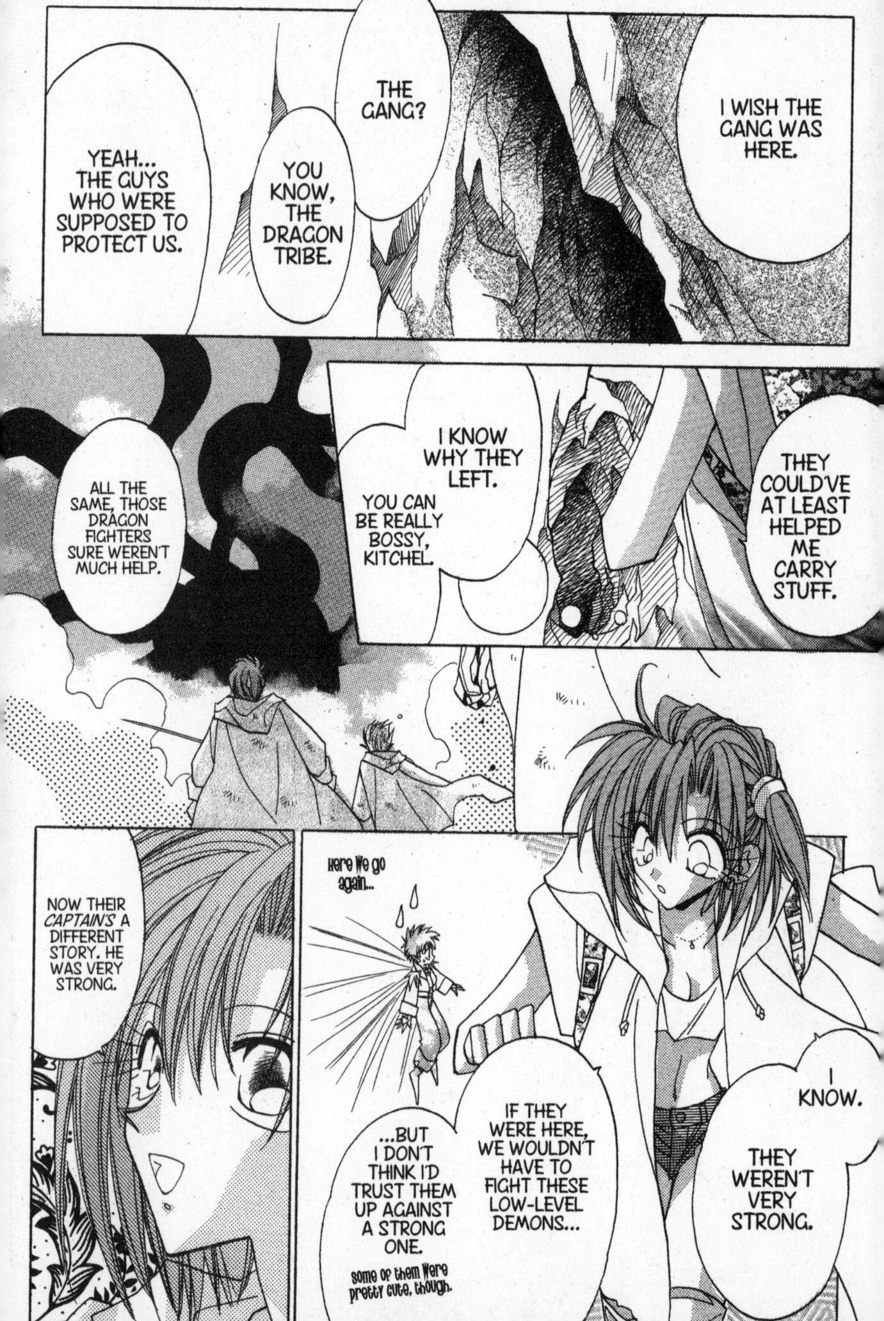
I WISH THE GANG WAS HERE.
THE GANG?
YOU KNOW, THE DRAGON TRIBE.
YEAH... THE GUYS WHO WERE SUPPOSED TO PROTECT US.
THEY COULD'VE AT LEAST HELPED ME CARRY STUFF.
I KNOW WHY THEY LEFT.
YOU CAN BE REALLY BOSSY, KITCHEL.
ALL THE SAME, THOSE DRAGON FIGHTERS SURE WEREN'T MUCH HELP.
I KNOW.
THEY WEREN'T VERY STRONG.
IF THEY WERE HERE, WE WOULDN'T HAVE TO FIGHT THESE LOW-LEVEL DEMONS...
...BUT I DON'T THINK I'D TRUST THEM UP AGAINST A STRONG ONE.
Some of them were pretty cute, though.
Here we go again...
NOW THEIR *CAPTAIN'S* A DIFFERENT STORY. HE WAS VERY STRONG.

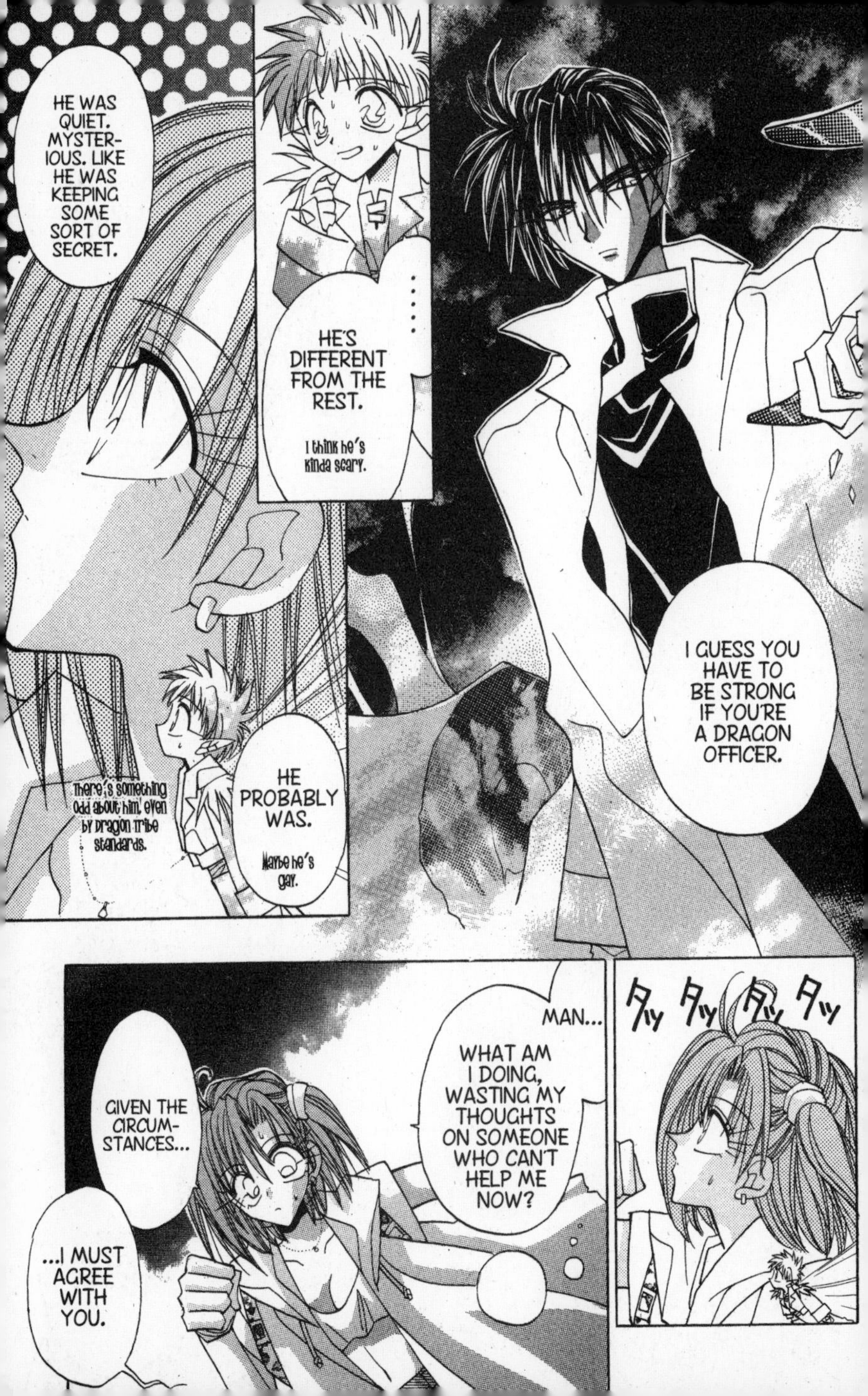
I GUESS YOU HAVE TO BE STRONG IF YOU'RE A DRAGON OFFICER.
......
HE'S DIFFERENT FROM THE REST.
I think he's kinda scary.
HE WAS QUIET. MYSTERIOUS. LIKE HE WAS KEEPING SOME SORT OF SECRET.
HE PROBABLY WAS.
Maybe he's gay.
There's something odd about him, even by Dragon Tribe standards.
タッ タッ タッ タッ
MAN...
WHAT AM I DOING, WASTING MY THOUGHTS ON SOMEONE WHO CAN'T HELP ME NOW?
GIVEN THE CIRCUMSTANCES...
...I MUST AGREE WITH YOU.

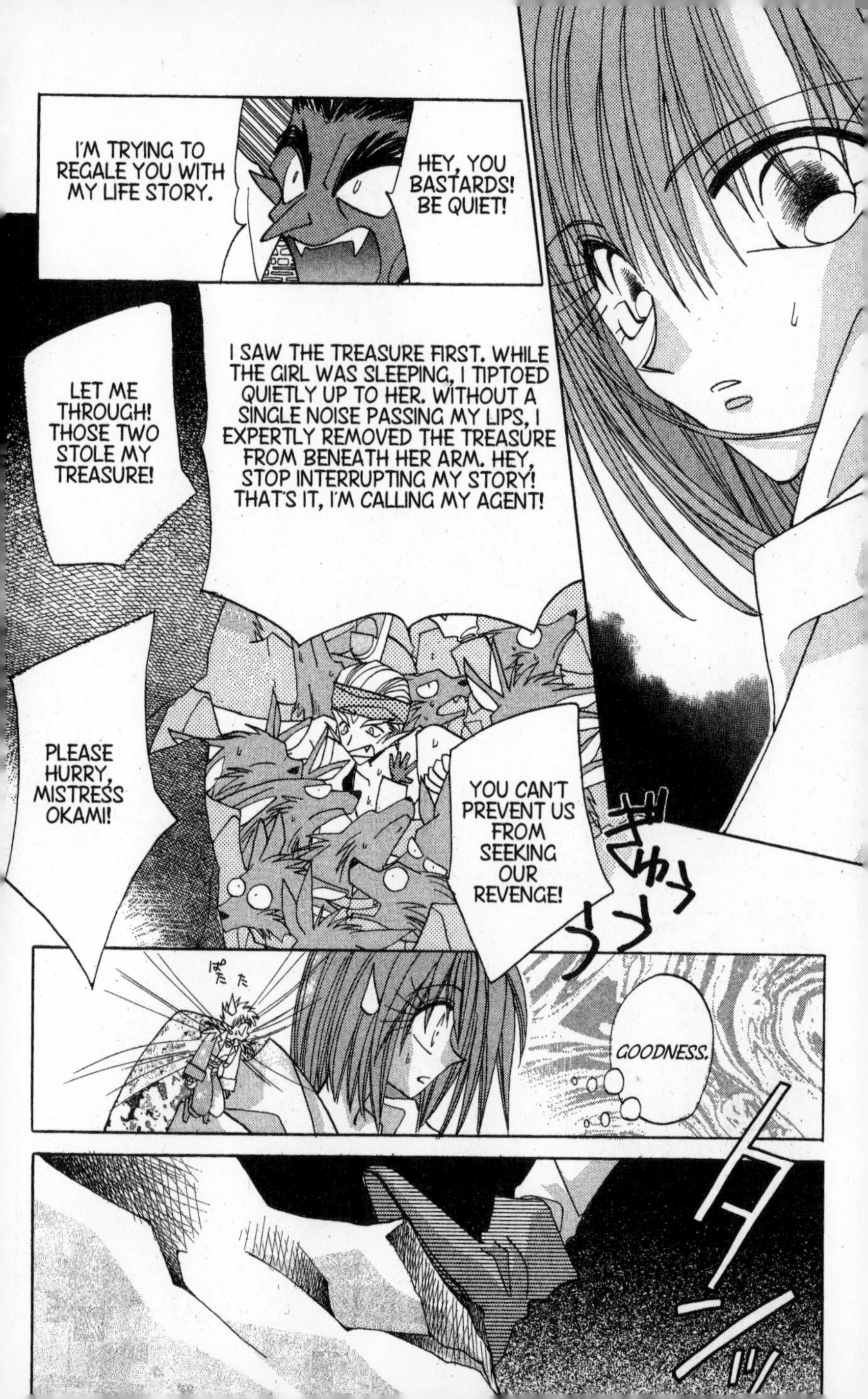
HEY, YOU BASTARDS! BE QUIET!
I'M TRYING TO REGALE YOU WITH MY LIFE STORY.
I SAW THE TREASURE FIRST. WHILE THE GIRL WAS SLEEPING, I TIPTOED QUIETLY UP TO HER. WITHOUT A SINGLE NOISE PASSING MY LIPS, I EXPERTLY REMOVED THE TREASURE FROM BENEATH HER ARM. HEY, STOP INTERRUPTING MY STORY! THAT'S IT, I'M CALLING MY AGENT!
LET ME THROUGH! THOSE TWO STOLE MY TREASURE!
YOU CAN'T PREVENT US FROM SEEKING OUR REVENGE!
PLEASE HURRY, MISTRESS OKAMI!
GOODNESS.
ぱたた

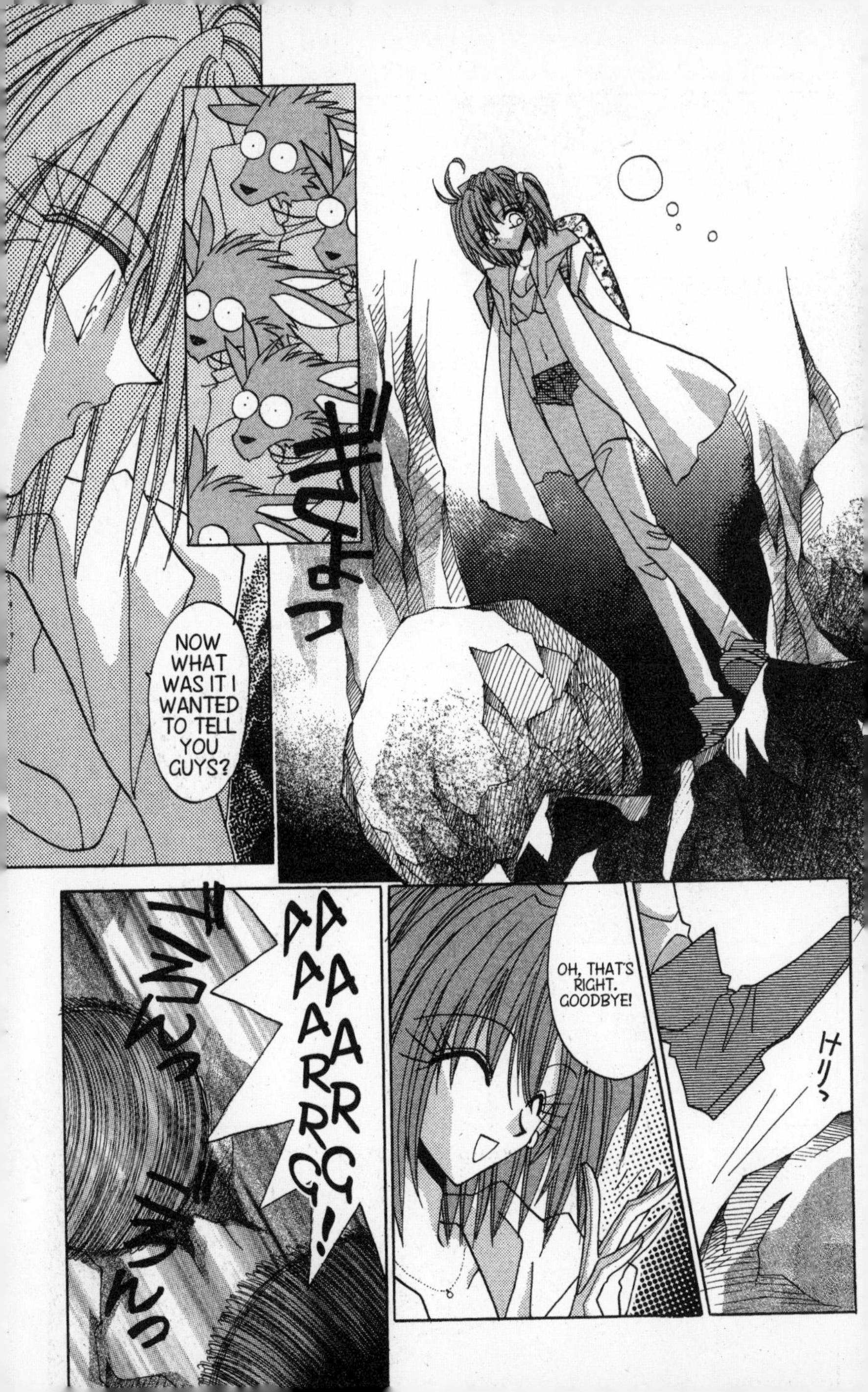
NOW WHAT WAS IT I WANTED TO TELL YOU GUYS?
ぎょっ
けりっ
OH, THAT'S RIGHT. GOODBYE!
AAAARRRG!!

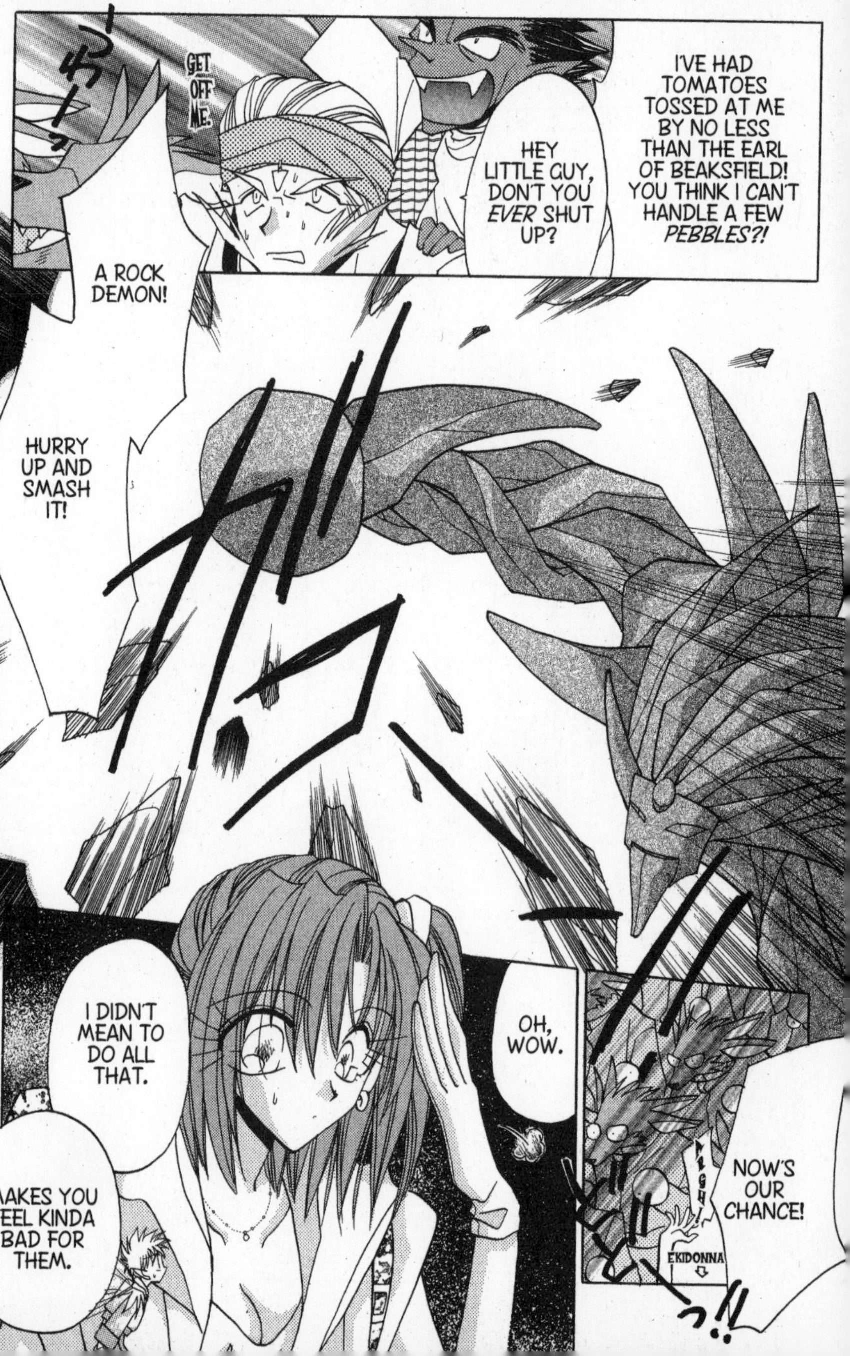
I'VE HAD TOMATOES TOSSED AT ME BY NO LESS THAN THE EARL OF BEAKSFIELD! YOU THINK I CAN'T HANDLE A FEW *PEBBLES?!*
HEY LITTLE GUY, DON'T YOU *EVER* SHUT UP?
GET OFF ME.
A ROCK DEMON!
HURRY UP AND SMASH IT!
NOW'S OUR CHANCE!
EKIDONNA
OH, WOW.
I DIDN'T MEAN TO DO ALL THAT.
MAKES YOU FEEL KINDA BAD FOR THEM.

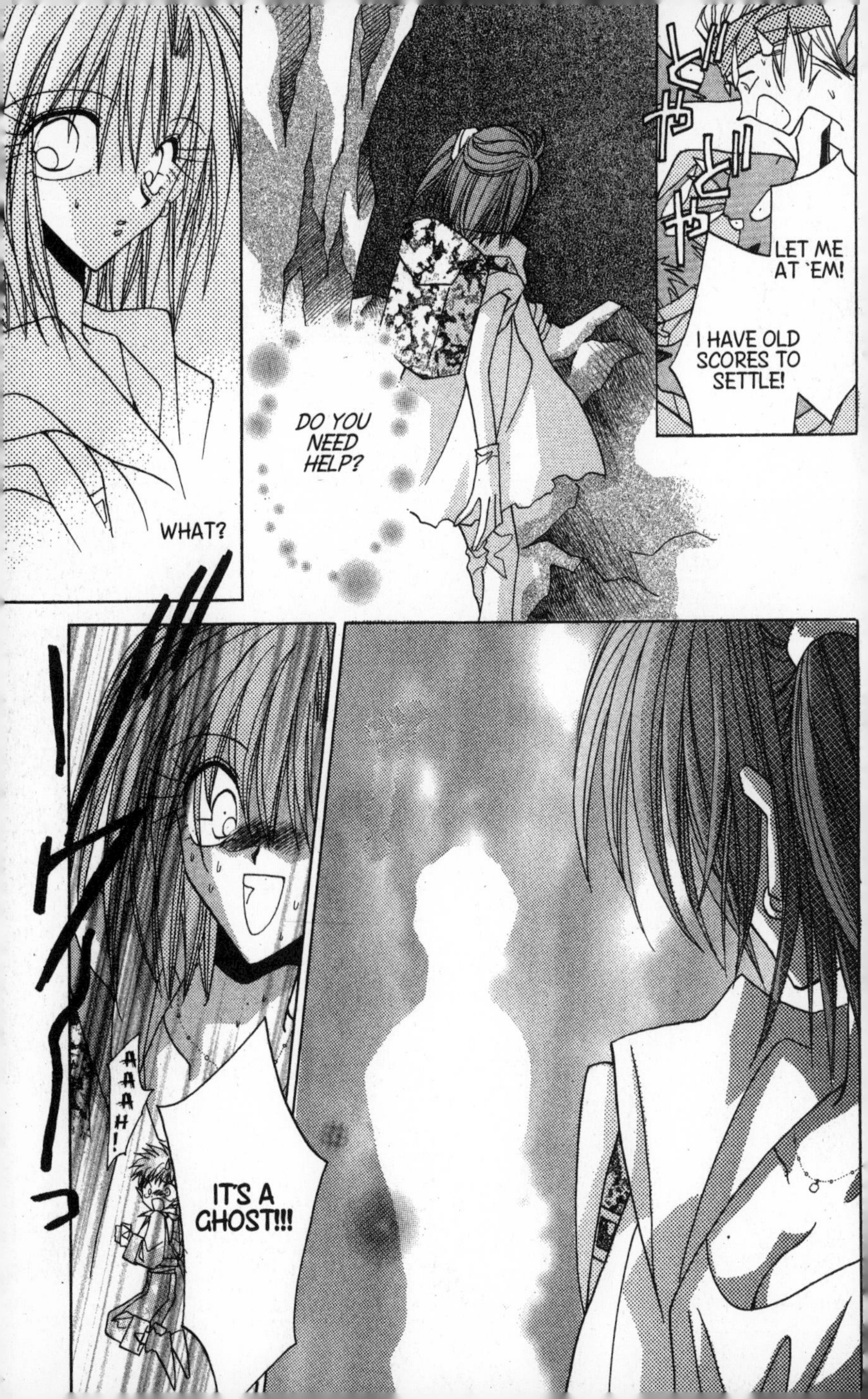
どやどやどや
LET ME AT `EM!
I HAVE OLD SCORES TO SETTLE!
DO YOU NEED HELP?
WHAT?
AAAH!
IT'S A GHOST!!!

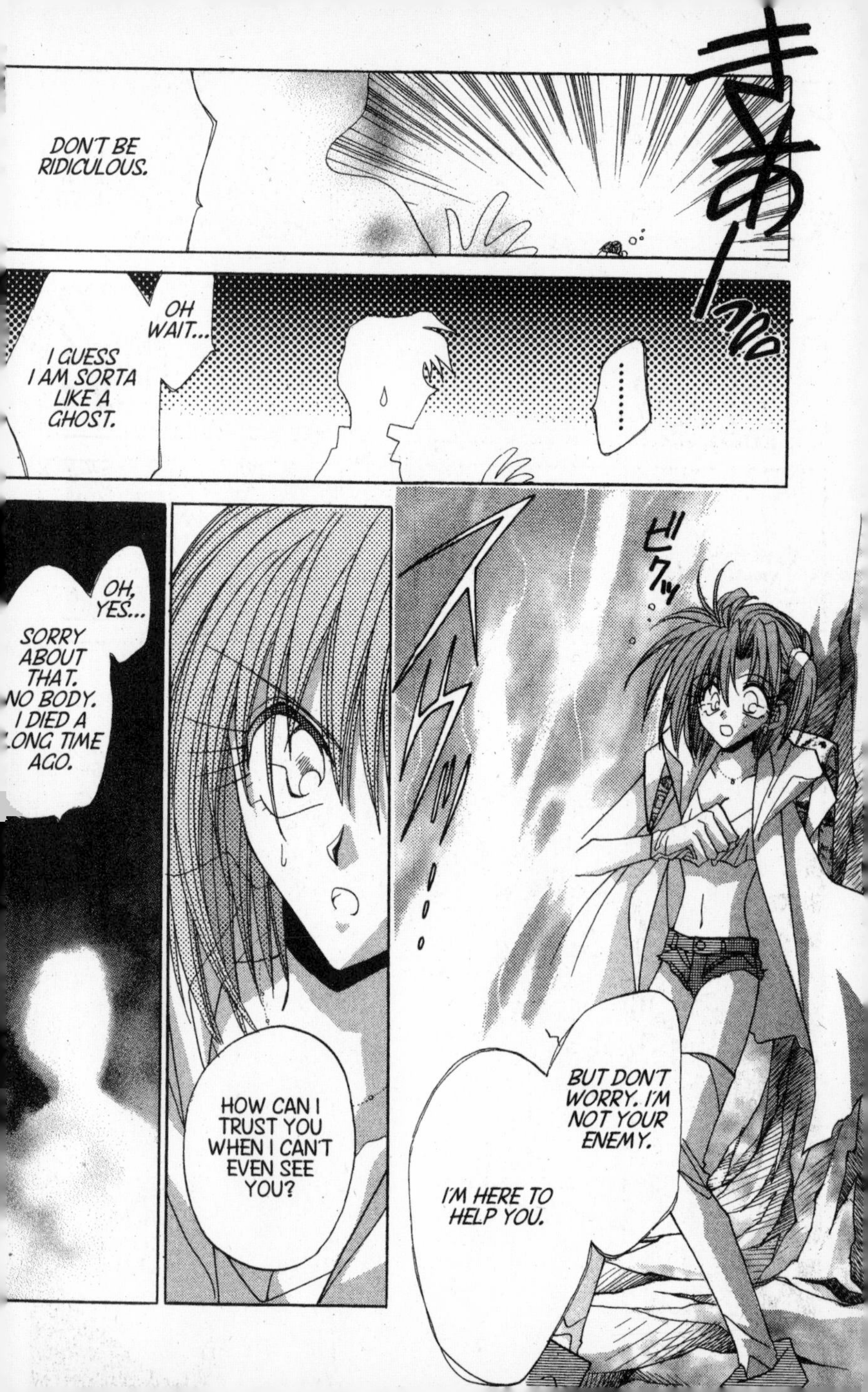

きあー
DON'T BE RIDICULOUS.
……
OH WAIT...
I GUESS I AM SORTA LIKE A GHOST.
ビクッ
BUT DON'T WORRY. I'M NOT YOUR ENEMY.
I'M HERE TO HELP YOU.
HOW CAN I TRUST YOU WHEN I CAN'T EVEN SEE YOU?
OH, YES...
SORRY ABOUT THAT. NO BODY. I DIED A LONG TIME AGO.

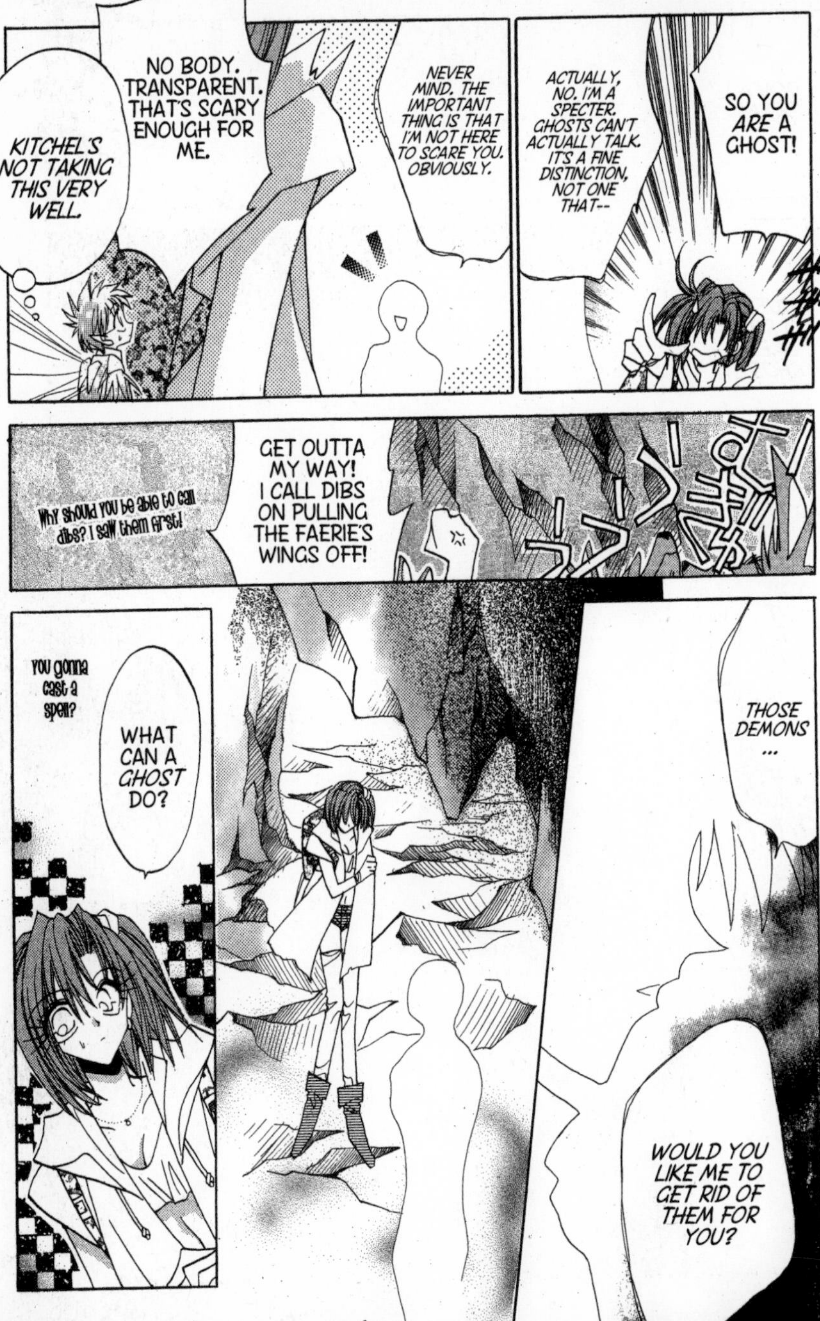
SO YOU ARE A GHOST!
ACTUALLY, NO. I'M A SPECTER. GHOSTS CAN'T ACTUALLY TALK. IT'S A FINE DISTINCTION, NOT ONE THAT--
NEVER MIND. THE IMPORTANT THING IS THAT I'M NOT HERE TO SCARE YOU. OBVIOUSLY.
NO BODY. TRANSPARENT. THAT'S SCARY ENOUGH FOR ME.
KITCHEL'S NOT TAKING THIS VERY WELL.
GET OUTTA MY WAY! I CALL DIBS ON PULLING THE FAERIE'S WINGS OFF!
Why should you be able to call dibs? I saw them first!
THOSE DEMONS ...
WOULD YOU LIKE ME TO GET RID OF THEM FOR YOU?
WHAT CAN A GHOST DO?
You gonna cast a spell?

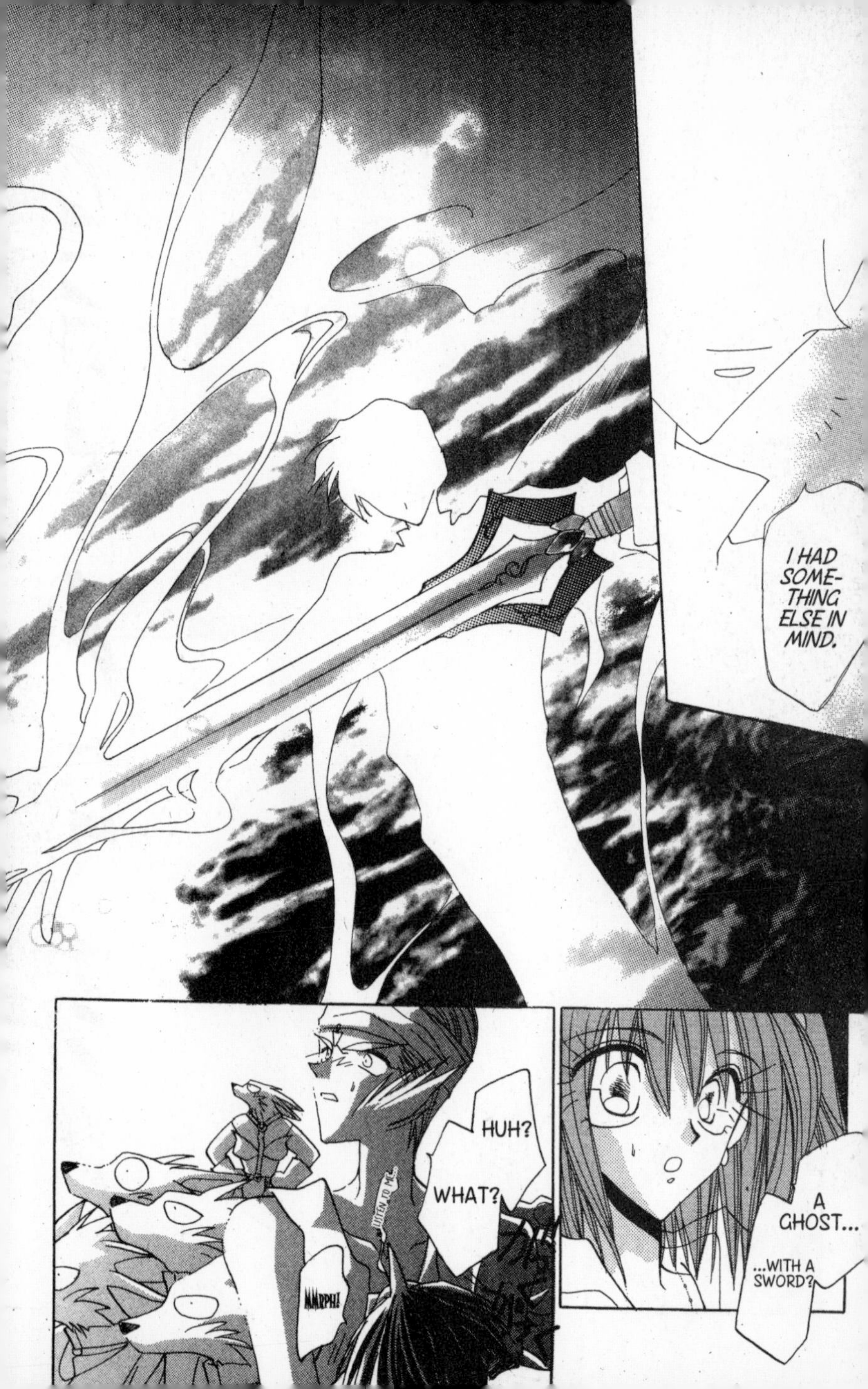
I HAD SOMETHING ELSE IN MIND.
A GHOST...
...WITH A SWORD?
HUH?
WHAT?
LISTEN TO ME...
MMRPH!

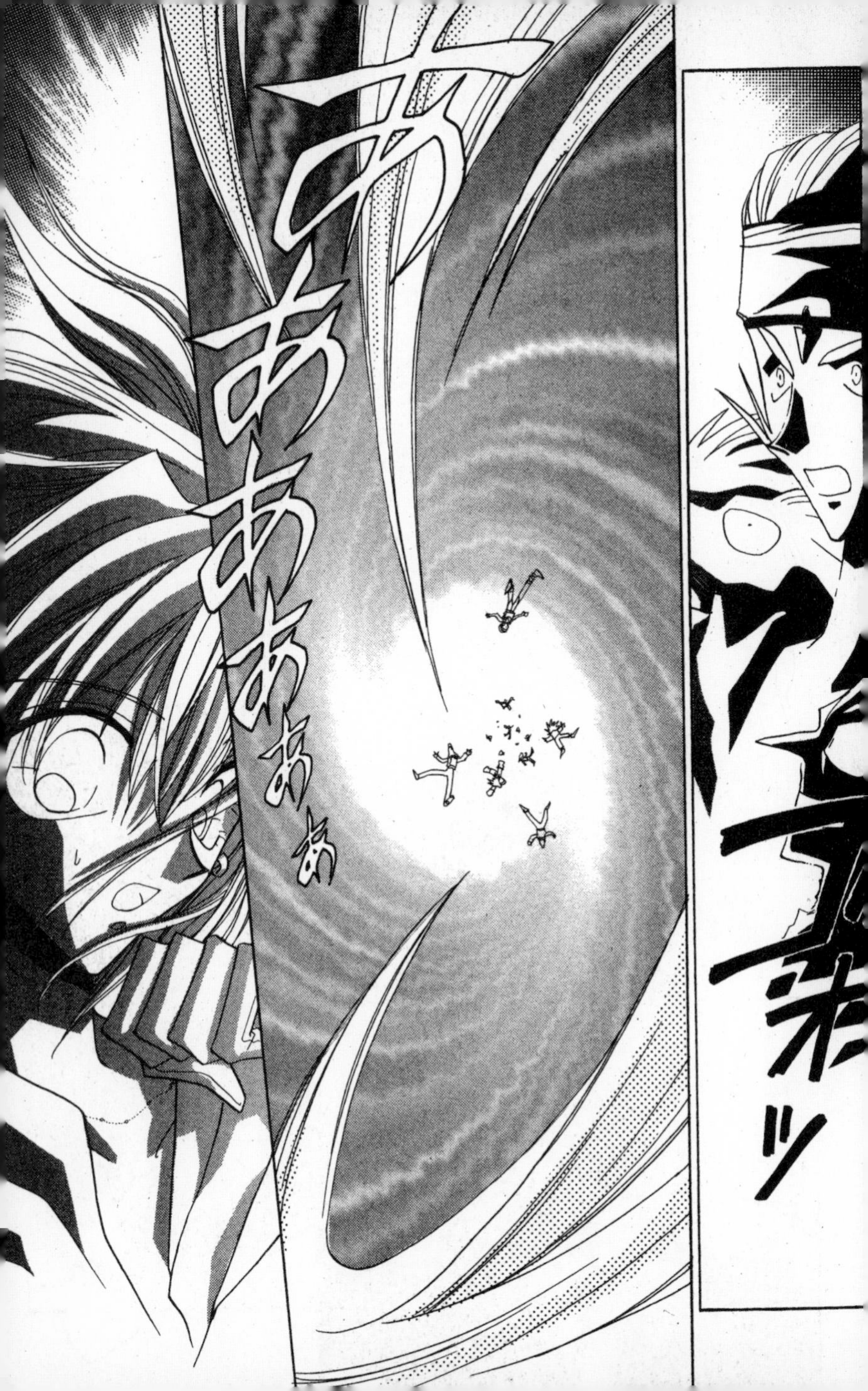
ズボッ
あああああぁ

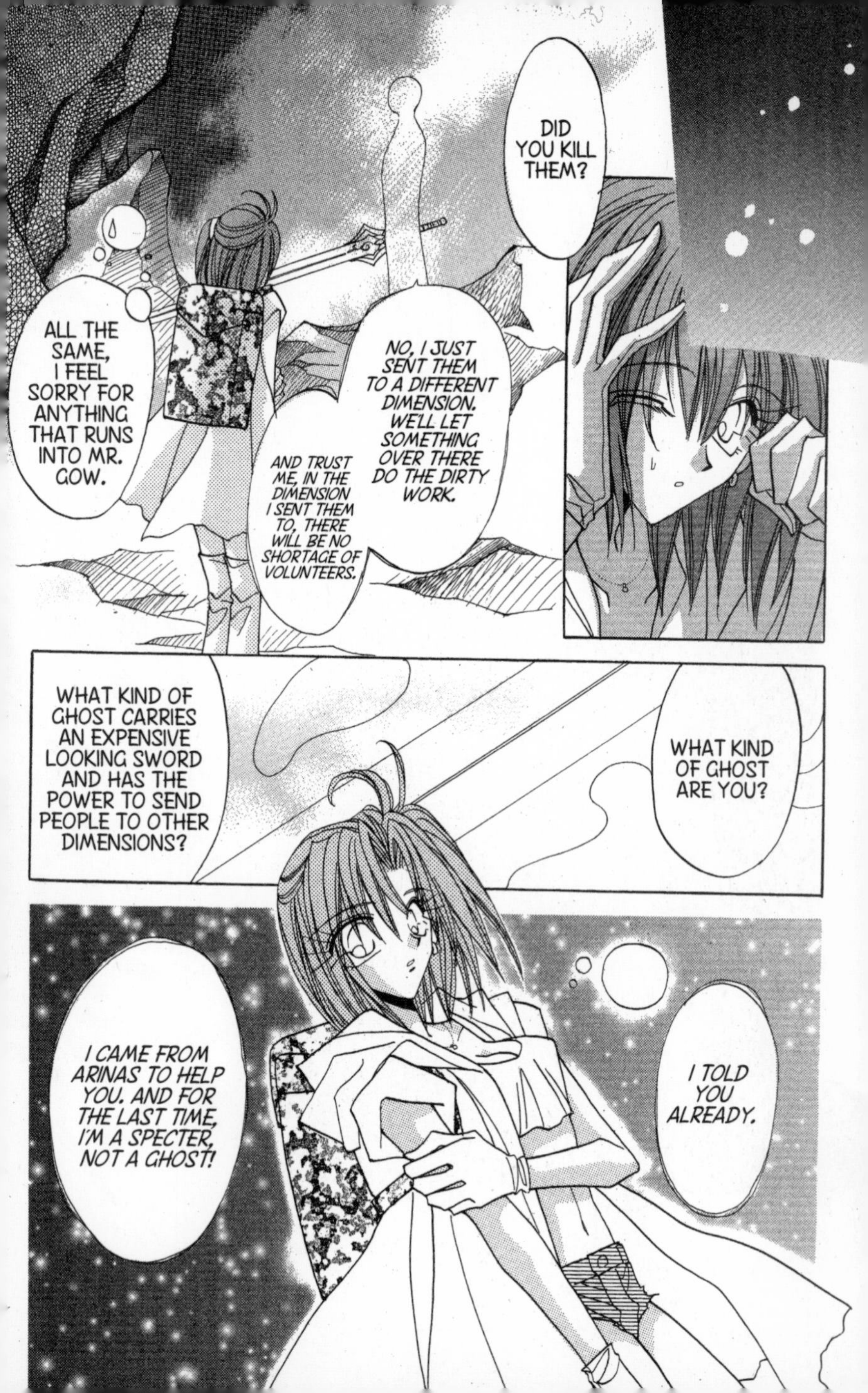
DID YOU KILL THEM?
NO, I JUST SENT THEM TO A DIFFERENT DIMENSION. WE'LL LET SOMETHING OVER THERE DO THE DIRTY WORK.
AND TRUST ME, IN THE DIMENSION I SENT THEM TO, THERE WILL BE NO SHORTAGE OF VOLUNTEERS.
ALL THE SAME, I FEEL SORRY FOR ANYTHING THAT RUNS INTO MR. GOW.
WHAT KIND OF GHOST ARE YOU?
WHAT KIND OF GHOST CARRIES AN EXPENSIVE LOOKING SWORD AND HAS THE POWER TO SEND PEOPLE TO OTHER DIMENSIONS?
I TOLD YOU ALREADY.
I CAME FROM ARINAS TO HELP YOU. AND FOR THE LAST TIME, I'M A SPECTER, NOT A GHOST!

KITCHEL
FREE STYLE

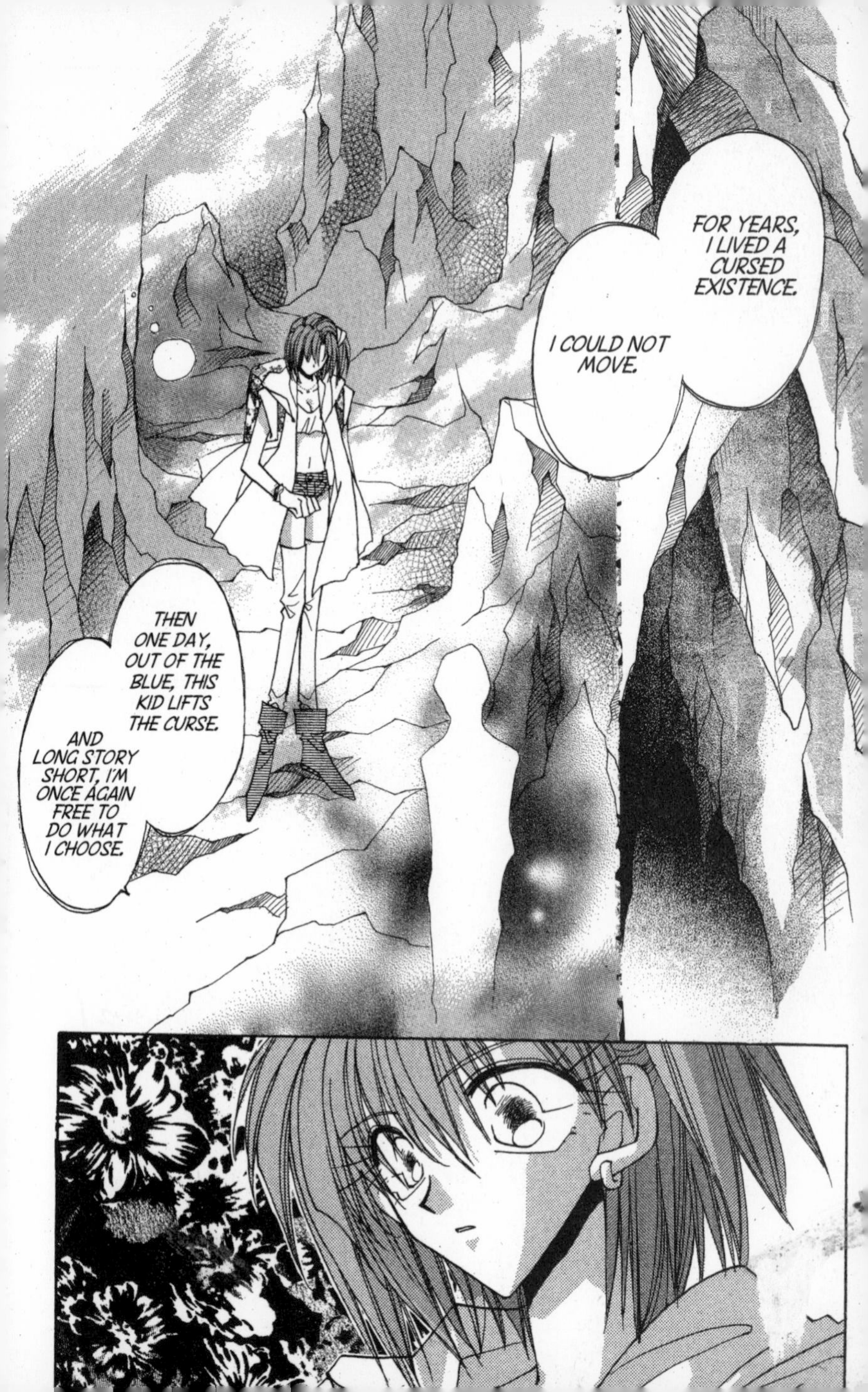
FOR YEARS, I LIVED A CURSED EXISTENCE.
I COULD NOT MOVE.
THEN ONE DAY, OUT OF THE BLUE, THIS KID LIFTS THE CURSE.
AND LONG STORY SHORT, I'M ONCE AGAIN FREE TO DO WHAT I CHOOSE.

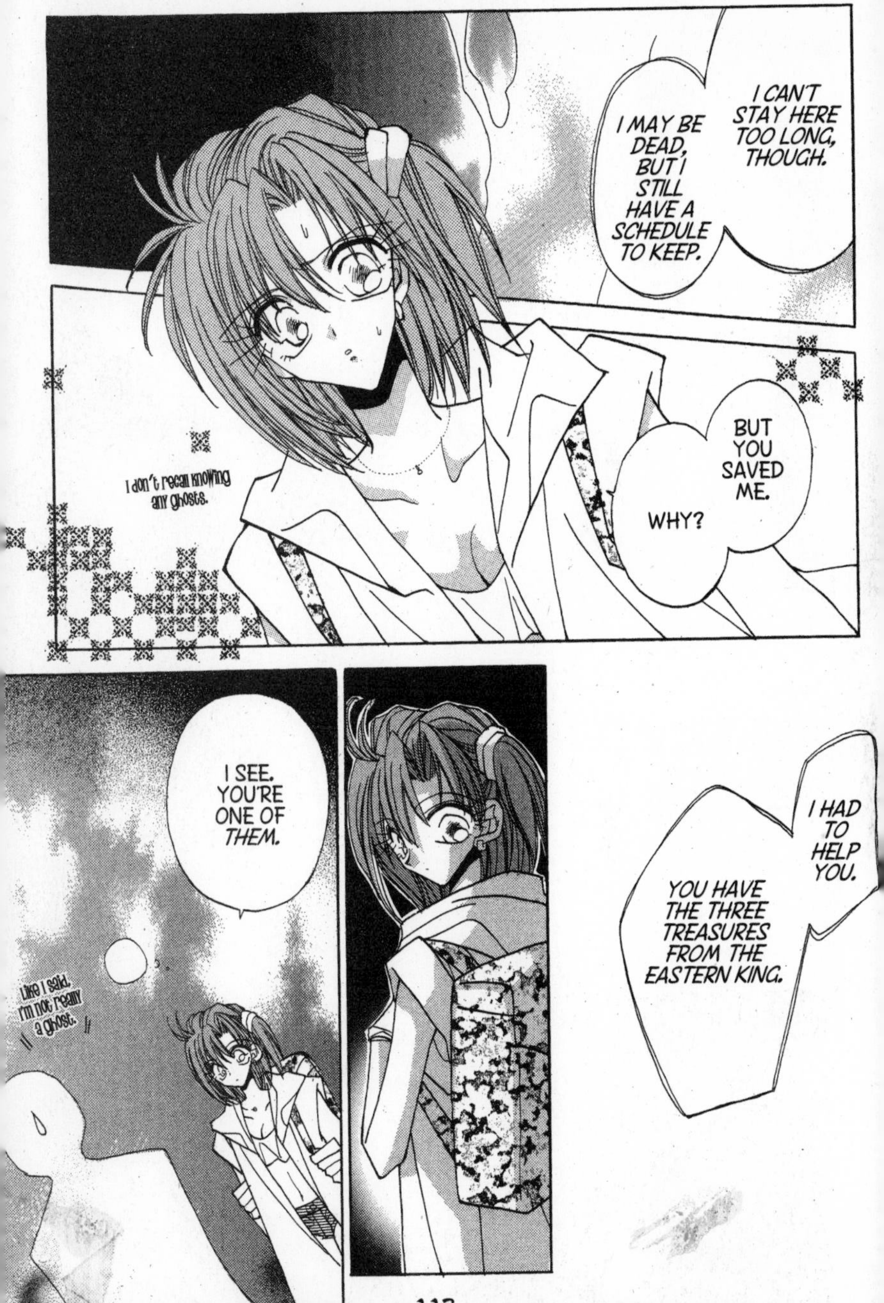
I CAN'T STAY HERE TOO LONG, THOUGH.
I MAY BE DEAD, BUT I STILL HAVE A SCHEDULE TO KEEP.
BUT YOU SAVED ME.
WHY?
I don't recall knowing any ghosts.
I HAD TO HELP YOU.
YOU HAVE THE THREE TREASURES FROM THE EASTERN KING.
I SEE. YOU'RE ONE OF THEM.
Like I said, I'm not really a ghost.

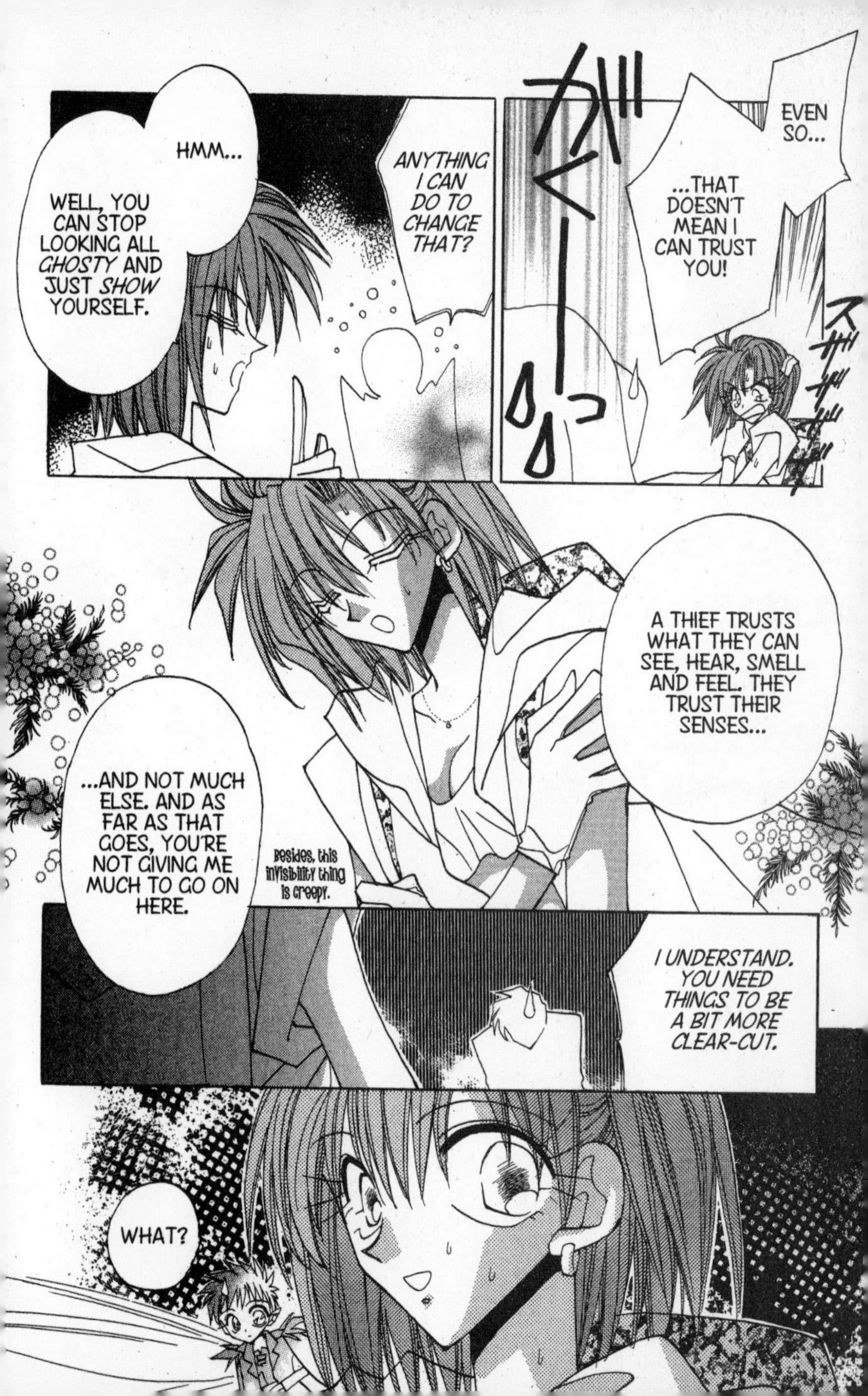
EVEN SO...
...THAT DOESN'T MEAN I CAN TRUST YOU!
ANYTHING I CAN DO TO CHANGE THAT?
HMM...
WELL, YOU CAN STOP LOOKING ALL GHOSTY AND JUST SHOW YOURSELF.
A THIEF TRUSTS WHAT THEY CAN SEE, HEAR, SMELL AND FEEL. THEY TRUST THEIR SENSES...
Besides, this invisibility thing is creepy.
...AND NOT MUCH ELSE. AND AS FAR AS THAT GOES, YOU'RE NOT GIVING ME MUCH TO GO ON HERE.
I UNDERSTAND. YOU NEED THINGS TO BE A BIT MORE CLEAR-CUT.
WHAT?

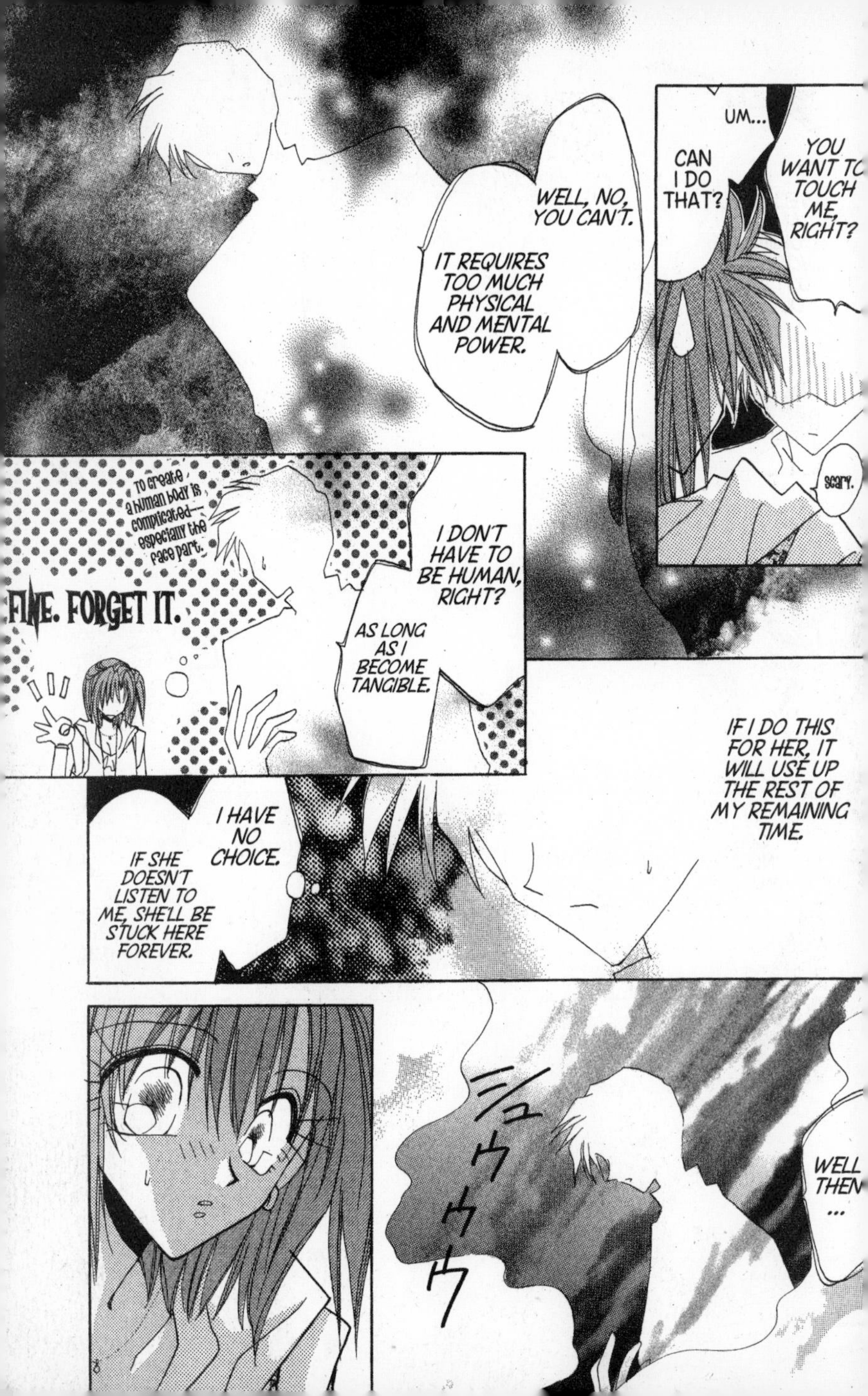
YOU WANT TO TOUCH ME, RIGHT?
UM...
CAN I DO THAT?
scary.
WELL, NO, YOU CAN'T.
IT REQUIRES TOO MUCH PHYSICAL AND MENTAL POWER.
I DON'T HAVE TO BE HUMAN, RIGHT?
AS LONG AS I BECOME TANGIBLE.
To create a human body is complicated—especially the face part.
FINE. FORGET IT.
IF I DO THIS FOR HER, IT WILL USE UP THE REST OF MY REMAINING TIME.
I HAVE NO CHOICE.
IF SHE DOESN'T LISTEN TO ME, SHE'LL BE STUCK HERE FOREVER.
WELL THEN...
シュウウウ

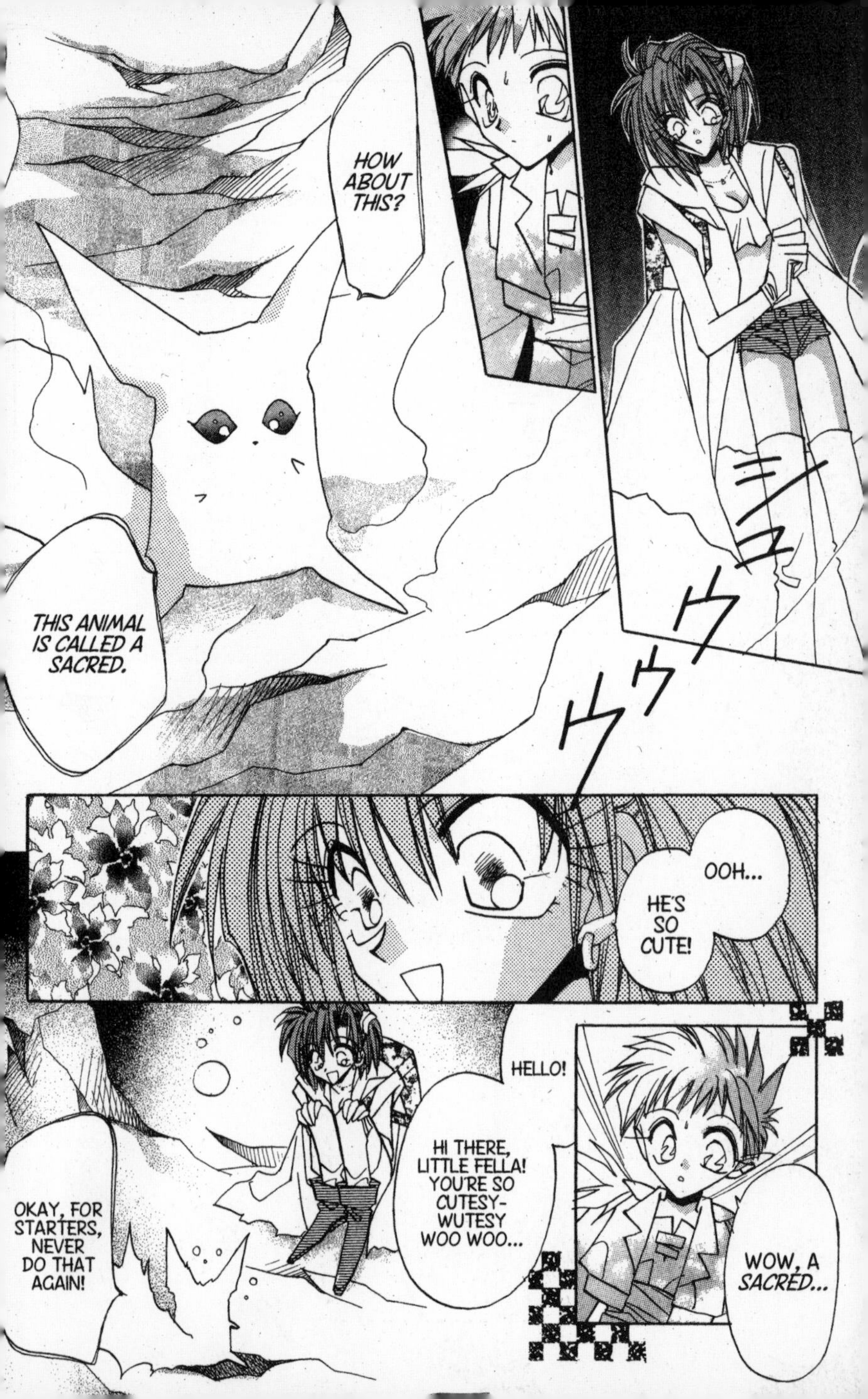
HOW ABOUT THIS?
THIS ANIMAL IS CALLED A SACRED.
ジュウウウ
OOH...
HE'S SO CUTE!
WOW, A SACRED...
HELLO!
HI THERE, LITTLE FELLA! YOU'RE SO CUTESY-WUTESY WOO WOO...
OKAY, FOR STARTERS, NEVER DO THAT AGAIN!

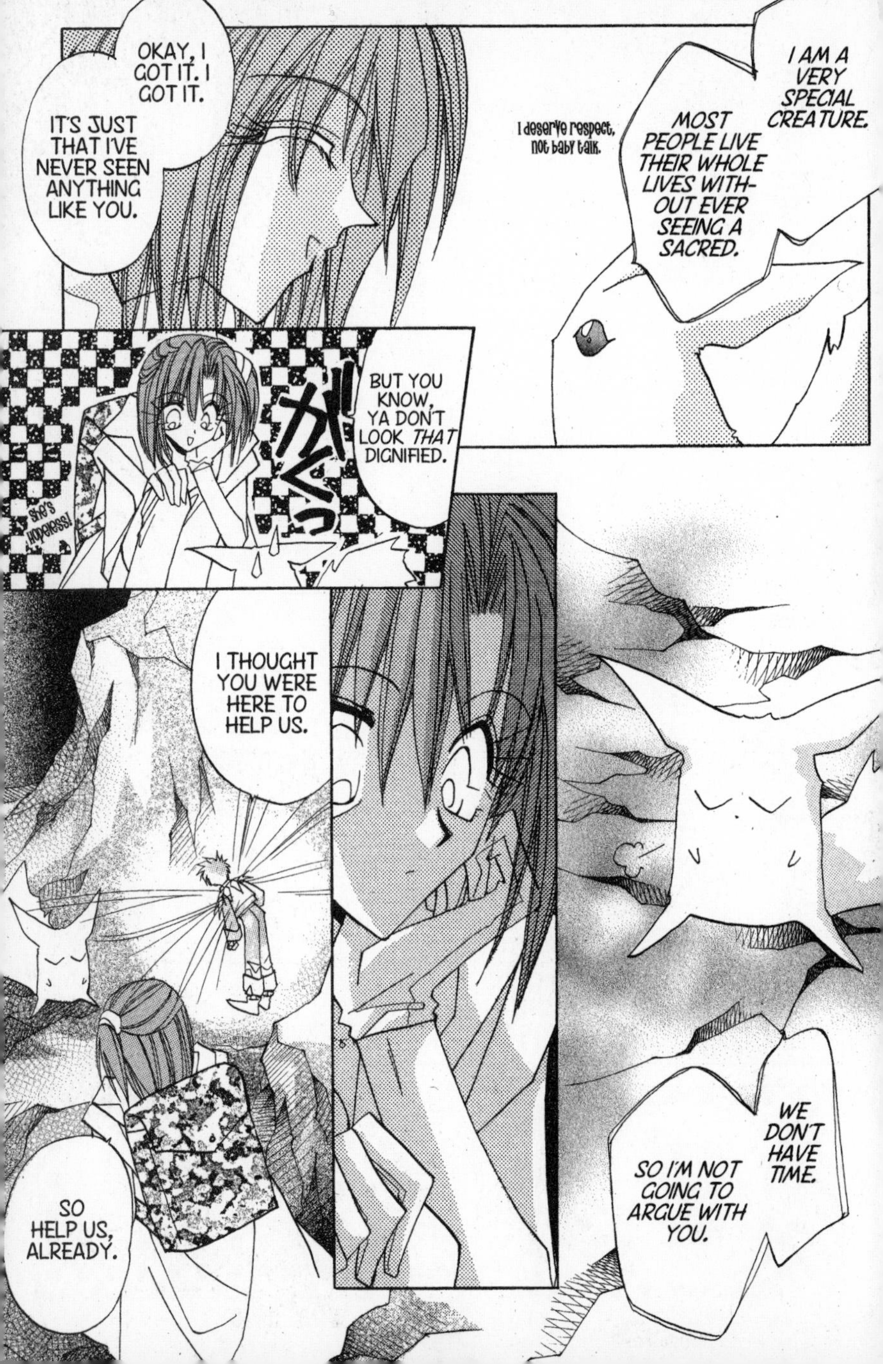
I AM A VERY SPECIAL CREATURE.
MOST PEOPLE LIVE THEIR WHOLE LIVES WITH-OUT EVER SEEING A SACRED.
I deserve respect, not baby talk.
OKAY, I GOT IT. I GOT IT.
IT'S JUST THAT I'VE NEVER SEEN ANYTHING LIKE YOU.
BUT YOU KNOW, YA DON'T LOOK *THAT* DIGNIFIED.
がくっ
She's hopeless!
WE DON'T HAVE TIME.
SO I'M NOT GOING TO ARGUE WITH YOU.
I THOUGHT YOU WERE HERE TO HELP US.
SO HELP US, ALREADY.

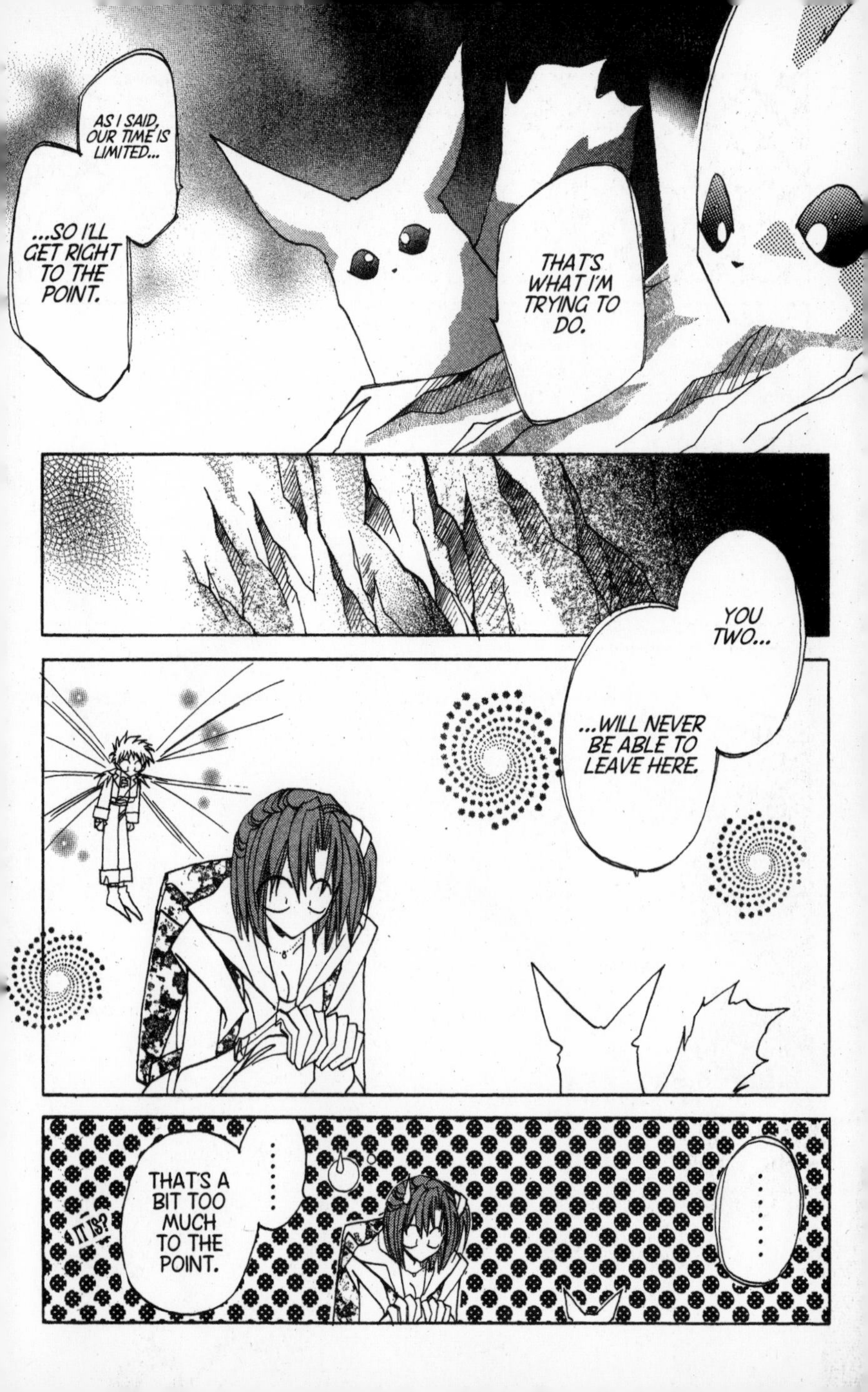
AS I SAID, OUR TIME IS LIMITED...
...SO I'LL GET RIGHT TO THE POINT.
THAT'S WHAT I'M TRYING TO DO.
YOU TWO...
...WILL NEVER BE ABLE TO LEAVE HERE.
......
......
THAT'S A BIT TOO MUCH TO THE POINT.
IT IS?

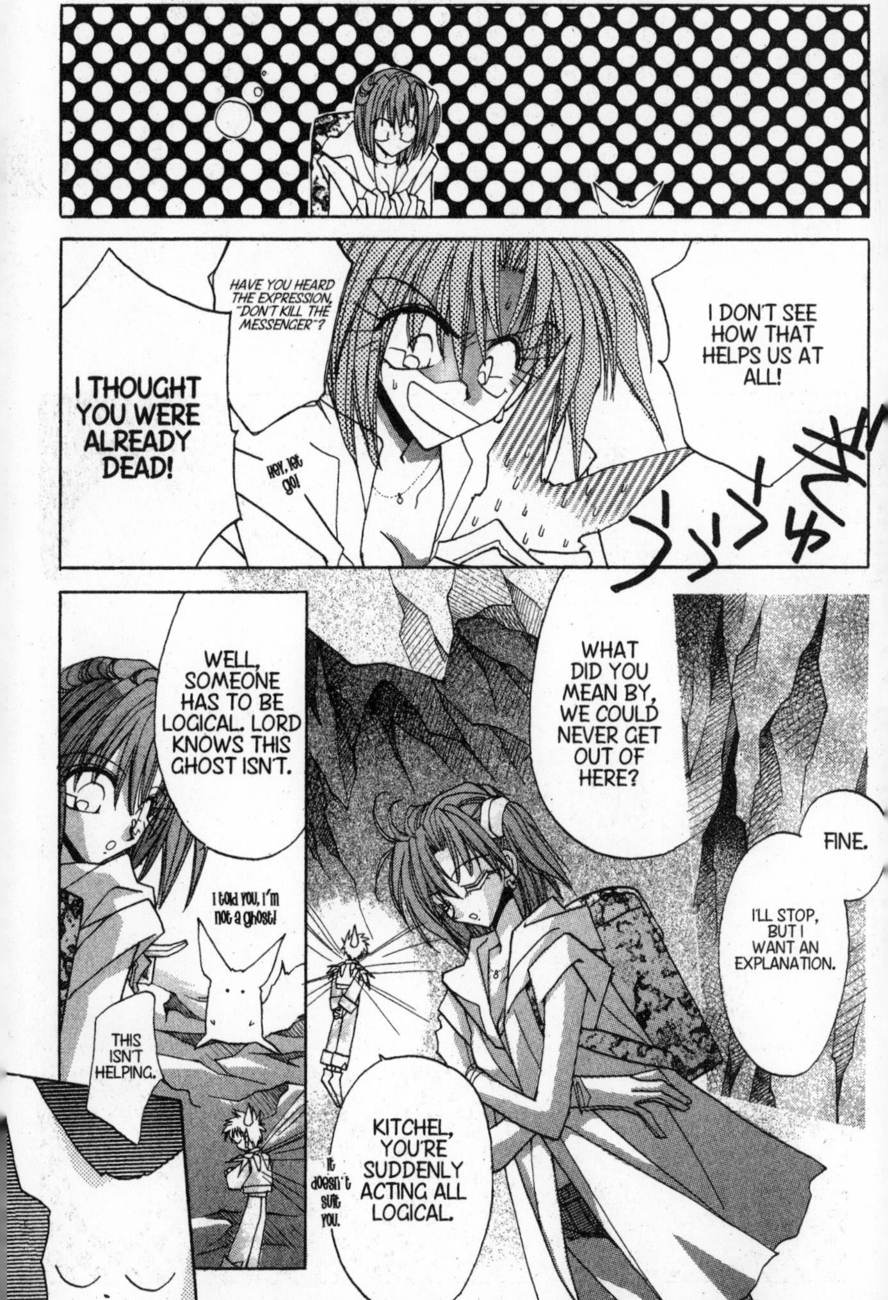
I DON'T SEE HOW THAT HELPS US AT ALL!
HAVE YOU HEARD THE EXPRESSION, "DON'T KILL THE MESSENGER"?
Hey, let go!
I THOUGHT YOU WERE ALREADY DEAD!
WHAT DID YOU MEAN BY, WE COULD NEVER GET OUT OF HERE?
FINE.
I'LL STOP, BUT I WANT AN EXPLANATION.
KITCHEL, YOU'RE SUDDENLY ACTING ALL LOGICAL.
It doesn't suit you.
WELL, SOMEONE HAS TO BE LOGICAL. LORD KNOWS THIS GHOST ISN'T.
I told you, I'm not a ghost!
THIS ISN'T HELPING.

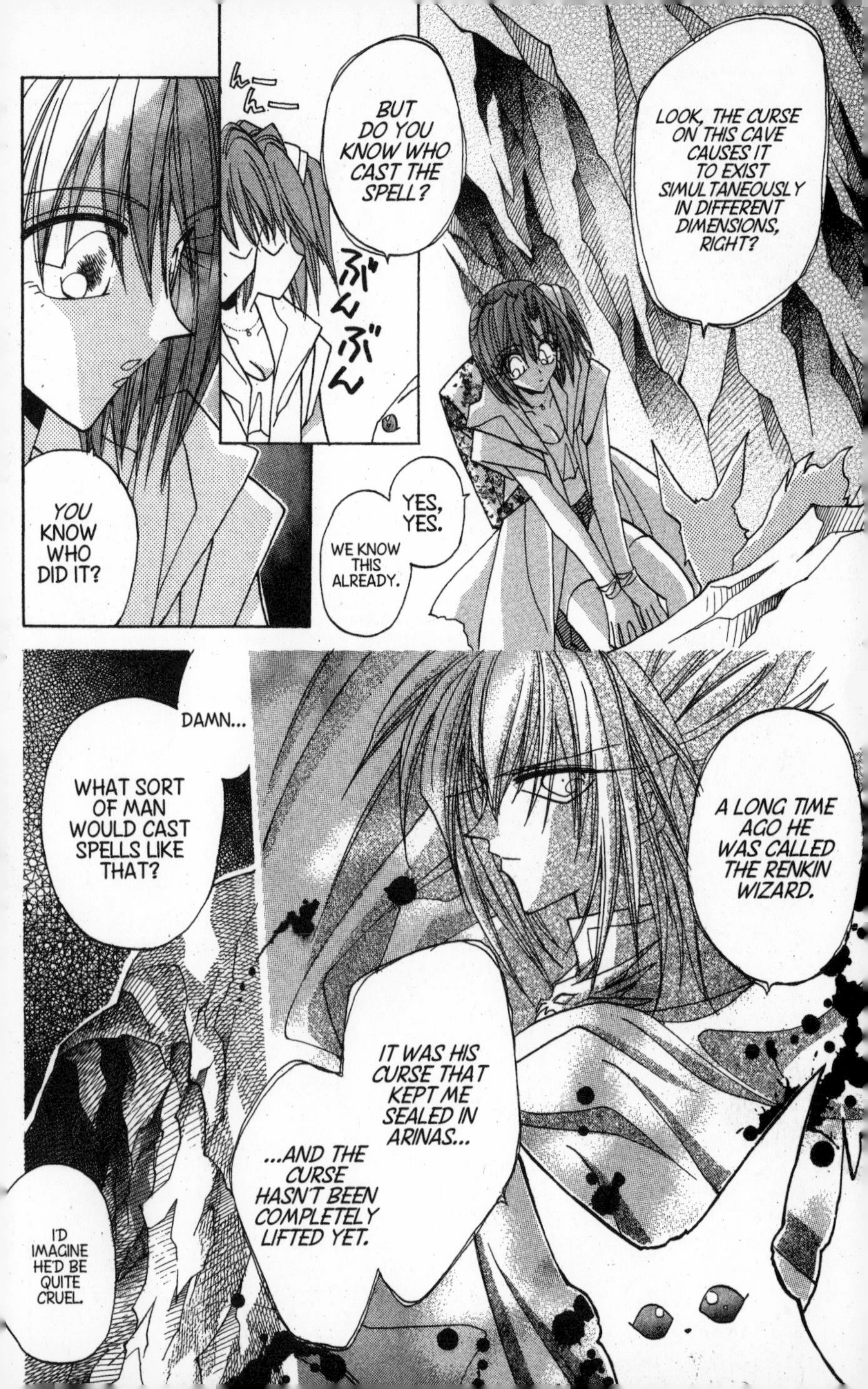
LOOK, THE CURSE ON THIS CAVE CAUSES IT TO EXIST SIMULTANEOUSLY IN DIFFERENT DIMENSIONS, RIGHT?
YES, YES.
WE KNOW THIS ALREADY.
んーんー
BUT DO YOU KNOW WHO CAST THE SPELL?
ぶんぶん
YOU KNOW WHO DID IT?
A LONG TIME AGO HE WAS CALLED THE RENKIN WIZARD.
IT WAS HIS CURSE THAT KEPT ME SEALED IN ARINAS...
...AND THE CURSE HASN'T BEEN COMPLETELY LIFTED YET.
DAMN...
WHAT SORT OF MAN WOULD CAST SPELLS LIKE THAT?
I'D IMAGINE HE'D BE QUITE CRUEL.

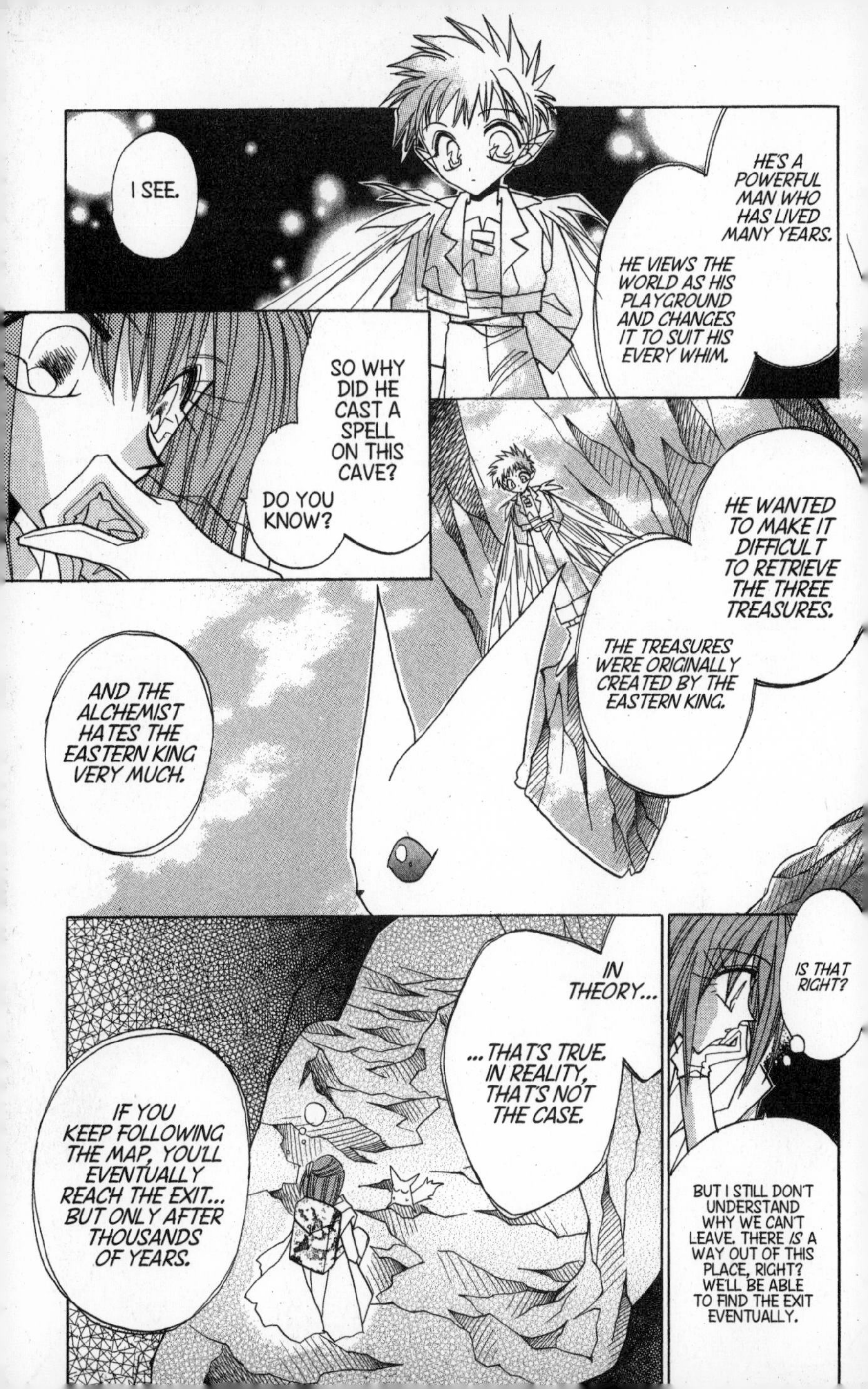
HE'S A POWERFUL MAN WHO HAS LIVED MANY YEARS.
HE VIEWS THE WORLD AS HIS PLAYGROUND AND CHANGES IT TO SUIT HIS EVERY WHIM.
I SEE.
SO WHY DID HE CAST A SPELL ON THIS CAVE?
DO YOU KNOW?
HE WANTED TO MAKE IT DIFFICULT TO RETRIEVE THE THREE TREASURES.
THE TREASURES WERE ORIGINALLY CREATED BY THE EASTERN KING.
AND THE ALCHEMIST HATES THE EASTERN KING VERY MUCH.
IS THAT RIGHT?
BUT I STILL DON'T UNDERSTAND WHY WE CAN'T LEAVE. THERE *IS* A WAY OUT OF THIS PLACE, RIGHT? WE'LL BE ABLE TO FIND THE EXIT EVENTUALLY.
IN THEORY...
...THAT'S TRUE. IN REALITY, THAT'S NOT THE CASE.
IF YOU KEEP FOLLOWING THE MAP, YOU'LL EVENTUALLY REACH THE EXIT... BUT ONLY AFTER THOUSANDS OF YEARS.

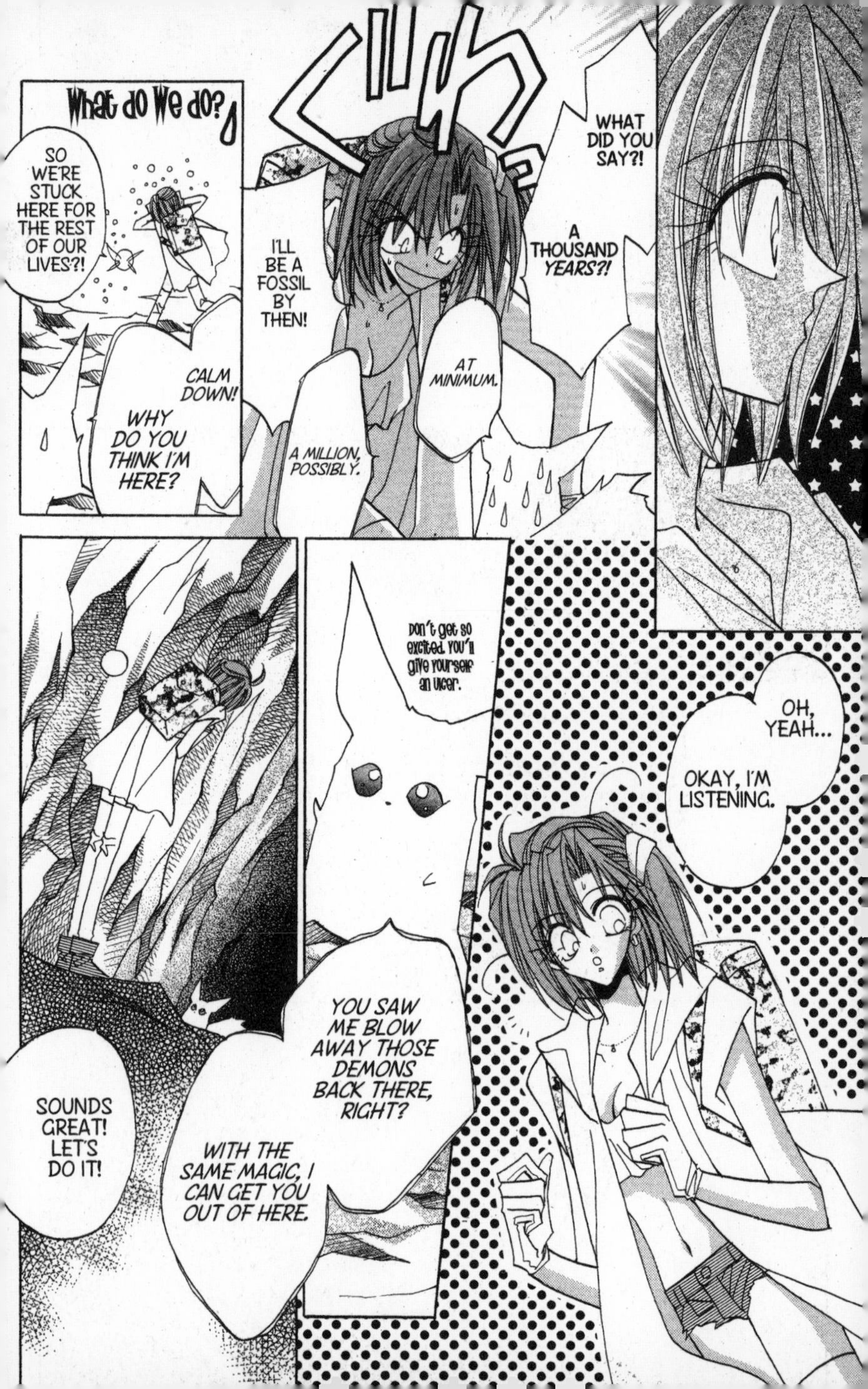
WHAT DID YOU SAY?!
A THOUSAND YEARS?!
I'LL BE A FOSSIL BY THEN!
AT MINIMUM.
A MILLION, POSSIBLY.
What do We do?
SO WE'RE STUCK HERE FOR THE REST OF OUR LIVES?!
CALM DOWN!
WHY DO YOU THINK I'M HERE?
OH, YEAH...
OKAY, I'M LISTENING.
Don't get so excited. You'll give yourself an ulcer.
YOU SAW ME BLOW AWAY THOSE DEMONS BACK THERE, RIGHT?
WITH THE SAME MAGIC, I CAN GET YOU OUT OF HERE.
SOUNDS GREAT! LET'S DO IT!

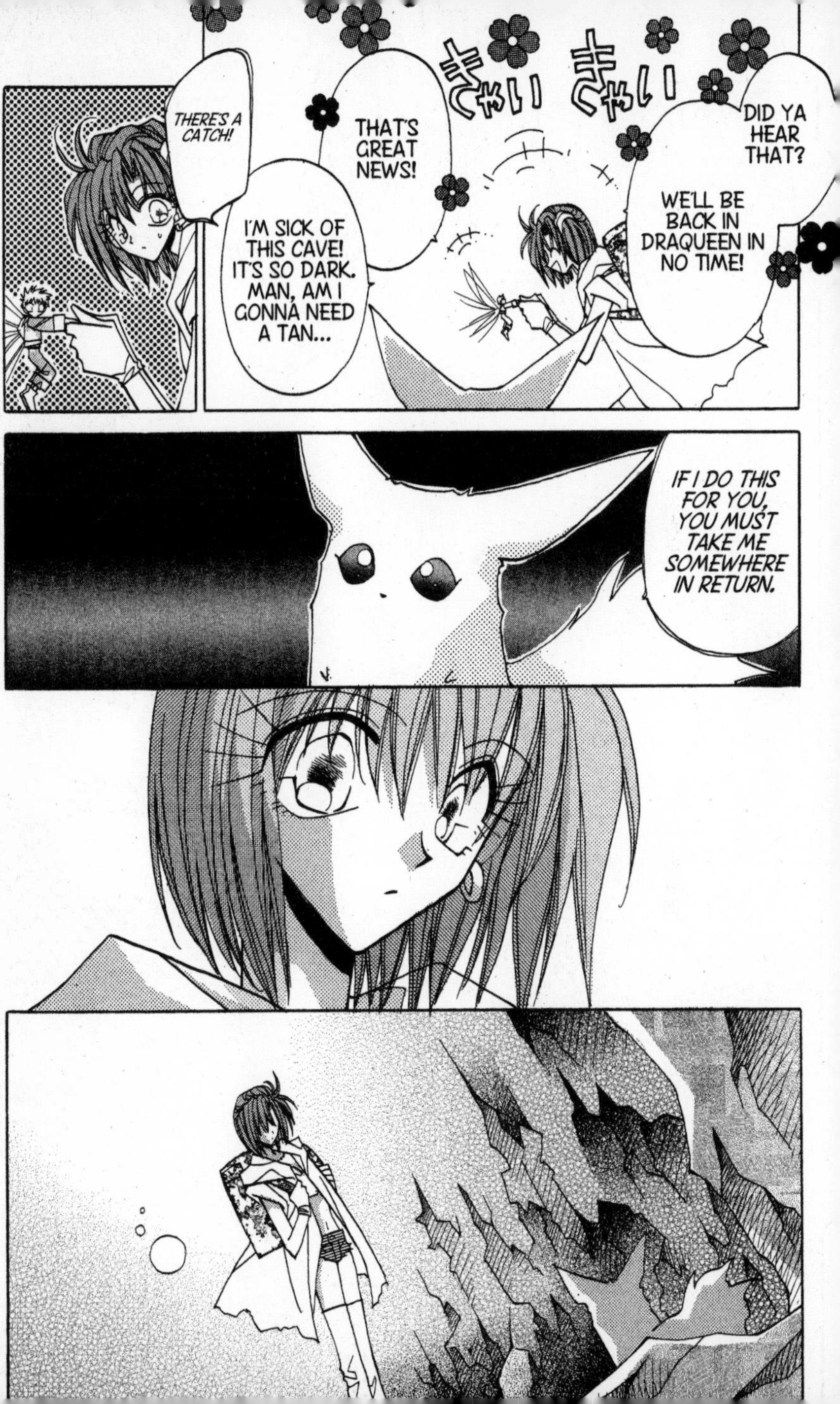
DID YA HEAR THAT?
WE'LL BE BACK IN DRAQUEEN IN NO TIME!
きゃい きゃい
THAT'S GREAT NEWS!
I'M SICK OF THIS CAVE! IT'S SO DARK. MAN, AM I GONNA NEED A TAN...
THERE'S A CATCH!
IF I DO THIS FOR YOU, YOU MUST TAKE ME SOMEWHERE IN RETURN.

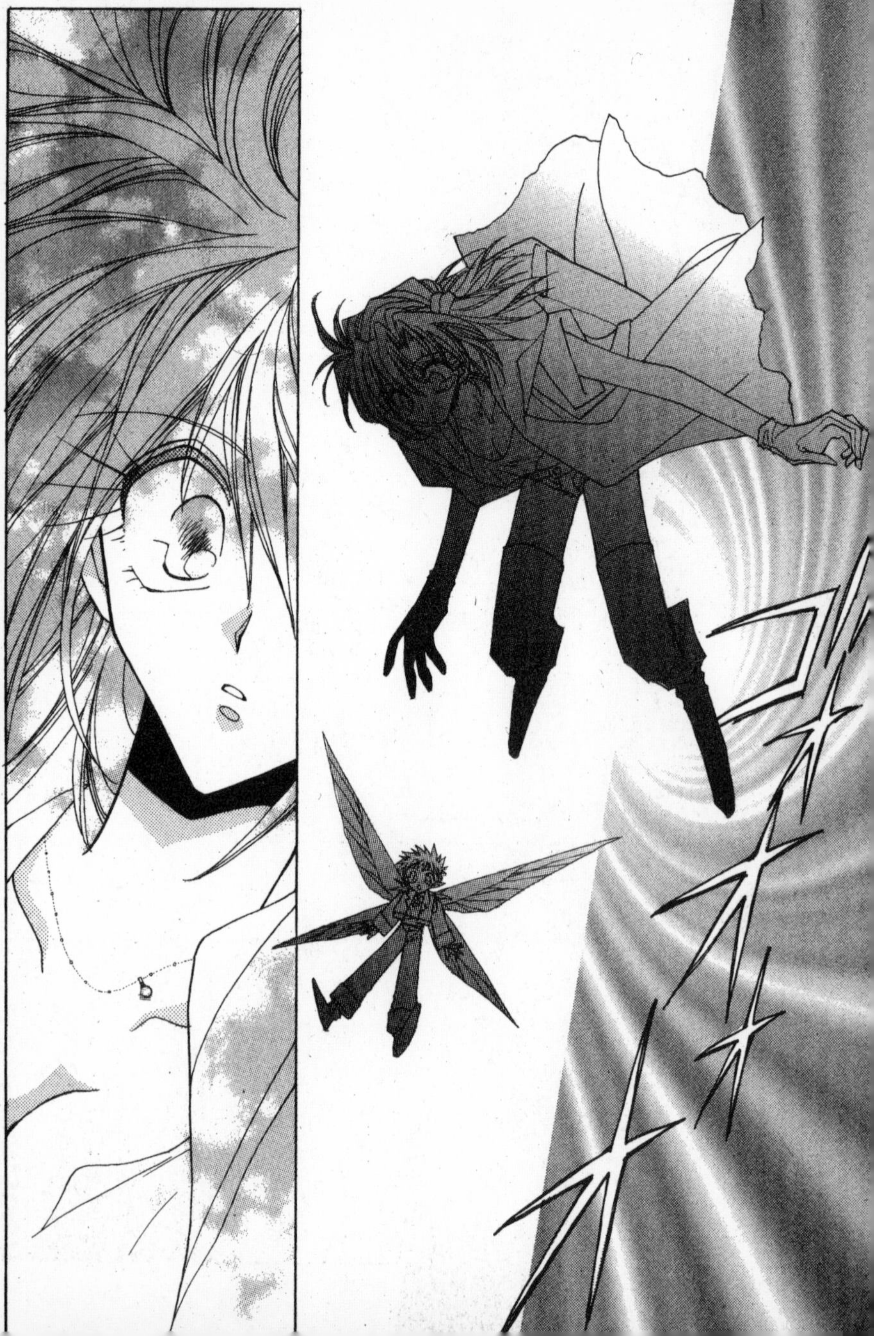

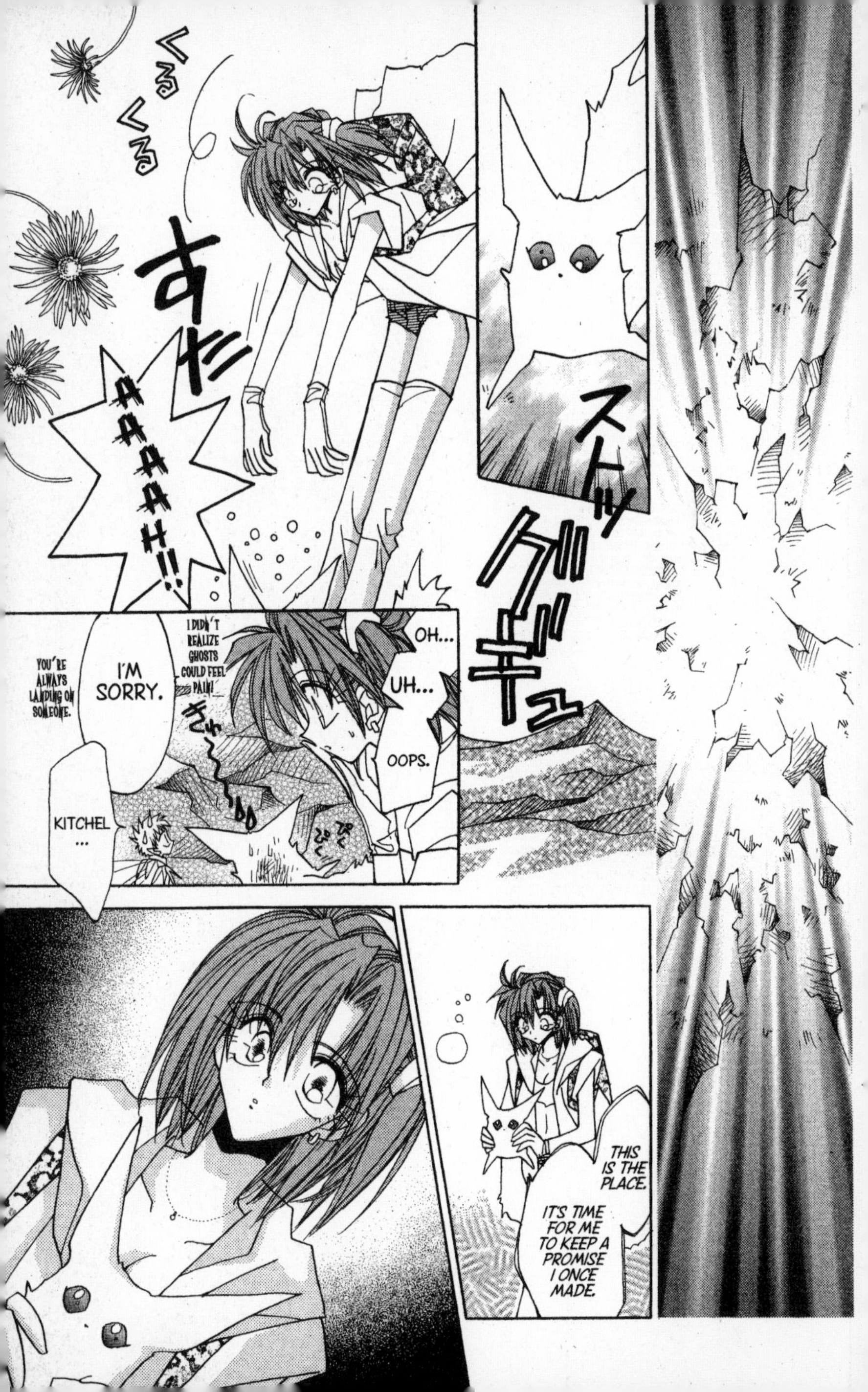
ストッ
グギュ
くるくる
すた
AAAAAH!!
OH...
UH...
OOPS.
I DIDN'T REALIZE GHOSTS COULD FEEL PAIN!
きゅ～～
I'M SORRY.
YOU'RE ALWAYS LANDING ON SOMEONE.
ぷくぷく
KITCHEL ...
THIS IS THE PLACE.
IT'S TIME FOR ME TO KEEP A PROMISE I ONCE MADE.

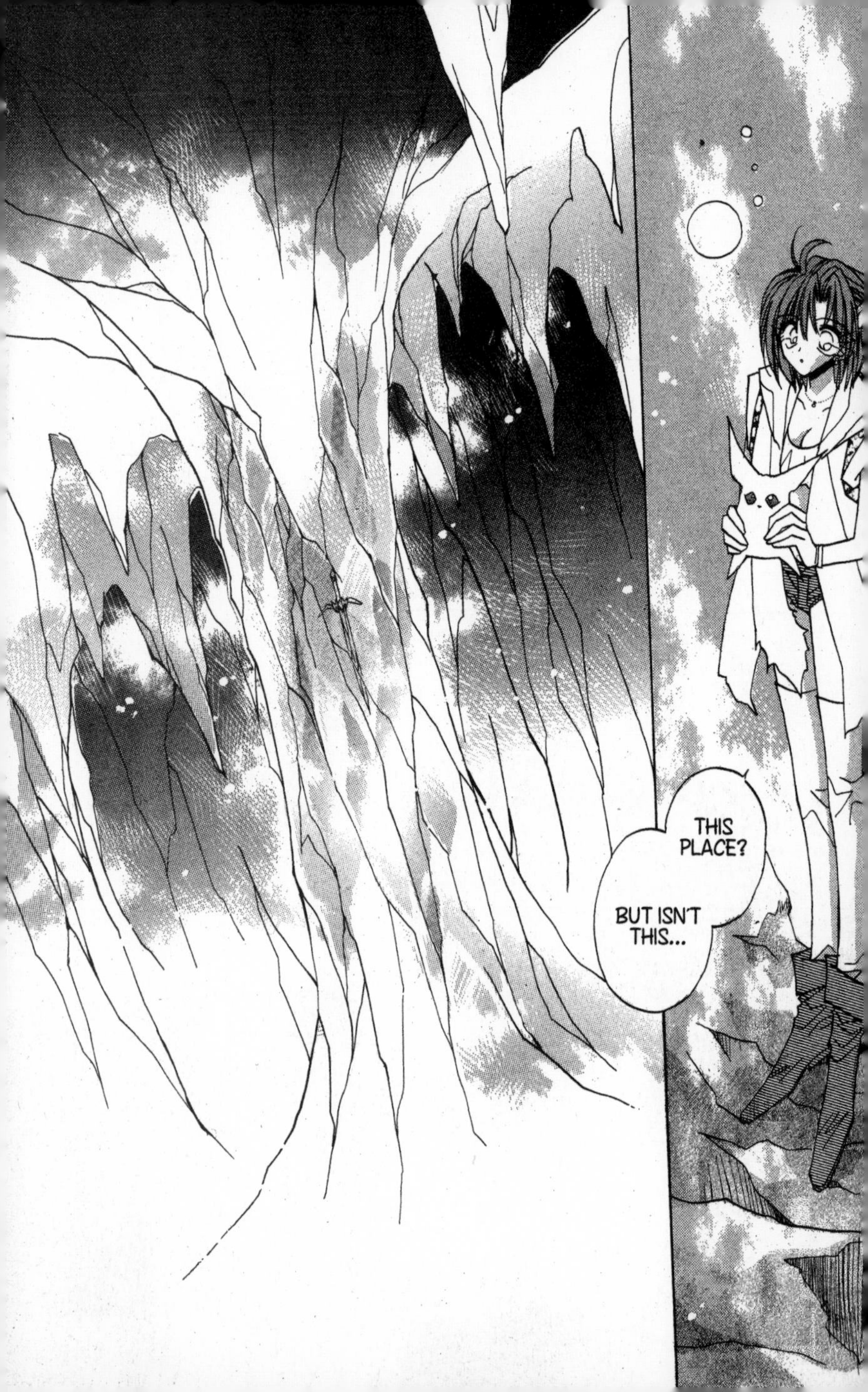
THIS PLACE?
BUT ISN'T THIS...

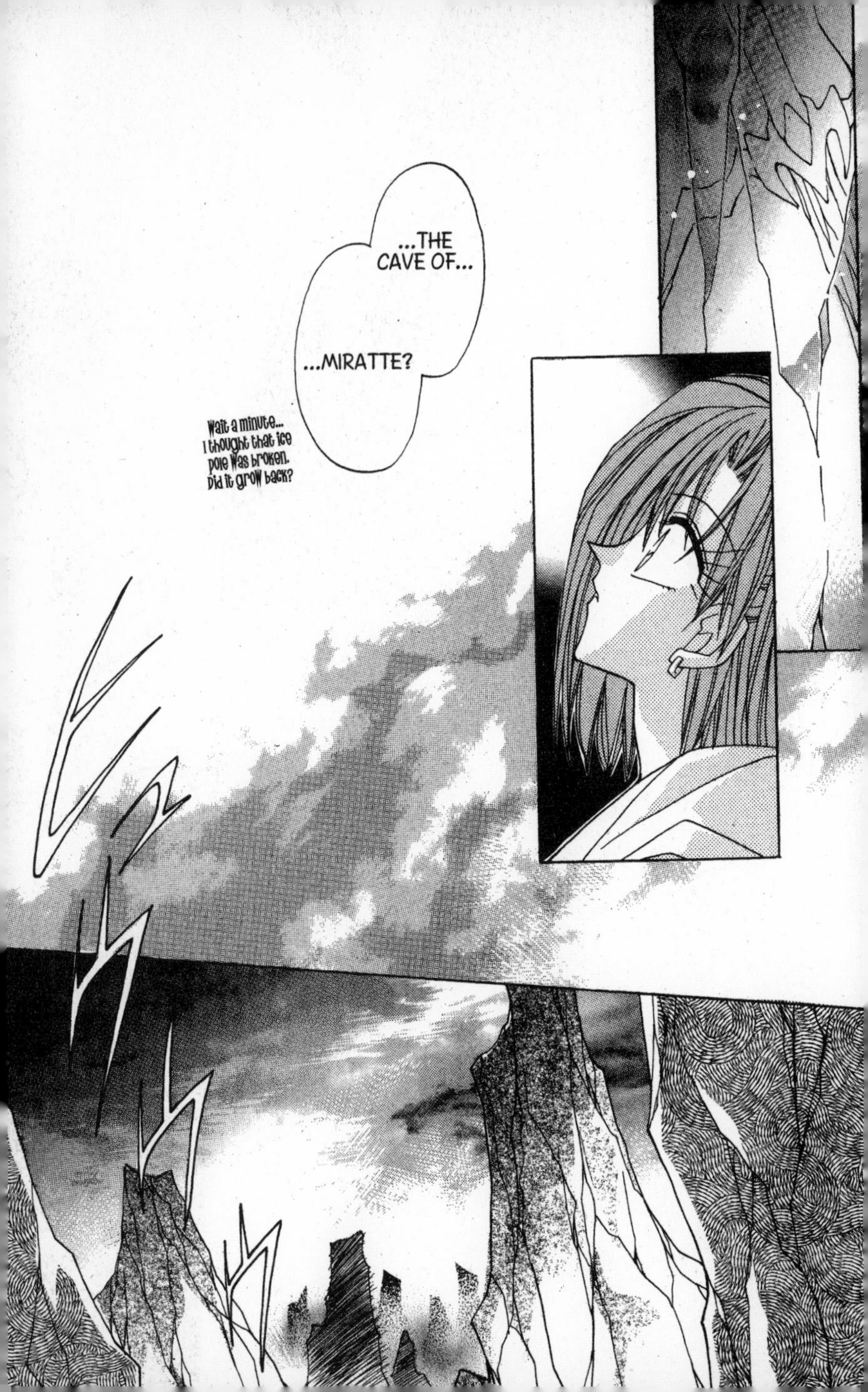
...THE CAVE OF...
...MIRATTE?
Wait a minute... I thought that ice pole was broken. Did it grow back?

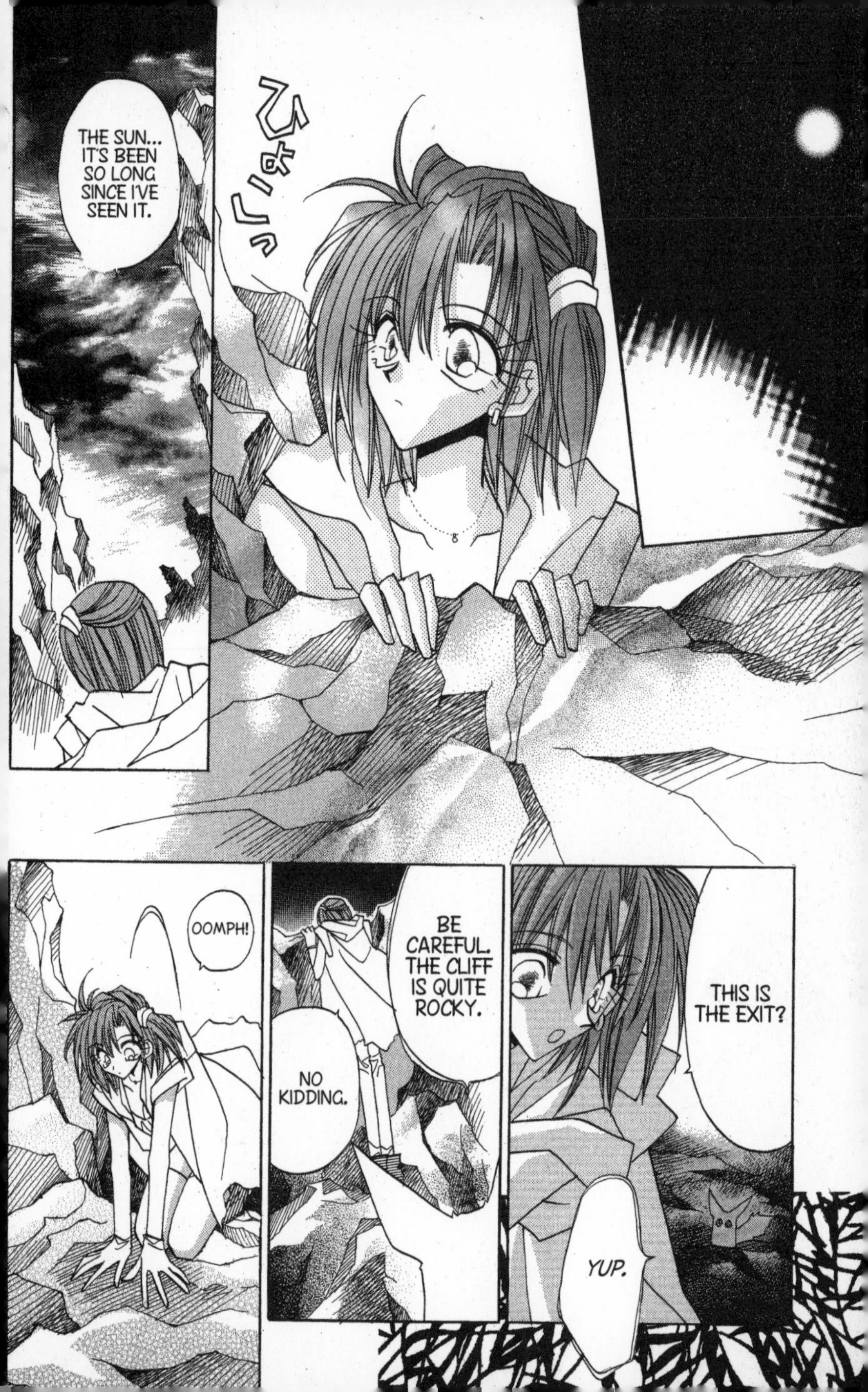
ひょこっ
THE SUN... IT'S BEEN SO LONG SINCE I'VE SEEN IT.
THIS IS THE EXIT?
YUP.
BE CAREFUL. THE CLIFF IS QUITE ROCKY.
NO KIDDING.
OOMPH!

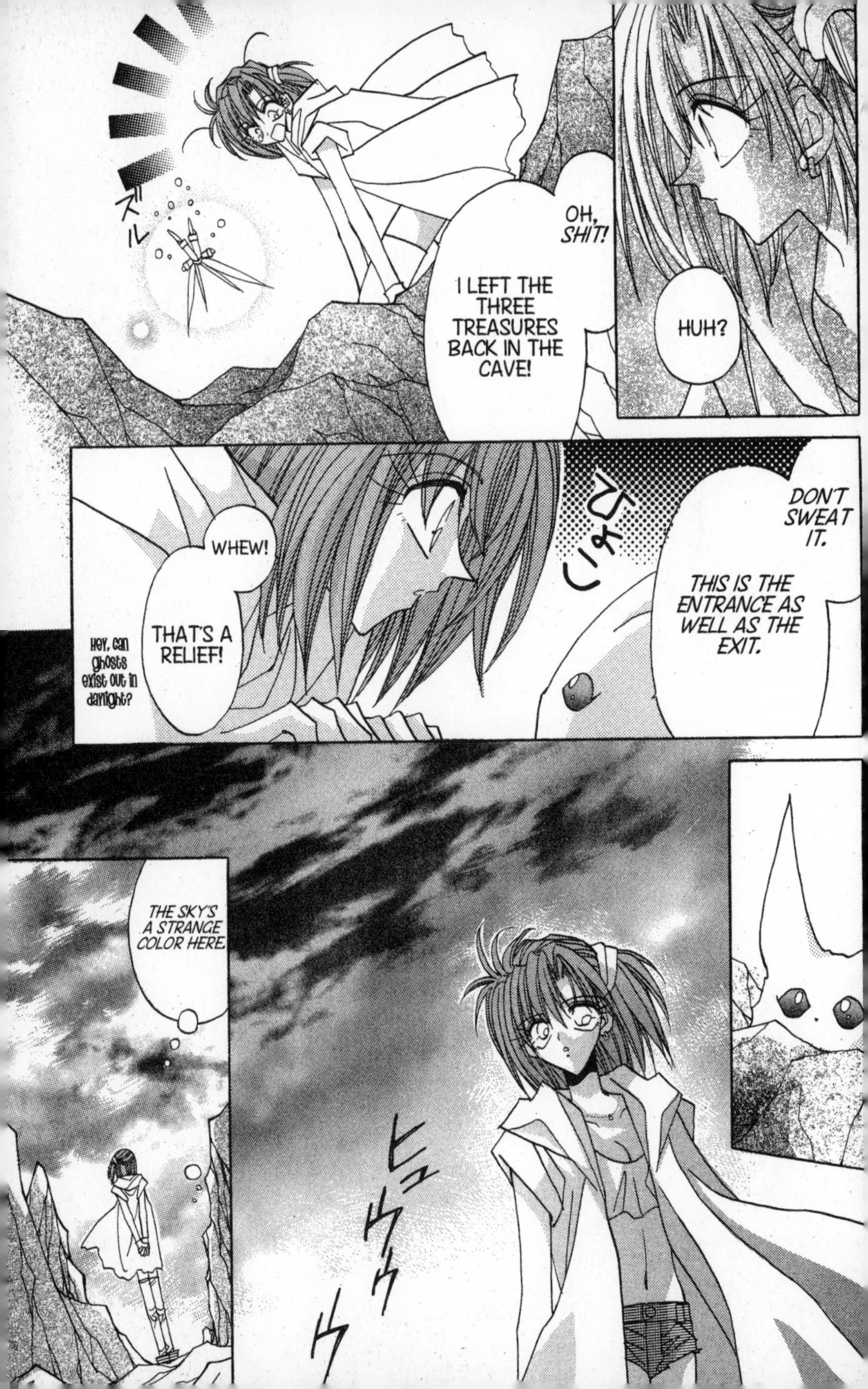
HUH?
OH, SHIT!
I LEFT THE THREE TREASURES BACK IN THE CAVE!
ズル
DON'T SWEAT IT.
THIS IS THE ENTRANCE AS WELL AS THE EXIT.
WHEW!
THAT'S A RELIEF!
Hey, can ghosts exist out in daylight?
THE SKY'S A STRANGE COLOR HERE.

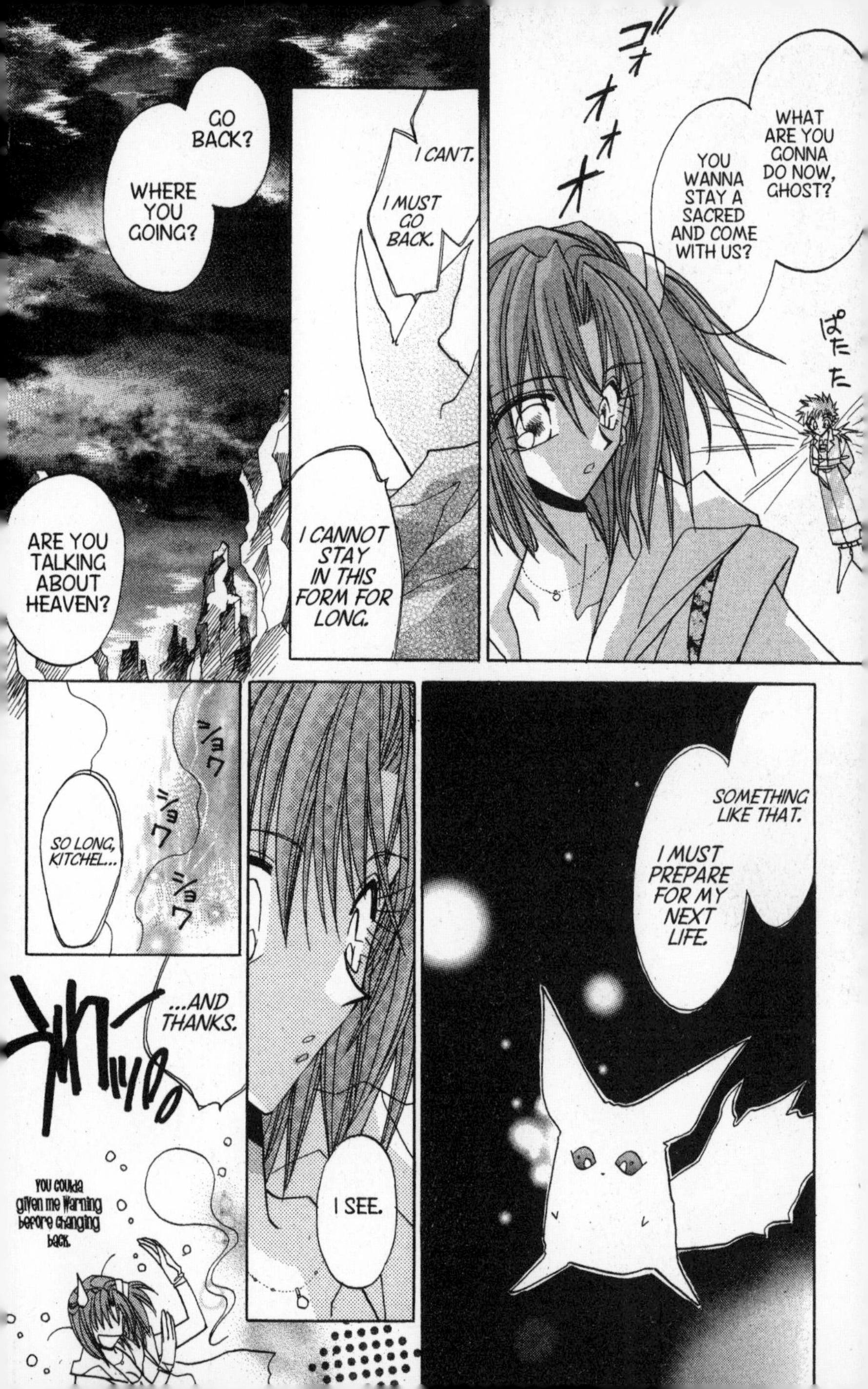
ゴォォォ
WHAT ARE YOU GONNA DO NOW, GHOST?
YOU WANNA STAY A SACRED AND COME WITH US?
ぱたた
I CAN'T.
I MUST GO BACK.
I CANNOT STAY IN THIS FORM FOR LONG.
GO BACK?
WHERE YOU GOING?
ARE YOU TALKING ABOUT HEAVEN?
SOMETHING LIKE THAT.
I MUST PREPARE FOR MY NEXT LIFE.
I SEE.
ショワ
ショワ
ショワ
SO LONG, KITCHEL...
...AND THANKS.
YOU COULDA GIVEN ME WARNING BEFORE CHANGING BACK.

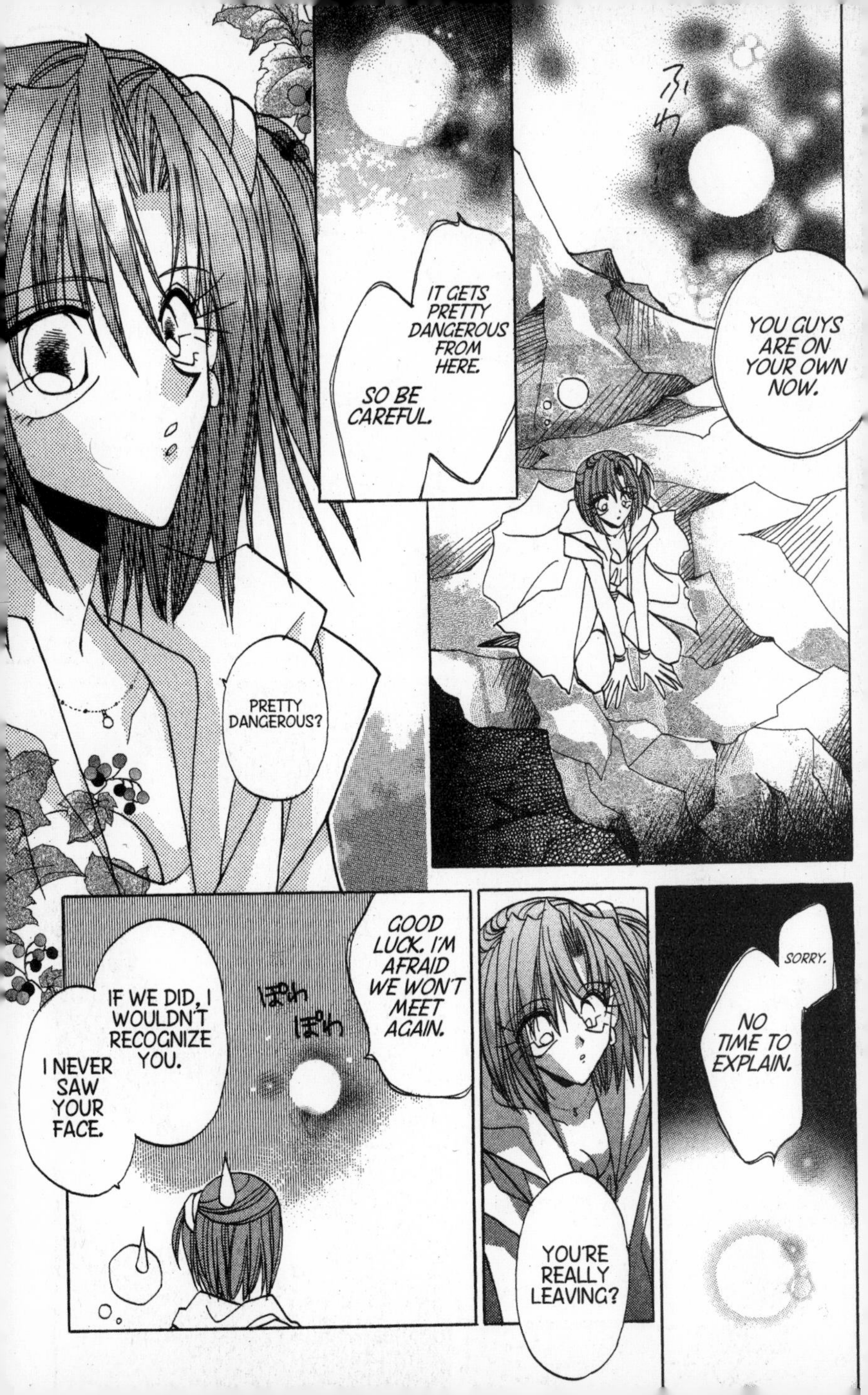
ふわ
YOU GUYS ARE ON YOUR OWN NOW.
IT GETS PRETTY DANGEROUS FROM HERE.
SO BE CAREFUL.
PRETTY DANGEROUS?
SORRY.
NO TIME TO EXPLAIN.
YOU'RE REALLY LEAVING?
GOOD LUCK. I'M AFRAID WE WON'T MEET AGAIN.
ぽわ ぽわ
IF WE DID, I WOULDN'T RECOGNIZE YOU.
I NEVER SAW YOUR FACE.

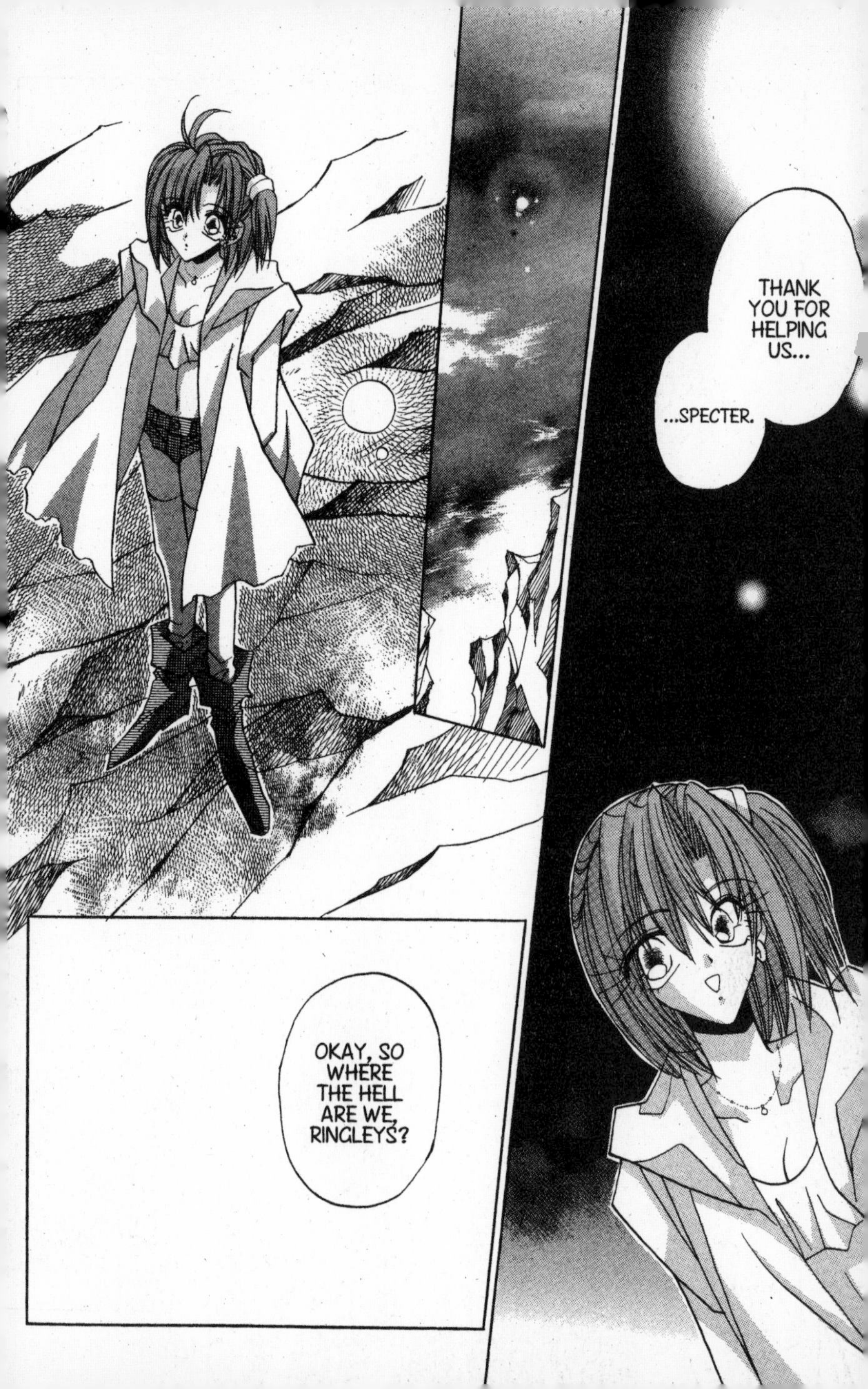
THANK YOU FOR HELPING US...
...SPECTER.
OKAY, SO WHERE THE HELL ARE WE, RINGLEYS?

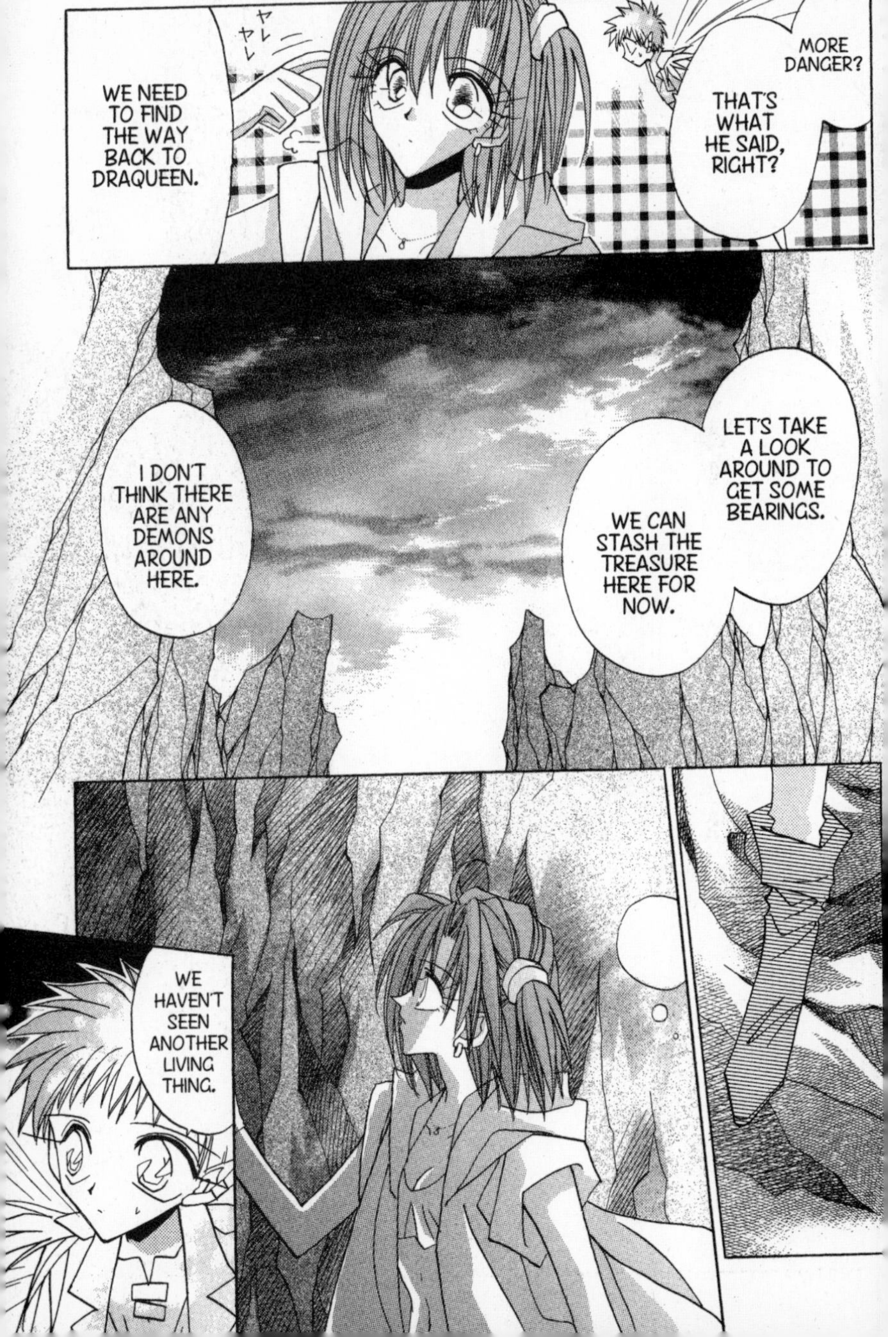
MORE DANGER?
THAT'S WHAT HE SAID, RIGHT?
ヤレ ヤレ
WE NEED TO FIND THE WAY BACK TO DRAQUEEN.
LET'S TAKE A LOOK AROUND TO GET SOME BEARINGS.
WE CAN STASH THE TREASURE HERE FOR NOW.
I DON'T THINK THERE ARE ANY DEMONS AROUND HERE.
WE HAVEN'T SEEN ANOTHER LIVING THING.

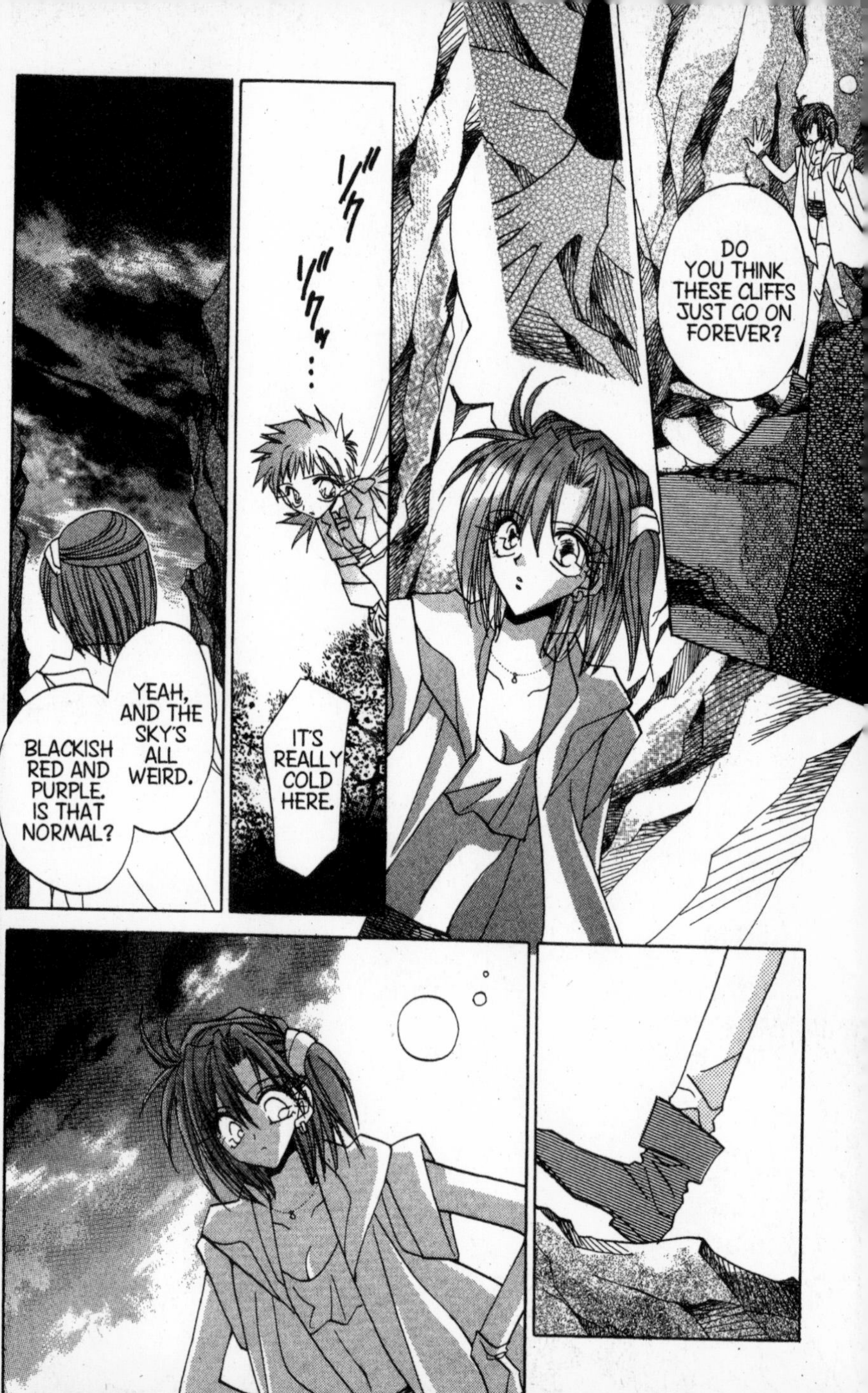

DO YOU THINK THESE CLIFFS JUST GO ON FOREVER?
ゾク ゾクッ…
IT'S REALLY COLD HERE.
YEAH, AND THE SKY'S ALL WEIRD.
BLACKISH RED AND PURPLE. IS THAT NORMAL?

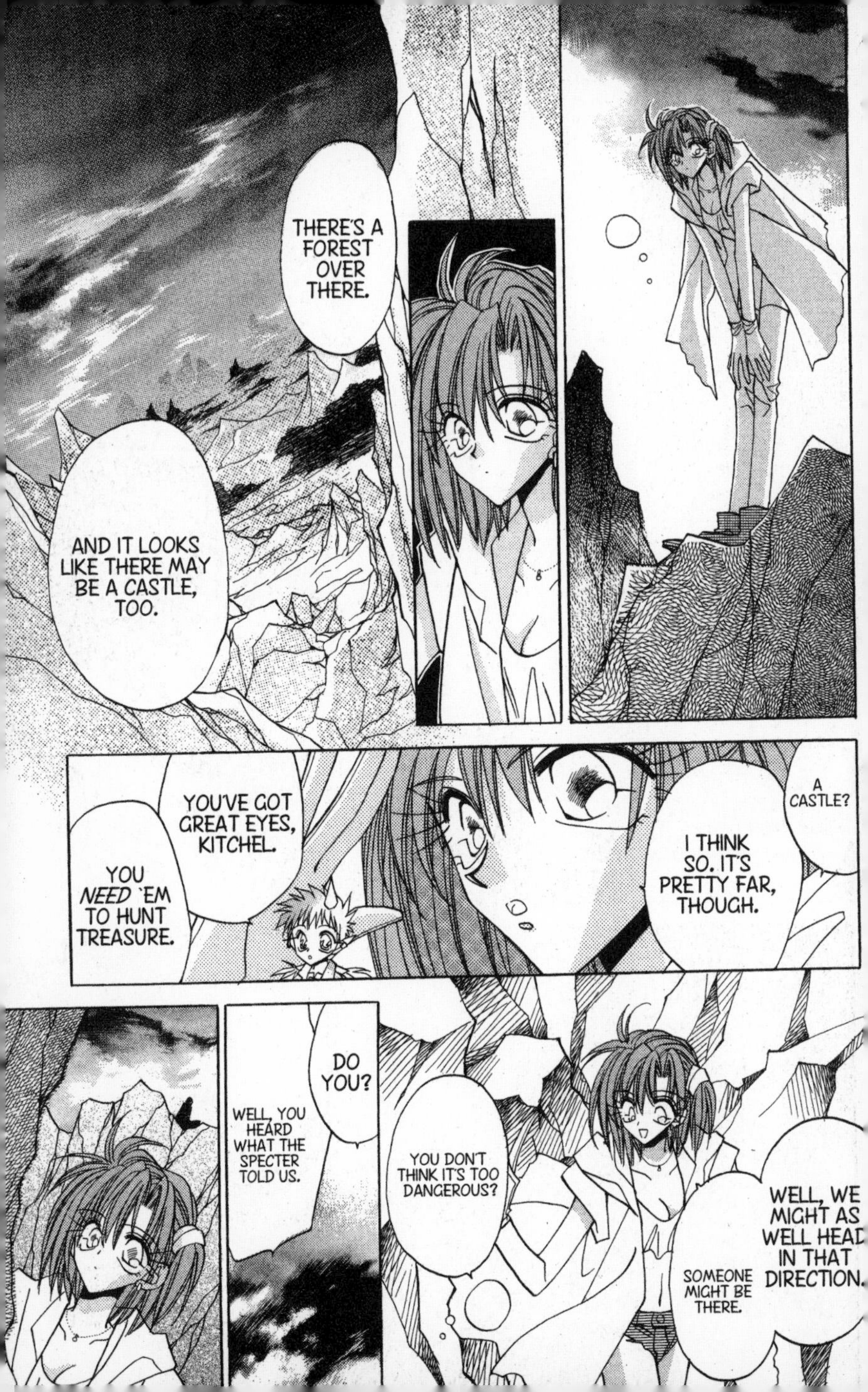
THERE'S A FOREST OVER THERE.
AND IT LOOKS LIKE THERE MAY BE A CASTLE, TOO.
A CASTLE?
I THINK SO. IT'S PRETTY FAR, THOUGH.
YOU'VE GOT GREAT EYES, KITCHEL.
YOU *NEED* `EM TO HUNT TREASURE.
WELL, WE MIGHT AS WELL HEAD IN THAT DIRECTION.
SOMEONE MIGHT BE THERE.
YOU DON'T THINK IT'S TOO DANGEROUS?
DO YOU?
WELL, YOU HEARD WHAT THE SPECTER TOLD US.

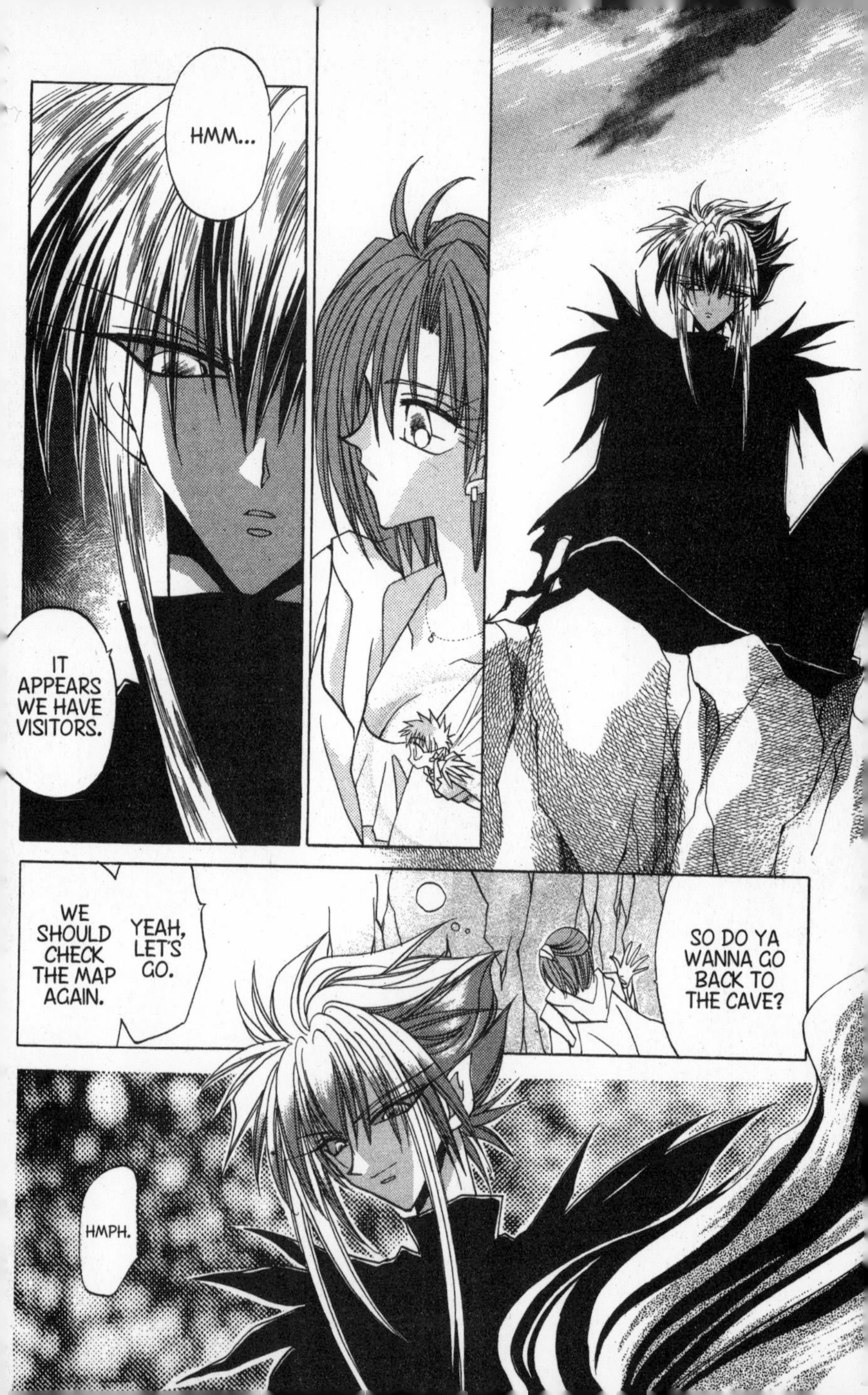
HMM...
IT APPEARS WE HAVE VISITORS.
SO DO YA WANNA GO BACK TO THE CAVE?
YEAH, LET'S GO.
WE SHOULD CHECK THE MAP AGAIN.
HMPH.

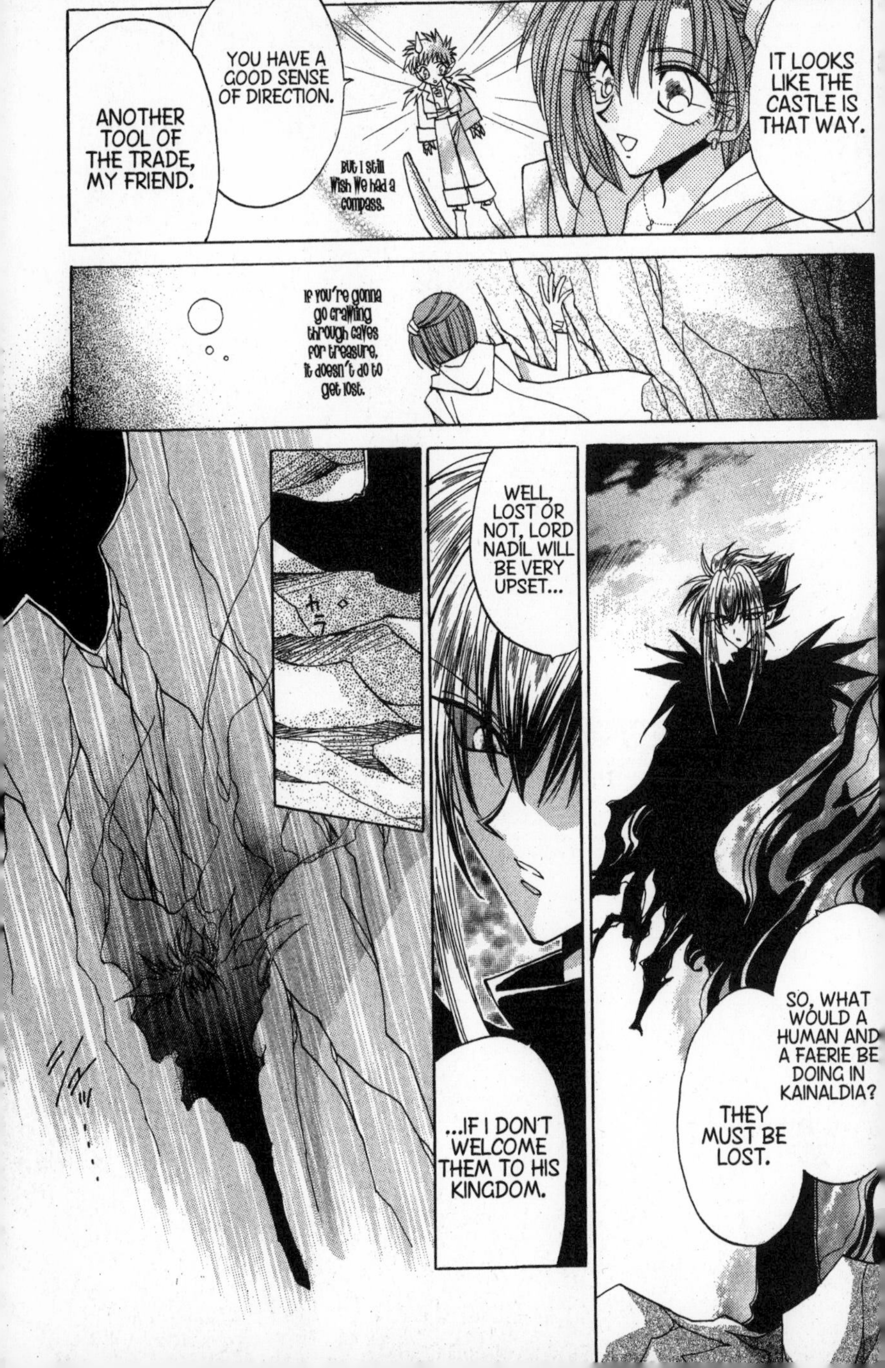
IT LOOKS LIKE THE CASTLE IS THAT WAY.
YOU HAVE A GOOD SENSE OF DIRECTION.
But I still Wish We had a compass.
ANOTHER TOOL OF THE TRADE, MY FRIEND.
If you're gonna go crawling through caves for treasure, it doesn't do to get lost.
SO, WHAT WOULD A HUMAN AND A FAERIE BE DOING IN KAINALDIA?
THEY MUST BE LOST.
WELL, LOST OR NOT, LORD NADIL WILL BE VERY UPSET...
...IF I DON'T WELCOME THEM TO HIS KINGDOM.

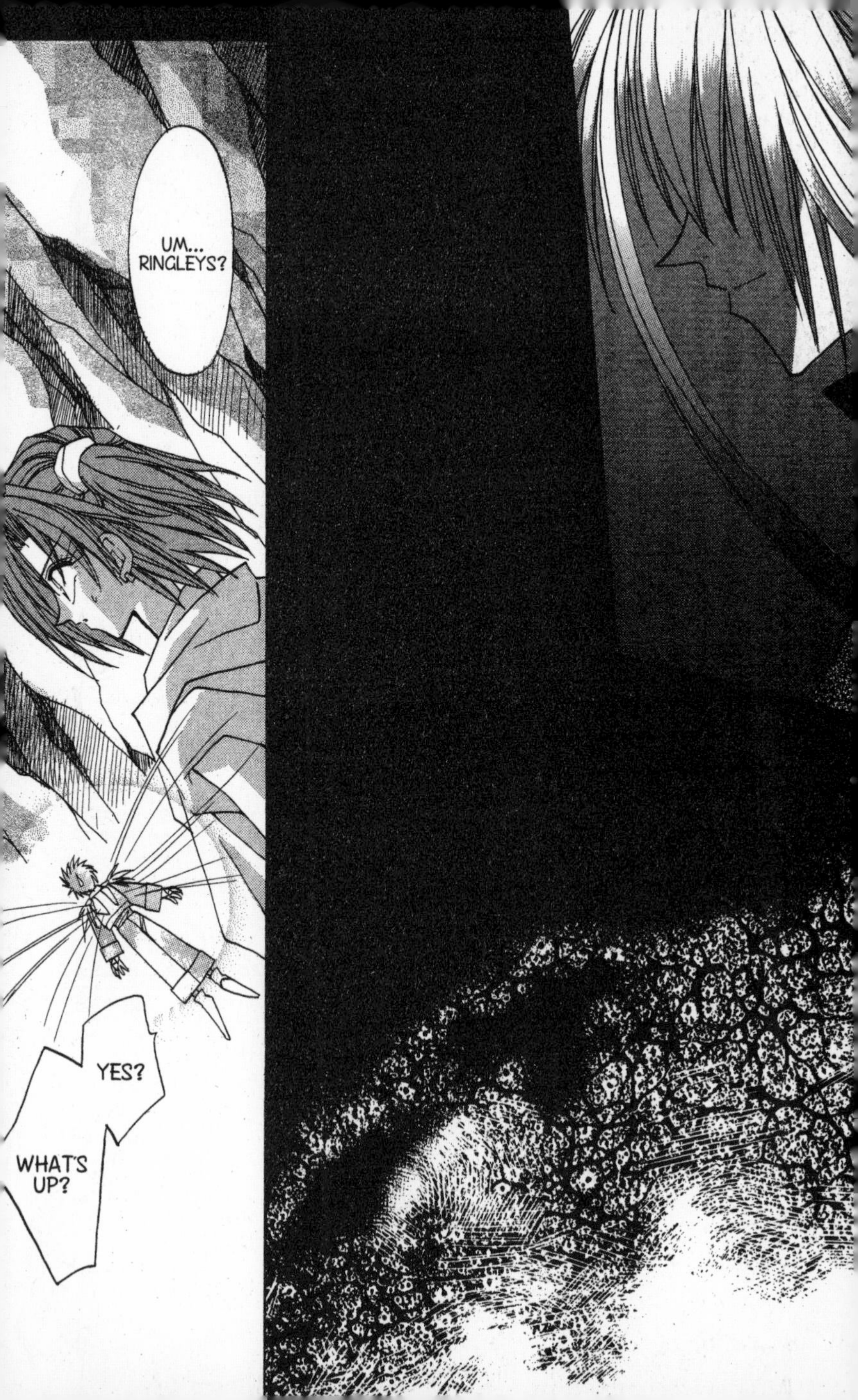
UM... RINGLEYS?
YES?
WHAT'S UP?

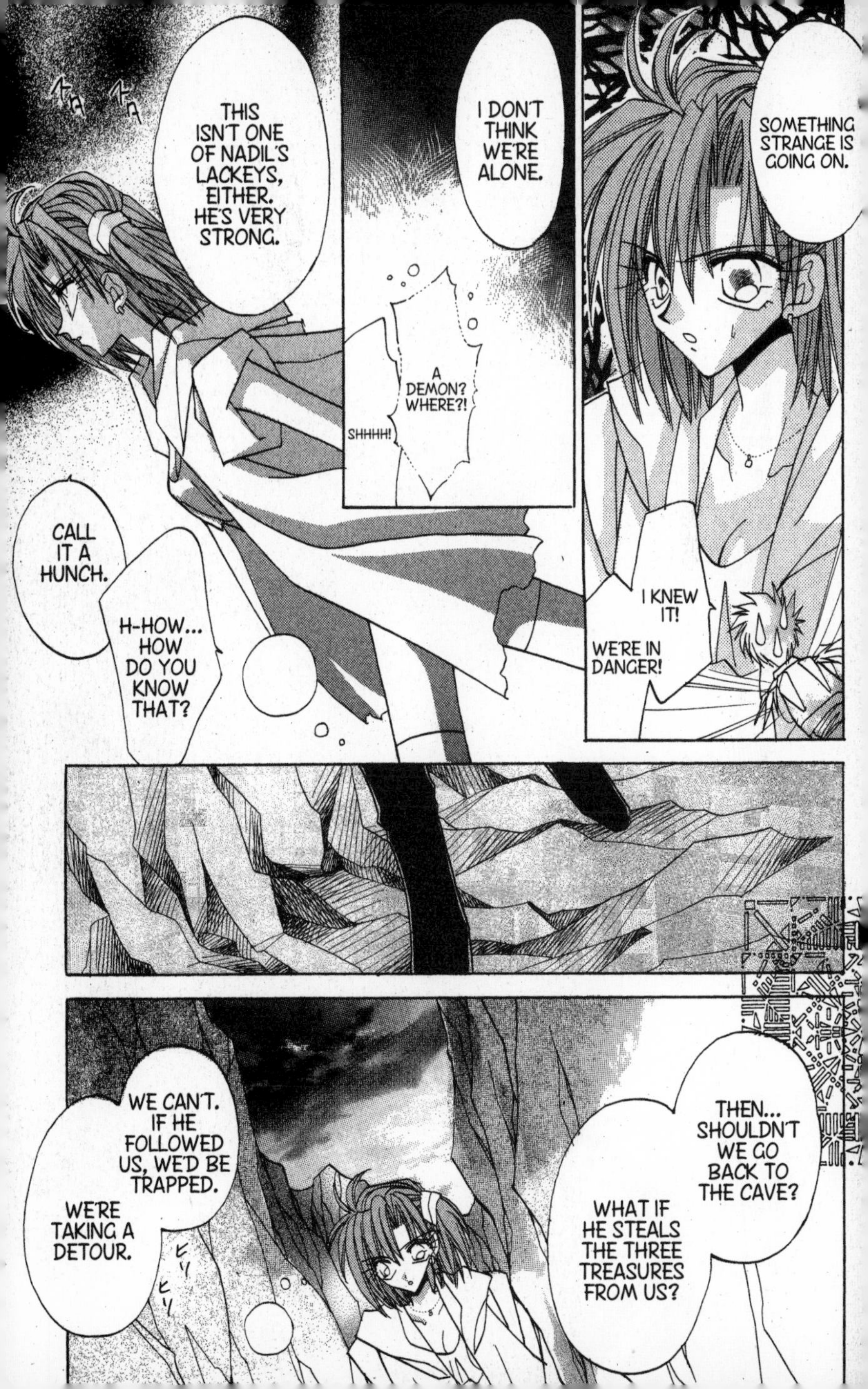
SOMETHING STRANGE IS GOING ON.
I KNEW IT!
WE'RE IN DANGER!
I DON'T THINK WE'RE ALONE.
A DEMON? WHERE?!
SHHHH!
THIS ISN'T ONE OF NADIL'S LACKEYS, EITHER. HE'S VERY STRONG.
H-HOW... HOW DO YOU KNOW THAT?
CALL IT A HUNCH.
THEN... SHOULDN'T WE GO BACK TO THE CAVE?
WHAT IF HE STEALS THE THREE TREASURES FROM US?
WE CAN'T. IF HE FOLLOWED US, WE'D BE TRAPPED.
WE'RE TAKING A DETOUR.

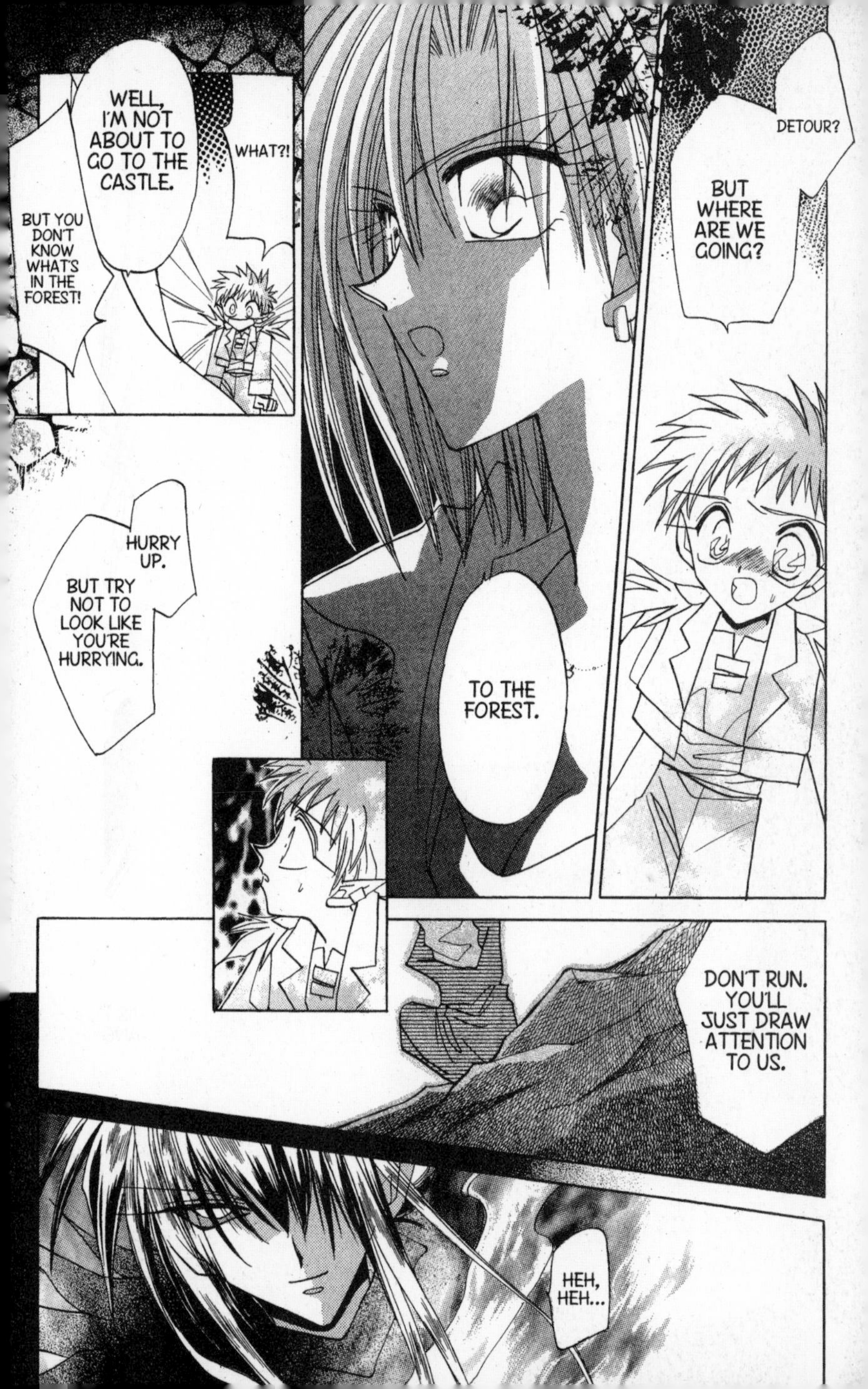
DETOUR?
BUT WHERE ARE WE GOING?
TO THE FOREST.
WHAT?!
BUT YOU DON'T KNOW WHAT'S IN THE FOREST!
WELL, I'M NOT ABOUT TO GO TO THE CASTLE.
HURRY UP.
BUT TRY NOT TO LOOK LIKE YOU'RE HURRYING.
DON'T RUN. YOU'LL JUST DRAW ATTENTION TO US.
HEH, HEH...

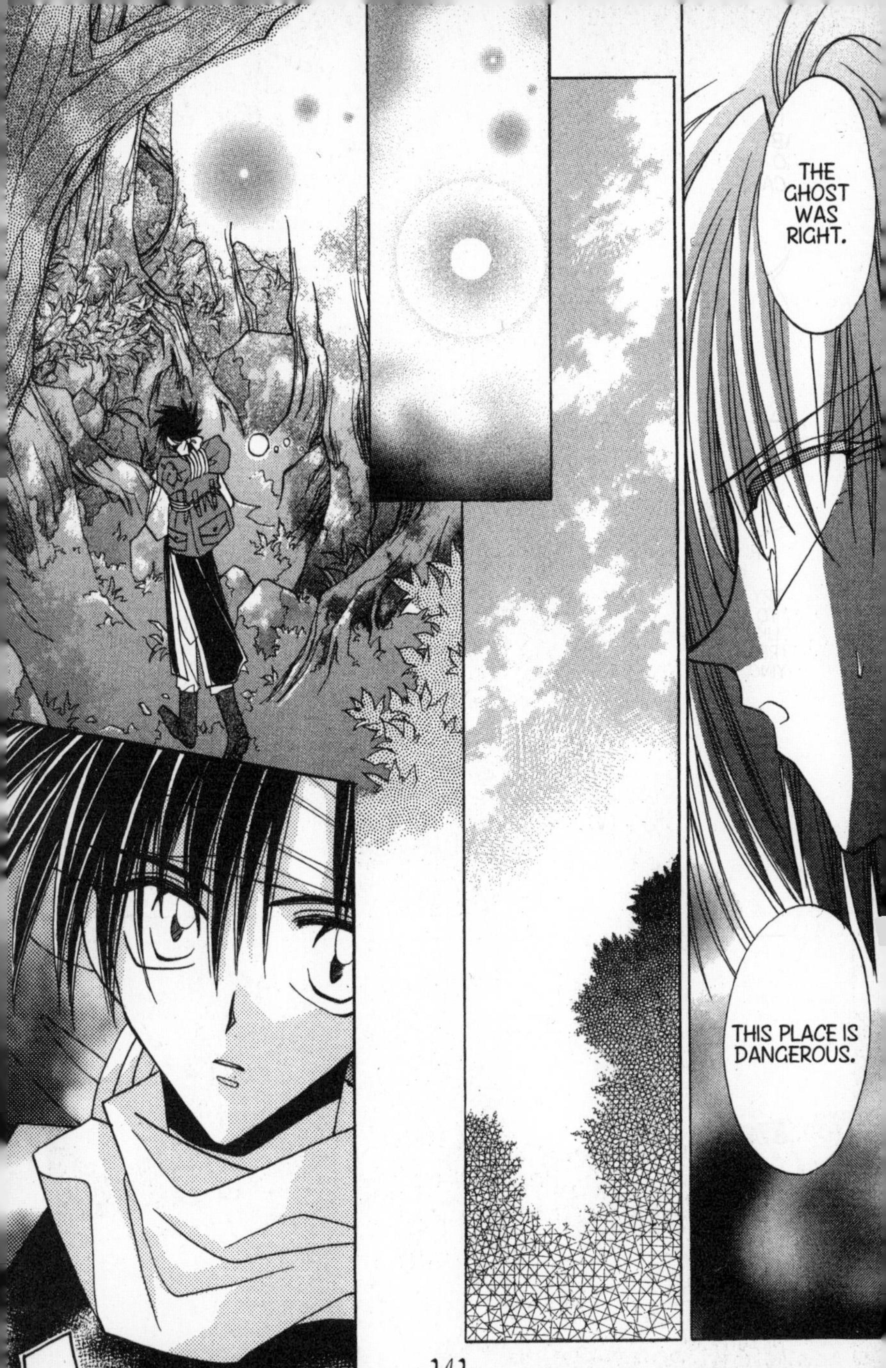
THE GHOST WAS RIGHT.
THIS PLACE IS DANGEROUS.

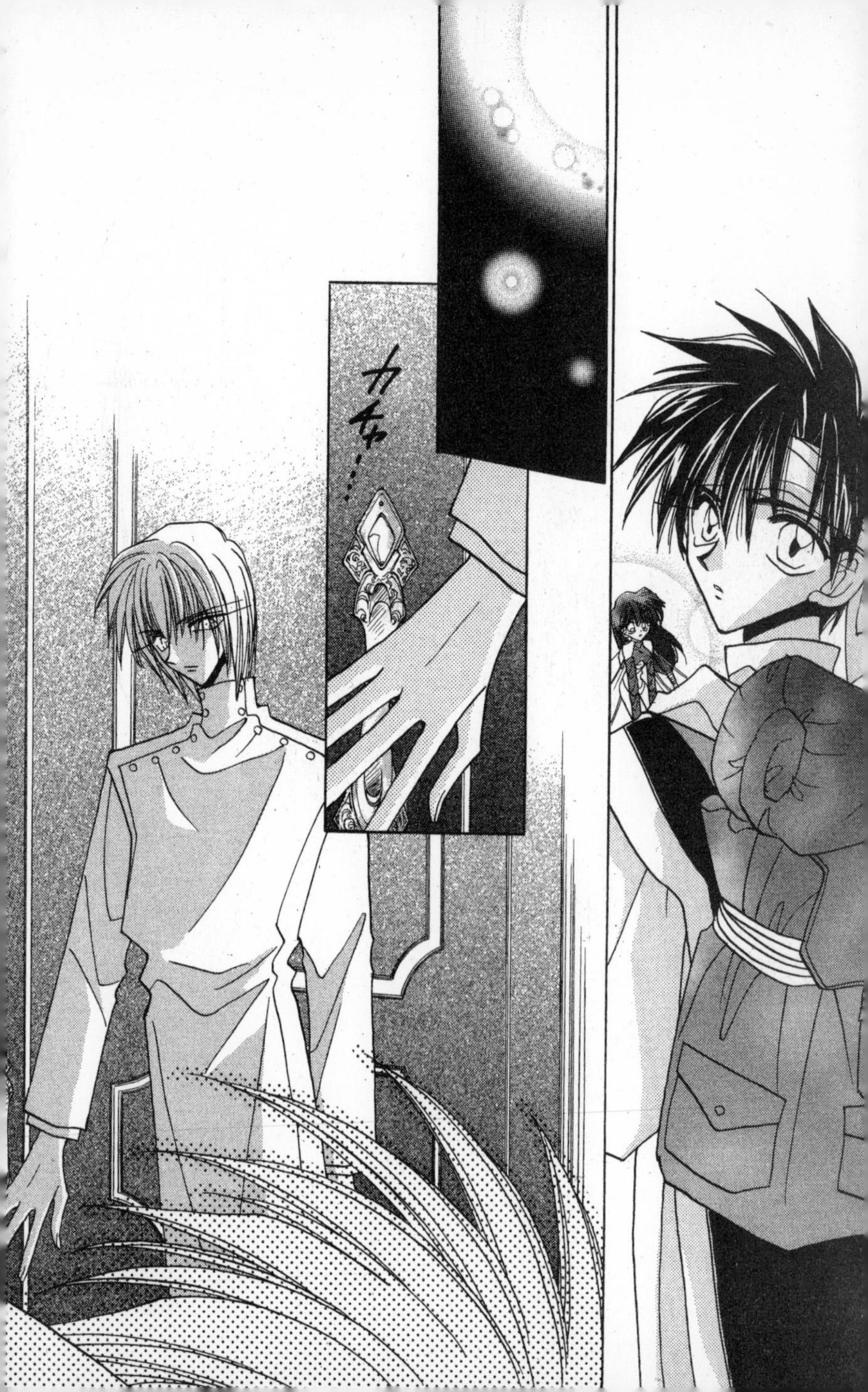
カチャ…

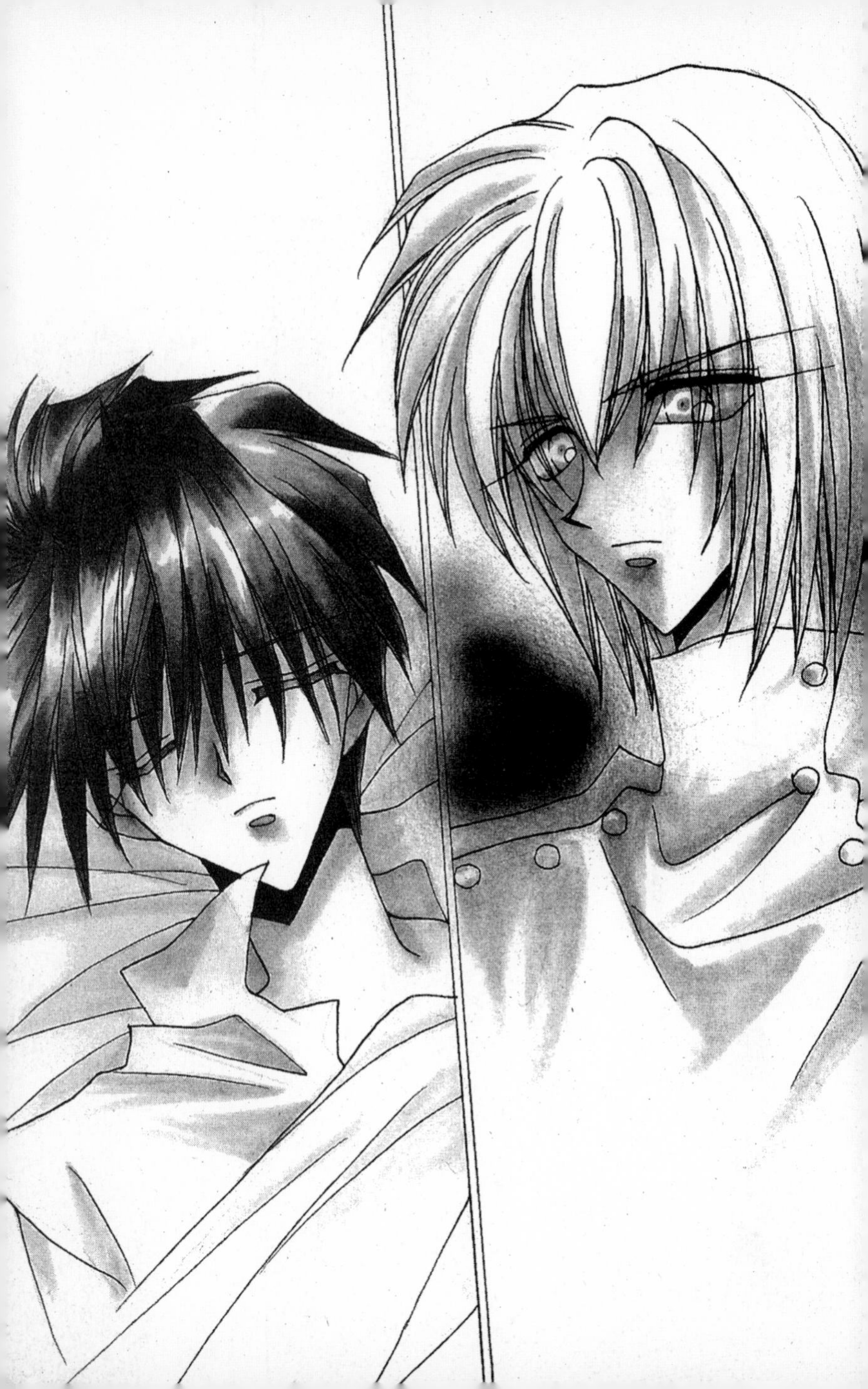

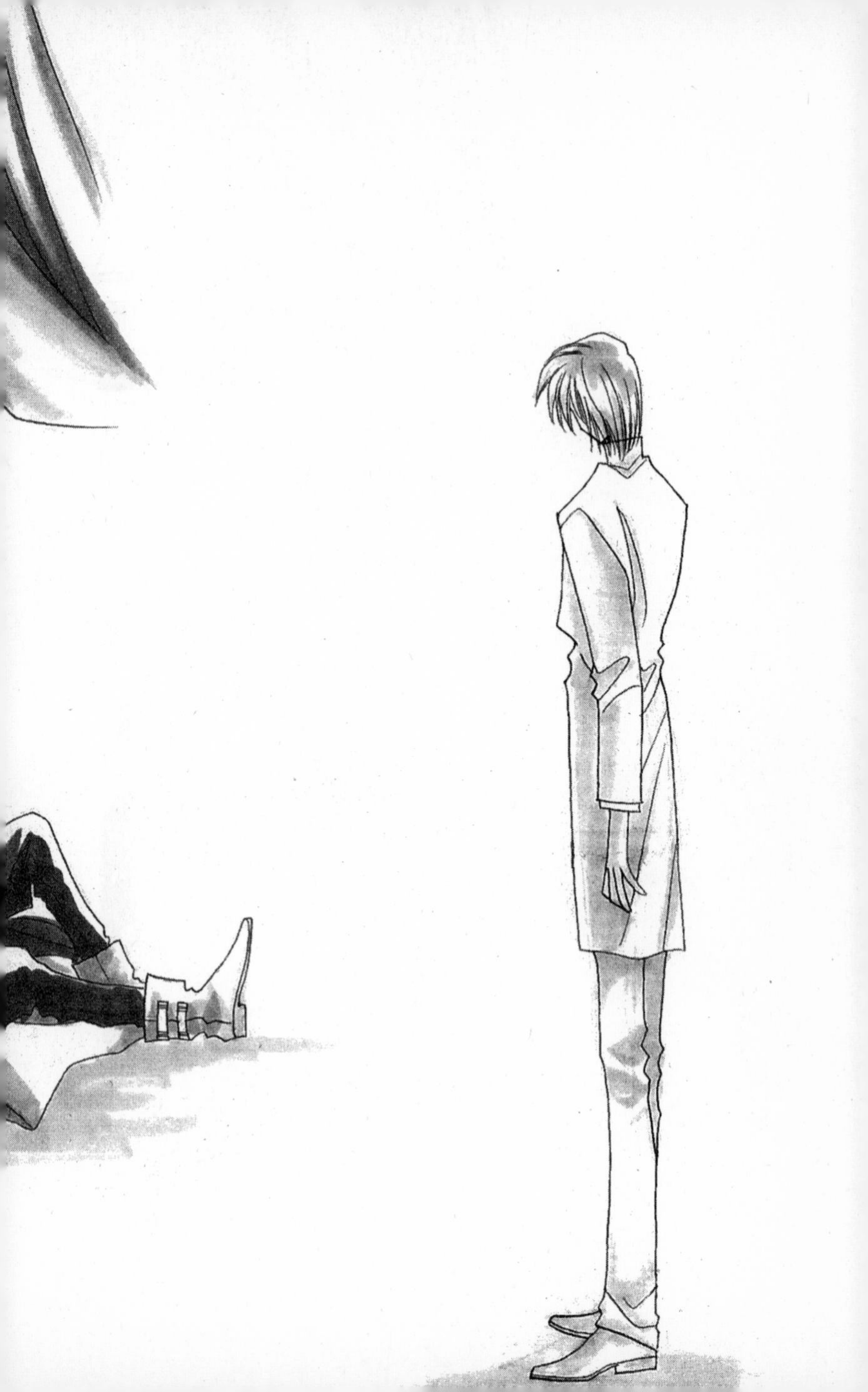

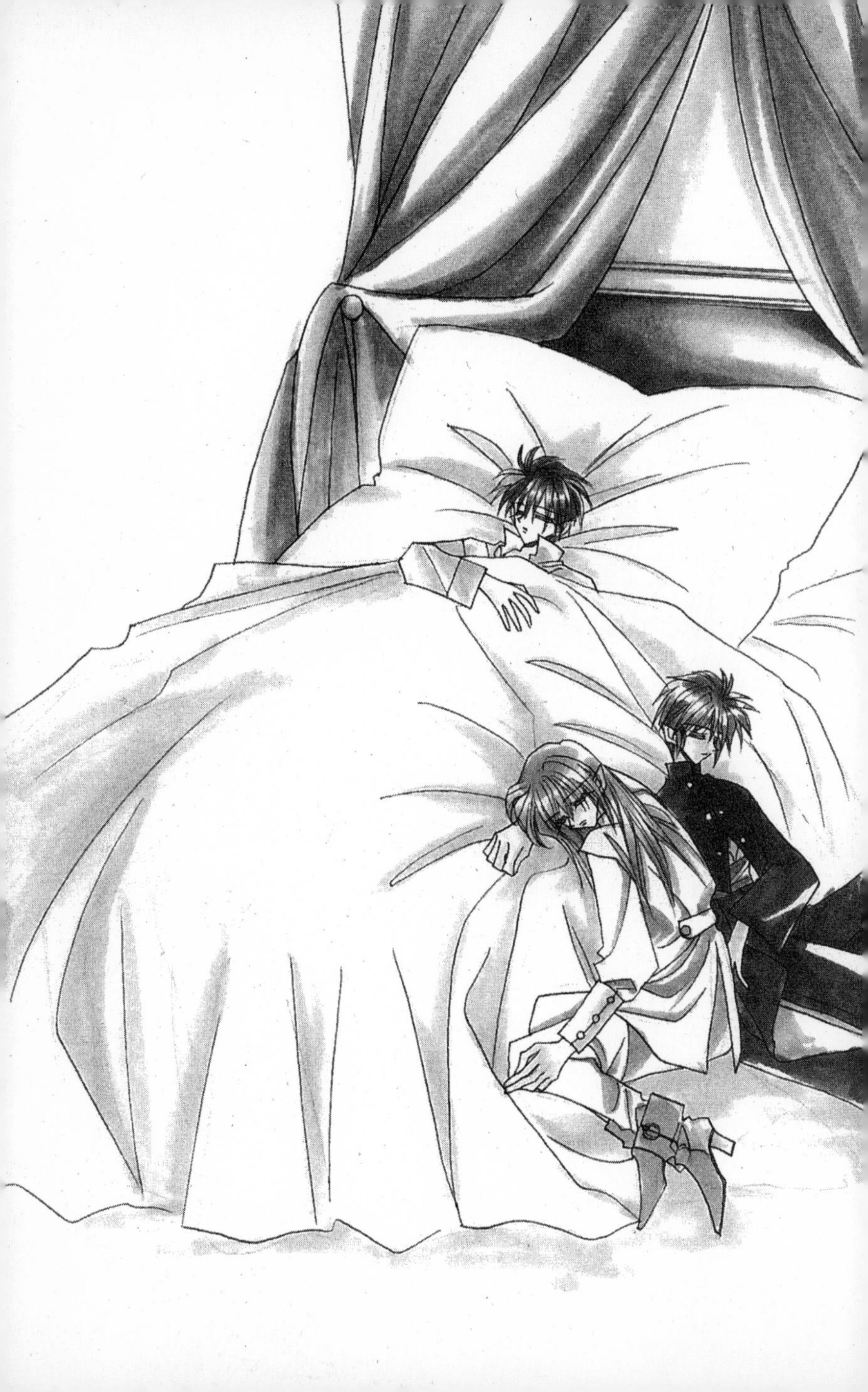

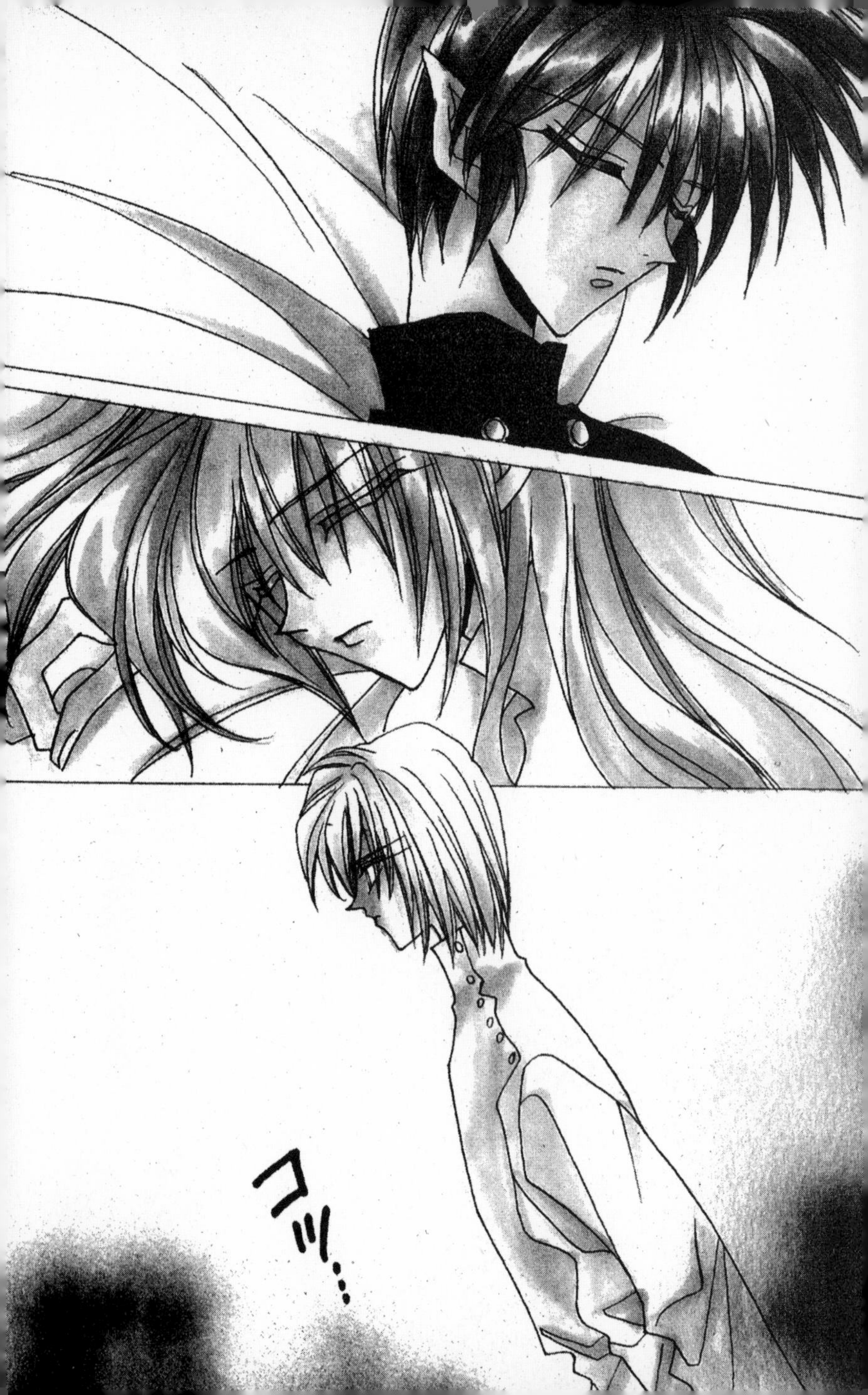
コツ…

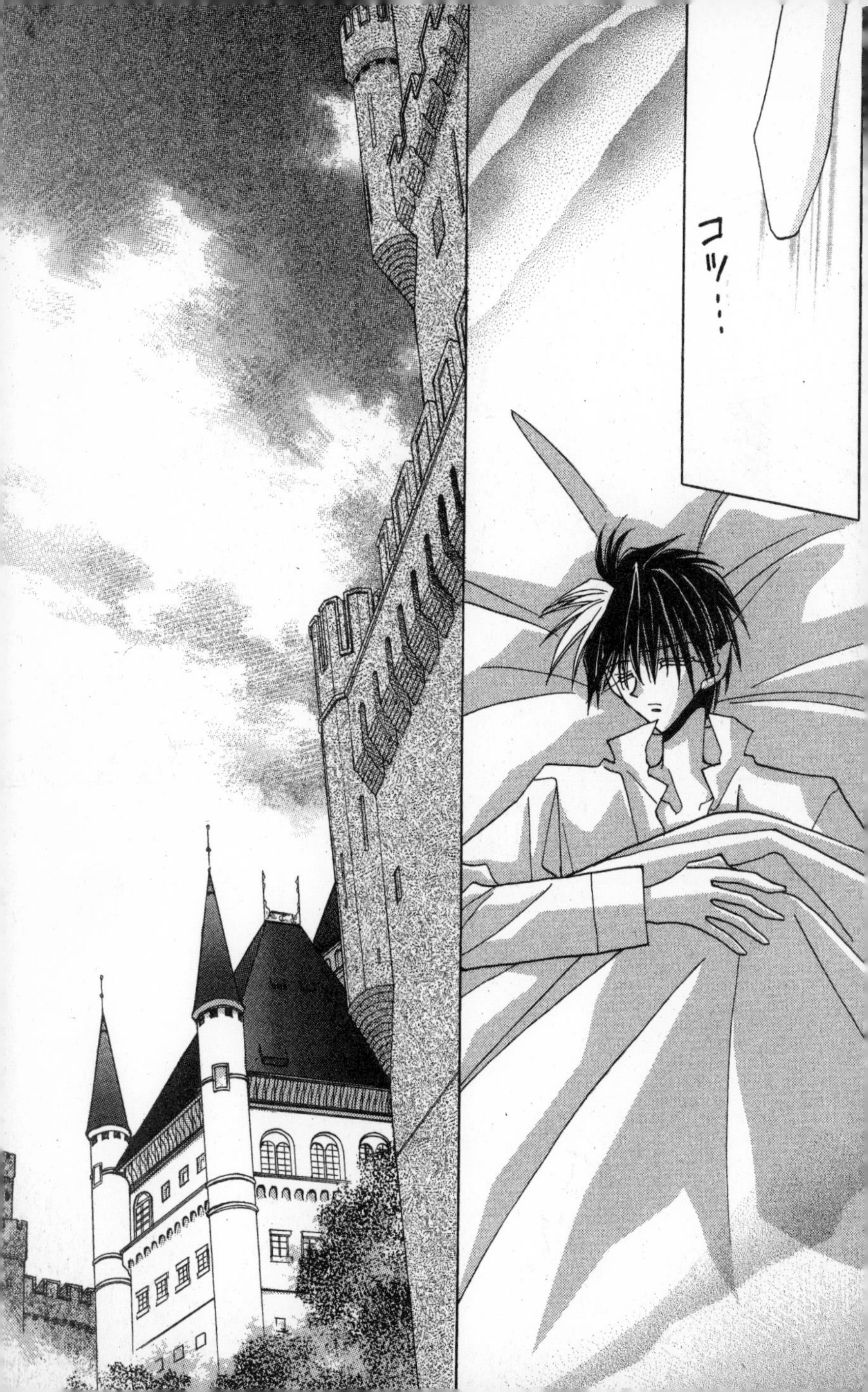
コツ…

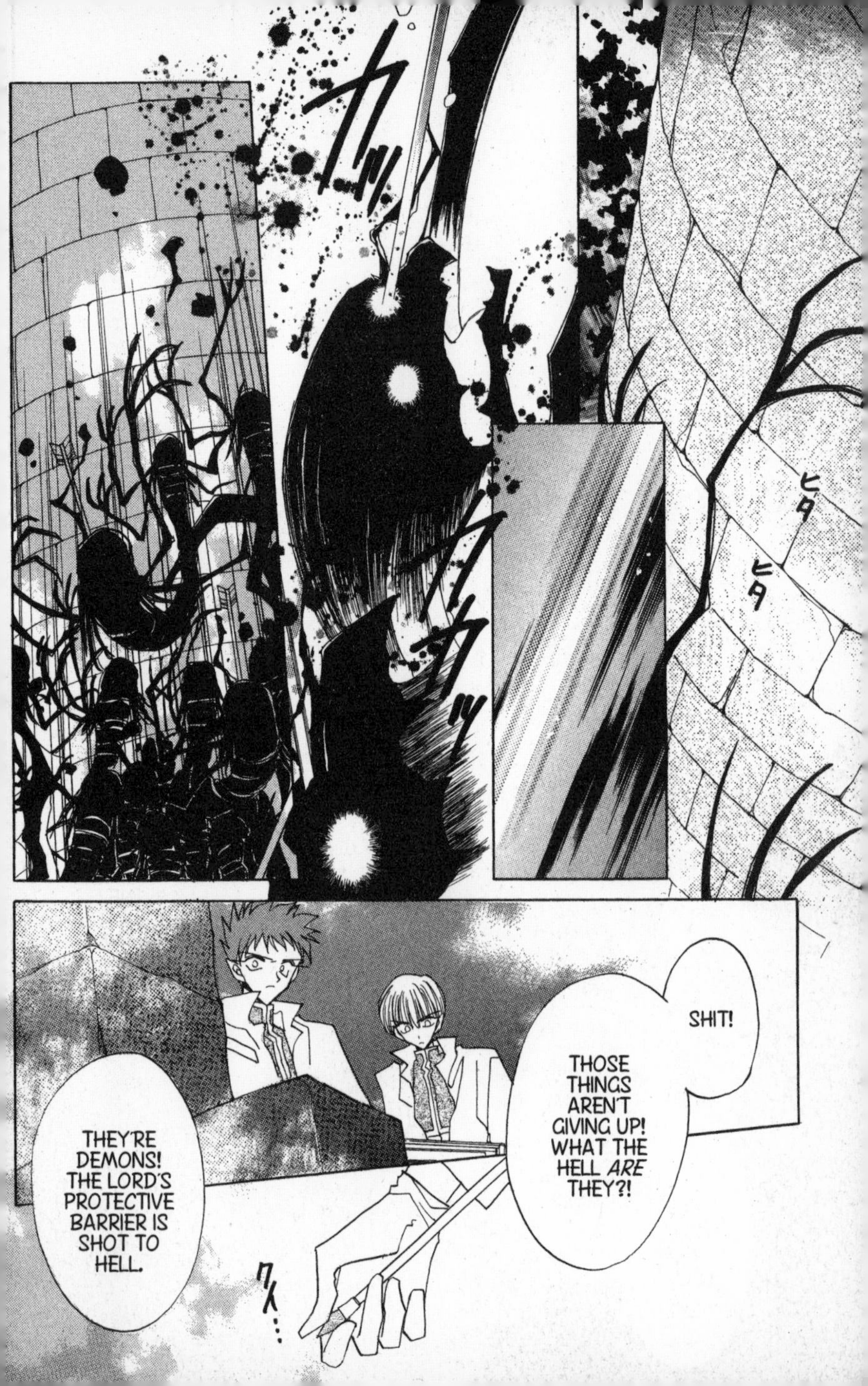
カッ
ヒタ
ヒタ
SHIT!
THOSE THINGS AREN'T GIVING UP! WHAT THE HELL *ARE* THEY?!
THEY'RE DEMONS! THE LORD'S PROTECTIVE BARRIER IS SHOT TO HELL.
クッ…

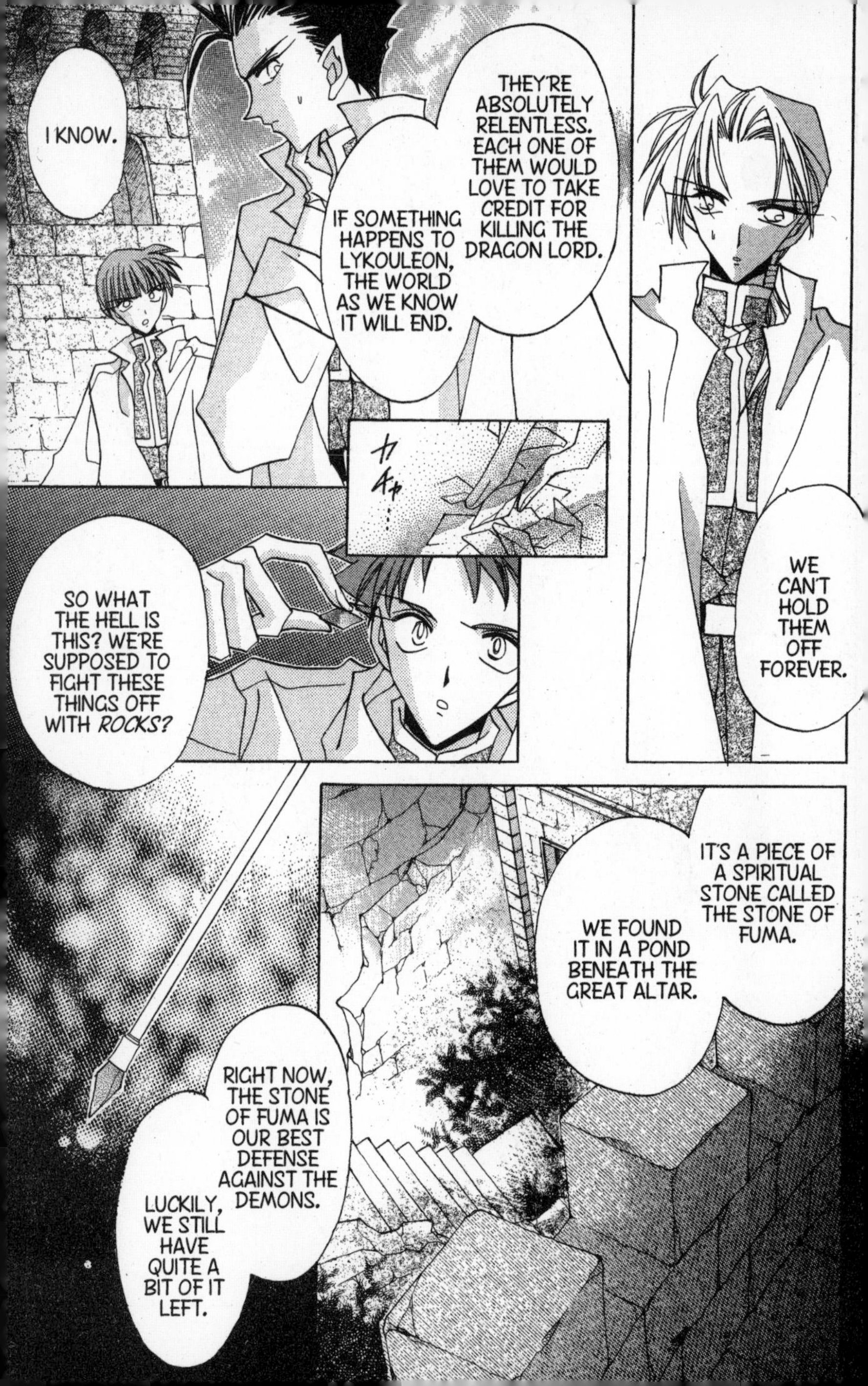
THEY'RE ABSOLUTELY RELENTLESS. EACH ONE OF THEM WOULD LOVE TO TAKE CREDIT FOR KILLING THE DRAGON LORD.
IF SOMETHING HAPPENS TO LYKOULEON, THE WORLD AS WE KNOW IT WILL END.
I KNOW.
WE CAN'T HOLD THEM OFF FOREVER.
カチャ…
SO WHAT THE HELL IS THIS? WE'RE SUPPOSED TO FIGHT THESE THINGS OFF WITH *ROCKS?*
IT'S A PIECE OF A SPIRITUAL STONE CALLED THE STONE OF FUMA.
WE FOUND IT IN A POND BENEATH THE GREAT ALTAR.
RIGHT NOW, THE STONE OF FUMA IS OUR BEST DEFENSE AGAINST THE DEMONS.
LUCKILY, WE STILL HAVE QUITE A BIT OF IT LEFT.

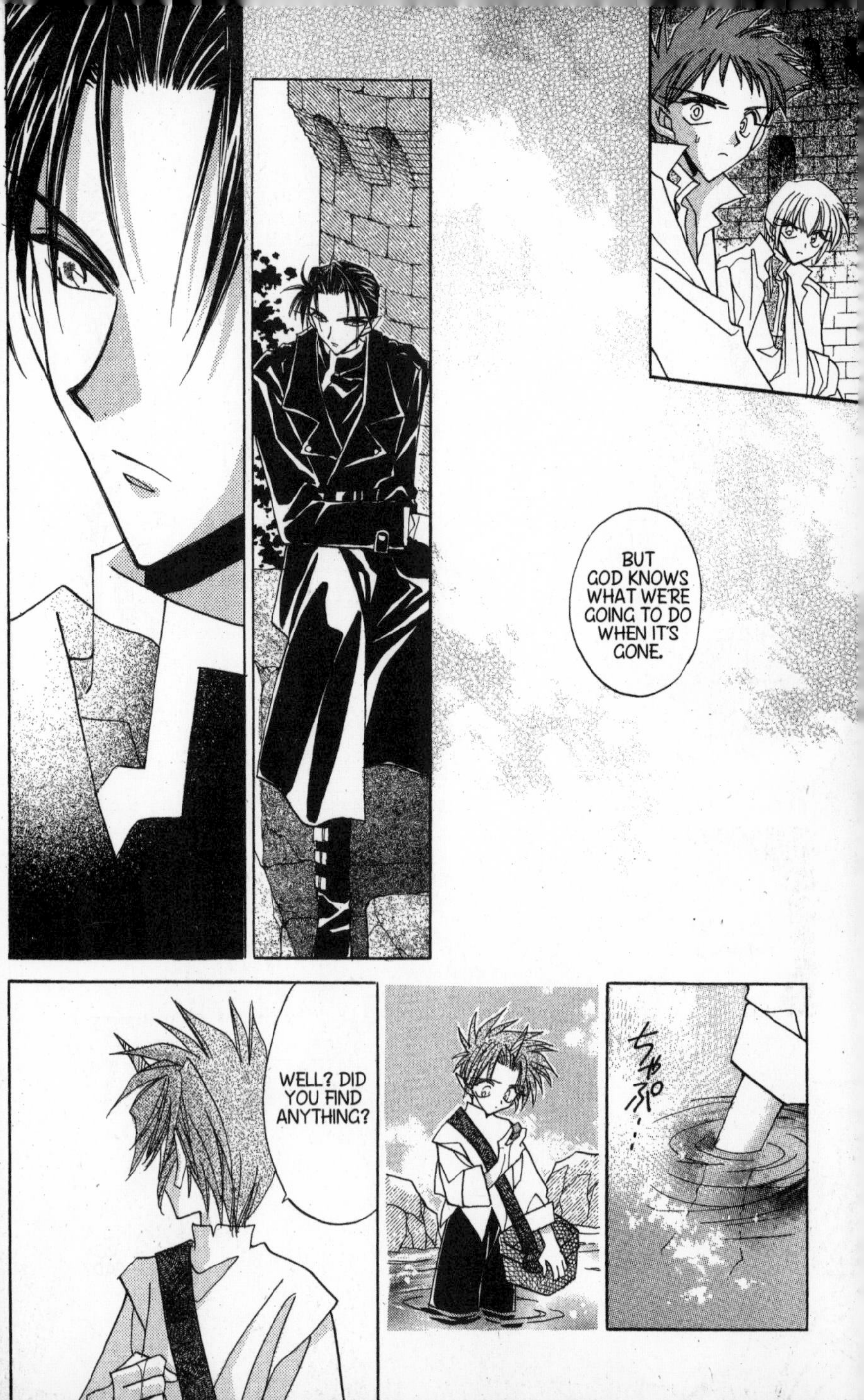
BUT GOD KNOWS WHAT WE'RE GOING TO DO WHEN IT'S GONE.
ちゃぷ…
WELL? DID YOU FIND ANYTHING?

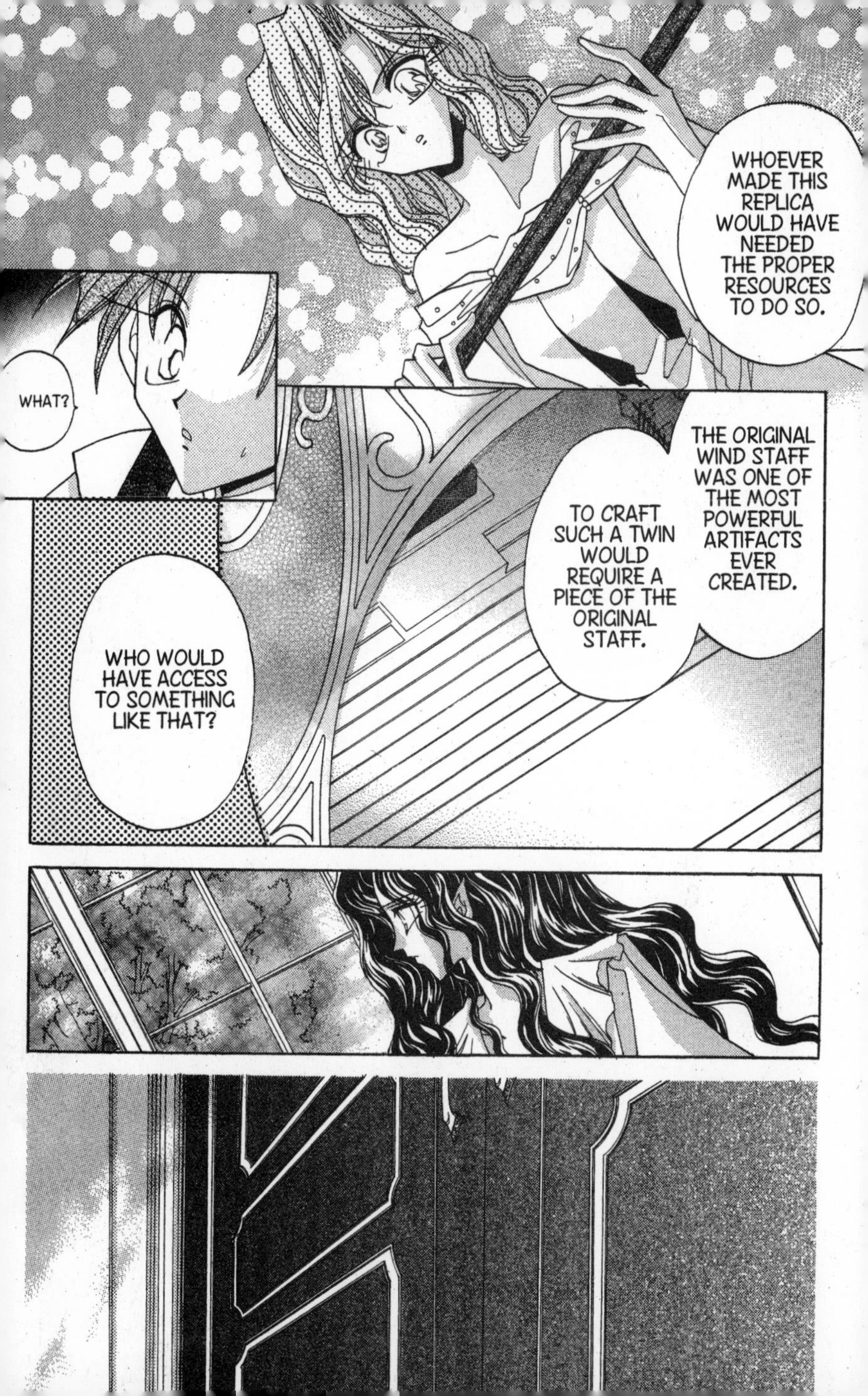
WHOEVER MADE THIS REPLICA WOULD HAVE NEEDED THE PROPER RESOURCES TO DO SO.
WHAT?
THE ORIGINAL WIND STAFF WAS ONE OF THE MOST POWERFUL ARTIFACTS EVER CREATED.
TO CRAFT SUCH A TWIN WOULD REQUIRE A PIECE OF THE ORIGINAL STAFF.
WHO WOULD HAVE ACCESS TO SOMETHING LIKE THAT?

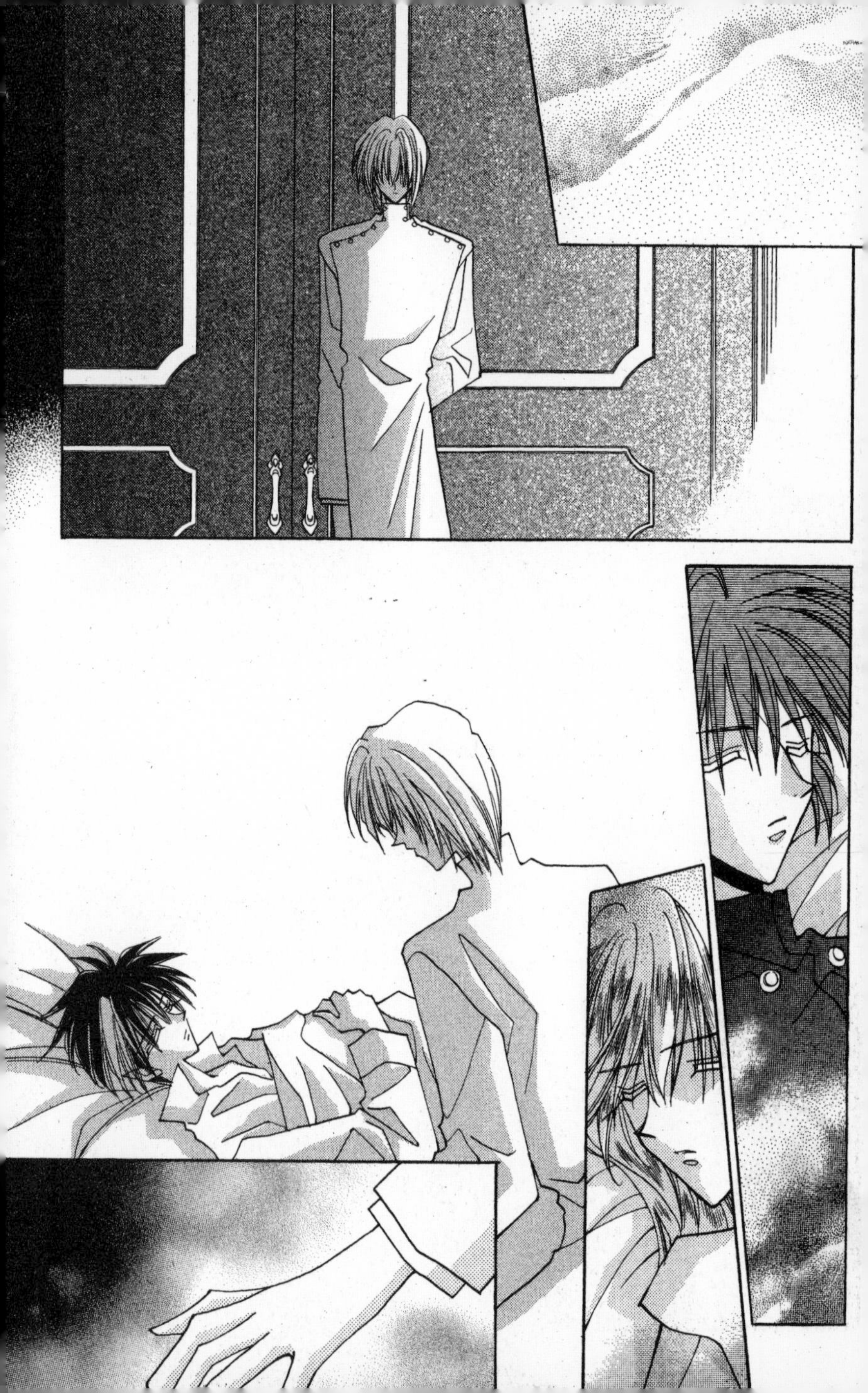

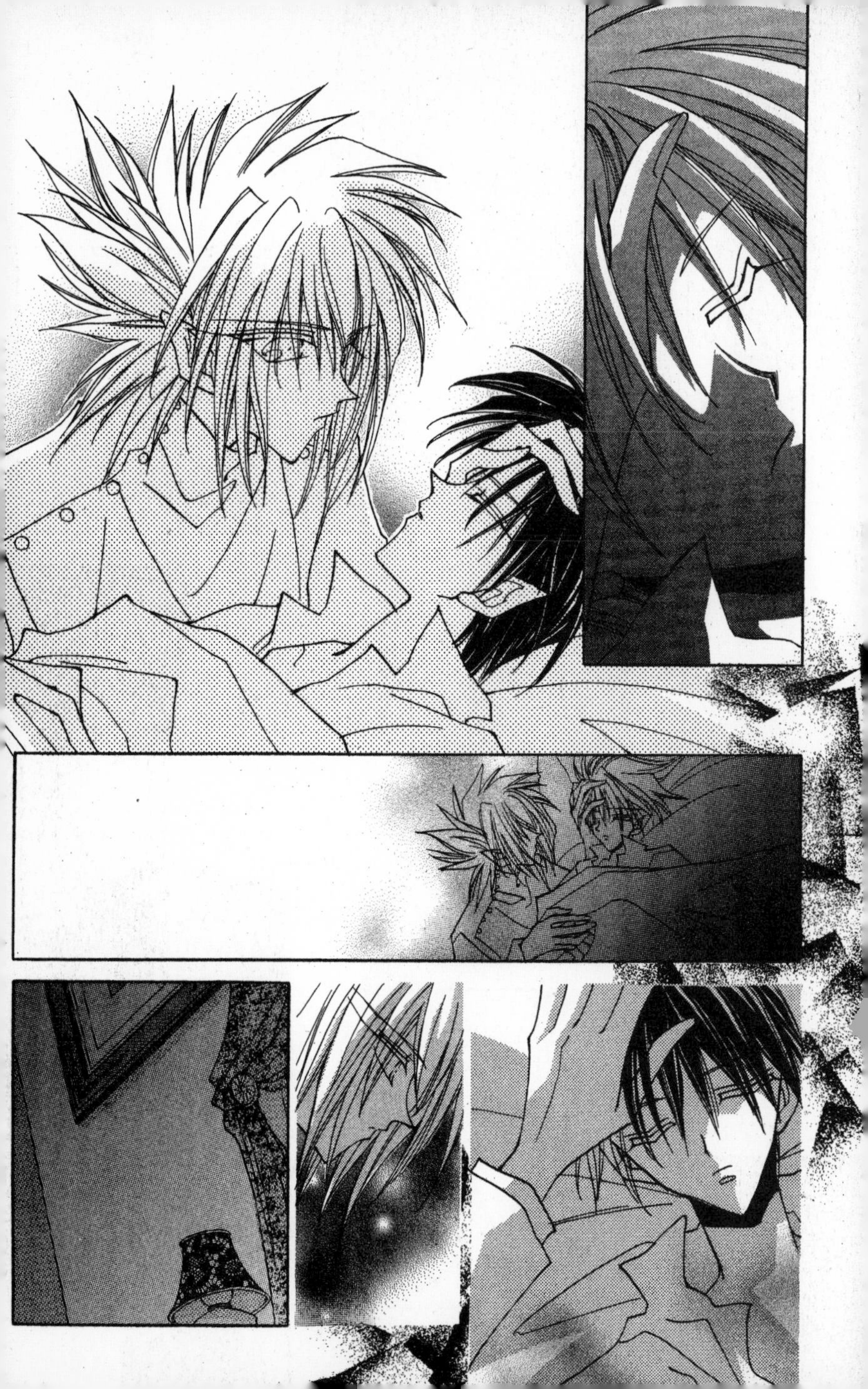

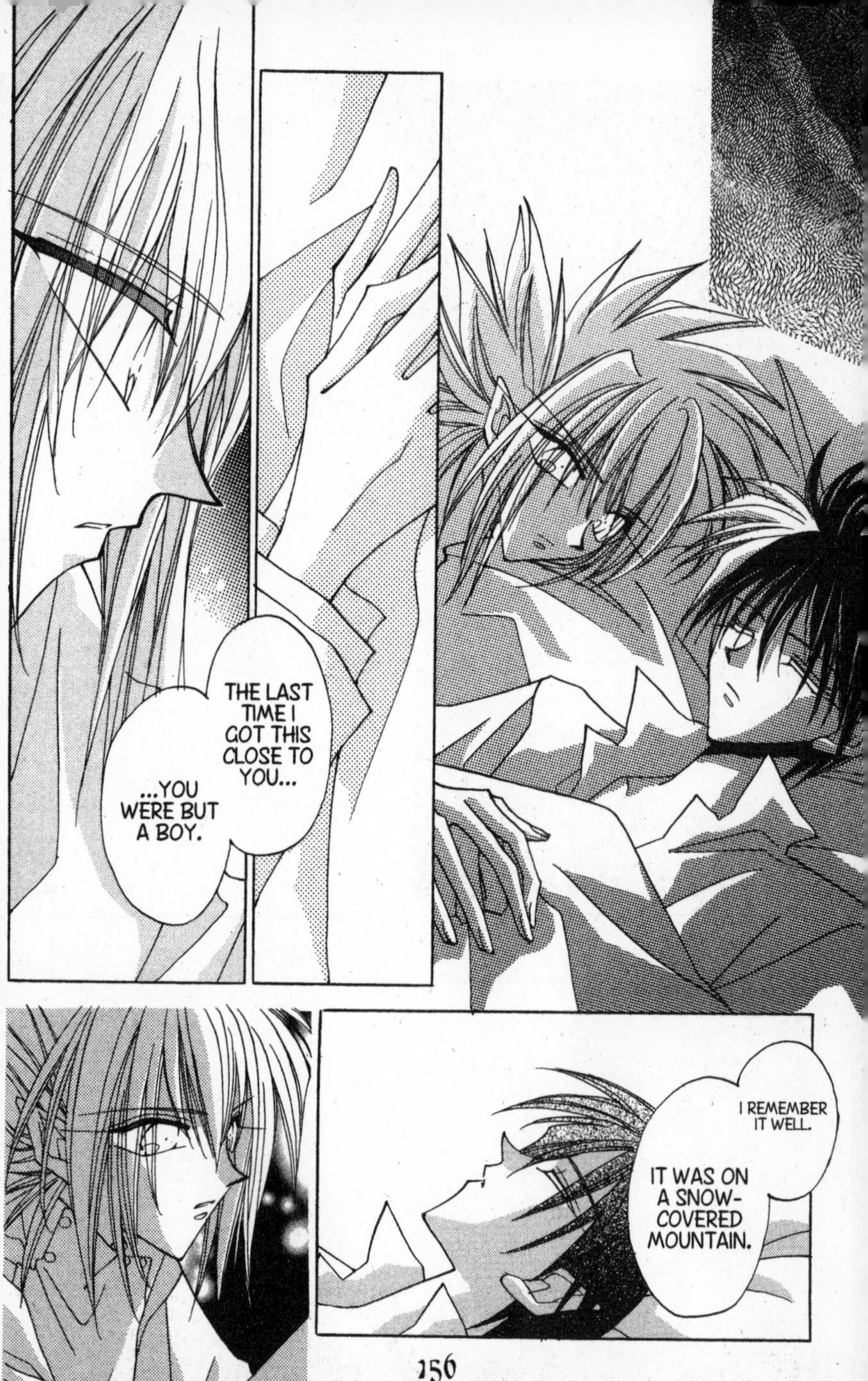
THE LAST TIME I GOT THIS CLOSE TO YOU...
...YOU WERE BUT A BOY.
I REMEMBER IT WELL.
IT WAS ON A SNOW-COVERED MOUNTAIN.

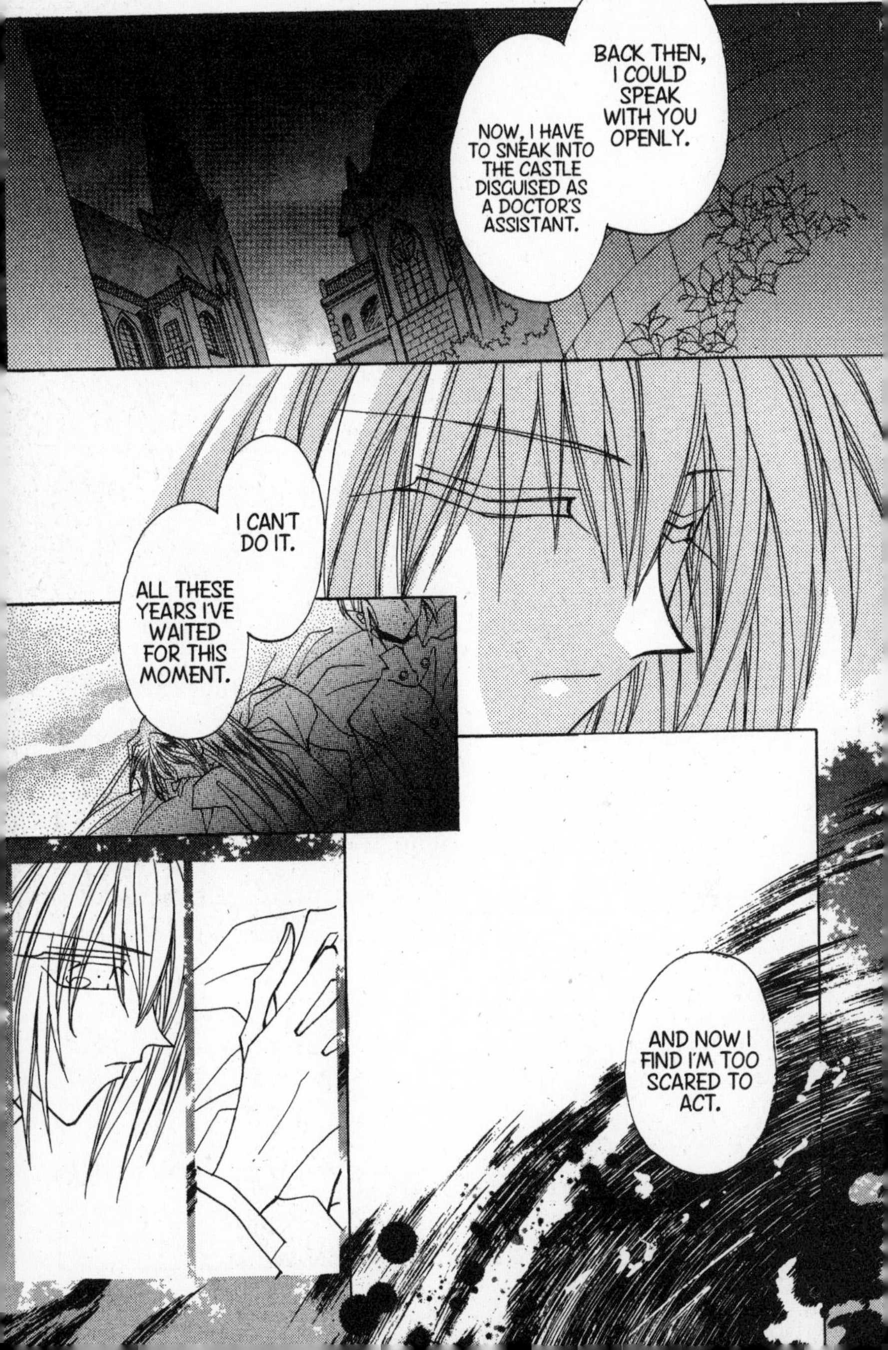
BACK THEN, I COULD SPEAK WITH YOU OPENLY.
NOW, I HAVE TO SNEAK INTO THE CASTLE DISGUISED AS A DOCTOR'S ASSISTANT.
I CAN'T DO IT.
ALL THESE YEARS I'VE WAITED FOR THIS MOMENT.
AND NOW I FIND I'M TOO SCARED TO ACT.

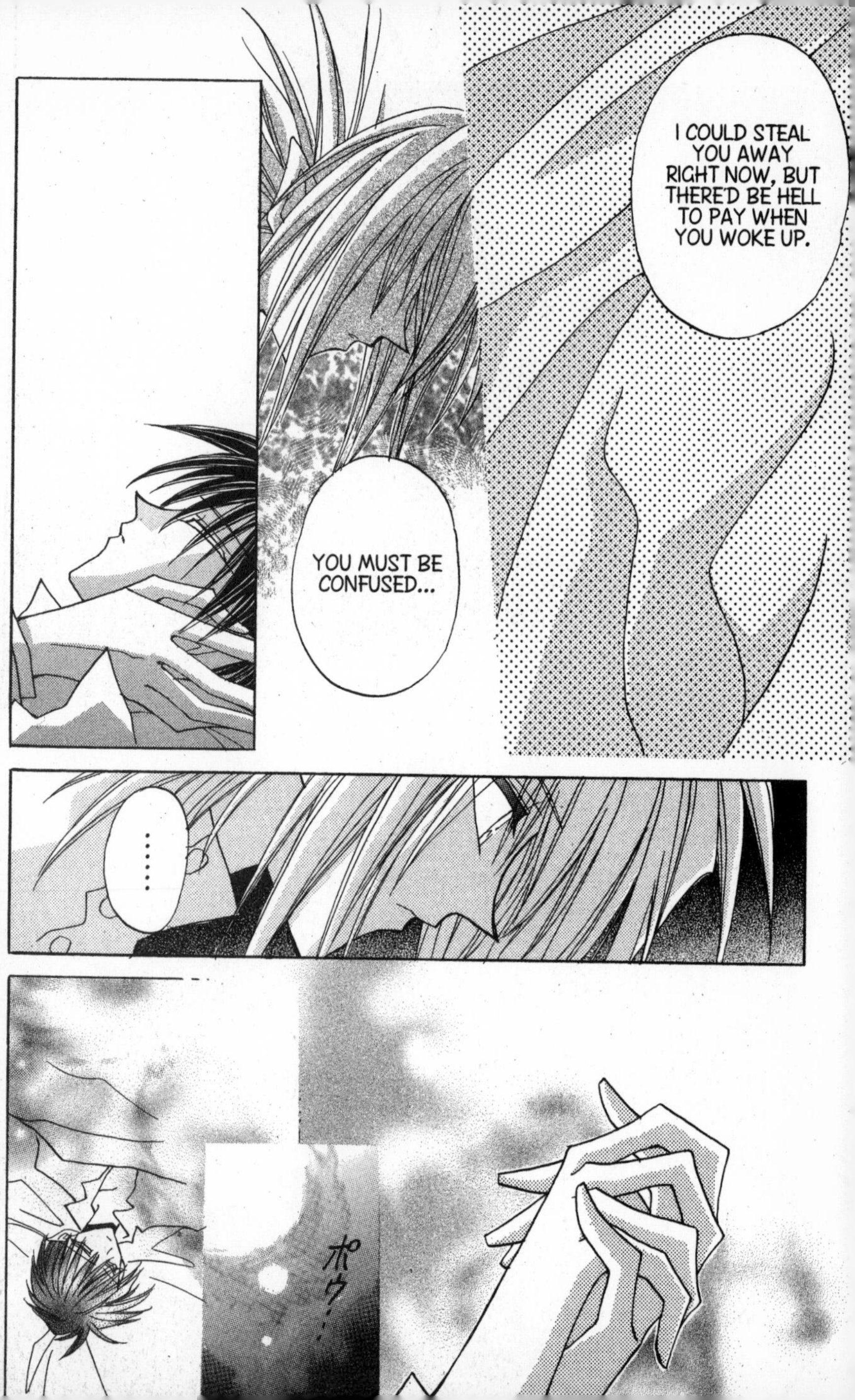
I COULD STEAL YOU AWAY RIGHT NOW, BUT THERE'D BE HELL TO PAY WHEN YOU WOKE UP.
YOU MUST BE CONFUSED...
......
ポウ…

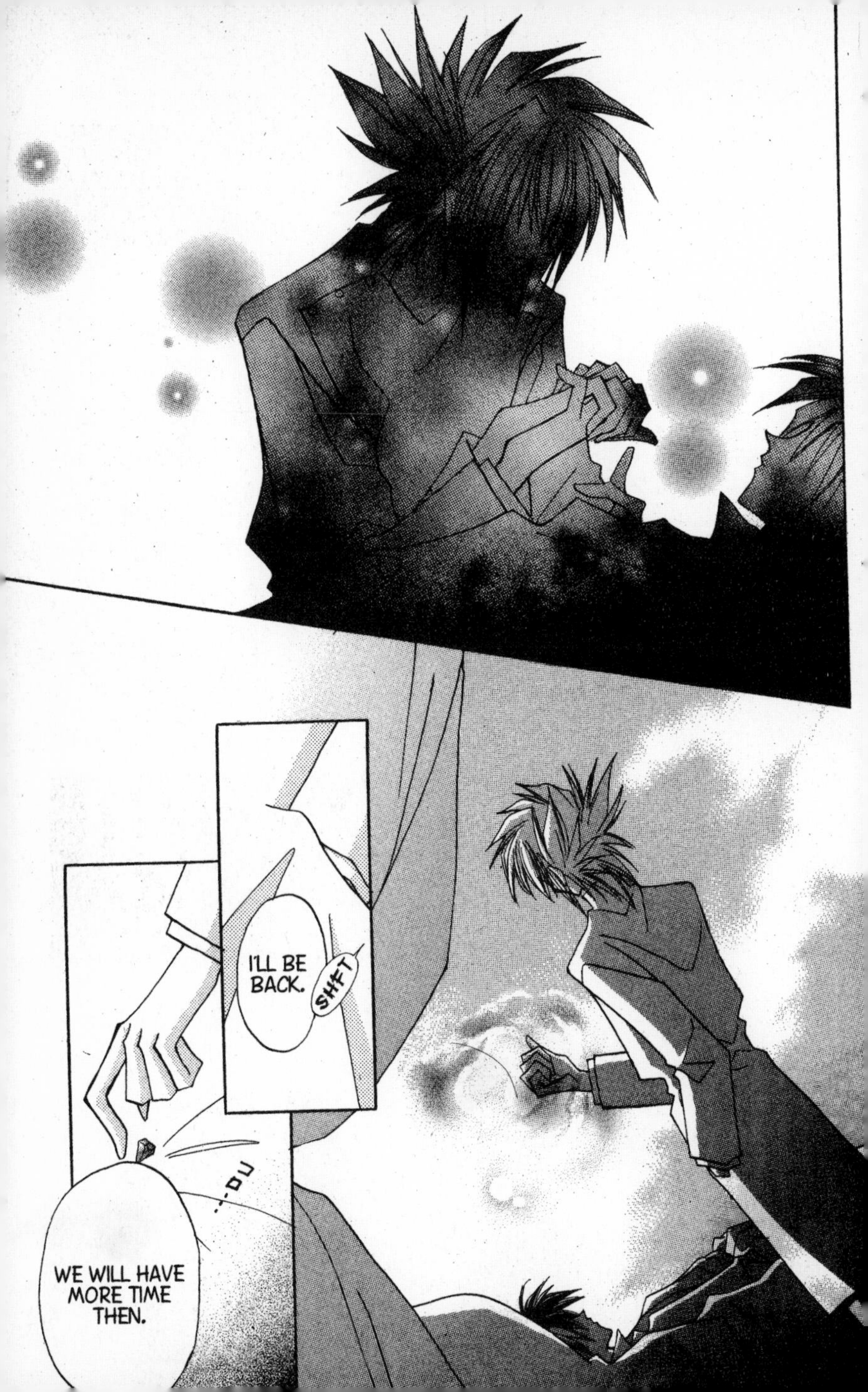
I'LL BE BACK.
SHFT
...DU
WE WILL HAVE MORE TIME THEN.

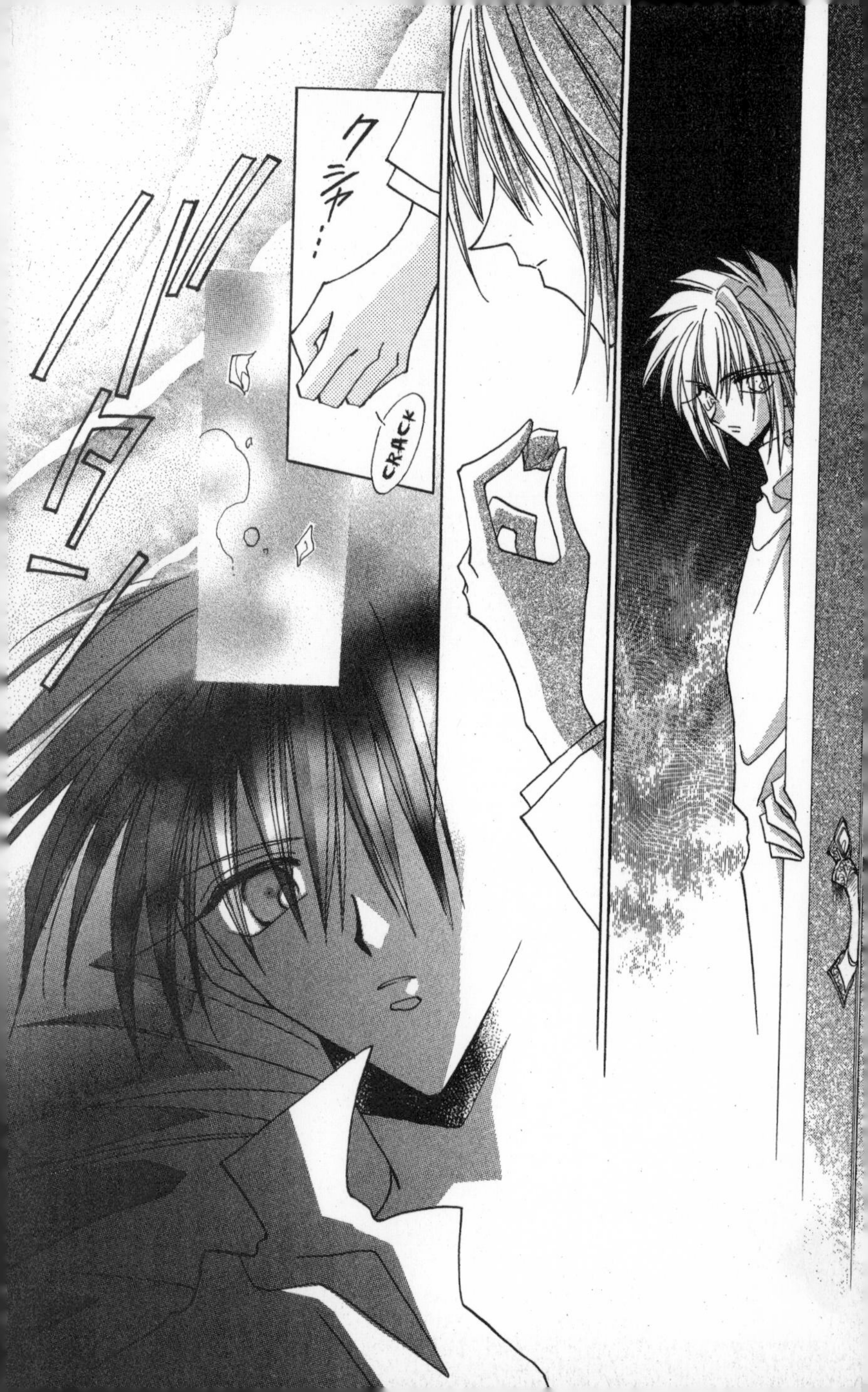
クシャ…
CRACK
バタン

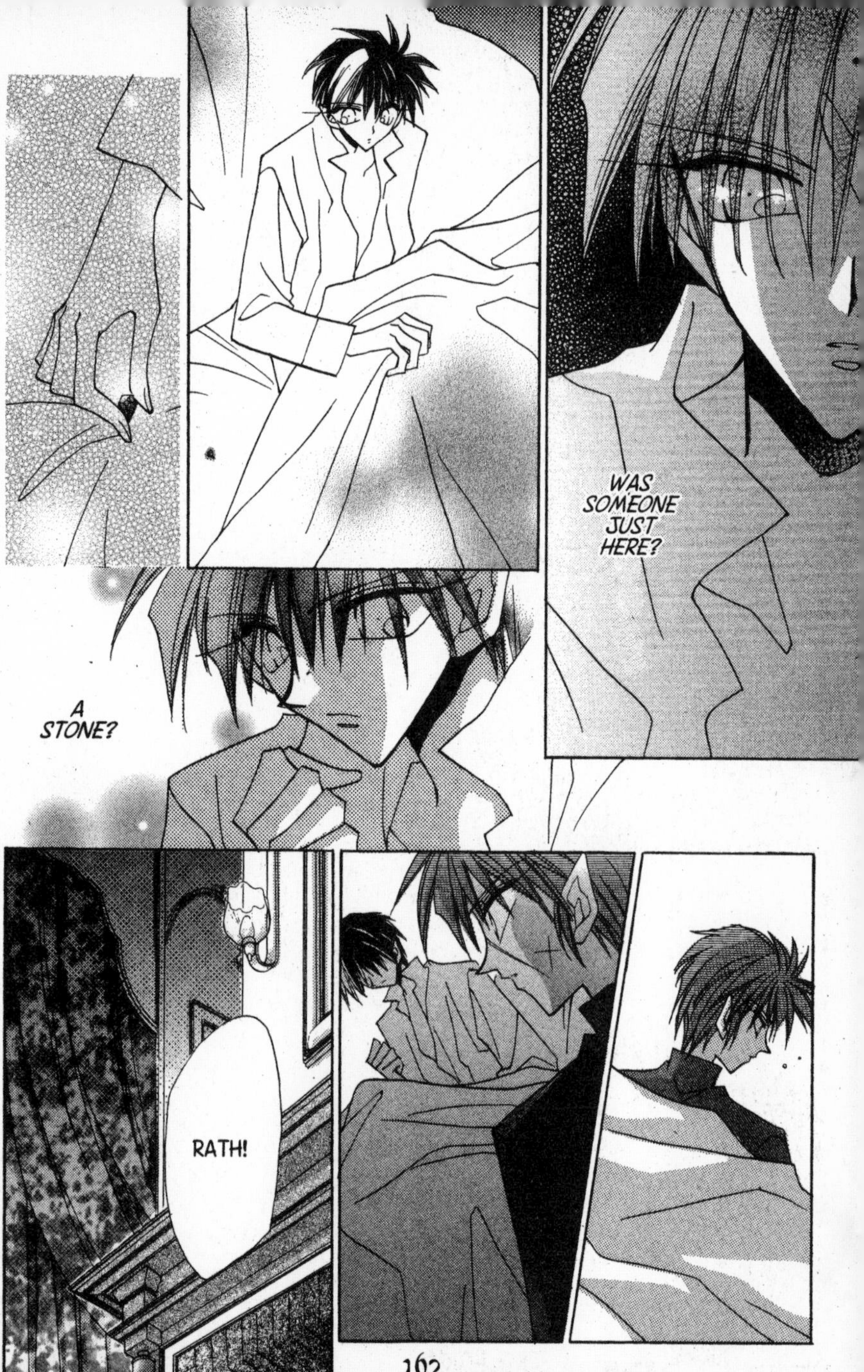
WAS SOMEONE JUST HERE?
A STONE?
RATH!

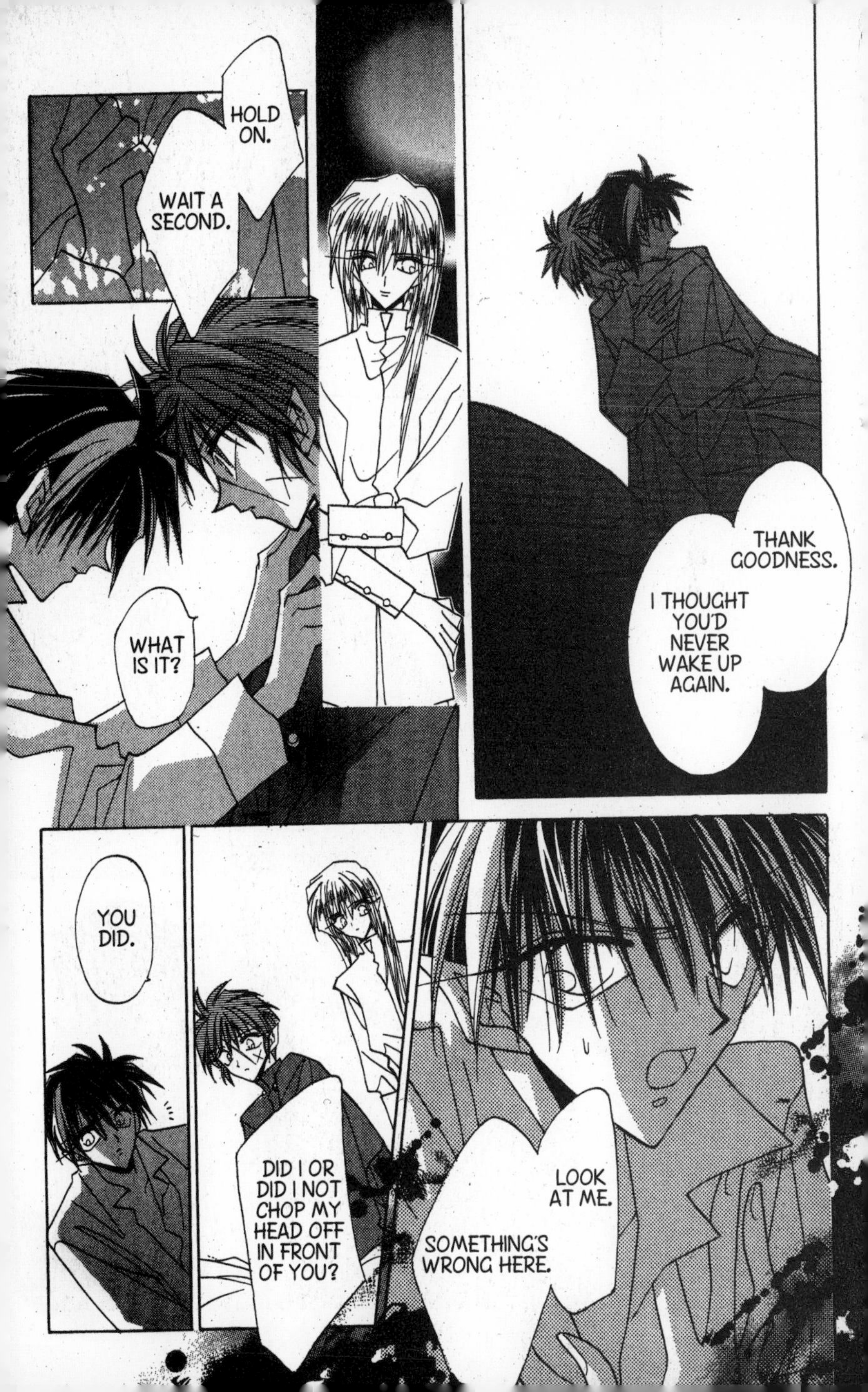
THANK GOODNESS.
I THOUGHT YOU'D NEVER WAKE UP AGAIN.
HOLD ON.
WAIT A SECOND.
WHAT IS IT?
LOOK AT ME.
SOMETHING'S WRONG HERE.
DID I OR DID I NOT CHOP MY HEAD OFF IN FRONT OF YOU?
YOU DID.

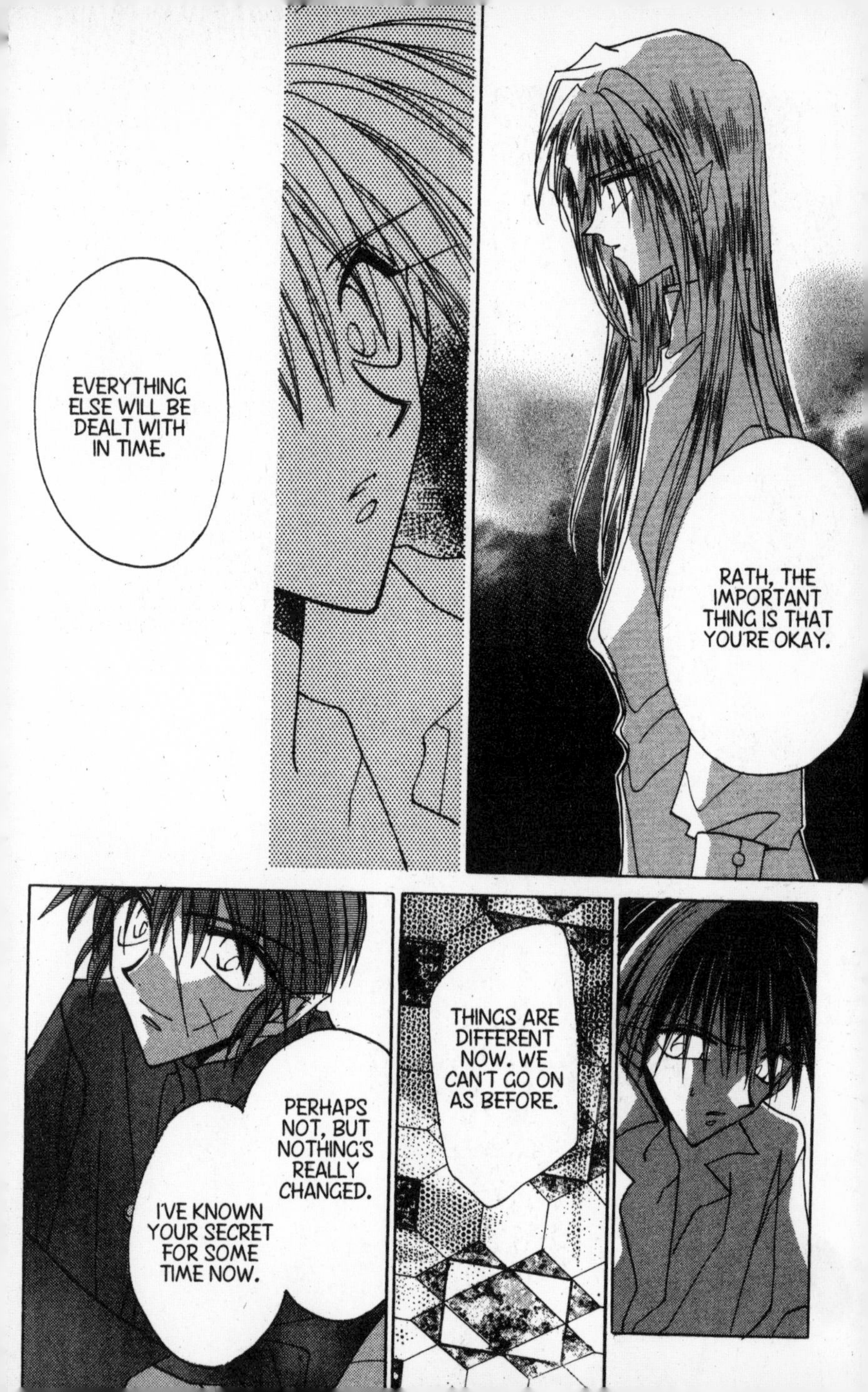
RATH, THE IMPORTANT THING IS THAT YOU'RE OKAY.
EVERYTHING ELSE WILL BE DEALT WITH IN TIME.
THINGS ARE DIFFERENT NOW. WE CAN'T GO ON AS BEFORE.
PERHAPS NOT, BUT NOTHING'S REALLY CHANGED.
I'VE KNOWN YOUR SECRET FOR SOME TIME NOW.

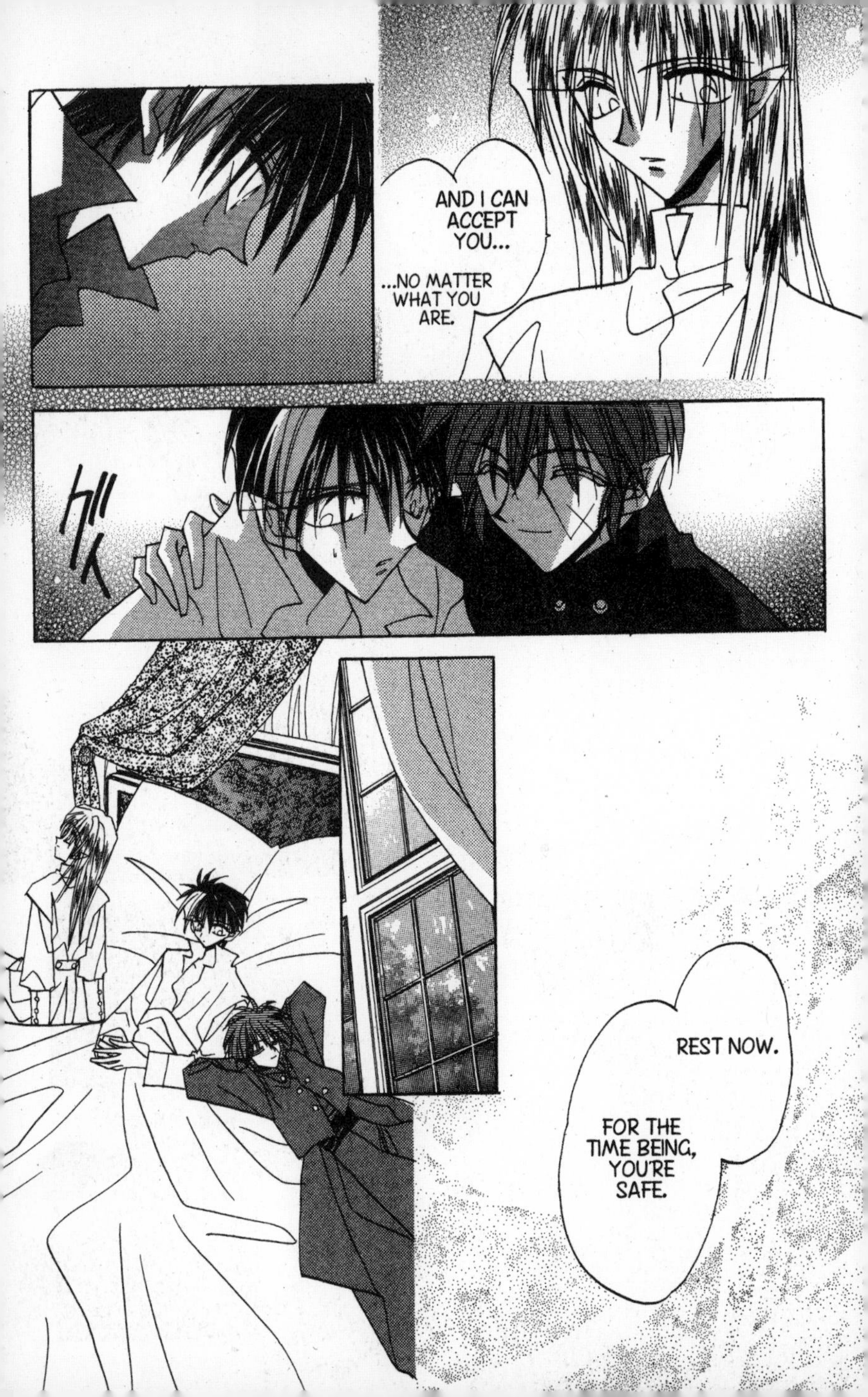
AND I CAN ACCEPT YOU...
...NO MATTER WHAT YOU ARE.
グイ
REST NOW.
FOR THE TIME BEING, YOU'RE SAFE.

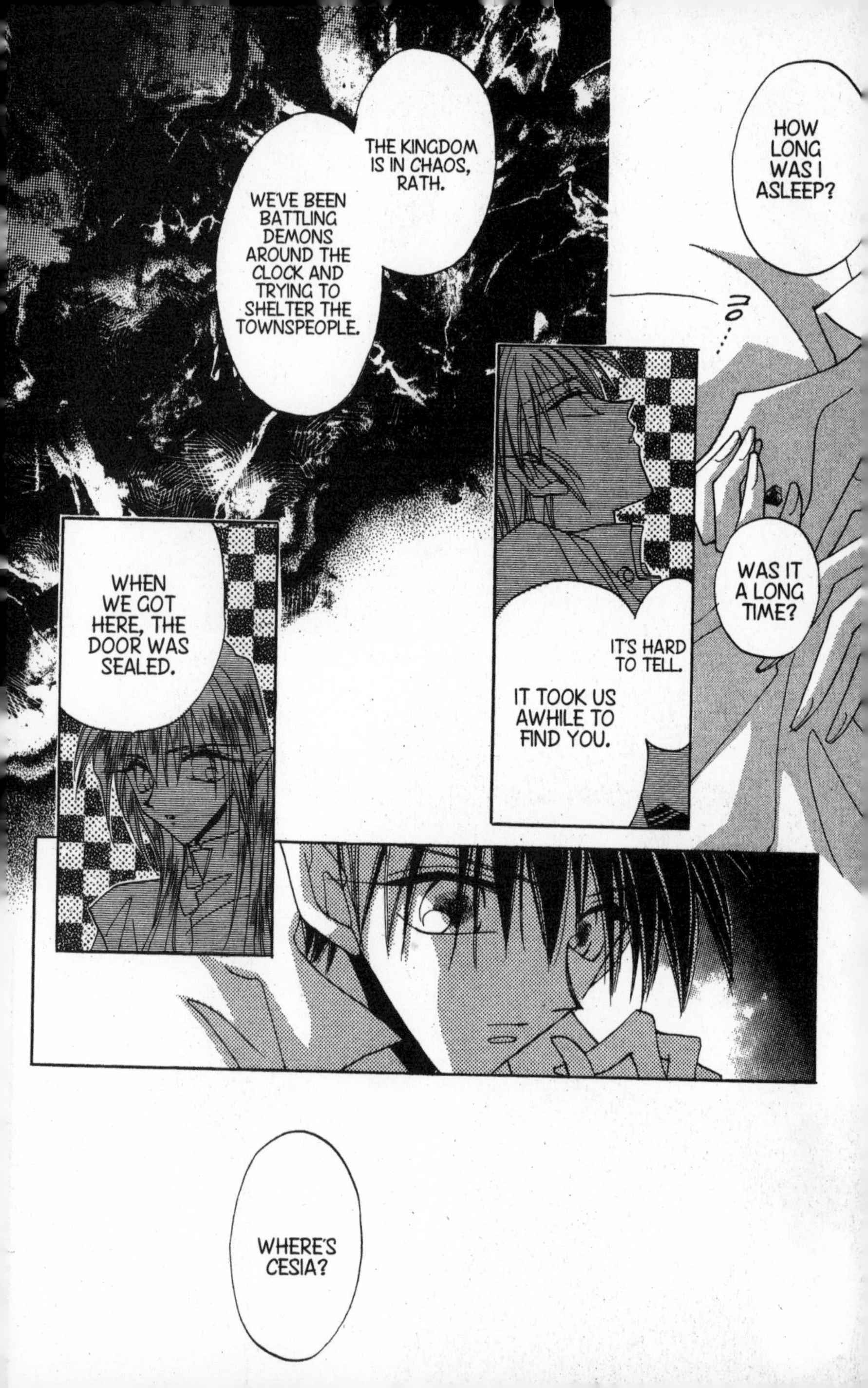
HOW LONG WAS I ASLEEP?
WAS IT A LONG TIME?
IT'S HARD TO TELL.
IT TOOK US AWHILE TO FIND YOU.
WHEN WE GOT HERE, THE DOOR WAS SEALED.
THE KINGDOM IS IN CHAOS, RATH.
WE'VE BEEN BATTLING DEMONS AROUND THE CLOCK AND TRYING TO SHELTER THE TOWNSPEOPLE.
WHERE'S CESIA?

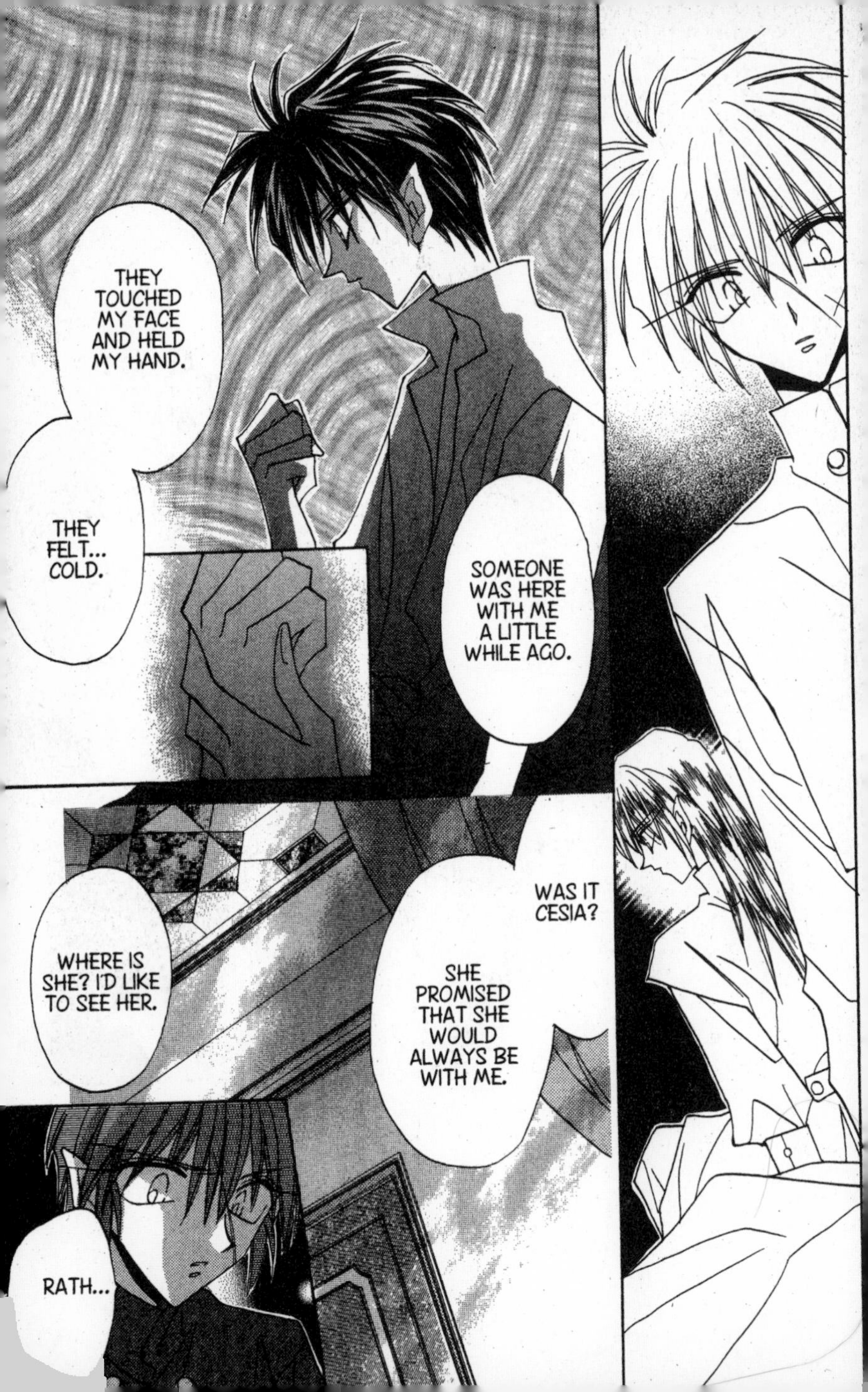
SOMEONE WAS HERE WITH ME A LITTLE WHILE AGO.
THEY TOUCHED MY FACE AND HELD MY HAND.
THEY FELT... COLD.
WAS IT CESIA?
SHE PROMISED THAT SHE WOULD ALWAYS BE WITH ME.
WHERE IS SHE? I'D LIKE TO SEE HER.
RATH...

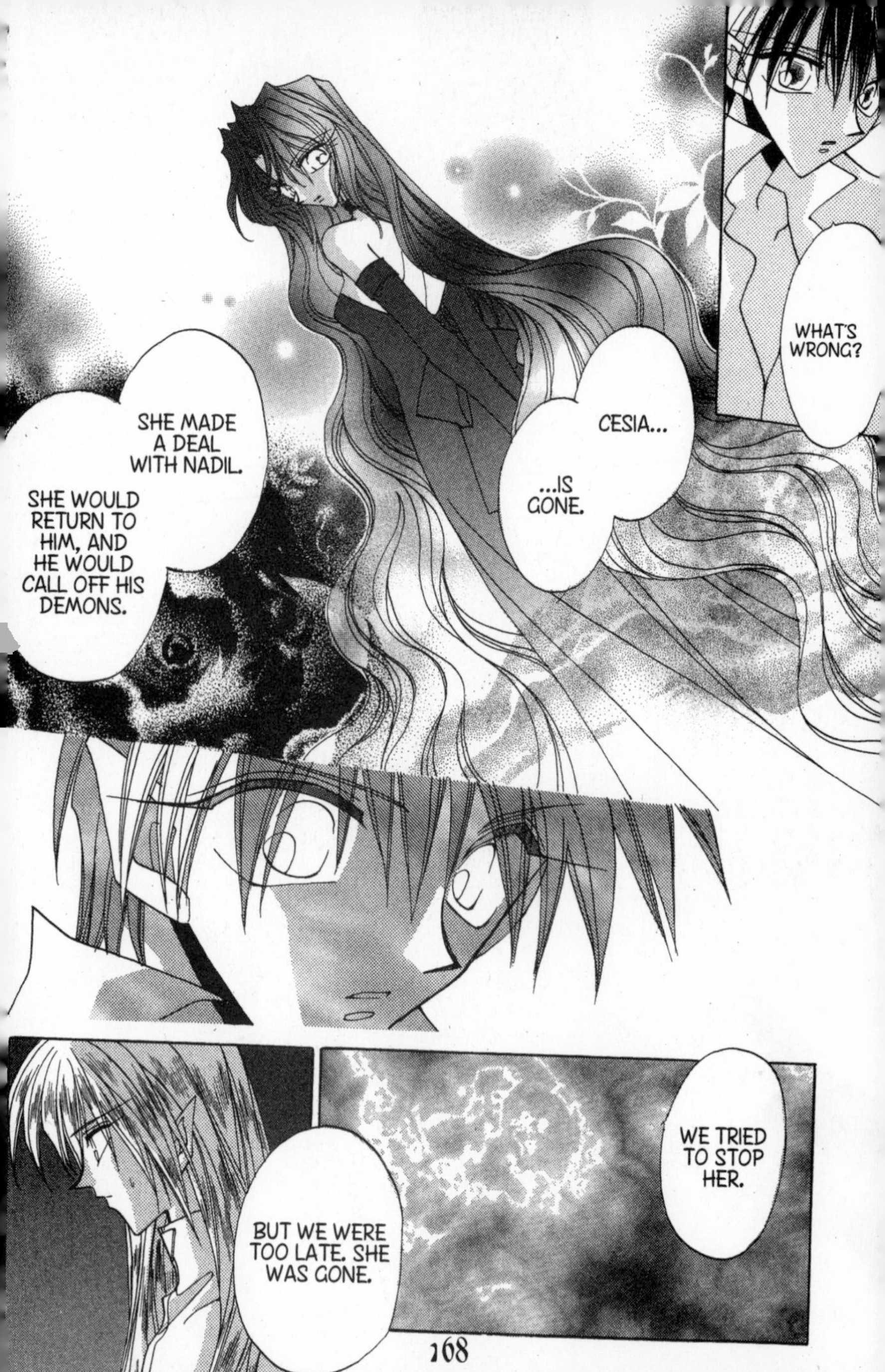
WHAT'S WRONG?
CESIA...
...IS GONE.
SHE MADE A DEAL WITH NADIL.
SHE WOULD RETURN TO HIM, AND HE WOULD CALL OFF HIS DEMONS.
WE TRIED TO STOP HER.
BUT WE WERE TOO LATE. SHE WAS GONE.

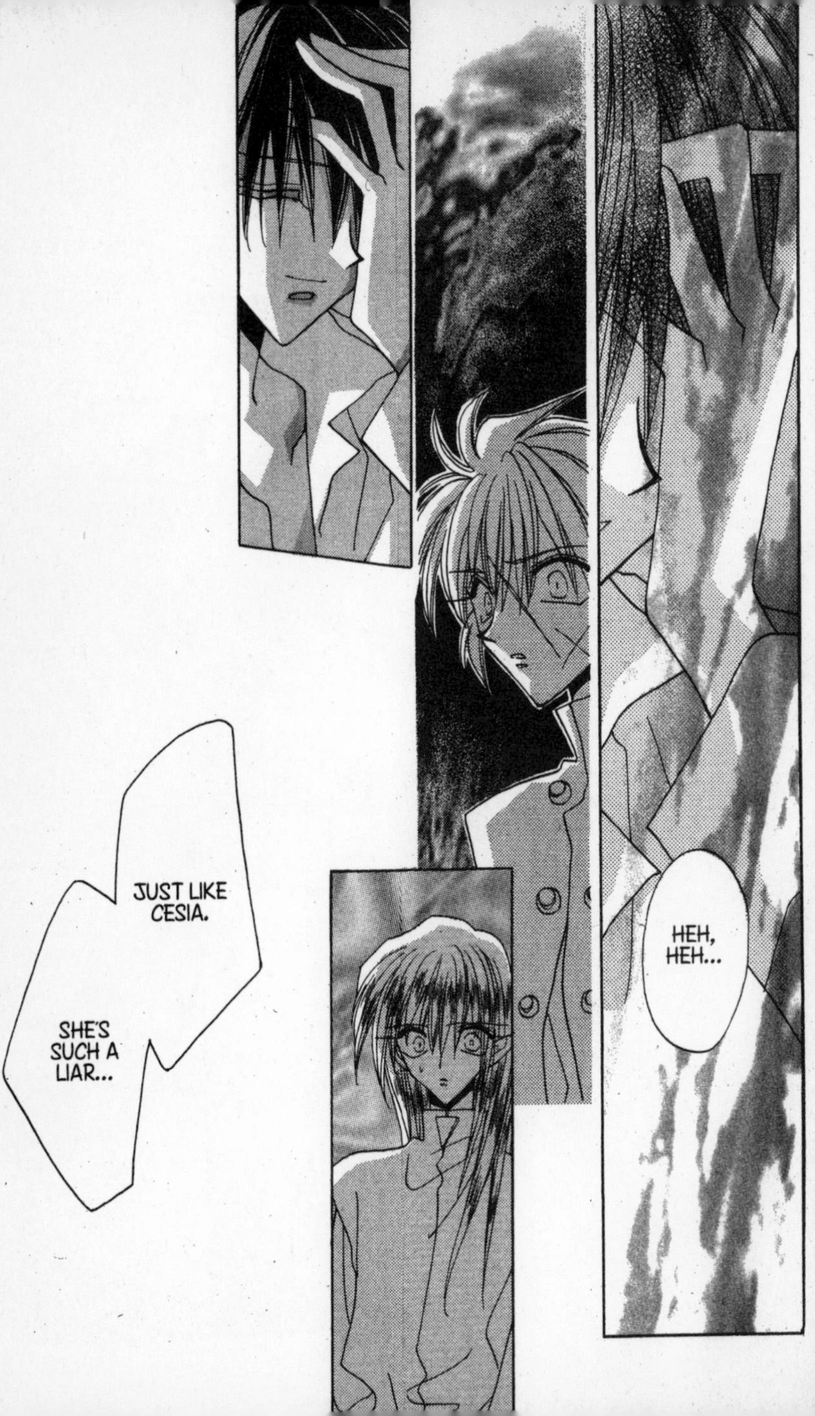
HEH, HEH...
JUST LIKE CESIA.
SHE'S SUCH A LIAR...

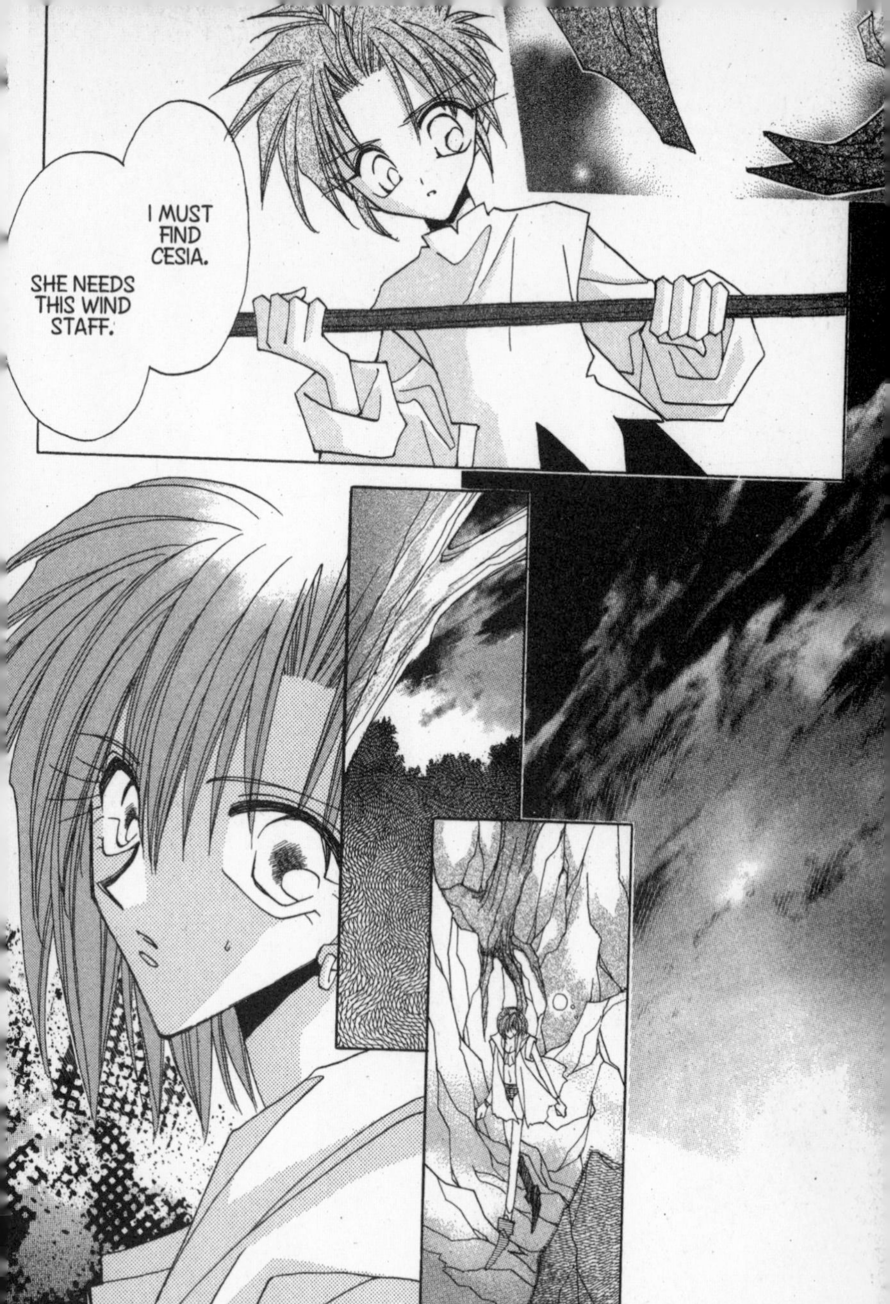
I MUST FIND CESIA.
SHE NEEDS THIS WIND STAFF.

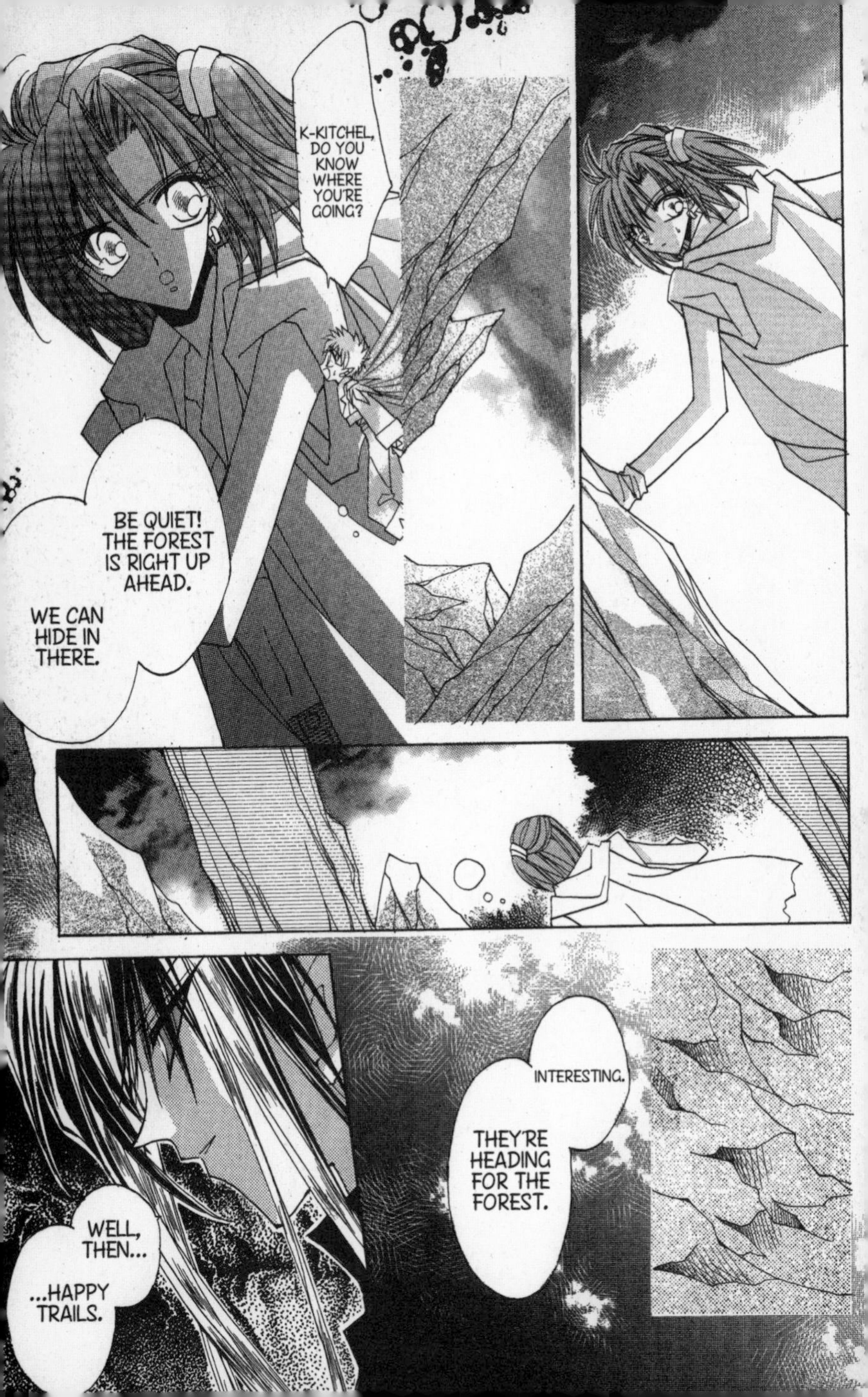
K-KITCHEL, DO YOU KNOW WHERE YOU'RE GOING?
BE QUIET! THE FOREST IS RIGHT UP AHEAD.
WE CAN HIDE IN THERE.
INTERESTING.
THEY'RE HEADING FOR THE FOREST.
WELL, THEN...
...HAPPY TRAILS.

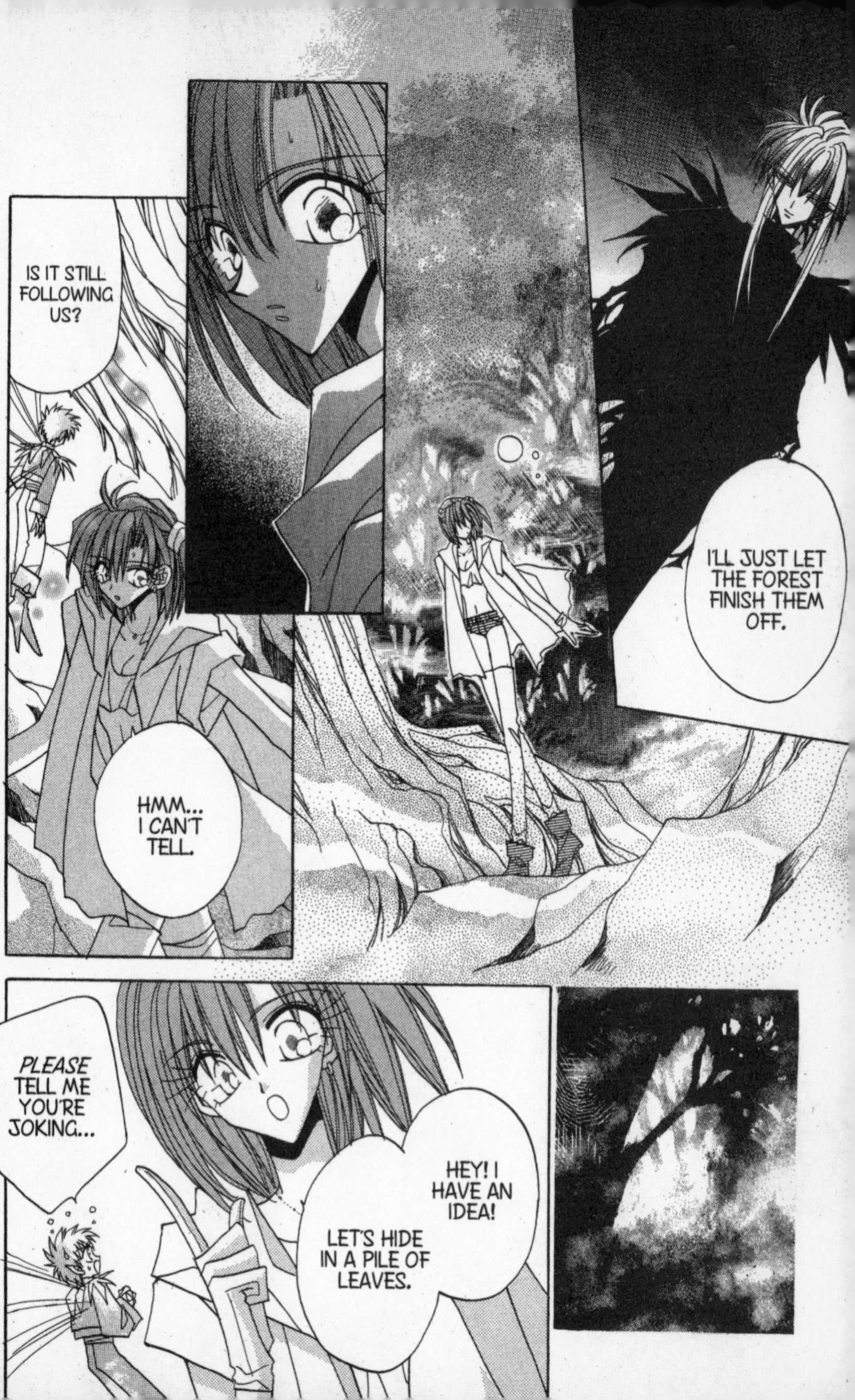
I'LL JUST LET THE FOREST FINISH THEM OFF.
IS IT STILL FOLLOWING US?
HMM... I CAN'T TELL.
HEY! I HAVE AN IDEA!
LET'S HIDE IN A PILE OF LEAVES.
PLEASE TELL ME YOU'RE JOKING...

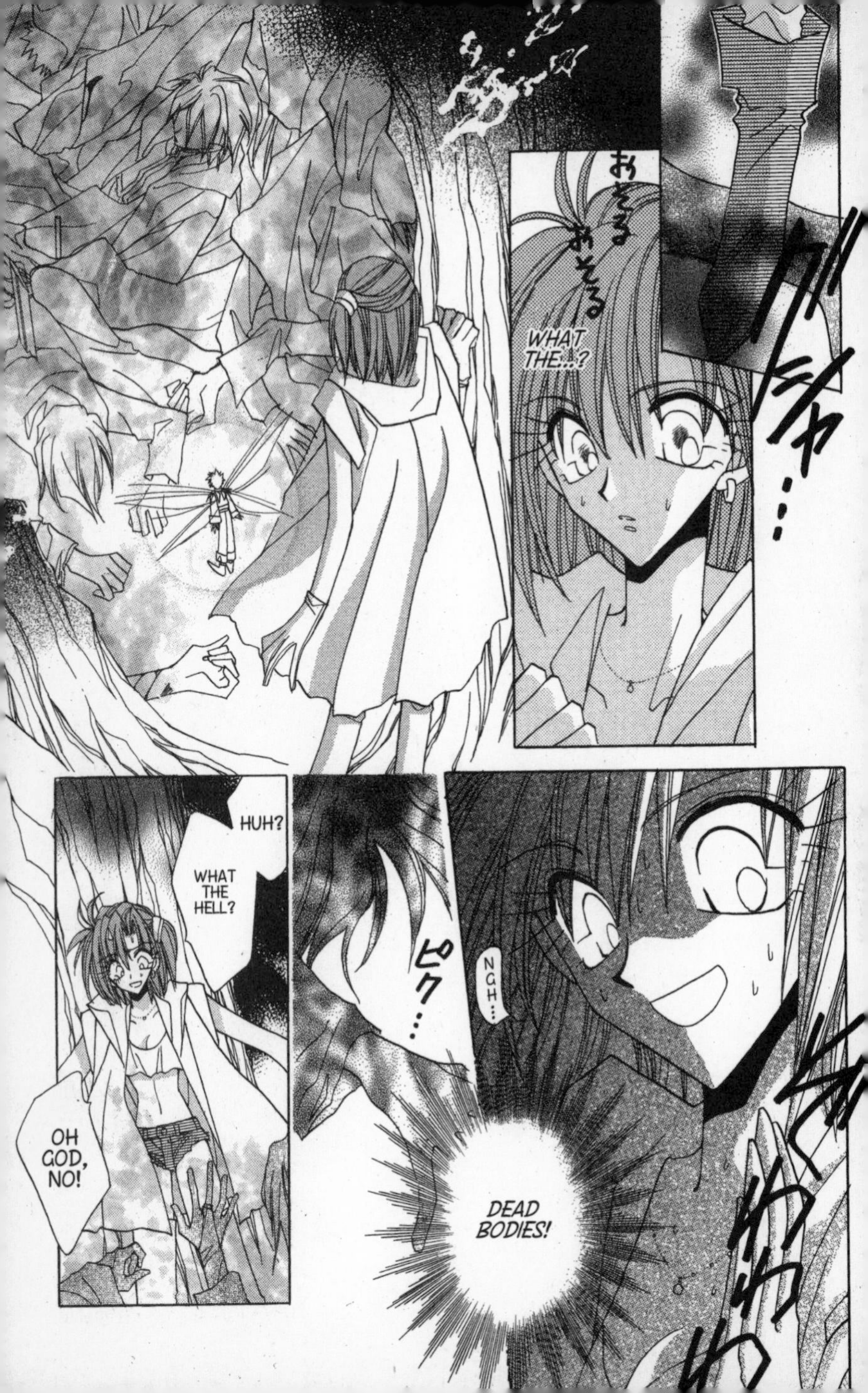
ガシャ…
おそる
おそる
WHAT THE...?
ピク…
NGH...
DEAD BODIES!
HUH?
WHAT THE HELL?
OH GOD, NO!

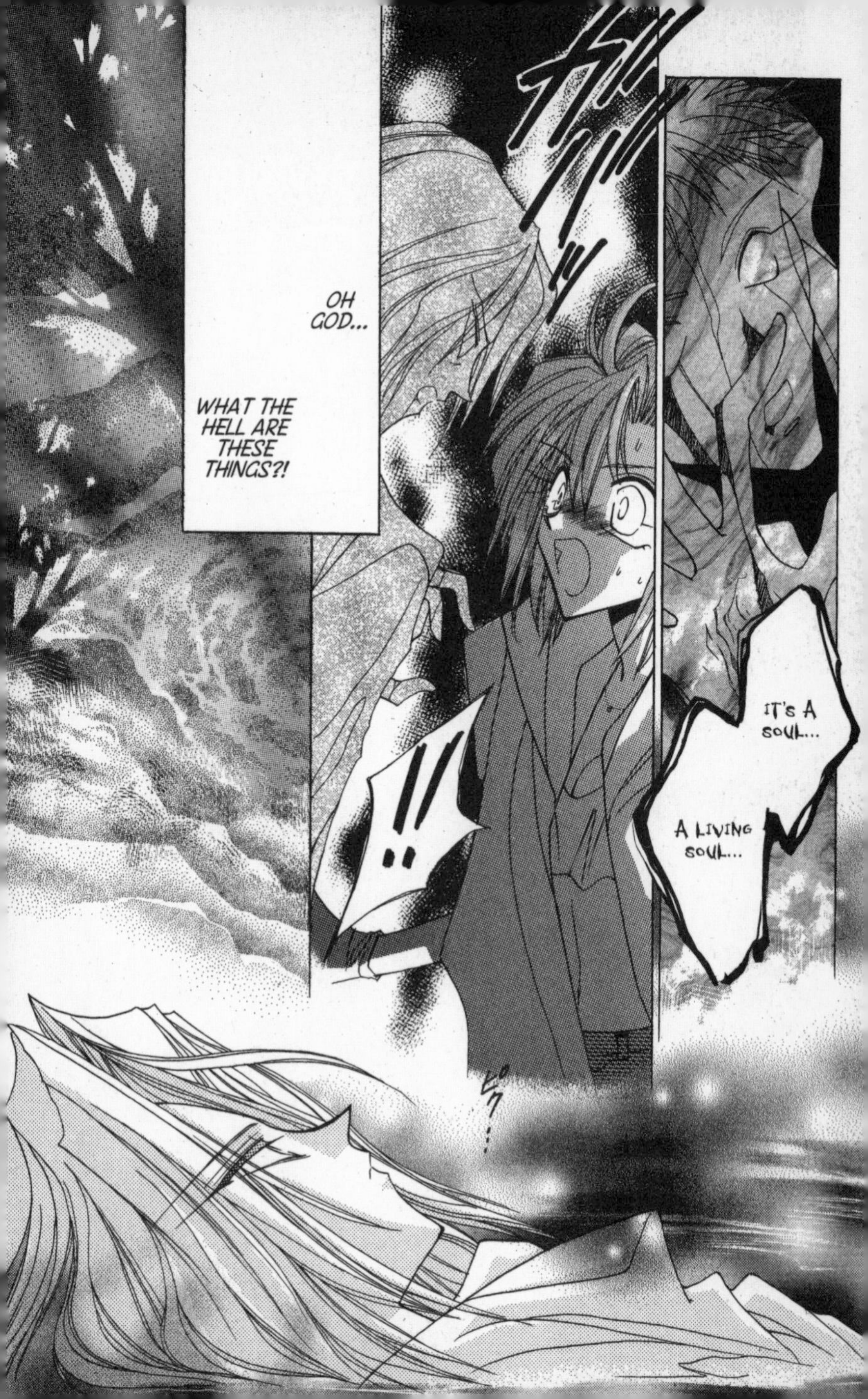
IT'S A SOUL...
A LIVING SOUL...
!!
OH GOD...
WHAT THE HELL ARE THESE THINGS?!

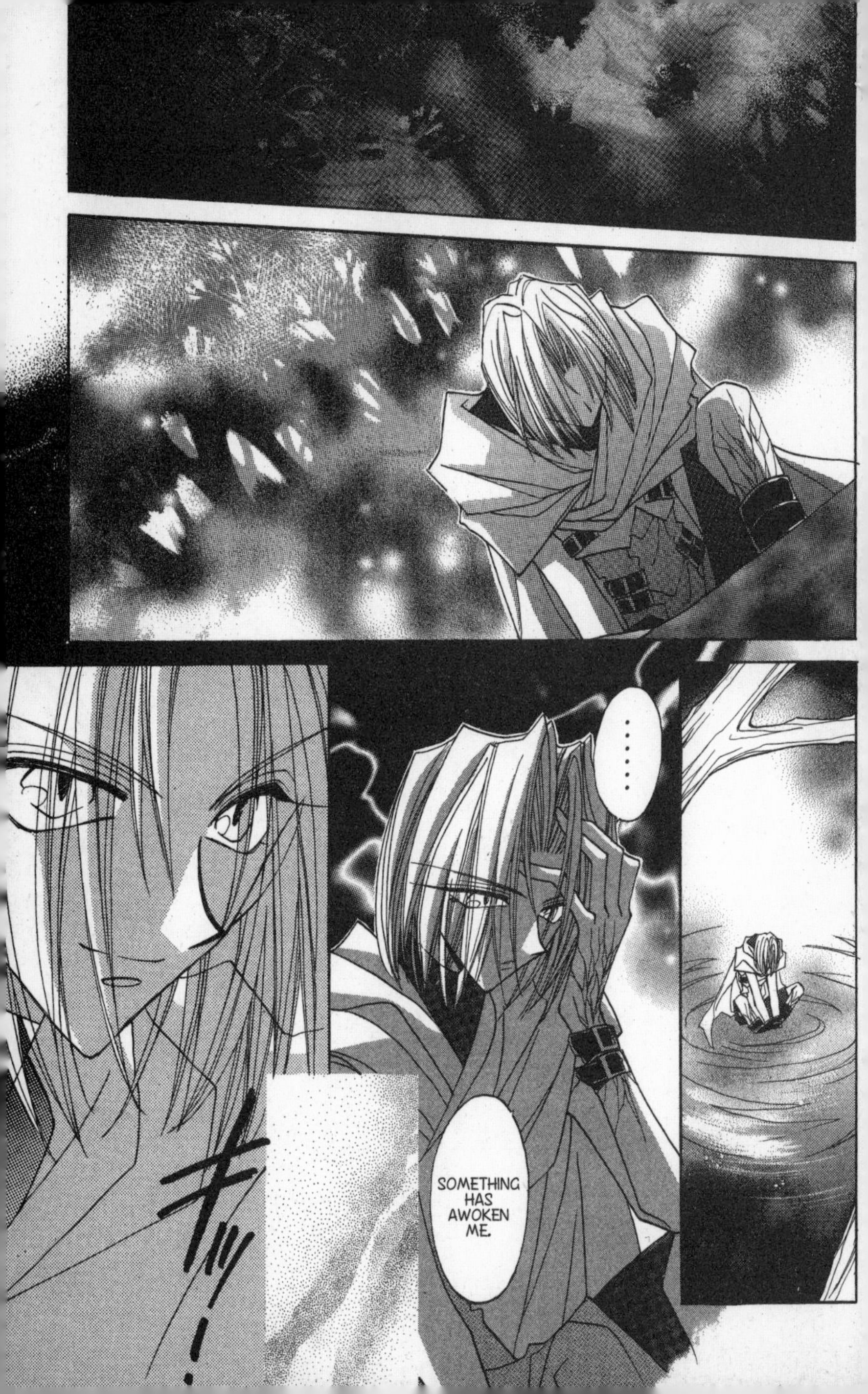
......
SOMETHING HAS AWOKEN ME.
キッ

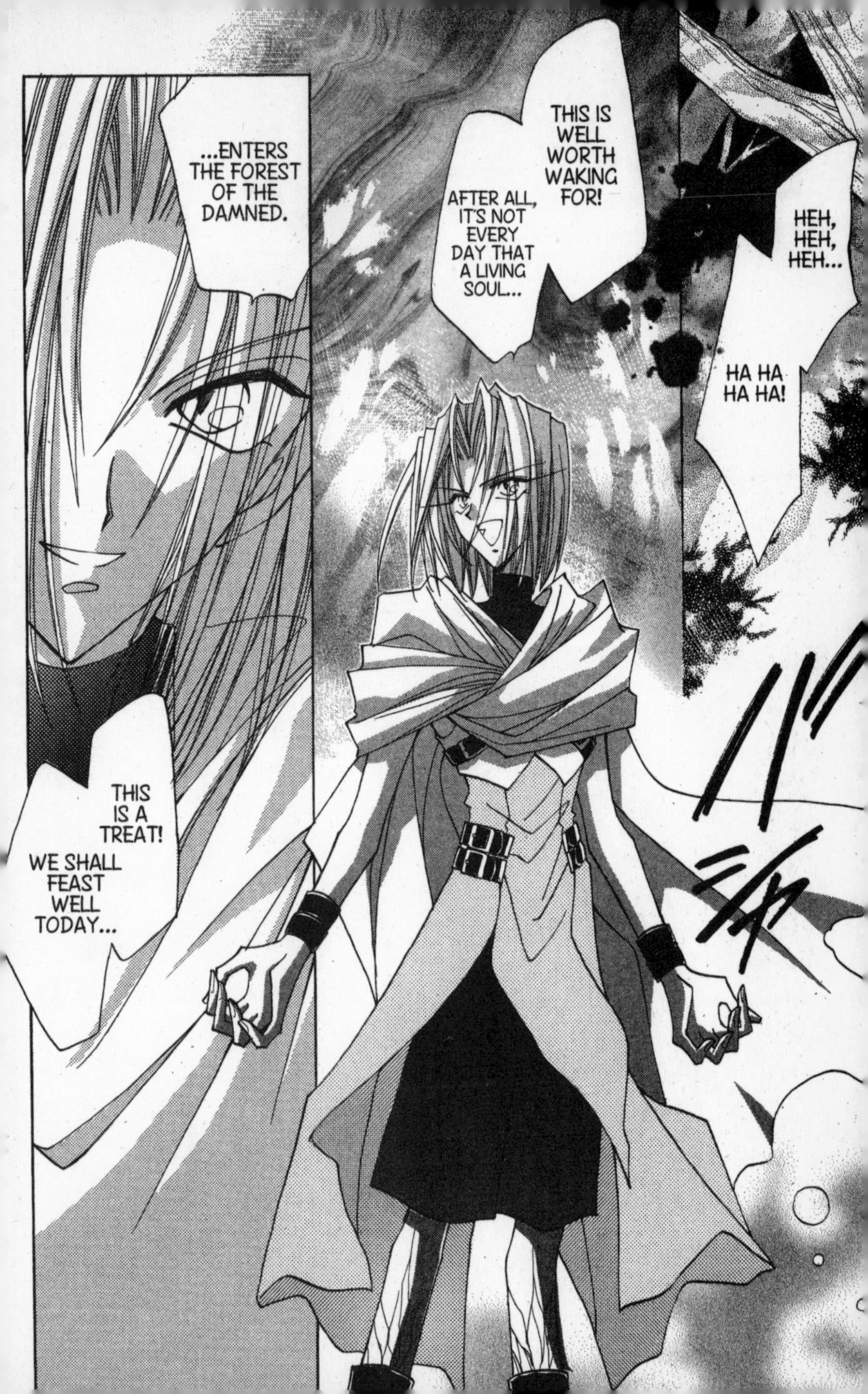
HEH, HEH, HEH...
HA HA HA HA!
THIS IS WELL WORTH WAKING FOR!
AFTER ALL, IT'S NOT EVERY DAY THAT A LIVING SOUL...
...ENTERS THE FOREST OF THE DAMNED.
THIS IS A TREAT!
WE SHALL FEAST WELL TODAY...

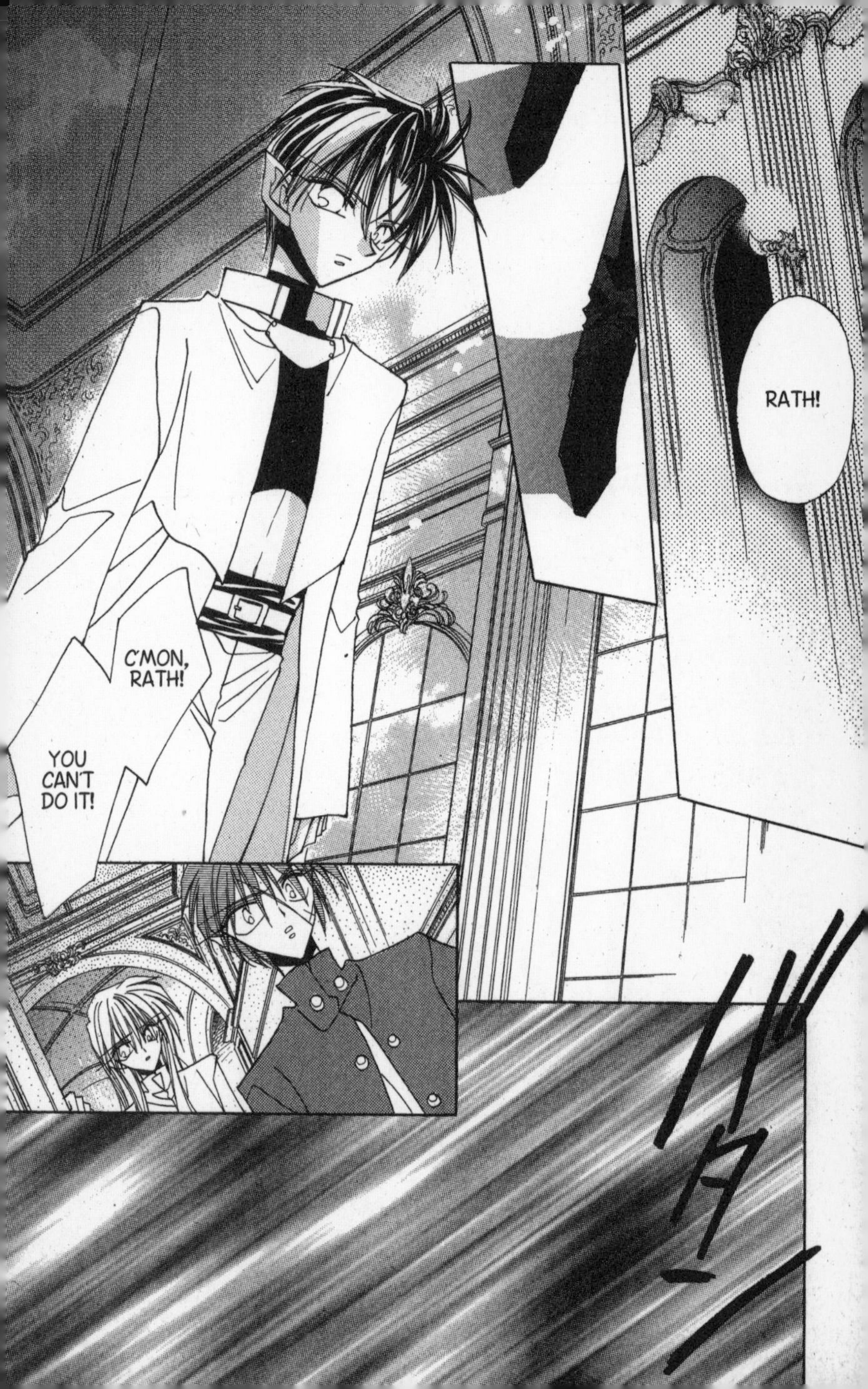
RATH!
C'MON, RATH!
YOU CAN'T DO IT!

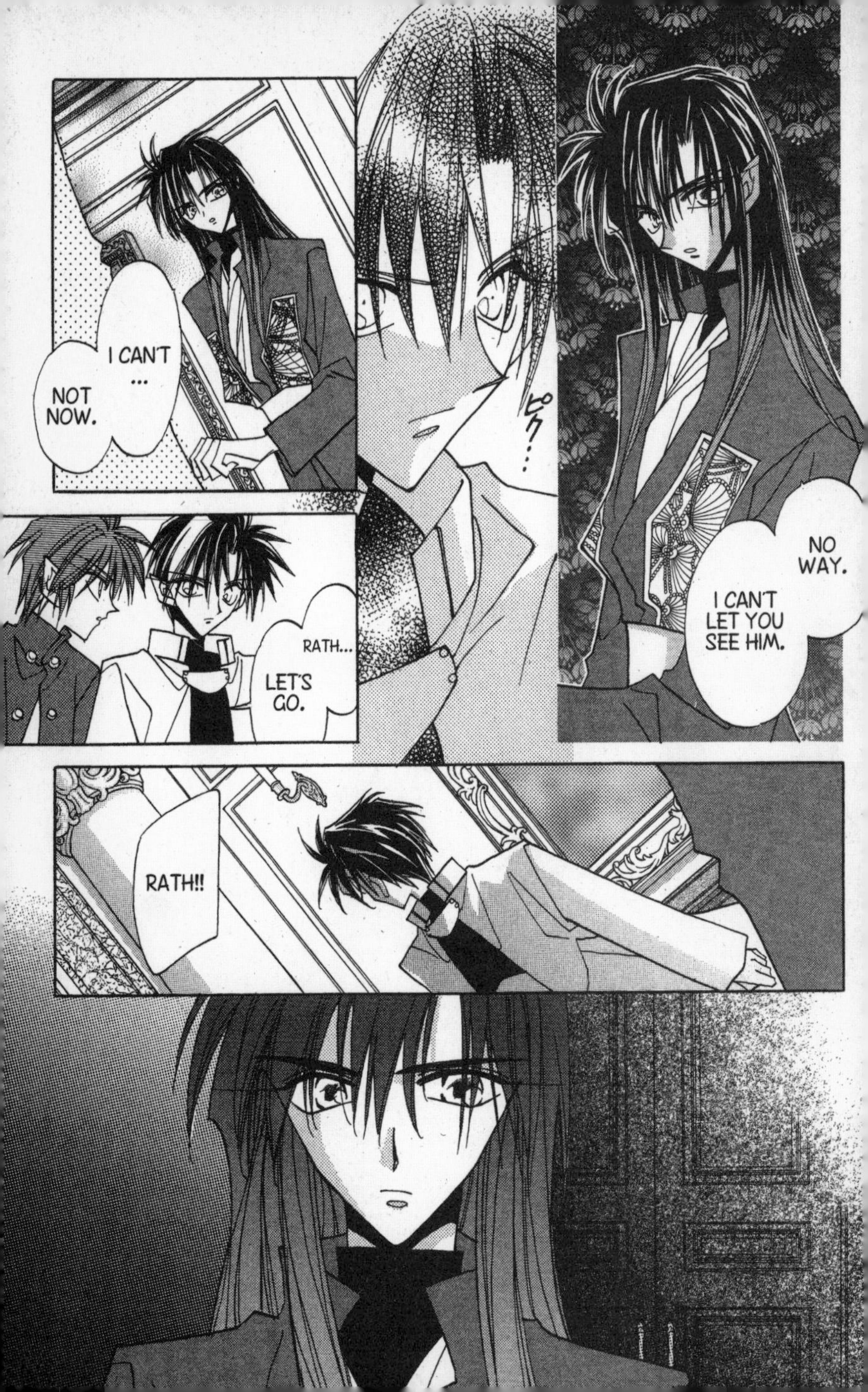
NO WAY.
I CAN'T LET YOU SEE HIM.
ピク…
I CAN'T ... NOT NOW.
RATH... LET'S GO.
RATH!!

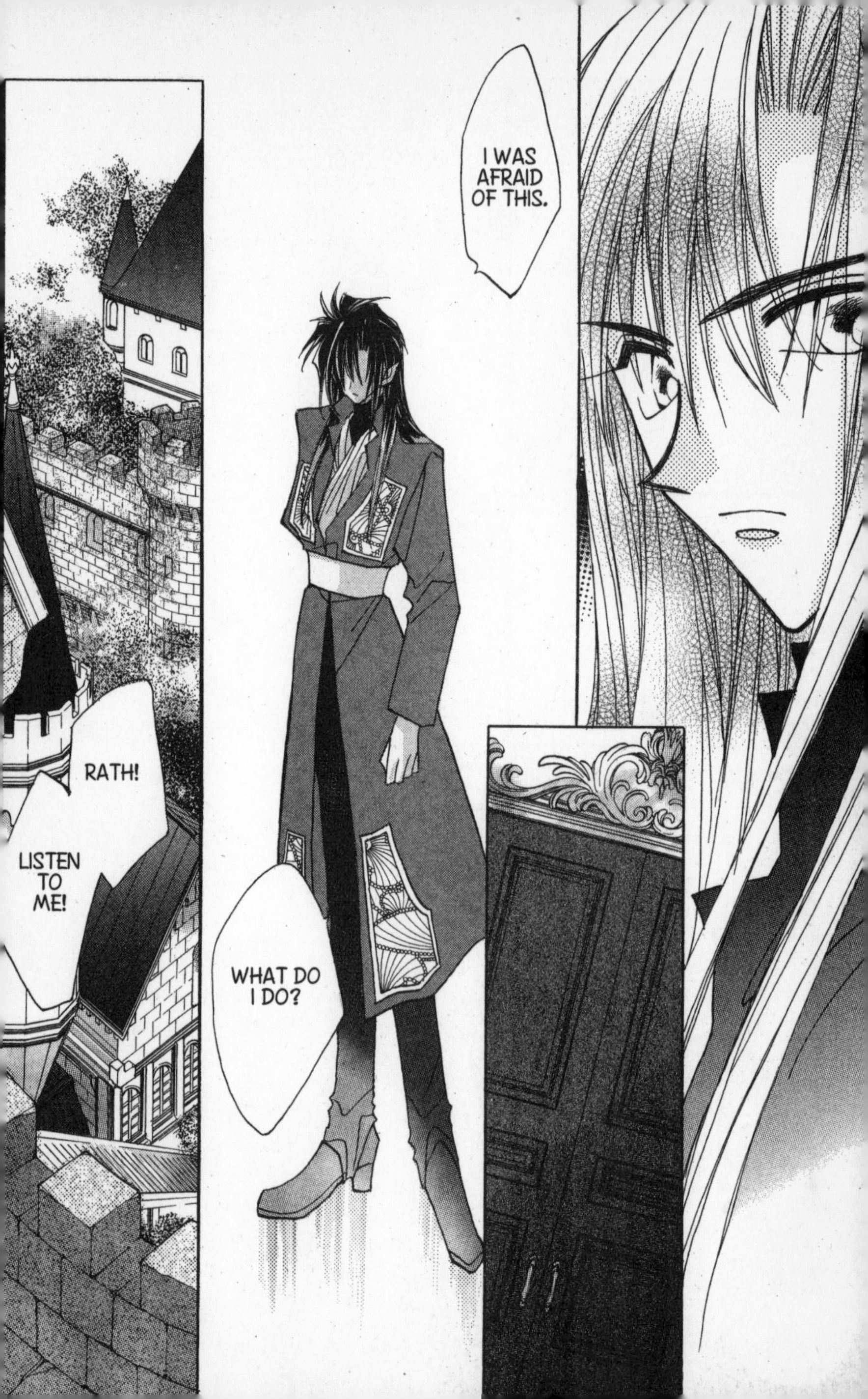
I WAS AFRAID OF THIS.
WHAT DO I DO?
RATH!
LISTEN TO ME!

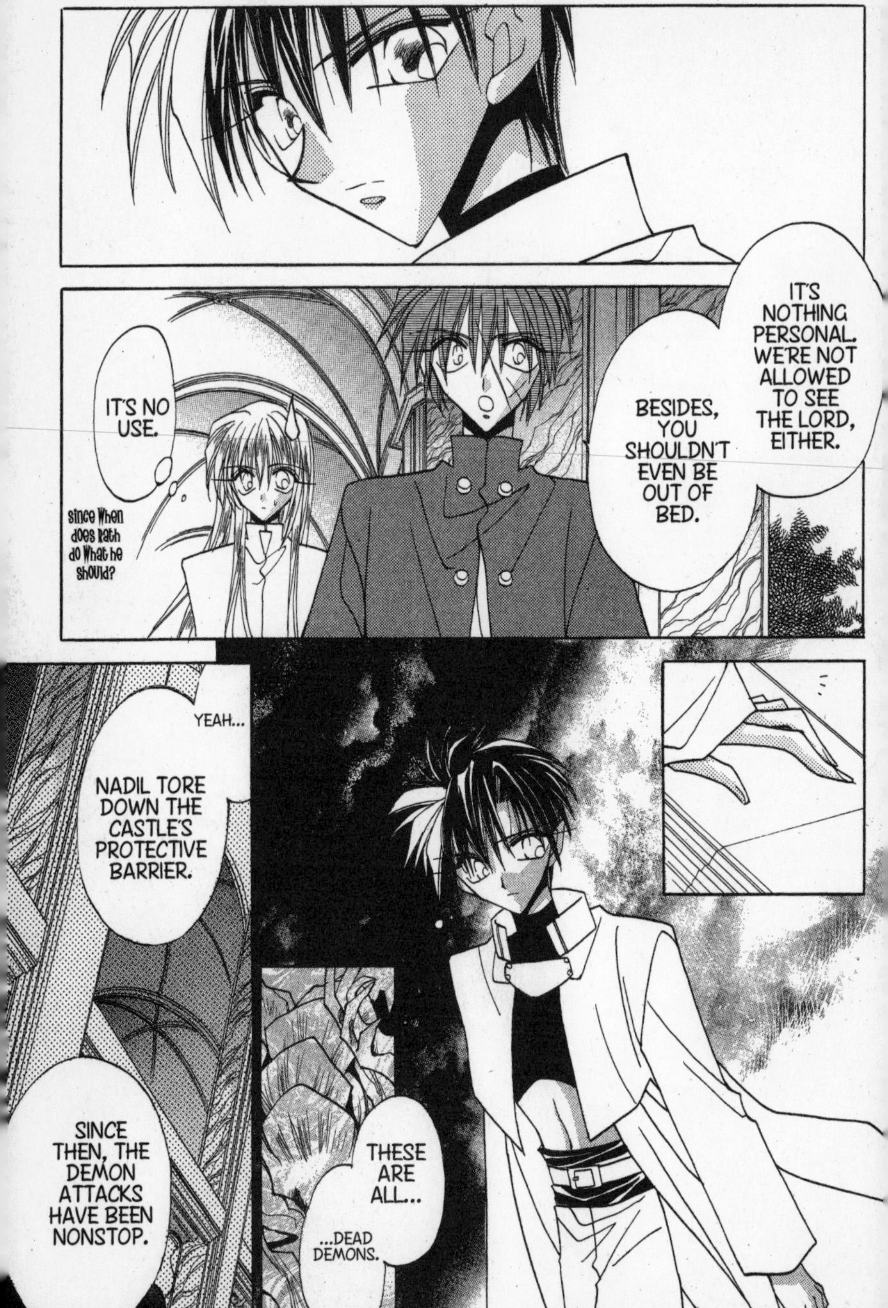
IT'S NOTHING PERSONAL. WE'RE NOT ALLOWED TO SEE THE LORD, EITHER.
BESIDES, YOU SHOULDN'T EVEN BE OUT OF BED.
IT'S NO USE.
since When does Rath do What he should?
THESE ARE ALL...
...DEAD DEMONS.
YEAH...
NADIL TORE DOWN THE CASTLE'S PROTECTIVE BARRIER.
SINCE THEN, THE DEMON ATTACKS HAVE BEEN NONSTOP.

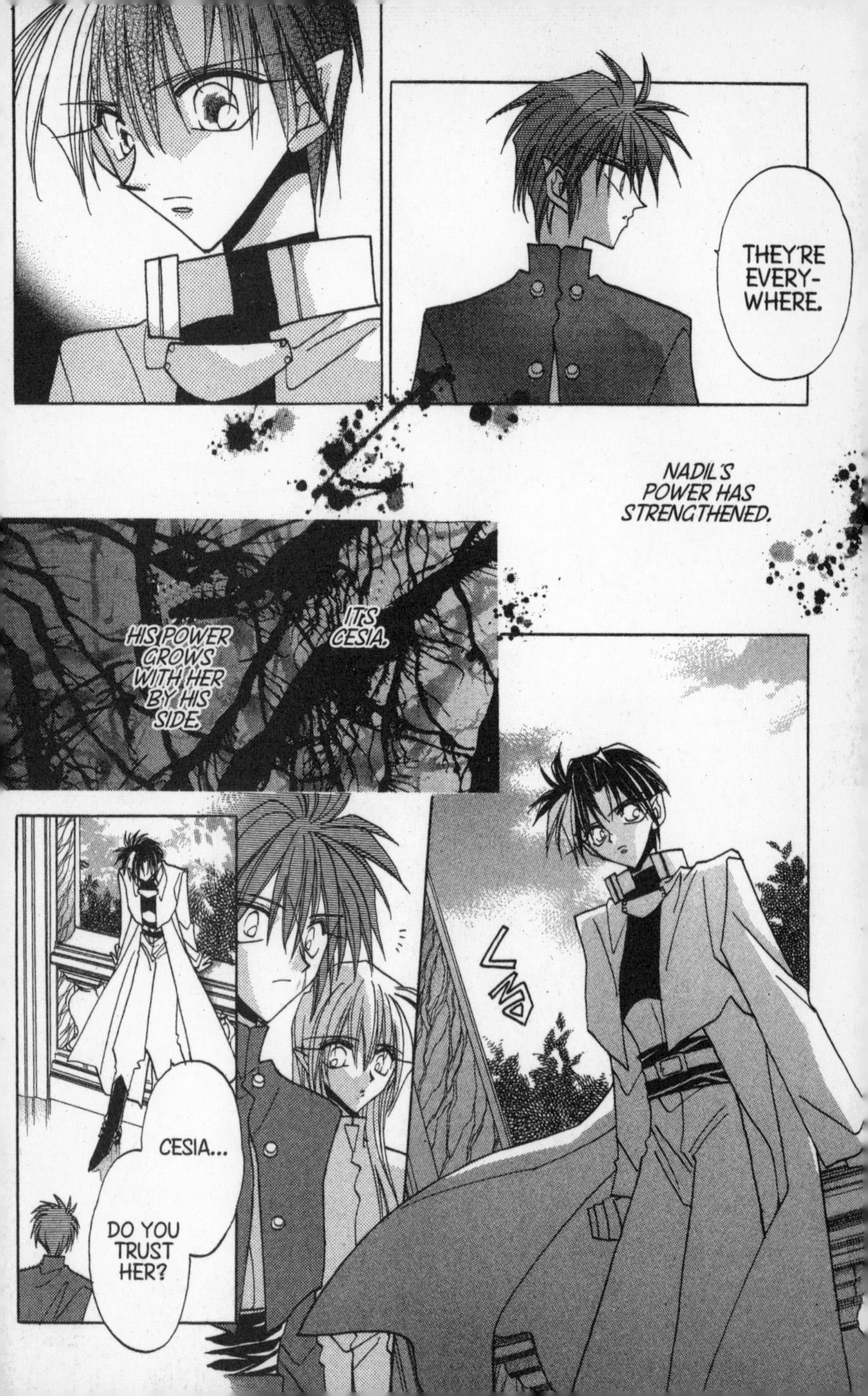
THEY'RE EVERY-WHERE.
NADIL'S POWER HAS STRENGTHENED.
IT'S CESIA.
HIS POWER GROWS WITH HER BY HIS SIDE.
CESIA...
DO YOU TRUST HER?

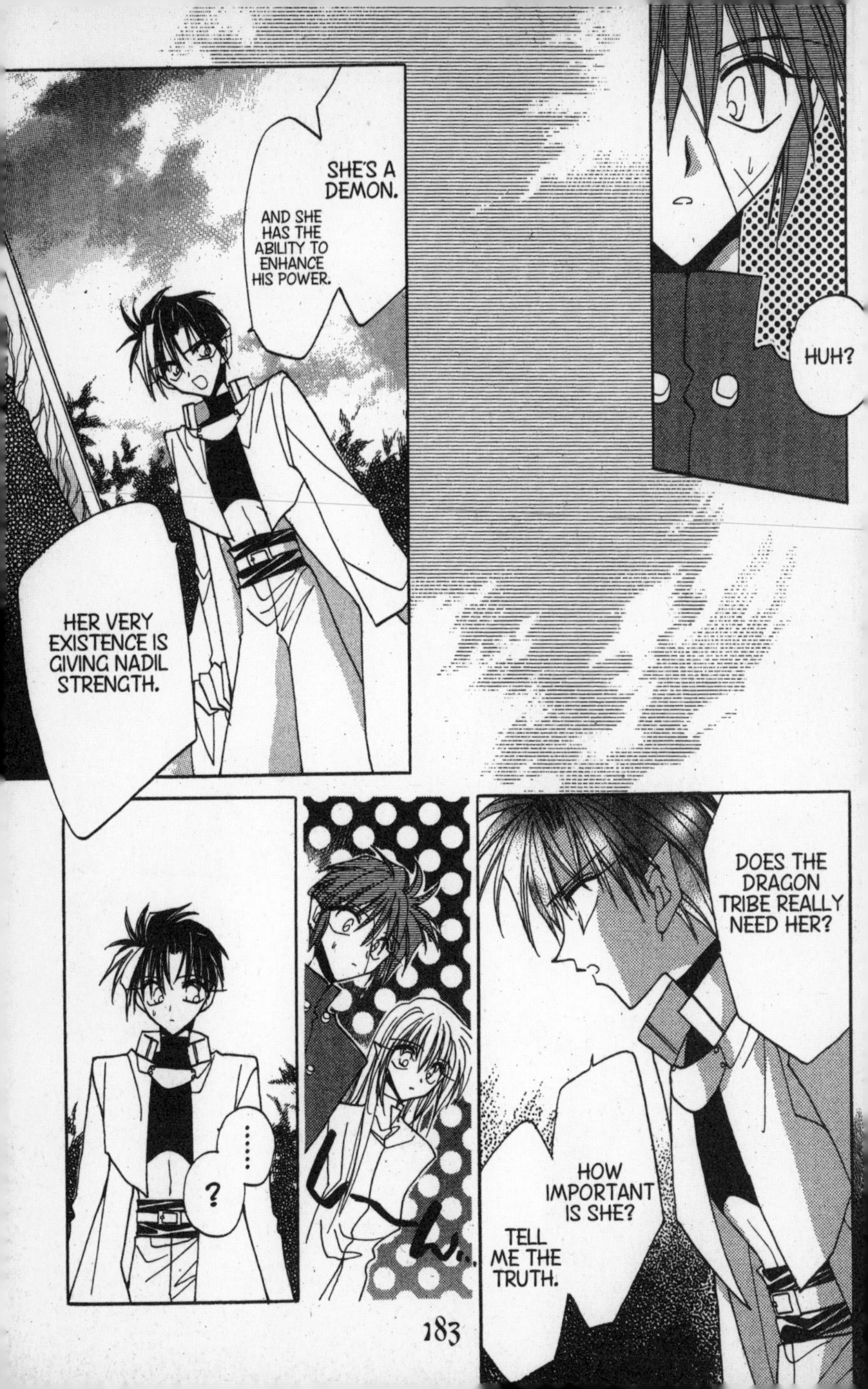
HUH?
SHE'S A DEMON.
AND SHE HAS THE ABILITY TO ENHANCE HIS POWER.
HER VERY EXISTENCE IS GIVING NADIL STRENGTH.
DOES THE DRAGON TRIBE REALLY NEED HER?
HOW IMPORTANT IS SHE?
TELL ME THE TRUTH.
......
?

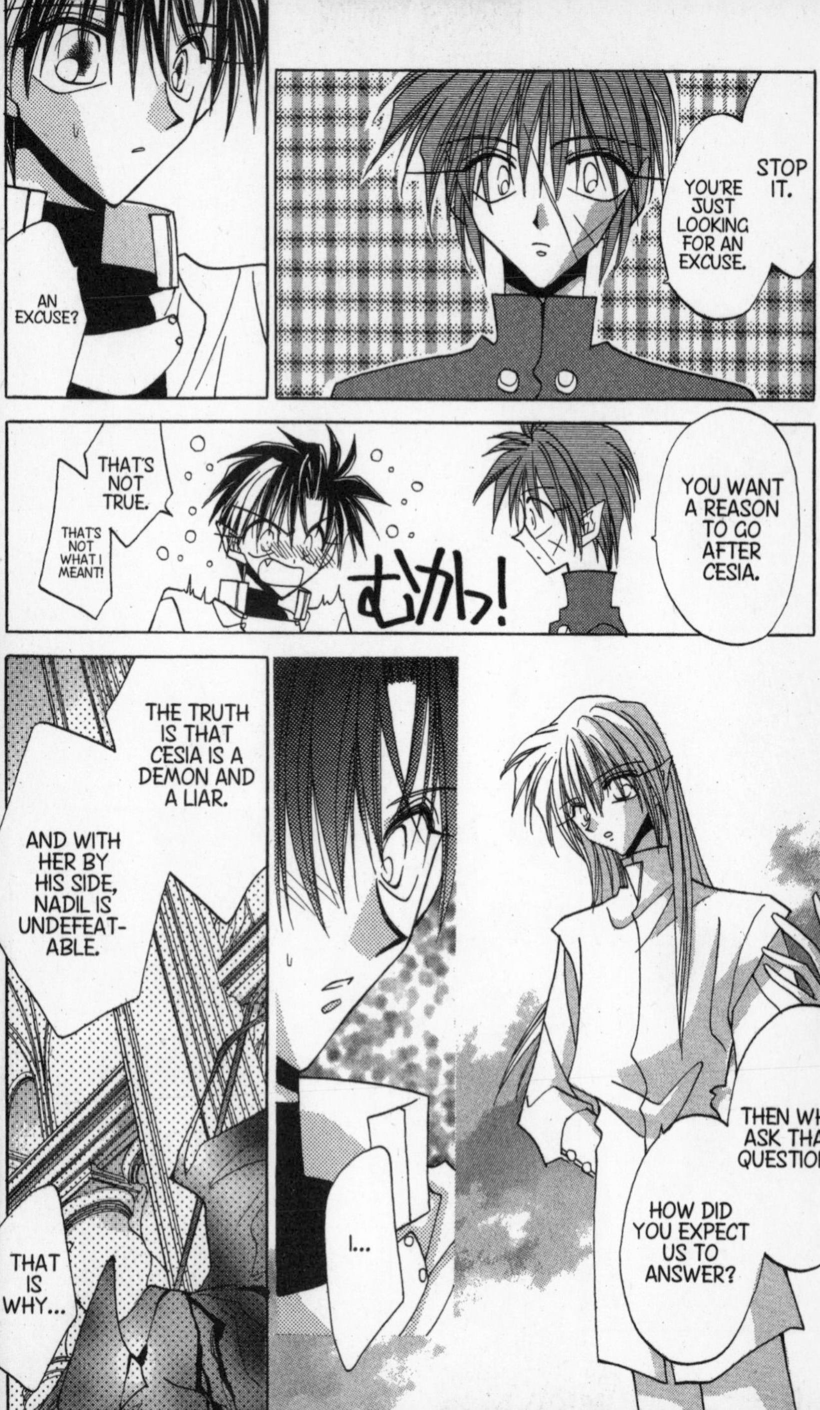
STOP IT.
YOU'RE JUST LOOKING FOR AN EXCUSE.
AN EXCUSE?
YOU WANT A REASON TO GO AFTER CESIA.
むかっ!
THAT'S NOT TRUE.
THAT'S NOT WHAT I MEANT!
THEN WHY ASK THAT QUESTION?
HOW DID YOU EXPECT US TO ANSWER?
I...
THE TRUTH IS THAT CESIA IS A DEMON AND A LIAR.
AND WITH HER BY HIS SIDE, NADIL IS UNDEFEAT-ABLE.
THAT IS WHY...

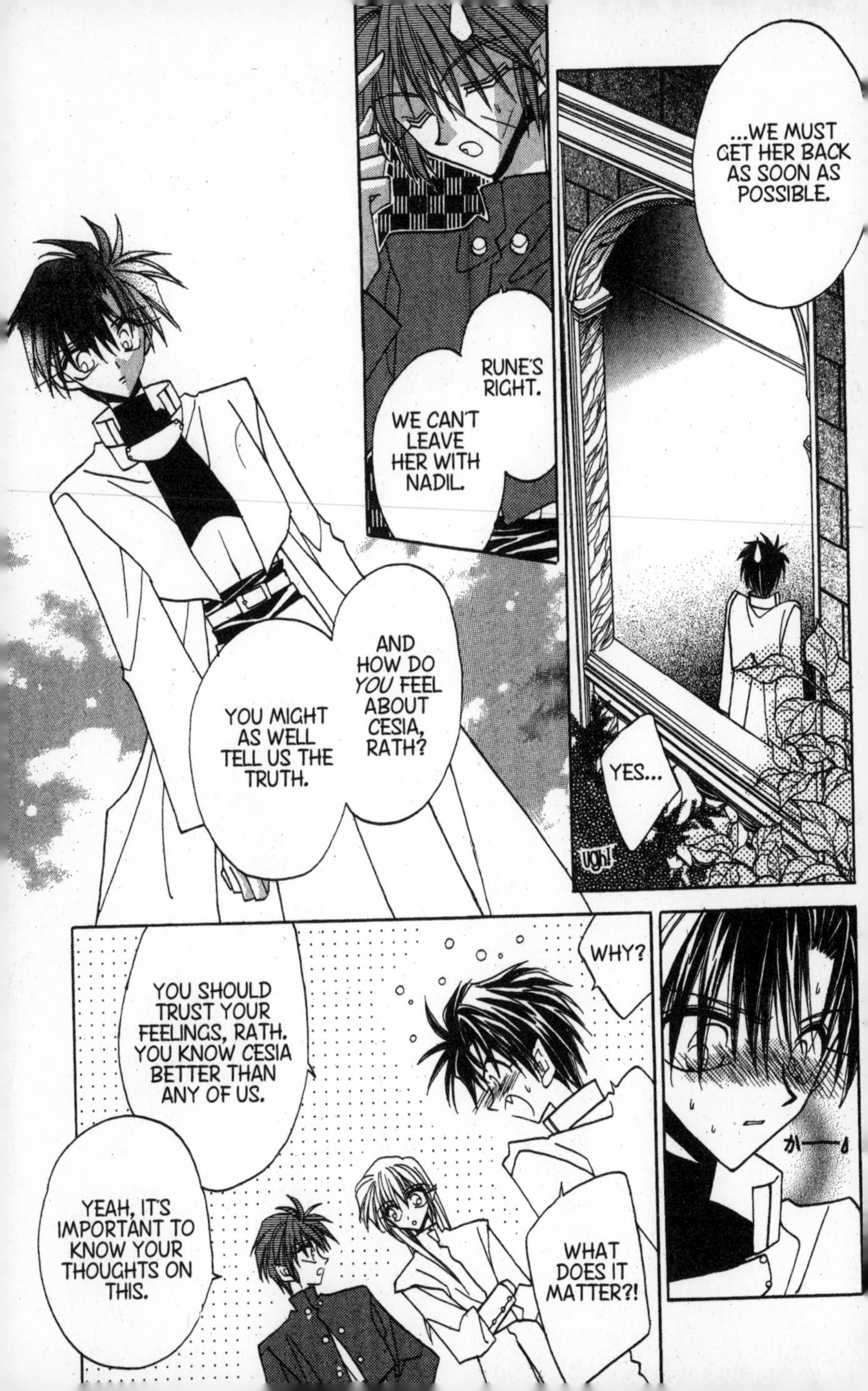
...WE MUST GET HER BACK AS SOON AS POSSIBLE.
YES...
UGH!
RUNE'S RIGHT.
WE CAN'T LEAVE HER WITH NADIL.
AND HOW DO *YOU* FEEL ABOUT CESIA, RATH?
YOU MIGHT AS WELL TELL US THE TRUTH.
か——
WHY?
WHAT DOES IT MATTER?!
YOU SHOULD TRUST YOUR FEELINGS, RATH. YOU KNOW CESIA BETTER THAN ANY OF US.
YEAH, IT'S IMPORTANT TO KNOW YOUR THOUGHTS ON THIS.

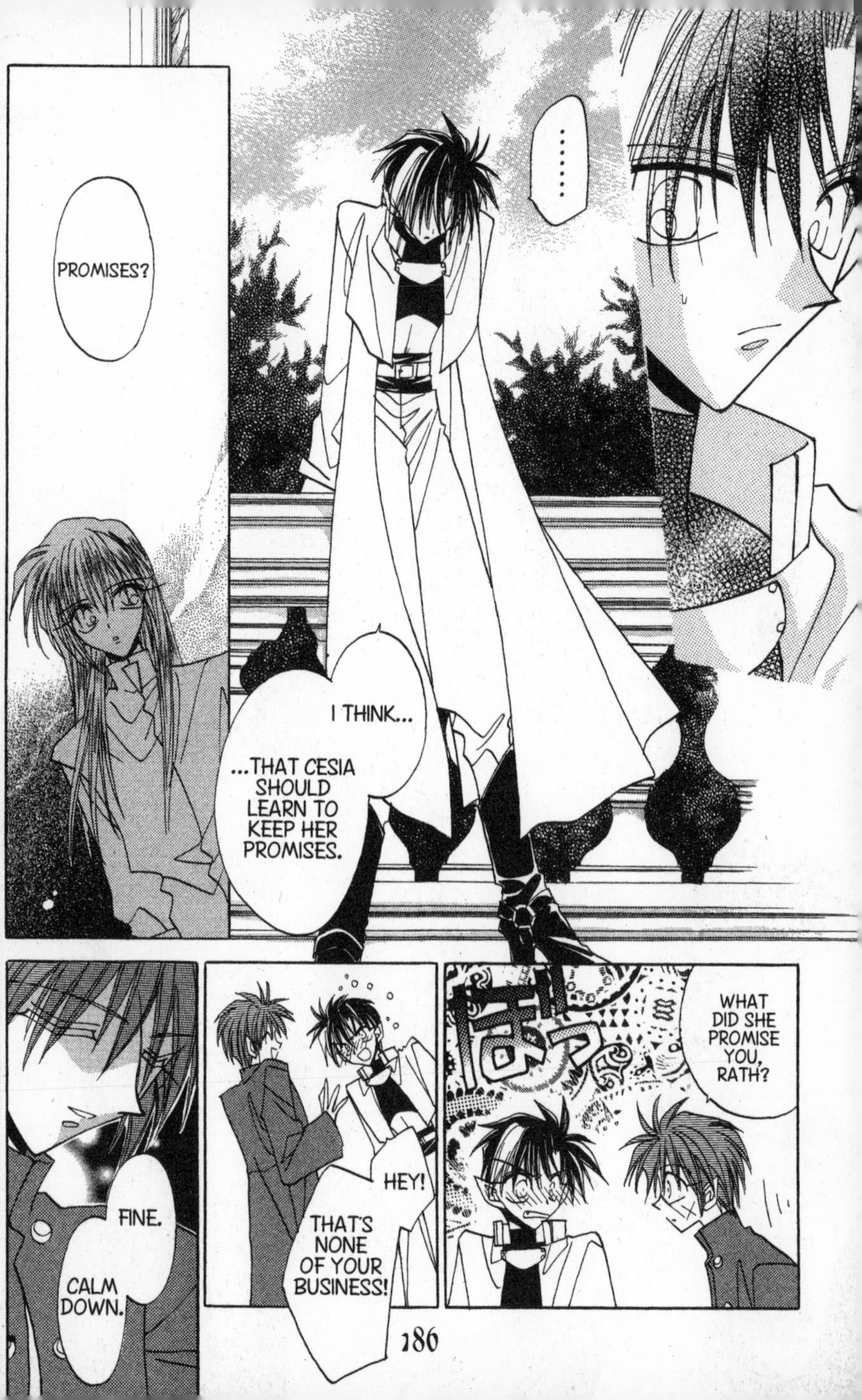
......
I THINK...
...THAT CESIA SHOULD LEARN TO KEEP HER PROMISES.
PROMISES?
WHAT DID SHE PROMISE YOU, RATH?
ぽっ
HEY!
THAT'S NONE OF YOUR BUSINESS!
FINE.
CALM DOWN.

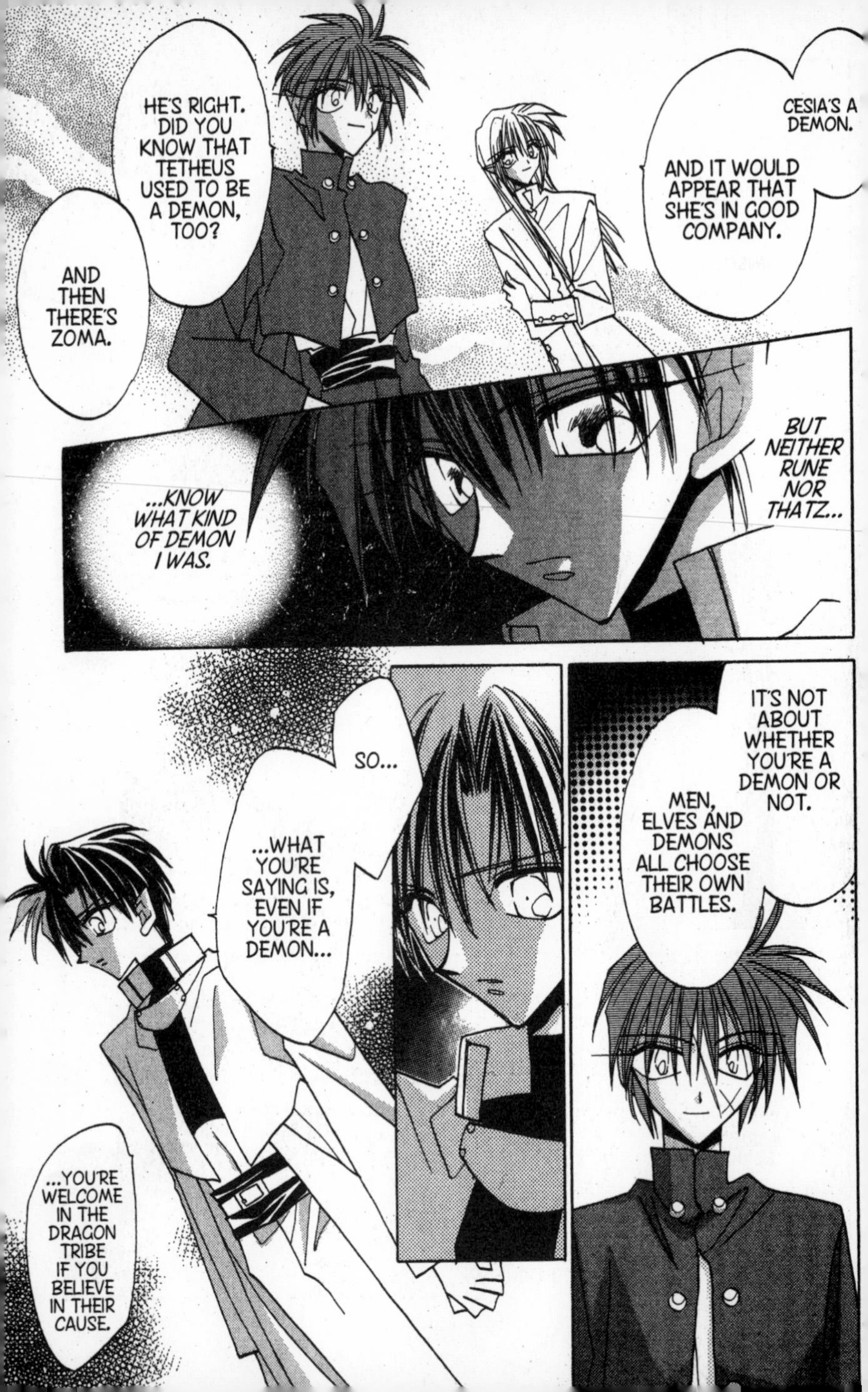
CESIA'S A DEMON.
AND IT WOULD APPEAR THAT SHE'S IN GOOD COMPANY.
HE'S RIGHT. DID YOU KNOW THAT TETHEUS USED TO BE A DEMON, TOO?
AND THEN THERE'S ZOMA.
BUT NEITHER RUNE NOR THATZ...
...KNOW WHAT KIND OF DEMON I WAS.
IT'S NOT ABOUT WHETHER YOU'RE A DEMON OR NOT.
MEN, ELVES AND DEMONS ALL CHOOSE THEIR OWN BATTLES.
SO...
...WHAT YOU'RE SAYING IS, EVEN IF YOU'RE A DEMON...
...YOU'RE WELCOME IN THE DRAGON TRIBE IF YOU BELIEVE IN THEIR CAUSE.

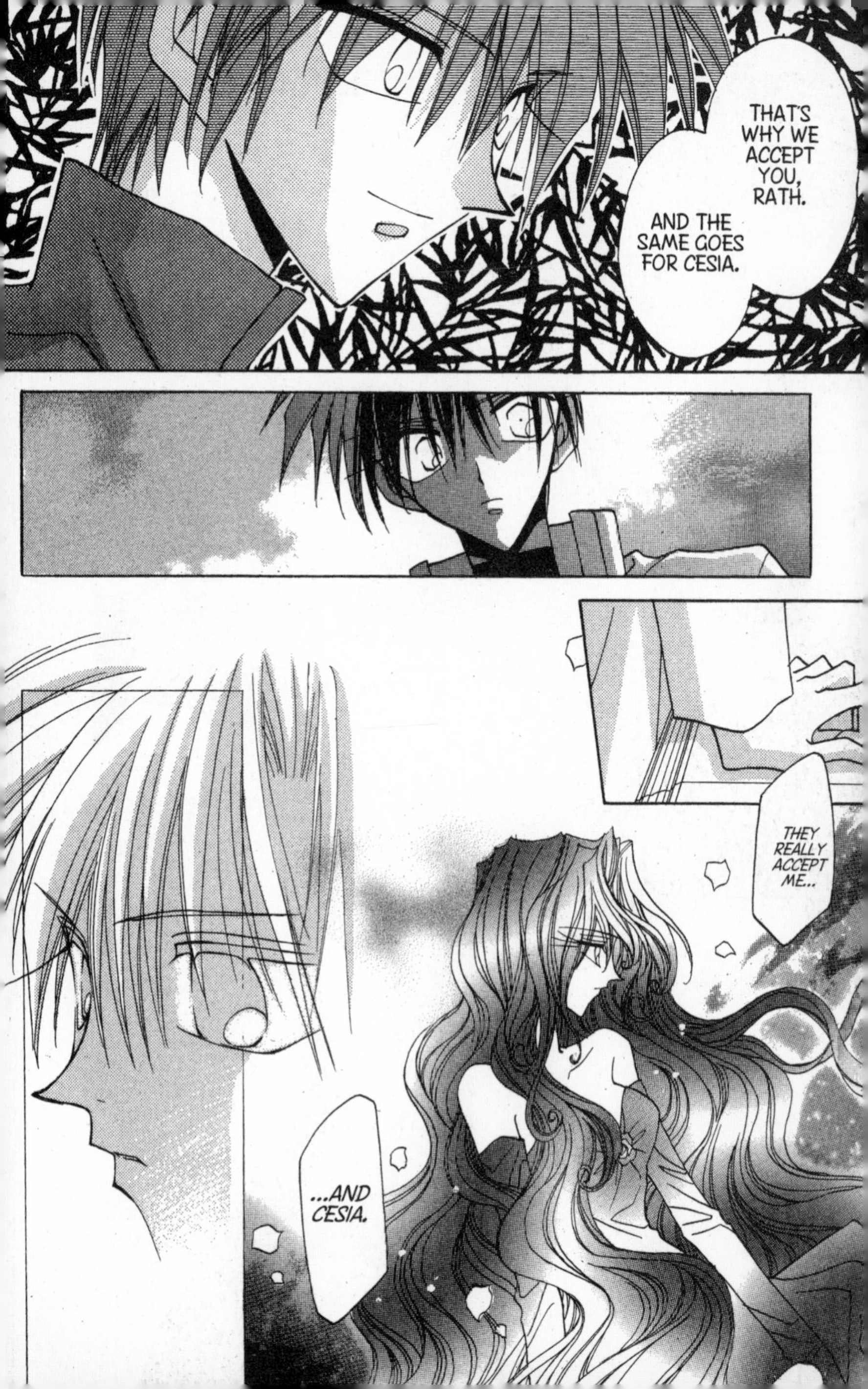
THAT'S WHY WE ACCEPT YOU, RATH.
AND THE SAME GOES FOR CESIA.
THEY REALLY ACCEPT ME...
...AND CESIA.

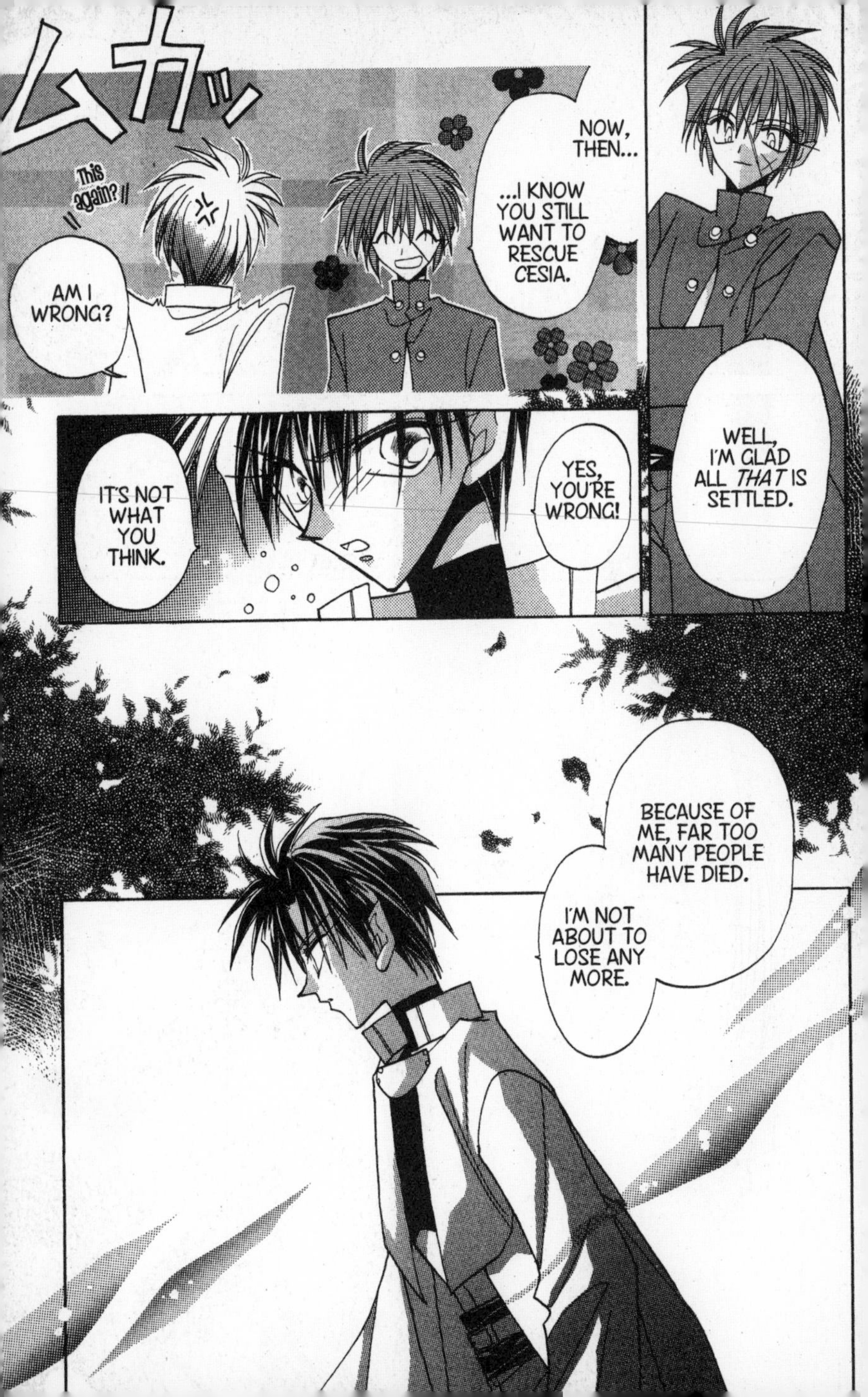
NOW, THEN...
...I KNOW YOU STILL WANT TO RESCUE CESIA.
ムカッ
This again?
AM I WRONG?
YES, YOU'RE WRONG!
IT'S NOT WHAT YOU THINK.
WELL, I'M GLAD ALL *THAT* IS SETTLED.
BECAUSE OF ME, FAR TOO MANY PEOPLE HAVE DIED.
I'M NOT ABOUT TO LOSE ANY MORE.

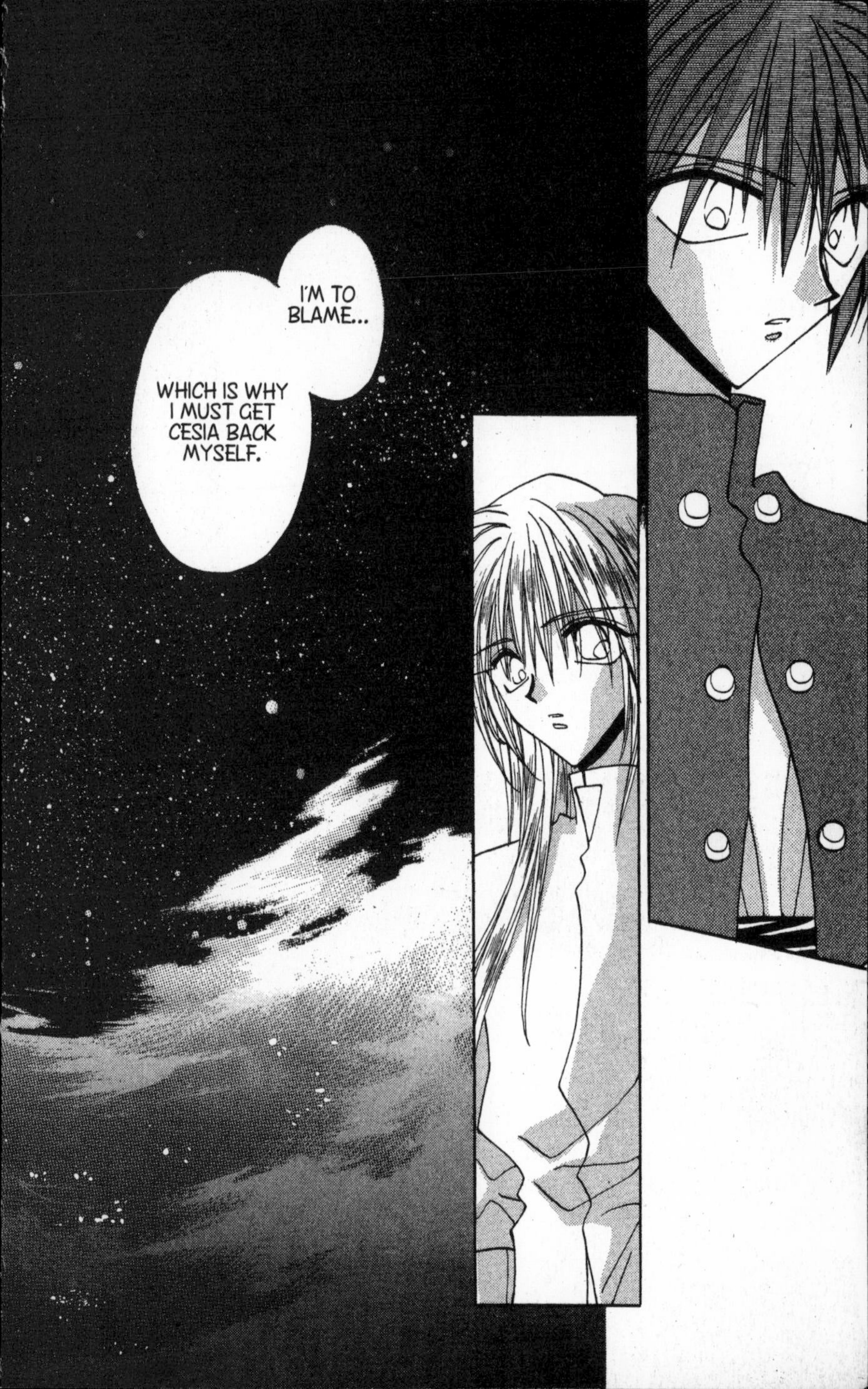
I'M TO BLAME...
WHICH IS WHY I MUST GET CESIA BACK MYSELF.

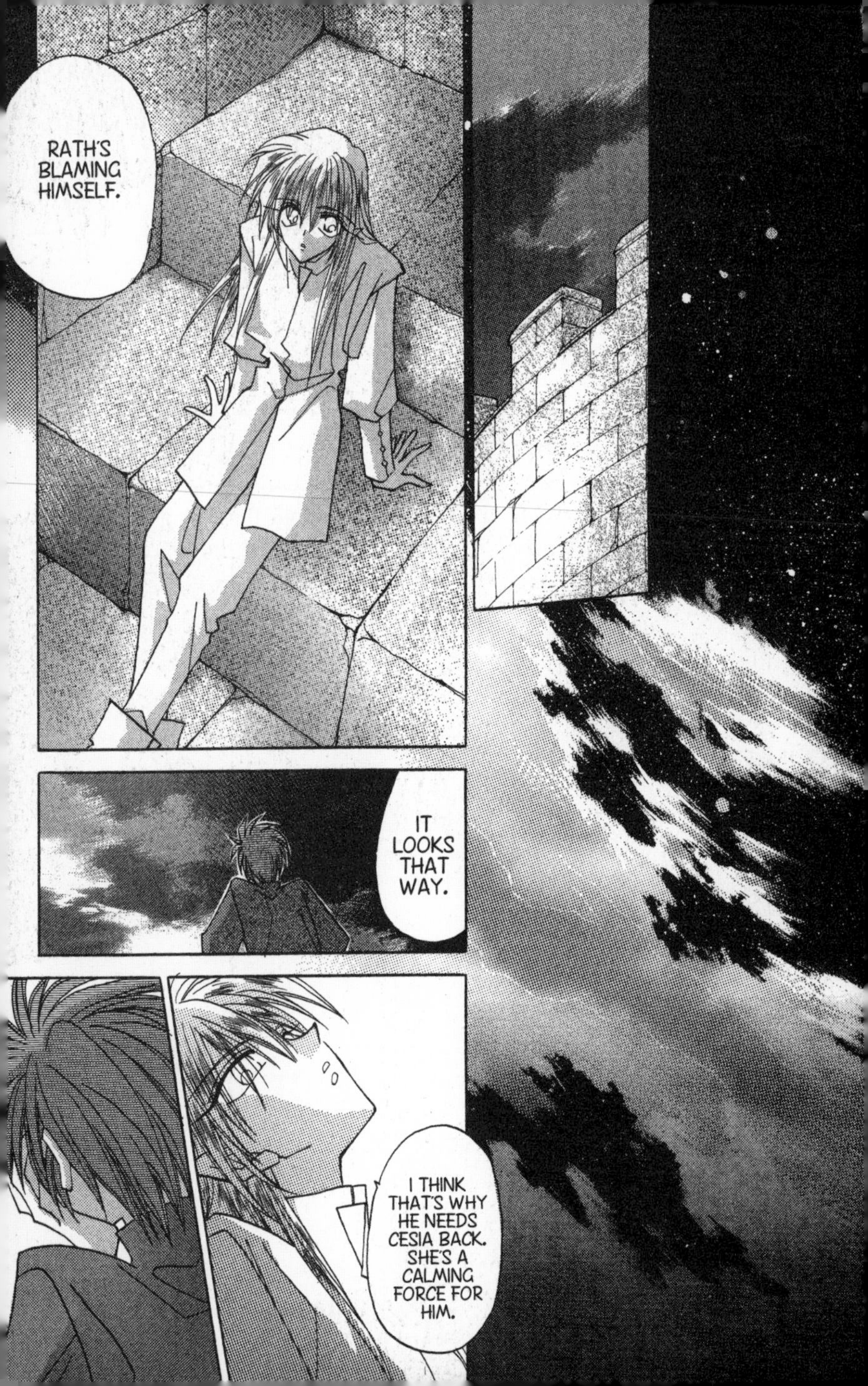
RATH'S BLAMING HIMSELF.
IT LOOKS THAT WAY.
I THINK THAT'S WHY HE NEEDS CESIA BACK. SHE'S A CALMING FORCE FOR HIM.

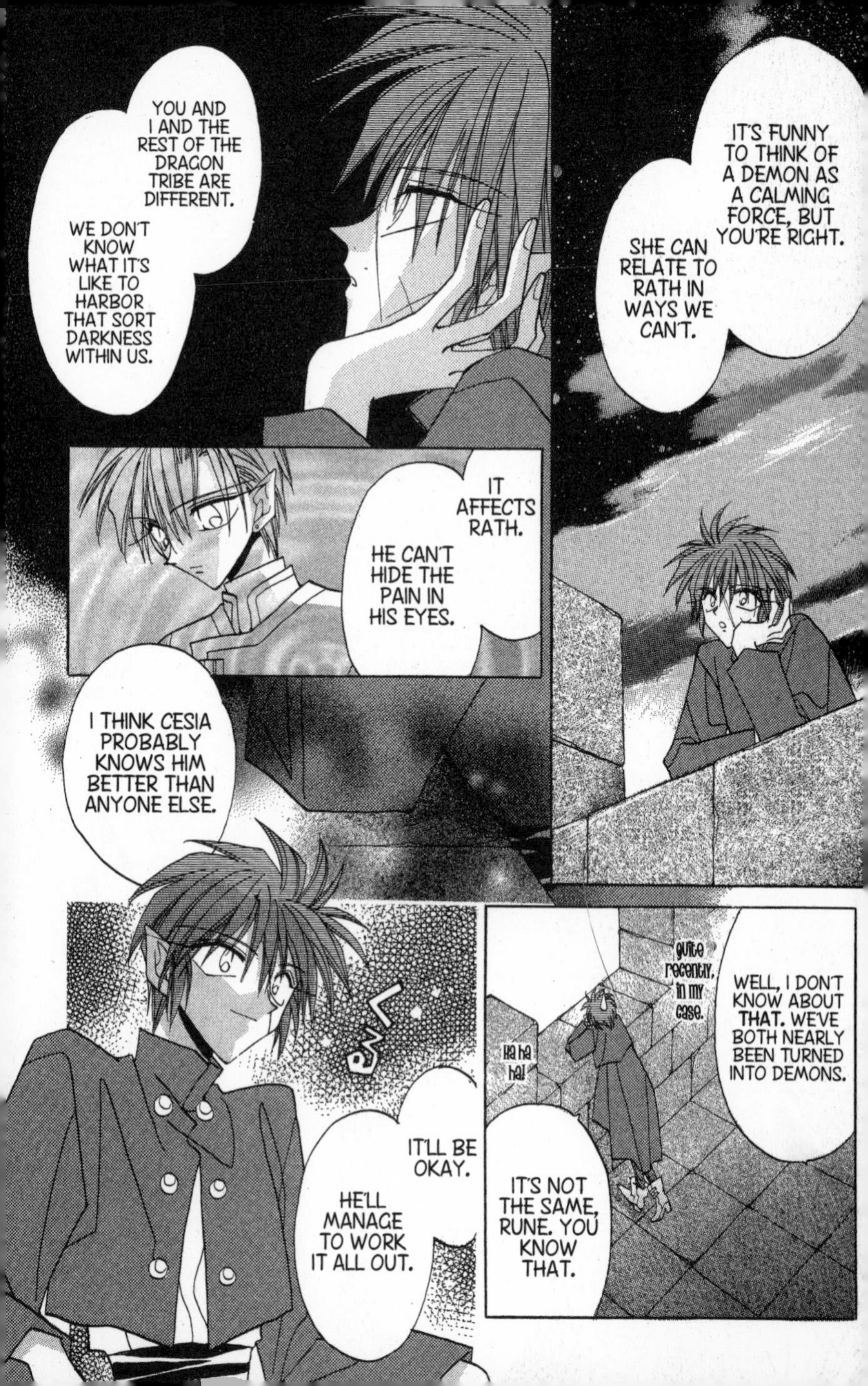
IT'S FUNNY TO THINK OF A DEMON AS A CALMING FORCE, BUT YOU'RE RIGHT.
SHE CAN RELATE TO RATH IN WAYS WE CAN'T.
YOU AND I AND THE REST OF THE DRAGON TRIBE ARE DIFFERENT.
WE DON'T KNOW WHAT IT'S LIKE TO HARBOR THAT SORT DARKNESS WITHIN US.
IT AFFECTS RATH.
HE CAN'T HIDE THE PAIN IN HIS EYES.
I THINK CESIA PROBABLY KNOWS HIM BETTER THAN ANYONE ELSE.
WELL, I DON'T KNOW ABOUT **THAT.** WE'VE BOTH NEARLY BEEN TURNED INTO DEMONS.
quite recently, in my case.
Ha ha ha!
IT'S NOT THE SAME, RUNE. YOU KNOW THAT.
IT'LL BE OKAY.
HE'LL MANAGE TO WORK IT ALL OUT.

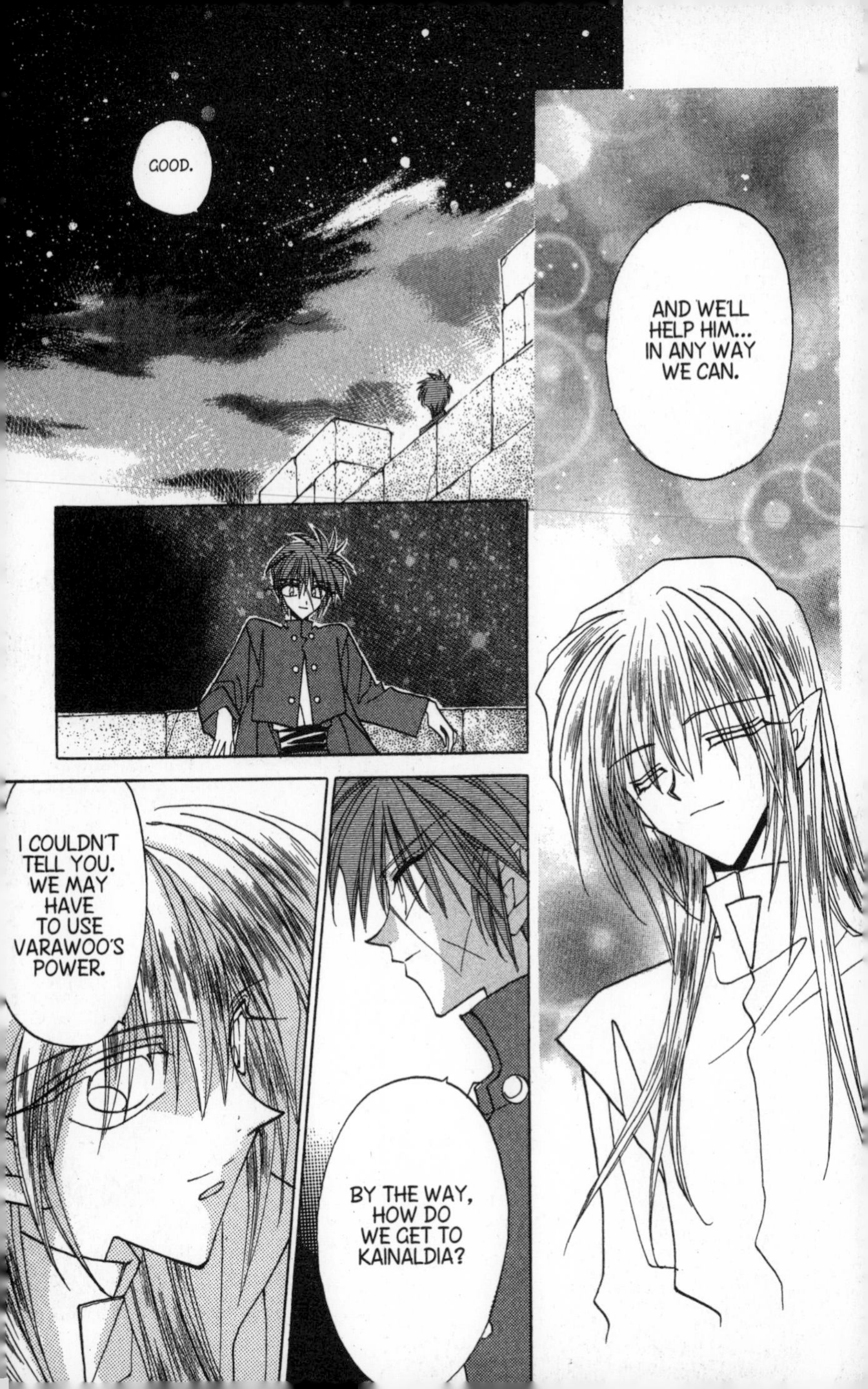
AND WE'LL HELP HIM... IN ANY WAY WE CAN.
GOOD.
BY THE WAY, HOW DO WE GET TO KAINALDIA?
I COULDN'T TELL YOU. WE MAY HAVE TO USE VARAWOO'S POWER.

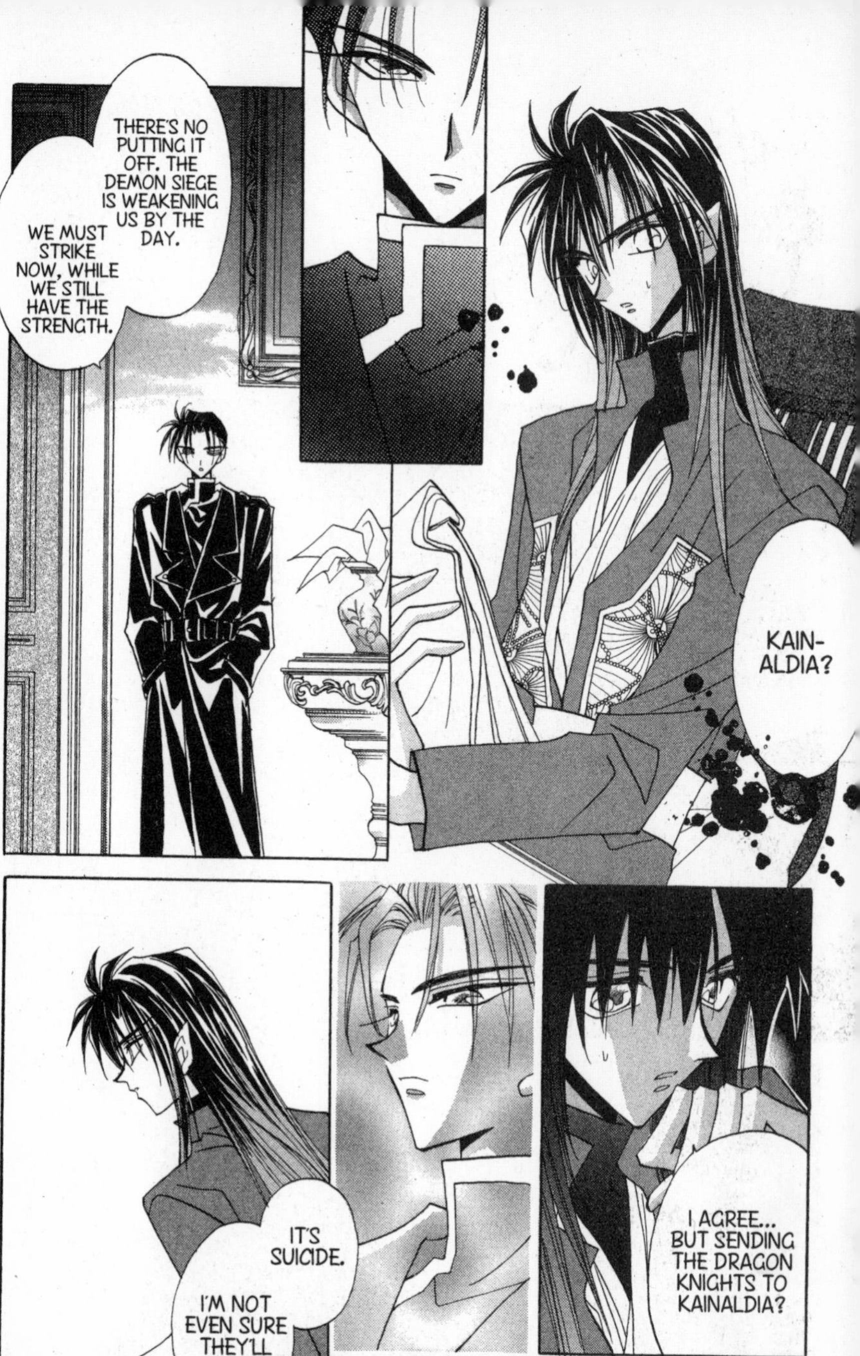
KAIN-ALDIA?
THERE'S NO PUTTING IT OFF. THE DEMON SIEGE IS WEAKENING US BY THE DAY.
WE MUST STRIKE NOW, WHILE WE STILL HAVE THE STRENGTH.
I AGREE... BUT SENDING THE DRAGON KNIGHTS TO KAINALDIA?
IT'S SUICIDE.
I'M NOT EVEN SURE THEY'LL DO IT.

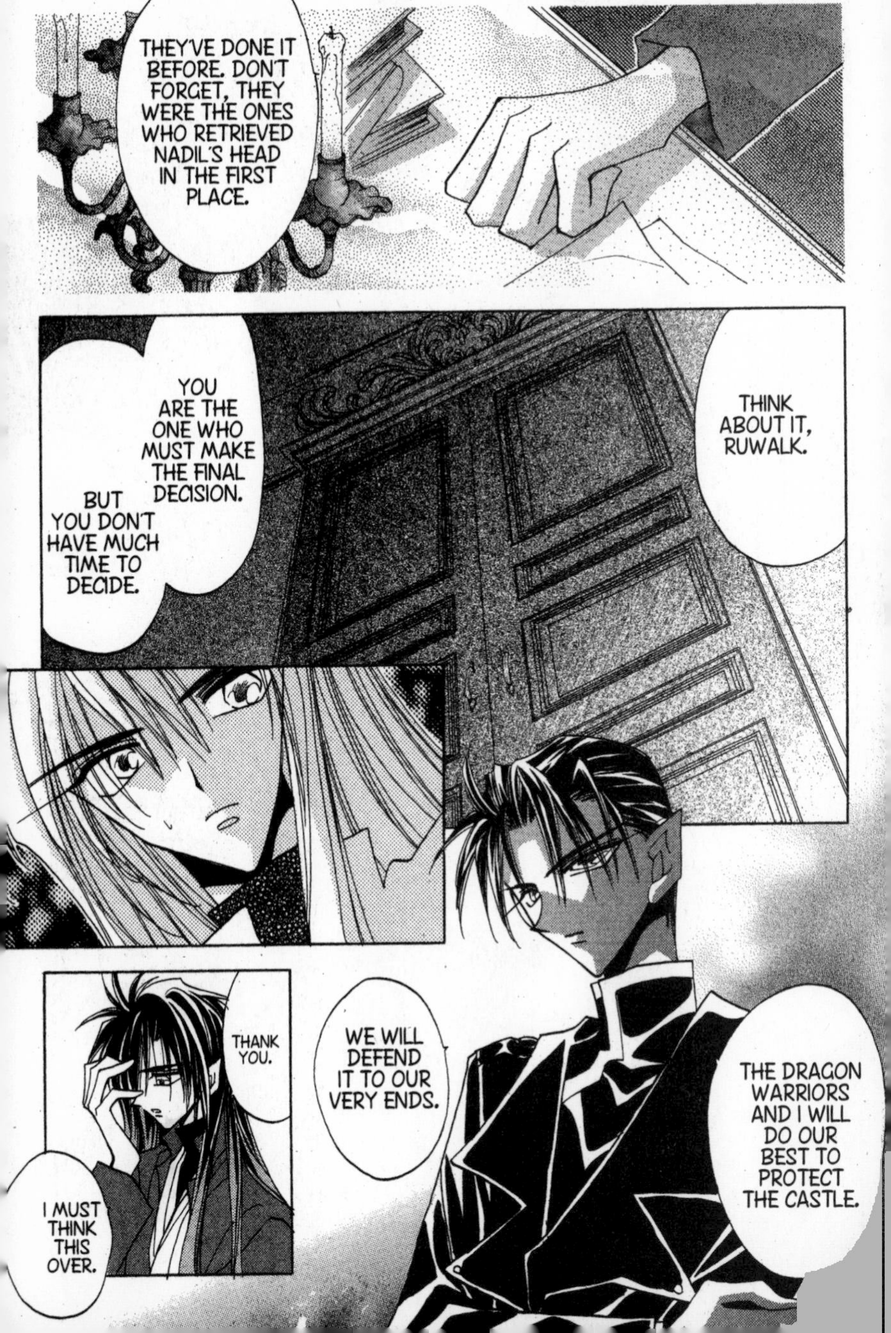
THEY'VE DONE IT BEFORE. DON'T FORGET, THEY WERE THE ONES WHO RETRIEVED NADIL'S HEAD IN THE FIRST PLACE.
THINK ABOUT IT, RUWALK.
YOU ARE THE ONE WHO MUST MAKE THE FINAL DECISION.
BUT YOU DON'T HAVE MUCH TIME TO DECIDE.
THE DRAGON WARRIORS AND I WILL DO OUR BEST TO PROTECT THE CASTLE.
WE WILL DEFEND IT TO OUR VERY ENDS.
THANK YOU.
I MUST THINK THIS OVER.

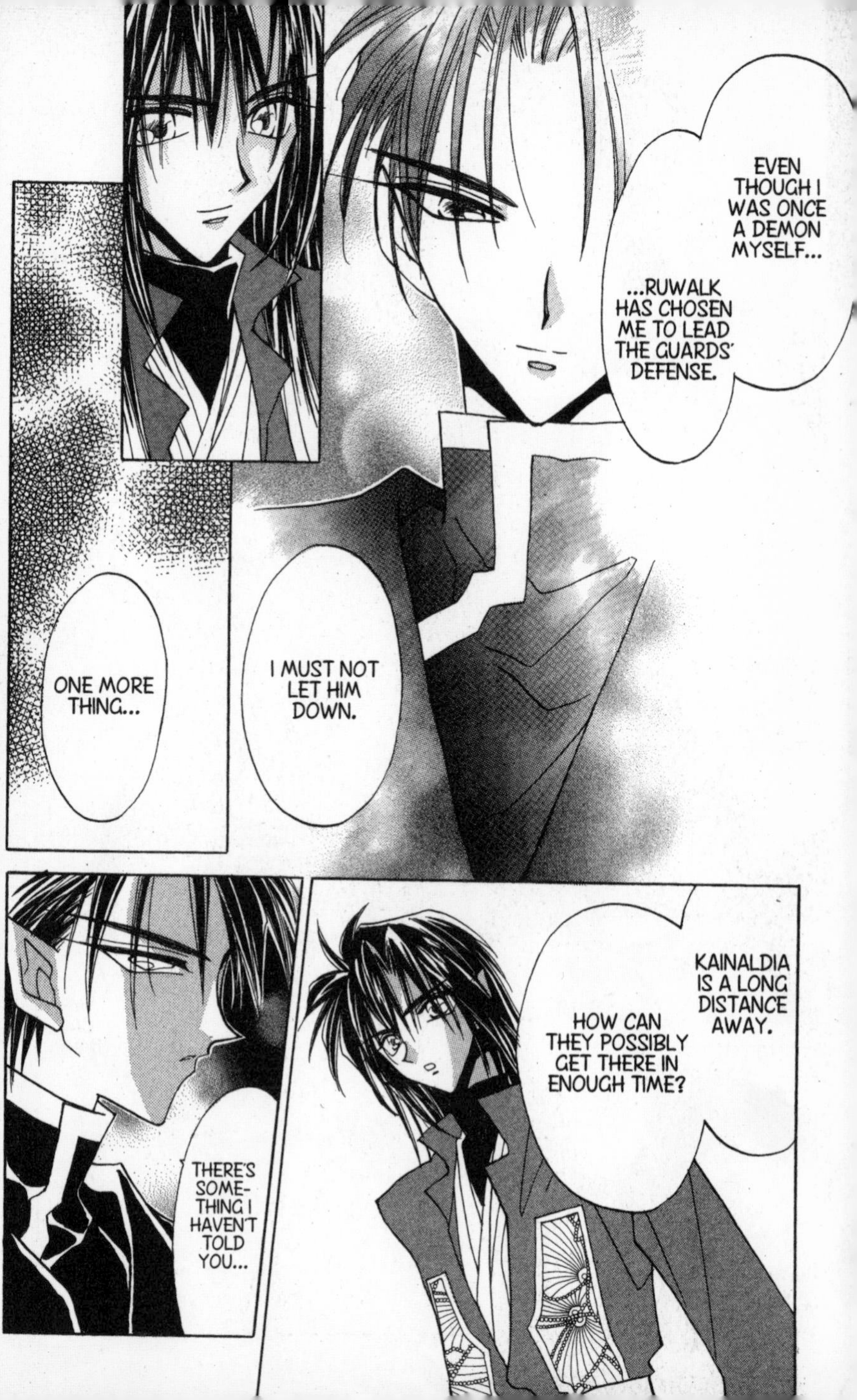
EVEN THOUGH I WAS ONCE A DEMON MYSELF...
...RUWALK HAS CHOSEN ME TO LEAD THE GUARDS' DEFENSE.
I MUST NOT LET HIM DOWN.
ONE MORE THING...
KAINALDIA IS A LONG DISTANCE AWAY.
HOW CAN THEY POSSIBLY GET THERE IN ENOUGH TIME?
THERE'S SOME-THING I HAVEN'T TOLD YOU...

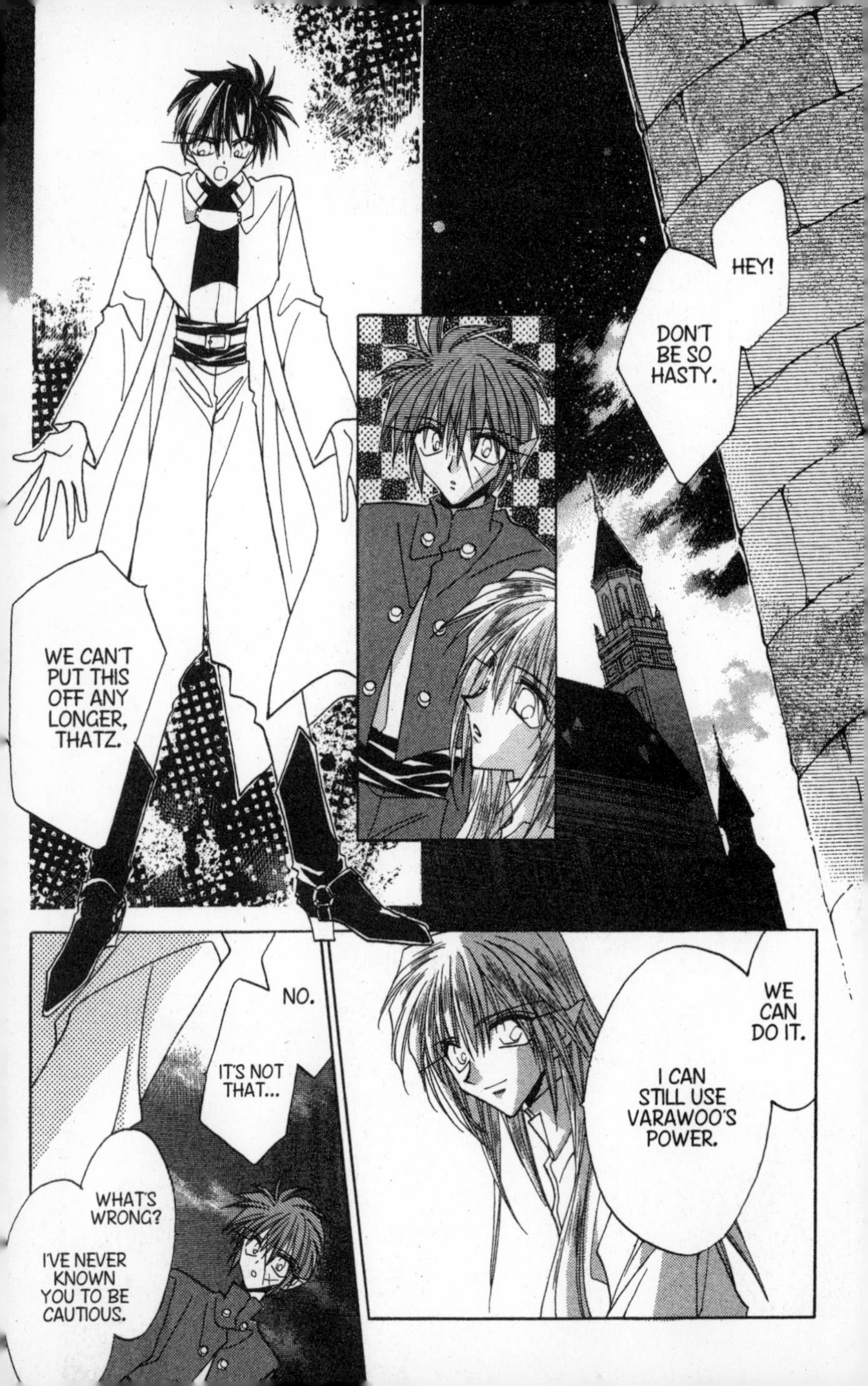
HEY!
DON'T BE SO HASTY.
WE CAN'T PUT THIS OFF ANY LONGER, THATZ.
WE CAN DO IT.
I CAN STILL USE VARAWOO'S POWER.
NO.
IT'S NOT THAT...
WHAT'S WRONG?
I'VE NEVER KNOWN YOU TO BE CAUTIOUS.

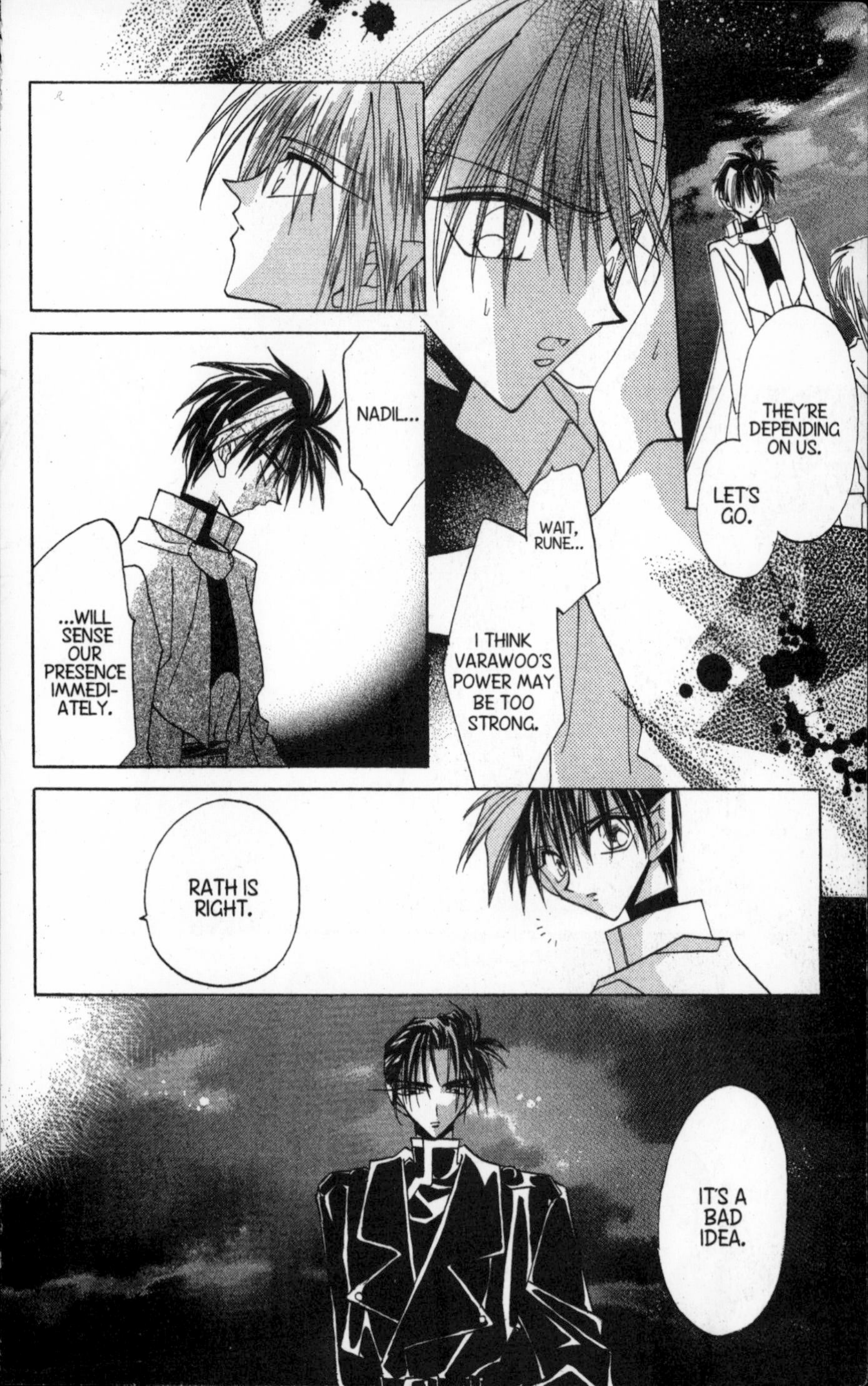
THEY'RE DEPENDING ON US.
LET'S GO.
WAIT, RUNE...
I THINK VARAWOO'S POWER MAY BE TOO STRONG.
NADIL...
...WILL SENSE OUR PRESENCE IMMEDIATELY.
RATH IS RIGHT.
IT'S A BAD IDEA.

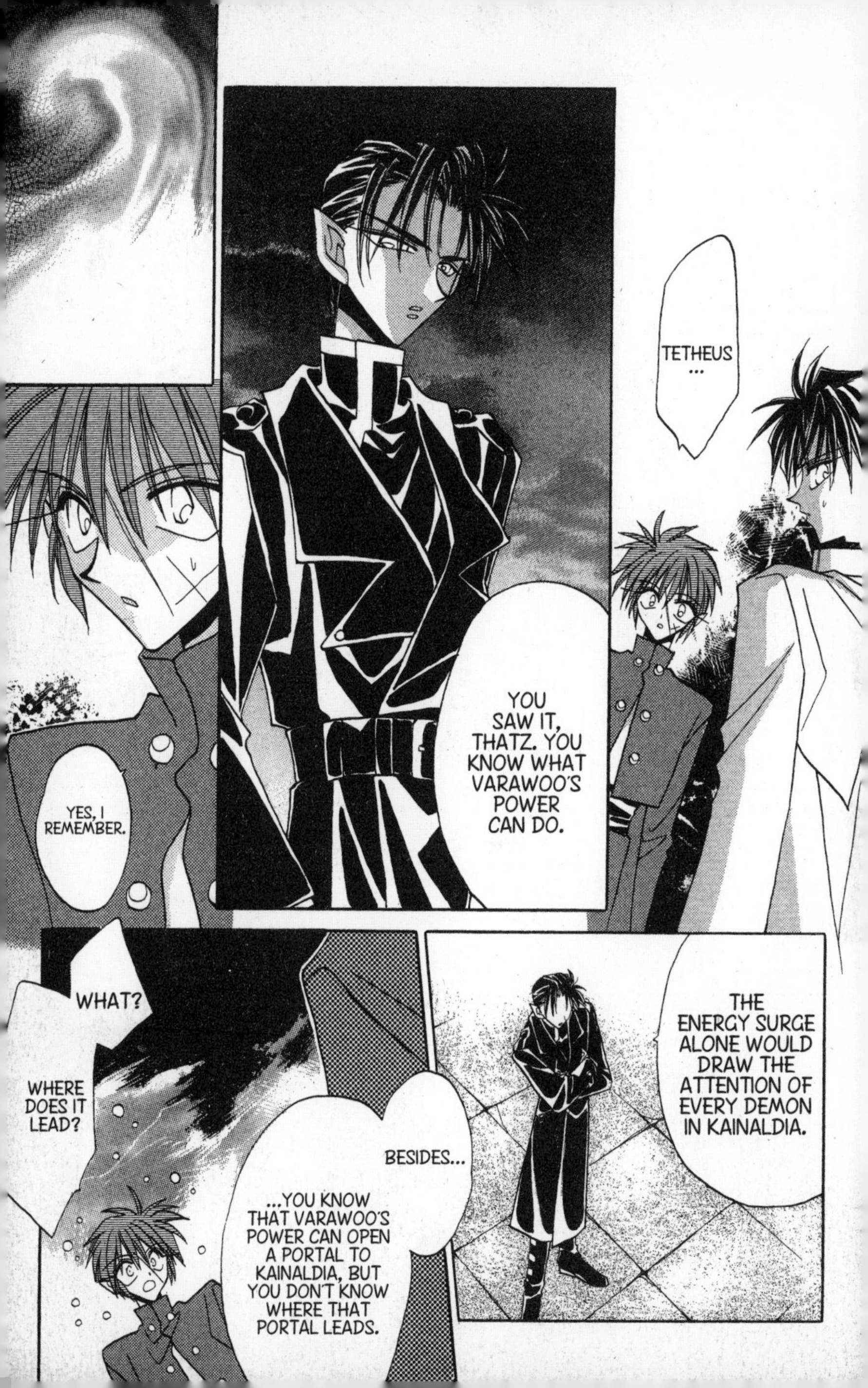
TETHEUS...
YOU SAW IT, THATZ. YOU KNOW WHAT VARAWOO'S POWER CAN DO.
YES, I REMEMBER.
THE ENERGY SURGE ALONE WOULD DRAW THE ATTENTION OF EVERY DEMON IN KAINALDIA.
BESIDES...
...YOU KNOW THAT VARAWOO'S POWER CAN OPEN A PORTAL TO KAINALDIA, BUT YOU DON'T KNOW WHERE THAT PORTAL LEADS.
WHAT?
WHERE DOES IT LEAD?

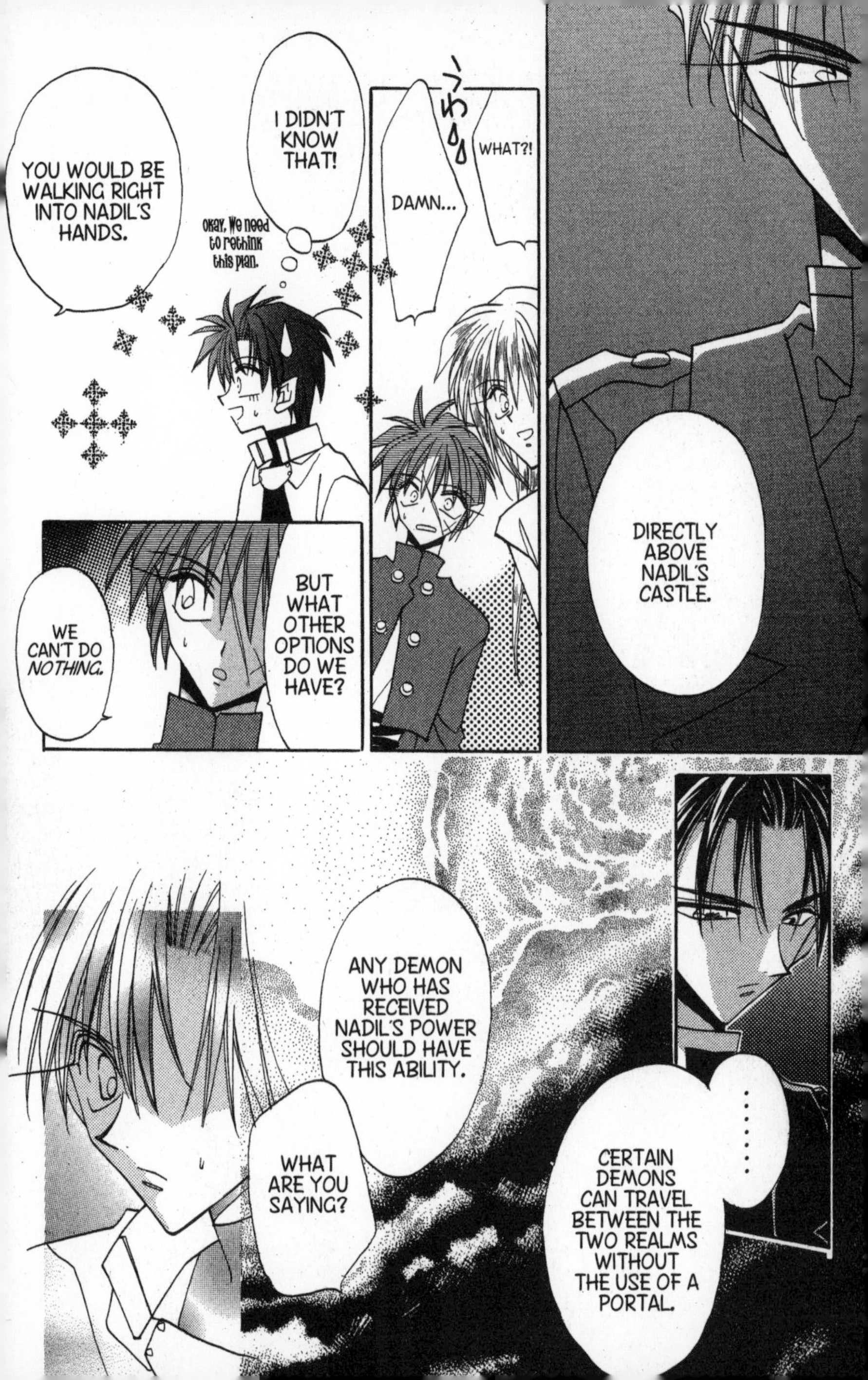
DIRECTLY ABOVE NADIL'S CASTLE.
WHAT?!
うわ
DAMN...
I DIDN'T KNOW THAT!
YOU WOULD BE WALKING RIGHT INTO NADIL'S HANDS.
Okay, We need to rethink this plan.
BUT WHAT OTHER OPTIONS DO WE HAVE?
WE CAN'T DO *NOTHING.*
......
CERTAIN DEMONS CAN TRAVEL BETWEEN THE TWO REALMS WITHOUT THE USE OF A PORTAL.
ANY DEMON WHO HAS RECEIVED NADIL'S POWER SHOULD HAVE THIS ABILITY.
WHAT ARE YOU SAYING?

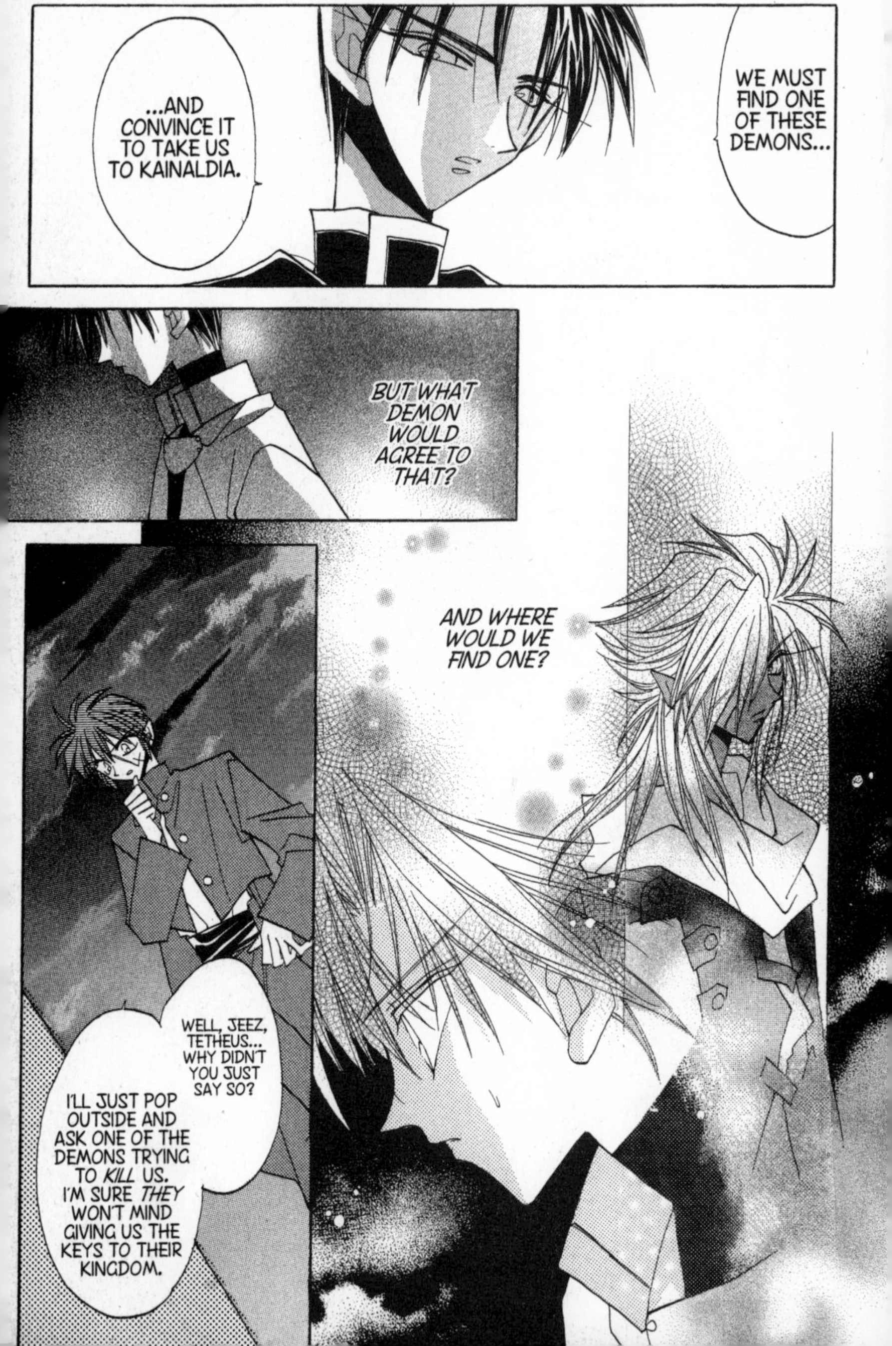
WE MUST FIND ONE OF THESE DEMONS...
...AND CONVINCE IT TO TAKE US TO KAINALDIA.
BUT WHAT DEMON WOULD AGREE TO THAT?
AND WHERE WOULD WE FIND ONE?
WELL, JEEZ, TETHEUS... WHY DIDN'T YOU JUST SAY SO?
I'LL JUST POP OUTSIDE AND ASK ONE OF THE DEMONS TRYING TO *KILL* US. I'M SURE *THEY* WON'T MIND GIVING US THE KEYS TO THEIR KINGDOM.

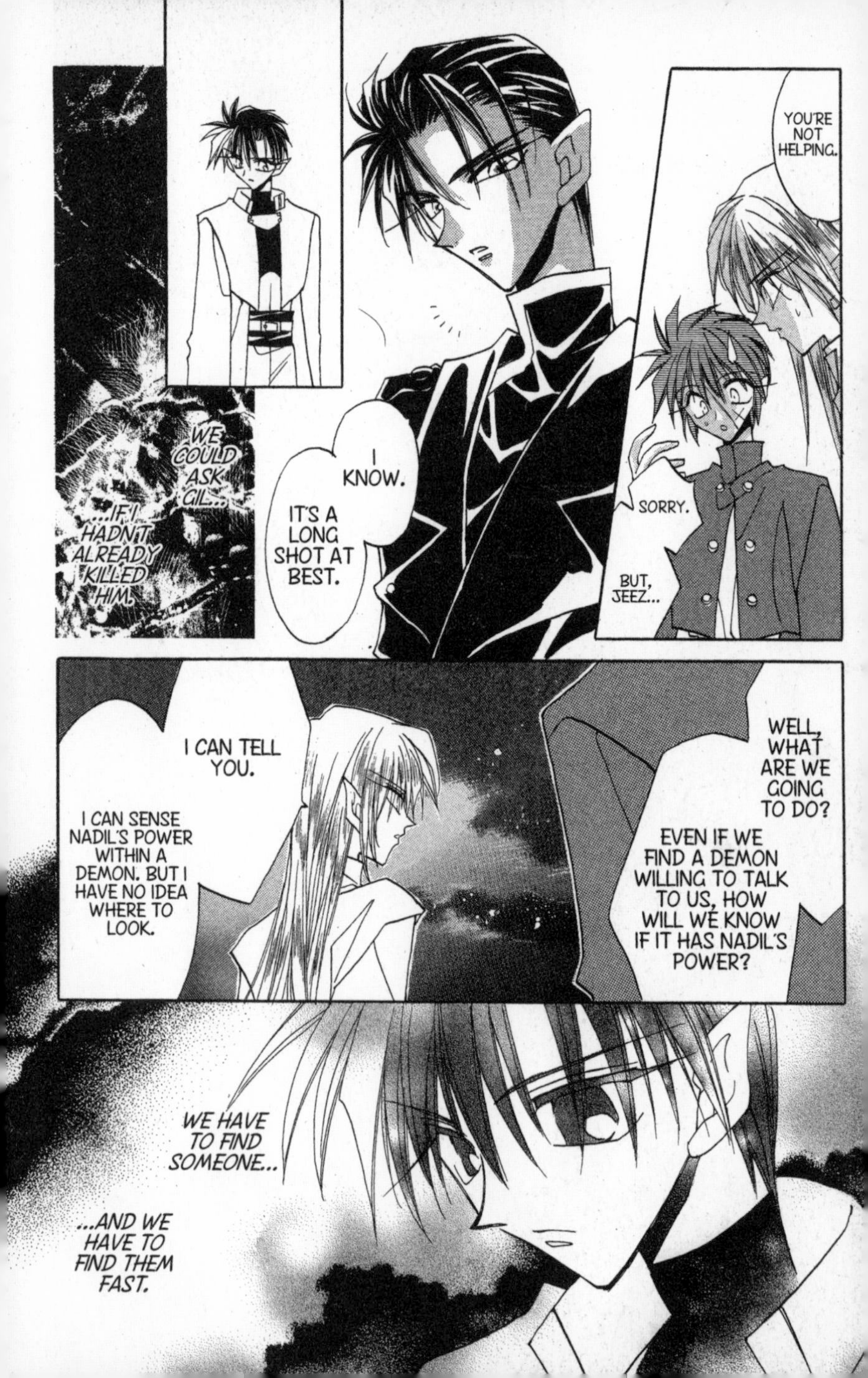
YOU'RE NOT HELPING.
SORRY.
BUT, JEEZ...
I KNOW.
IT'S A LONG SHOT AT BEST.
WE COULD ASK GIL...
...IF I HADN'T ALREADY KILLED HIM.
WELL, WHAT ARE WE GOING TO DO?
EVEN IF WE FIND A DEMON WILLING TO TALK TO US, HOW WILL WE KNOW IF IT HAS NADIL'S POWER?
I CAN TELL YOU.
I CAN SENSE NADIL'S POWER WITHIN A DEMON. BUT I HAVE NO IDEA WHERE TO LOOK.
WE HAVE TO FIND SOMEONE...
...AND WE HAVE TO FIND THEM FAST.

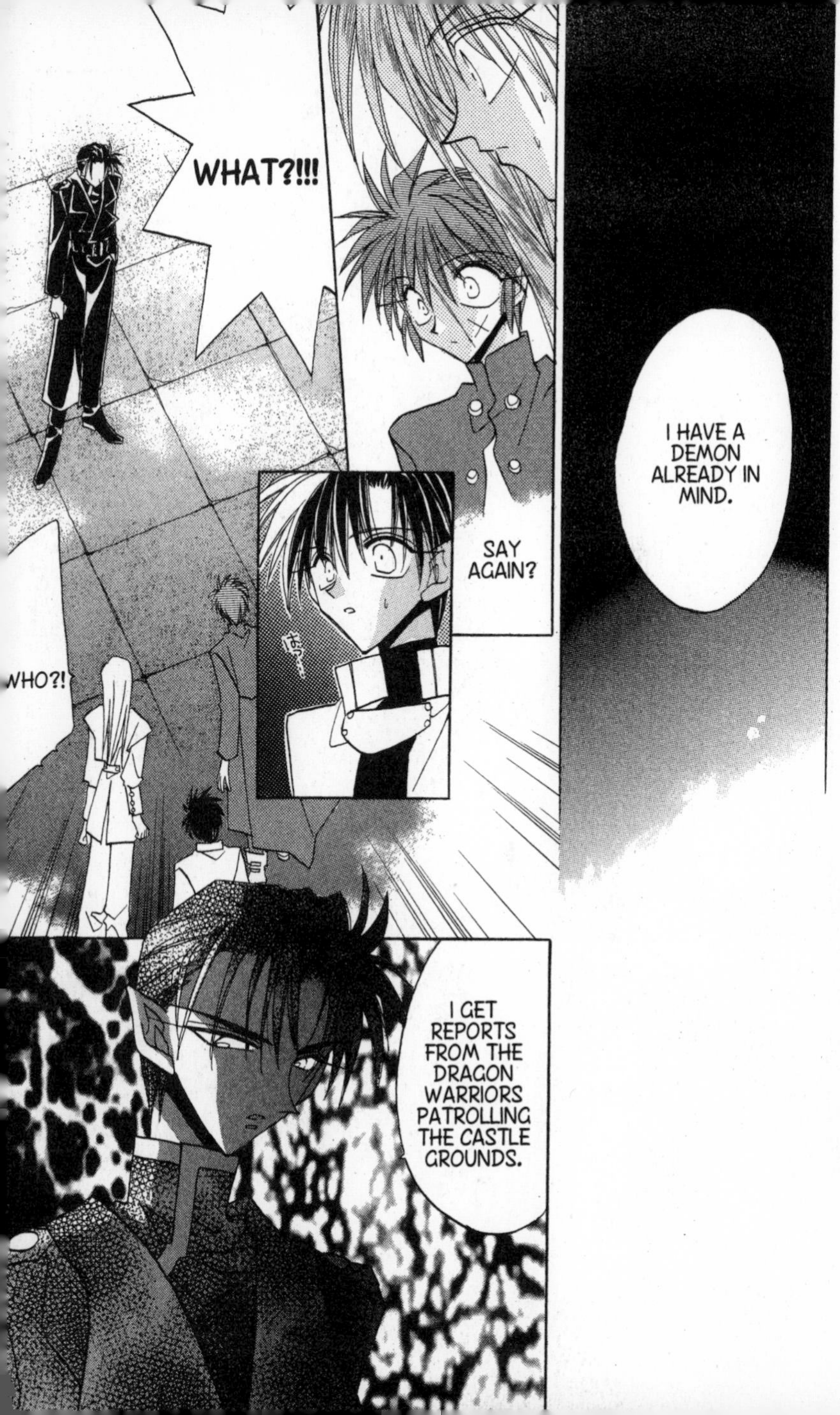
I HAVE A DEMON ALREADY IN MIND.
SAY AGAIN?
WHAT?!!!
WHO?!
I GET REPORTS FROM THE DRAGON WARRIORS PATROLLING THE CASTLE GROUNDS.

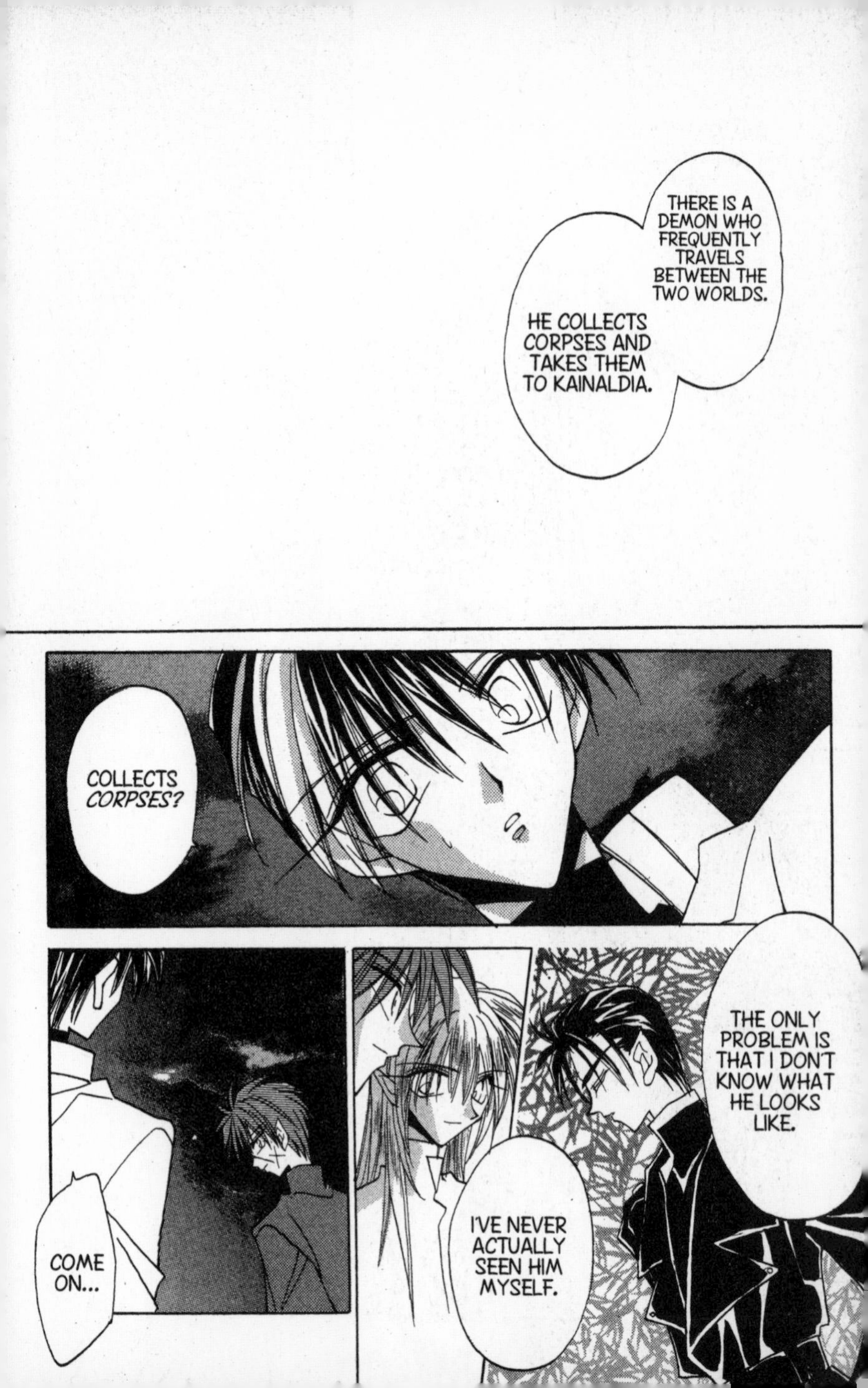
THERE IS A DEMON WHO FREQUENTLY TRAVELS BETWEEN THE TWO WORLDS.
HE COLLECTS CORPSES AND TAKES THEM TO KAINALDIA.
COLLECTS *CORPSES?*
THE ONLY PROBLEM IS THAT I DON'T KNOW WHAT HE LOOKS LIKE.
I'VE NEVER ACTUALLY SEEN HIM MYSELF.
COME ON...

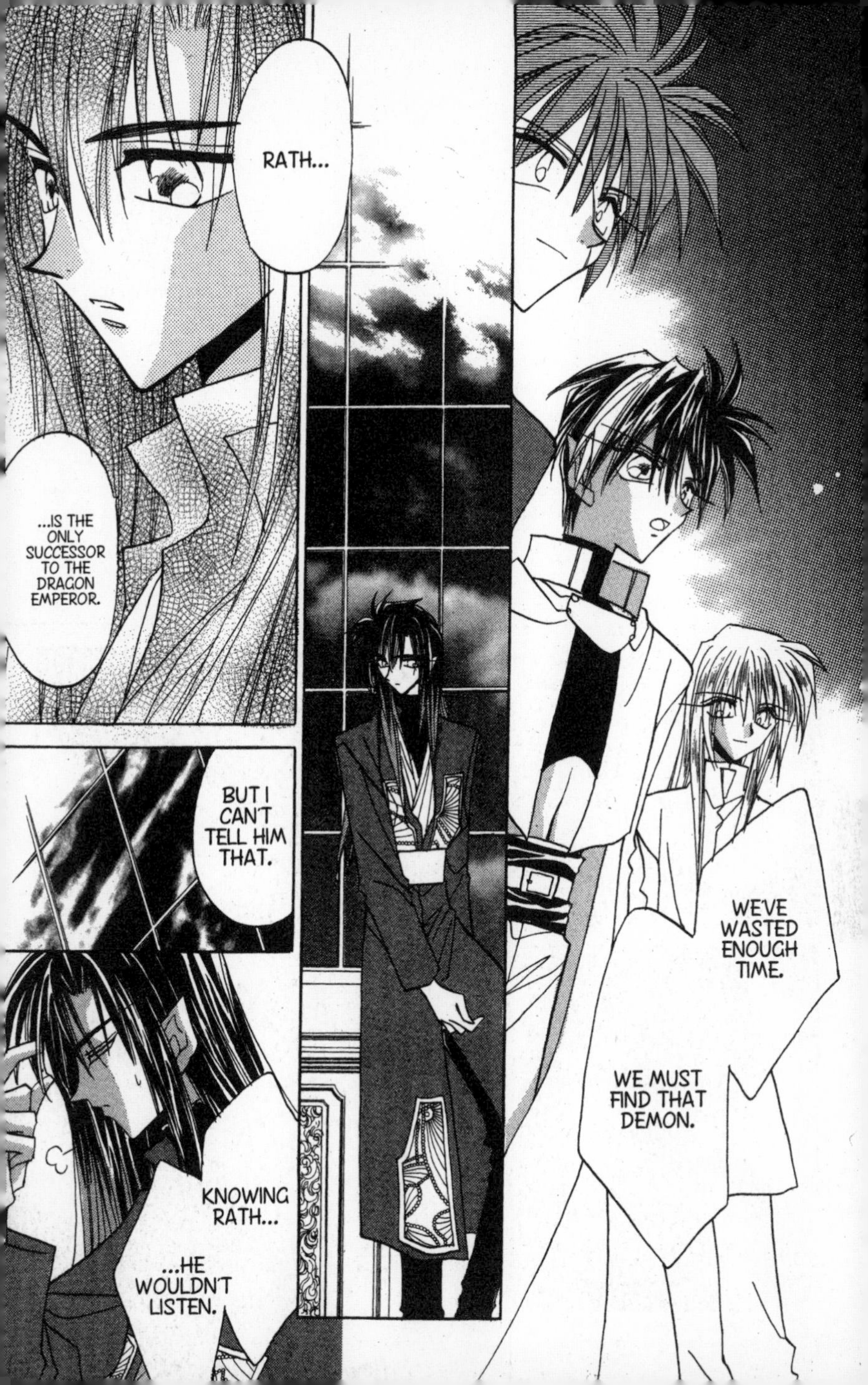
WE'VE WASTED ENOUGH TIME.
WE MUST FIND THAT DEMON.
RATH...
...IS THE ONLY SUCCESSOR TO THE DRAGON EMPEROR.
BUT I CAN'T TELL HIM THAT.
KNOWING RATH...
...HE WOULDN'T LISTEN.

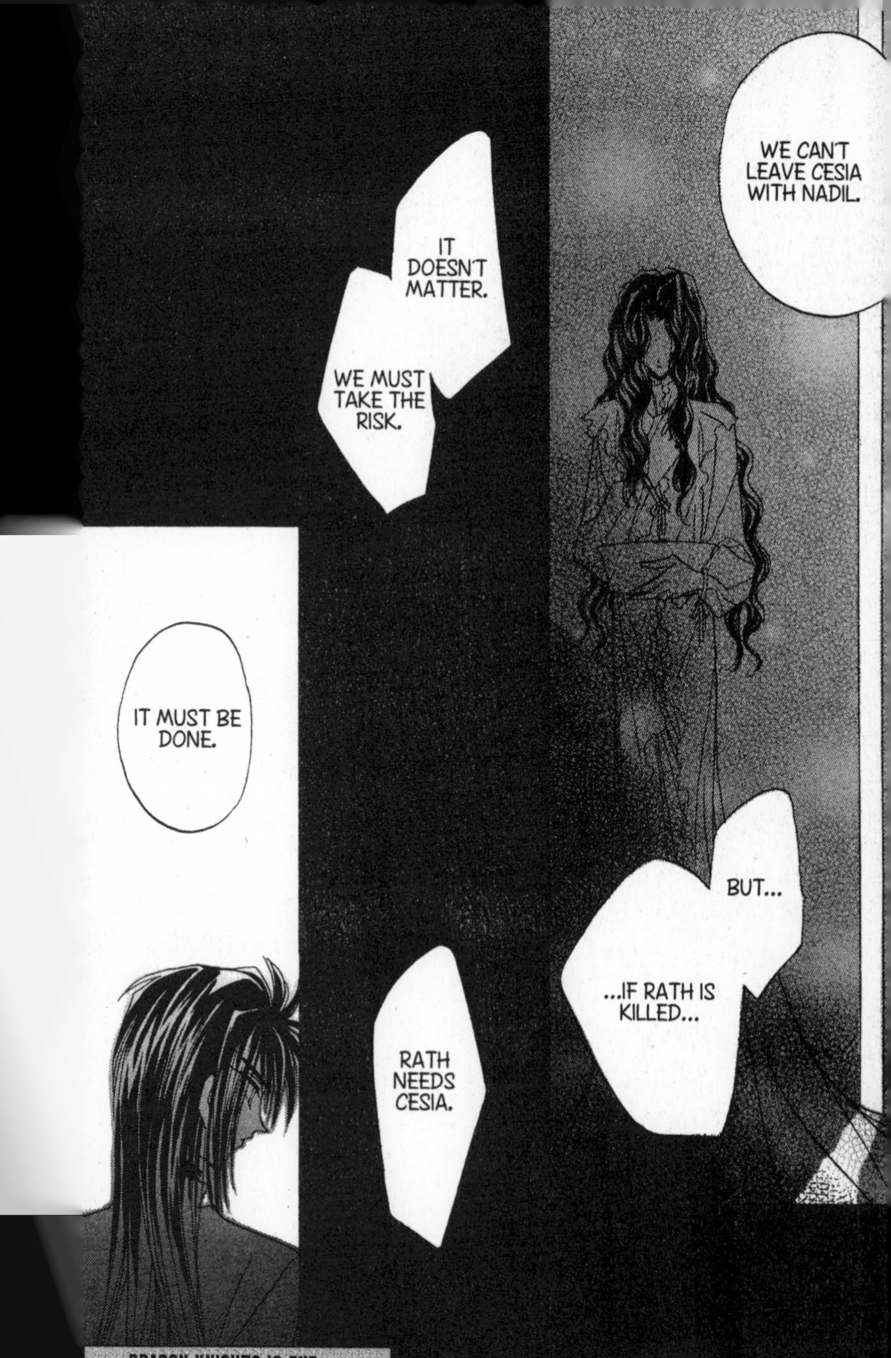
WE CAN'T LEAVE CESIA WITH NADIL.
BUT...
...IF RATH IS KILLED...
IT DOESN'T MATTER.
WE MUST TAKE THE RISK.
RATH NEEDS CESIA.
IT MUST BE DONE.
DRAGON KNIGHTS 13 END

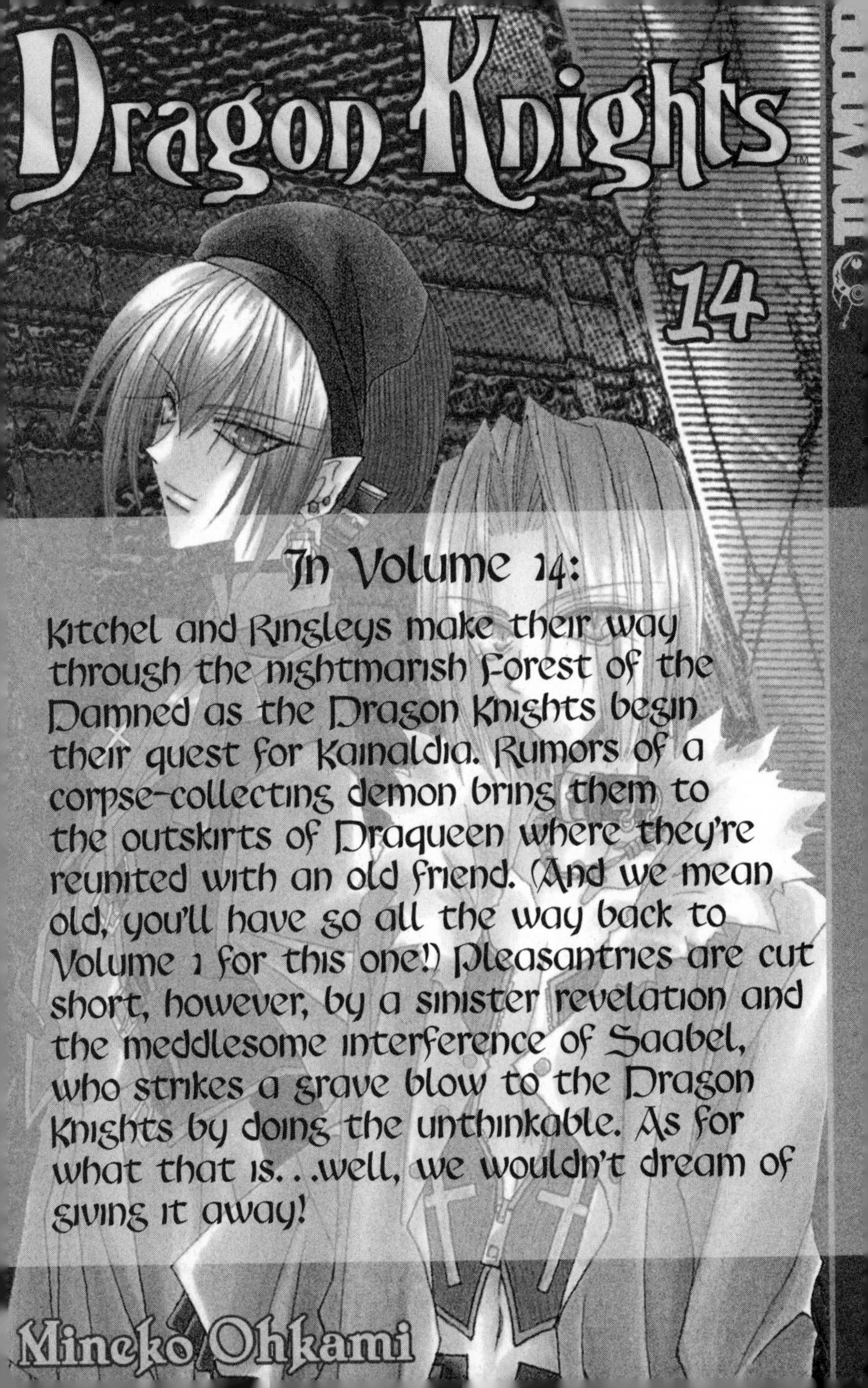
Dragon Knights™
TOKYOPOP
14
In Volume 14:
Kitchel and Ringleys make their way through the nightmarish Forest of the Damned as the Dragon Knights begin their quest for Kainaldia. Rumors of a corpse-collecting demon bring them to the outskirts of Draqueen where they're reunited with an old friend. (And we mean old, you'll have go all the way back to Volume 1 for this one!) Pleasantries are cut short, however, by a sinister revelation and the meddlesome interference of Saabel, who strikes a grave blow to the Dragon Knights by doing the unthinkable. As for what that is. . .well, we wouldn't dream of giving it away!
Mineko Ohkami

ALSO AVAILABLE FROM TOKYOPOP®

For more information visit www.TOKYOPOP.com

02.03.04T

ALSO AVAILABLE FROM TOKYOPOP®

MANGA

.HACK//LEGEND OF THE TWILIGHT
@LARGE
ABENOBASHI: MAGICAL SHOPPING ARCADE
A.I. LOVE YOU
AI YORI AOSHI
ANGELIC LAYER
ARM OF KANNON
BABY BIRTH
BATTLE ROYALE
BATTLE VIXENS
BRAIN POWERED
BRIGADOON
B'TX
CANDIDATE FOR GODDESS, THE
CARDCAPTOR SAKURA
CARDCAPTOR SAKURA - MASTER OF THE CLOW
CHOBITS
CHRONICLES OF THE CURSED SWORD
CLAMP SCHOOL DETECTIVES
CLOVER
COMIC PARTY
CONFIDENTIAL CONFESSIONS
CORRECTOR YUI
COWBOY BEBOP
COWBOY BEBOP: SHOOTING STAR
CRAZY LOVE STORY
CRESCENT MOON
CULDCEPT
CYBORG 009
D•N•ANGEL
DEMON DIARY
DEMON ORORON, THE
DEUS VITAE
DIGIMON
DIGIMON TAMERS
DIGIMON ZERO TWO
DOLL
DRAGON HUNTER
DRAGON KNIGHTS
DRAGON VOICE
DREAM SAGA
DUKLYON: CLAMP SCHOOL DEFENDERS
EERIE QUEERIE!
ERICA SAKURAZAWA: COLLECTED WORKS
ET CETERA
ETERNITY
EVIL'S RETURN
FAERIES' LANDING
FAKE
FLCL
FORBIDDEN DANCE
FRUITS BASKET
G GUNDAM
GATEKEEPERS
GETBACKERS

GIRL GOT GAME
GRAVITATION
GTO
GUNDAM BLUE DESTINY
GUNDAM SEED ASTRAY
GUNDAM WING
GUNDAM WING: BATTLEFIELD OF PACIFISTS
GUNDAM WING: ENDLESS WALTZ
GUNDAM WING: THE LAST OUTPOST (G-UNIT)
HANDS OFF!
HAPPY MANIA
HARLEM BEAT
I.N.V.U.
IMMORTAL RAIN
INITIAL D
INSTANT TEEN: JUST ADD NUTS
ISLAND
JING: KING OF BANDITS
JING: KING OF BANDITS - TWILIGHT TALES
JULINE
KARE KANO
KILL ME, KISS ME
KINDAICHI CASE FILES, THE
KING OF HELL
KODOCHA: SANA'S STAGE
LAMENT OF THE LAMB
LEGAL DRUG
LEGEND OF CHUN HYANG, THE
LES BIJOUX
LOVE HINA
LUPIN III
LUPIN III: WORLD'S MOST WANTED
MAGIC KNIGHT RAYEARTH I
MAGIC KNIGHT RAYEARTH II
MAHOROMATIC: AUTOMATIC MAIDEN
MAN OF MANY FACES
MARMALADE BOY
MARS
MARS: HORSE WITH NO NAME
METROID
MINK
MIRACLE GIRLS
MIYUKI-CHAN IN WONDERLAND
MODEL
ONE
ONE I LOVE, THE
PARADISE KISS
PARASYTE
PASSION FRUIT
PEACH GIRL
PEACH GIRL: CHANGE OF HEART
PET SHOP OF HORRORS
PITA-TEN
PLANET LADDER
PLANETES
PRIEST

02.03.04T

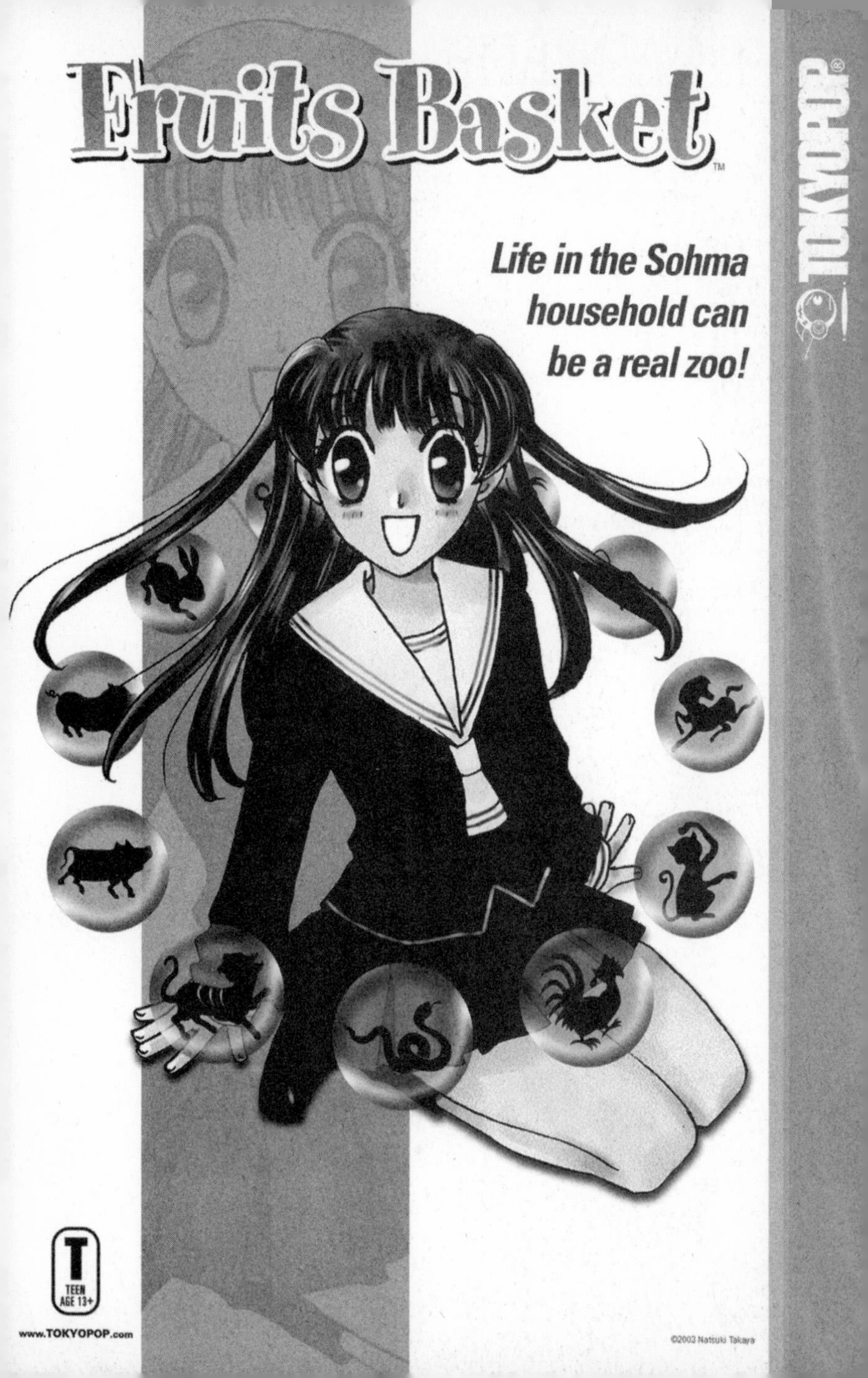
Fruits Basket™
Life in the Sohma household can be a real zoo!
TOKYOPOP®
T
TEEN
AGE 13+
www.TOKYOPOP.com
©2003 Natsuki Takaya

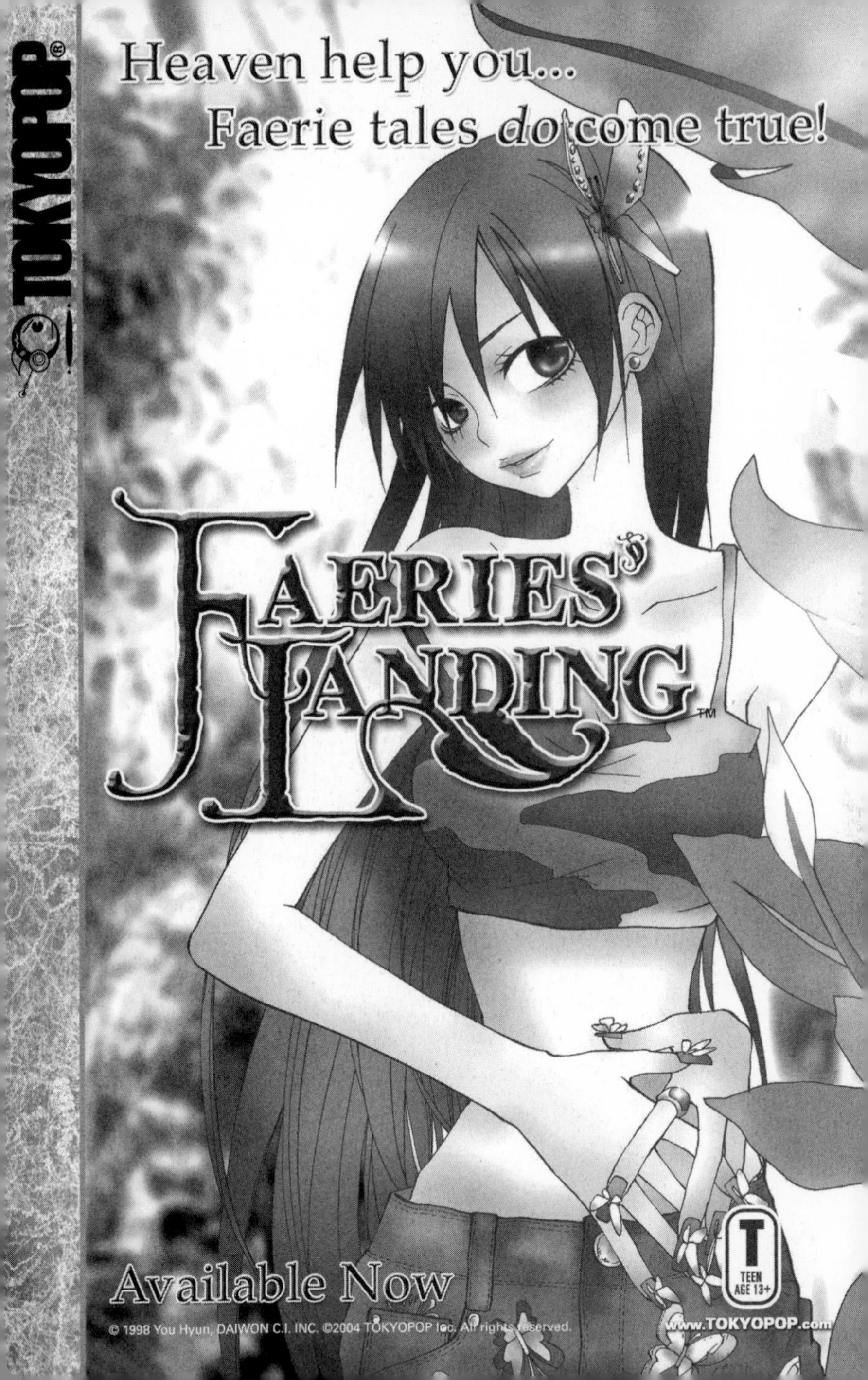
TOKYOPOP®
Heaven help you...
Faerie tales *do* come true!
FAERIES' LANDING™
Available Now
T TEEN AGE 13+
© 1998 You Hyun, DAIWON C.I. INC. ©2004 TOKYOPOP Inc. All rights reserved.
www.TOKYOPOP.com

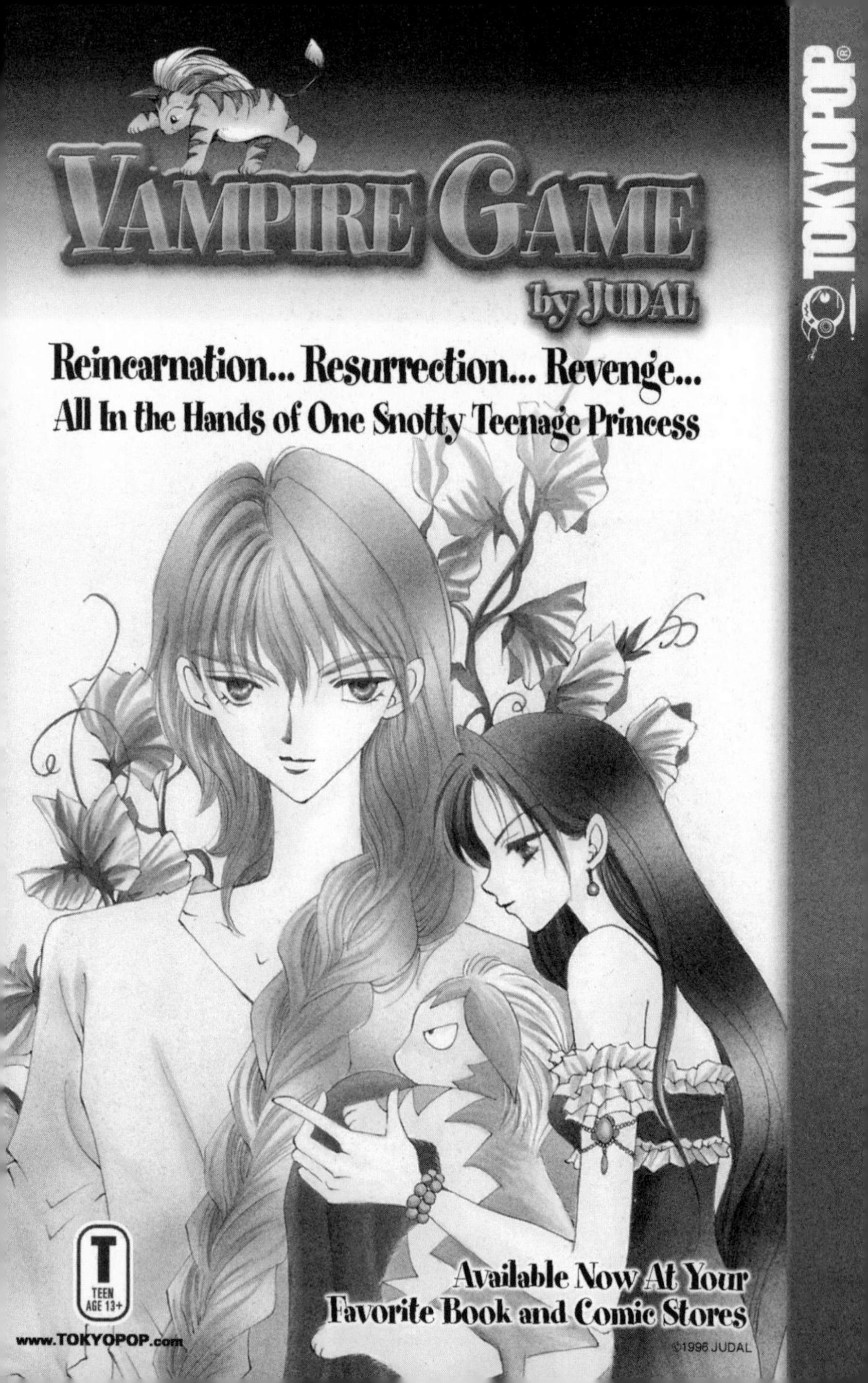
TOKYOPOP
VAMPIRE GAME
by JUDAL
Reincarnation... Resurrection... Revenge...
All In the Hands of One Snotty Teenage Princess
T
TEEN
AGE 13+
Available Now At Your
Favorite Book and Comic Stores
www.TOKYOPOP.com
©1996 JUDAL

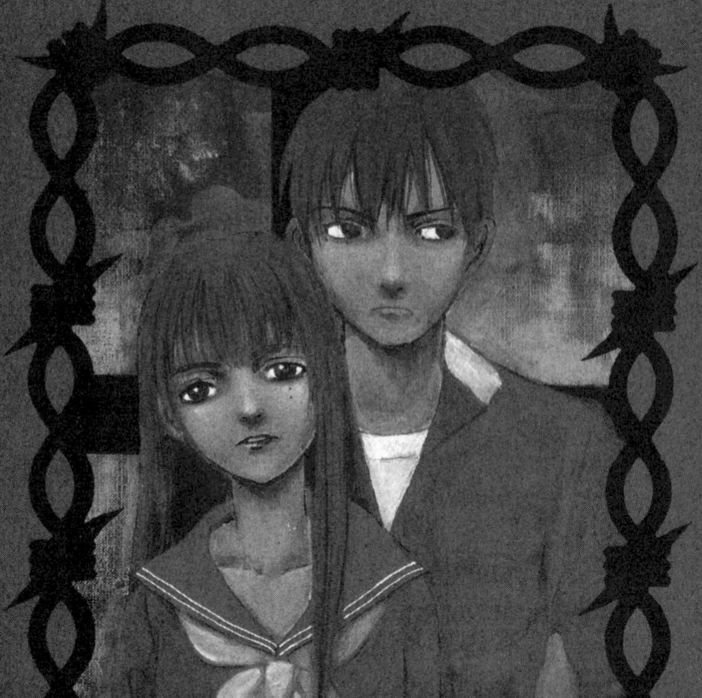

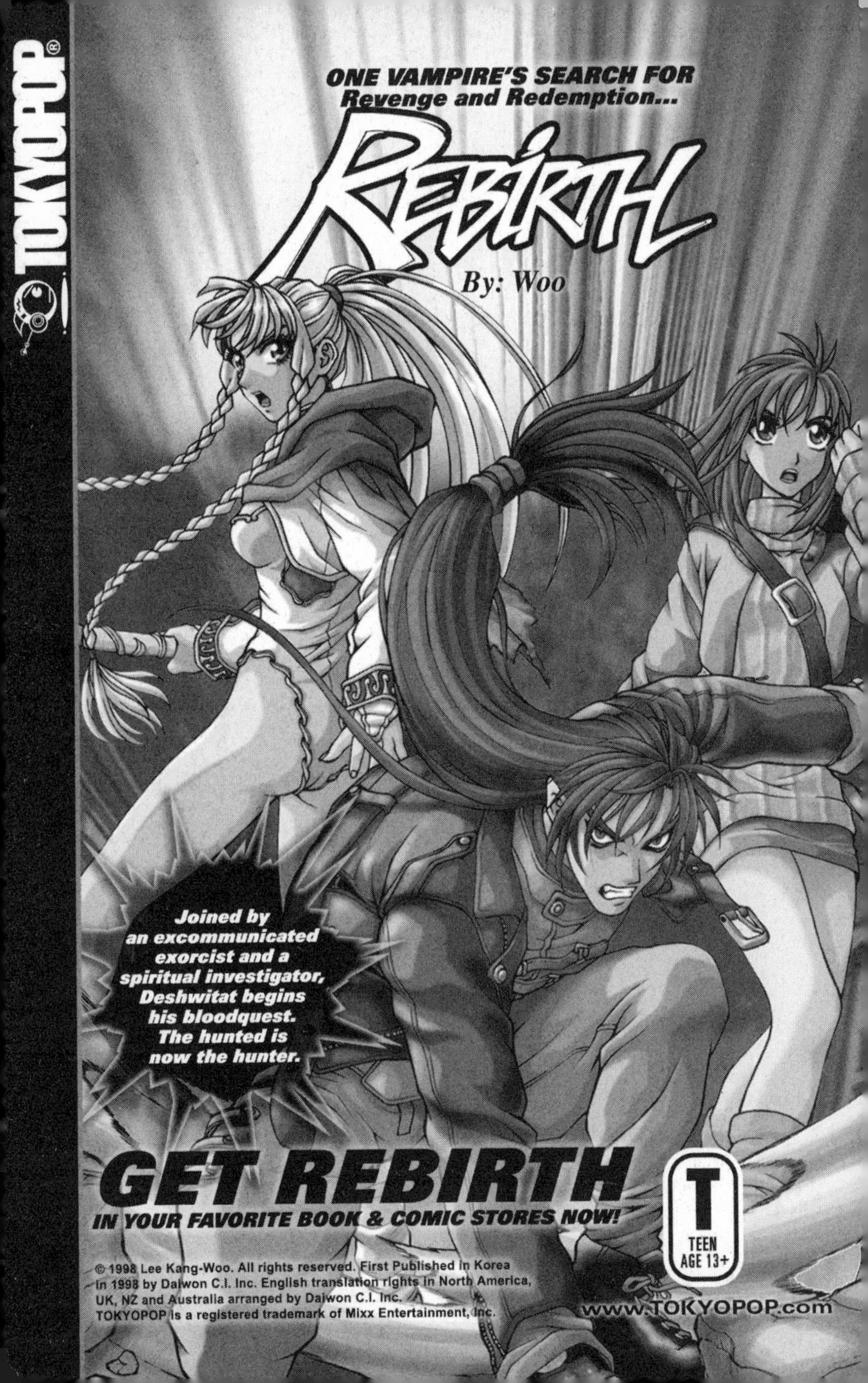
TOKYOPOP®
ONE VAMPIRE'S SEARCH FOR
Revenge and Redemption...
REBIRTH
By: Woo
Joined by an excommunicated exorcist and a spiritual investigator, Deshwitat begins his bloodquest. The hunted is now the hunter.
GET REBIRTH
IN YOUR FAVORITE BOOK & COMIC STORES NOW!
T
TEEN
AGE 13+
© 1998 Lee Kang-Woo. All rights reserved. First Published in Korea in 1998 by Daiwon C.I. Inc. English translation rights in North America, UK, NZ and Australia arranged by Daiwon C.I. Inc.
TOKYOPOP is a registered trademark of Mixx Entertainment, Inc.
www.TOKYOPOP.com

STOP!

This is the back of the book.
You wouldn't want to spoil a great ending!

This book is printed "manga-style," in the authentic Japanese right-to-left format. Since none of the artwork has been flipped or altered, readers get to experience the story just as the creator intended. You've been asking for it, so TOKYOPOP® delivered: authentic, hot-off-the-press, and far more fun!

DIRECTIONS

If this is your first time reading manga-style, here's a quick guide to help you understand how it works.

It's easy... just start in the top right panel and follow the numbers. Have fun, and look for more 100% authentic manga from TOKYOPOP®!